SAP PRESS e-books

Print or e-book, Kindle or iPad, workplace or airplane: Choose where and how to read your SAP PRESS books! You can now get all our titles as e-books, too:

▸ By download and online access
▸ For all popular devices
▸ And, of course, DRM-free

Convinced? Then go to **www.sap-press.com** and get your e-book today.

SAP Fiori® Implementation and Development

SAP PRESS is a joint initiative of SAP and Rheinwerk Publishing. The know-how offered by SAP specialists combined with the expertise of Rheinwerk Publishing offers the reader expert books in the field. SAP PRESS features first-hand information and expert advice, and provides useful skills for professional decision-making.

SAP PRESS offers a variety of books on technical and business-related topics for the SAP user. For further information, please visit our website: *www.sap-press.com*.

Goebels, Nepraunig, Seidel
SAPUI5: The Comprehensive Guide
2016, 672 pages, hardcover and e-book
www.sap-press.com/3980

Bardhan, Baumgartl, Choi, Dudgeon, Lahiri, Meijerink, Worsley-Tonks
SAP S/4HANA: An Introduction (3rd Edition)
2018, 647 pages, hardcover and e-book
www.sap-press.com/4782

Steve Guo
SAP Fiori Launchpad: Development and Extensibility
2018, 304 pages, hardcover and e-book
www.sap-press.com/4556

Stefan Haas, Bince Mathew
ABAP Development for SAP S/4HANA: ABAP Programming Model for SAP Fiori
2018, 461 pages, hardcover and e-book
www.sap-press.com/4766

Editor Will Jobst
Acquisitions Editor Hareem Shafi
Copyeditor Melinda Rankin
Cover Design Graham Geary
Photo Credit Shutterstock.com/72580192/© Nejron Photo
Layout Design Vera Brauner
Production Marissa Fritz
Typesetting SatzPro (Germany)
Printed and bound in the United States of America, on paper from sustainable sources

ISBN 978-1-4932-1541-6
© 2019 by Rheinwerk Publishing, Inc., Boston (MA)
2nd edition 2017, 1st reprint 2019

Library of Congress Cataloging-in-Publication Data
Names: Bavaraju, Anil.
Title: SAP Fiori implementation and development / Anil Bavaraju.
Description: 2nd edition. | Bonn ; Boston : SAP Press, Rheinwerk Publishing,
   2017. | Includes index.
Identifiers: LCCN 2017010639 | ISBN 9781493215416 (alk. paper)
Subjects: LCSH: SAP Fiori. | Enterprise application integration (Computer
   systems) | Cross-platform software development. | User interfaces
   (Computer systems) | Business enterprises--Data processing.
Classification: LCC QA76.76.A65 B378 2017 | DDC 005.4/37--dc23
LC record available at https://lccn.loc.gov/2017010639

Anil Bavaraju

SAP Fiori® Implementation and Development

Rheinwerk
Publishing

2.2	**Implementation Options**	78
	2.2.1	ABAP Environment	78
	2.2.2	SAP HANA Database	80
	2.2.3	SAP HANA XS	81
	2.2.4	SAP S/4HANA	84
2.3	**Deployment Options**	85
	2.3.1	Central Hub Deployment	85
	2.3.2	Embedded Deployment	87
2.4	**Apps Reference Library**	88
2.5	**Installation**	89
	2.5.1	ABAP Environment	89
	2.5.2	SAP Web Dispatcher	105
	2.5.3	SAP HANA Server	106
2.6	**Configuration**	108
	2.6.1	SAP Fiori Launchpad	108
	2.6.2	SAP Gateway	122
	2.6.3	Embedded Search	128
	2.6.4	SAP HANA	134
	2.6.5	Configuration Using the Task List	137
2.7	**Upgrading to SAP Fiori 2.0**	146
	2.7.1	SAP Fiori 2.0 for SAP S/4HANA	146
	2.7.2	SAP Fiori 2.0 for SAP Business Suite Powered by SAP HANA or AnyDB	147
2.8	**Summary**	147

PART II Implementation

3 SAP Fiori Security

151

3.1	**Communication Channel Security and Encryption**	152
	3.1.1	Client to SAP Web Dispatcher	155
	3.1.2	SAP Web Dispatcher to ABAP Servers	155

Contents

Foreword 15

Preface 17

Acknowledgments 23

PART I   Getting Started

1   Introduction to SAP Fiori   27

1.1   SAP Fiori and the Evolution of User Experience 27

    1.1.1   SAP UX Strategy 28

    1.1.2   SAP Fiori UX Design Principles 29

1.2   Architecture and Integration 30

    1.2.1   SAP Fiori Launchpad 32

    1.2.2   SAP Web Dispatcher 42

    1.2.3   Communication Channels 44

    1.2.4   SAP Fiori App-Supported Browsers and OS 45

    1.2.5   SAP Fiori, Cloud Edition 47

1.3   Types of SAP Fiori Apps 50

    1.3.1   Transactional Apps 53

    1.3.2   Fact Sheet Apps 54

    1.3.3   Analytical Apps 55

1.4   Related SAP Technologies 57

    1.4.1   SAPUI5 57

    1.4.2   OData and SAP Gateway 68

    1.4.3   SAP HANA XS 74

1.5   Summary 75

2   Installation and Configuration   77

2.1   Prerequisites 77

Dear Reader,

Sometimes, the sequel is better. The Godfather Part II. Led Zeppelin II. Web 2.0. You're not working from scratch. You can innovate inside the constraints of what has come before. Coppola found the Mafia story he wanted to tell. Zeppelin toured and found their sound. The internet moved away from static websites to dynamic, user-generated content. Updates are fresh, revitalizing, and important for longevity.

All of this remains true for the SAP Fiori 2.0 design concept (the next stage for UX throughout SAP) and the second edition of our bestselling *SAP Fiori Implementation and Development* guide.

Inside this updated edition, SAP Fiori ace Anil Bavaraju has dispensed the implementation and development information you need to know, including step-by-step instructions and screenshots.

What did you think about *SAP Fiori Implementation and Development*? Your comments and suggestions are the most useful tools to help us make our books the best they can be. Please feel free to contact me and share any praise or criticism you may have.

Thank you for purchasing a book from SAP PRESS!

Will Jobst
Editor, SAP PRESS

willj@rheinwerk-publishing.com
www.sap-press.com
Rheinwerk Publishing · Boston, MA

Contents at a Glance

PART I   Getting Started

1   Introduction to SAP Fiori   27

2   Installation and Configuration   77

PART II   Implementation

3   SAP Fiori Security   151

4   Implementing Transactional Apps   175

5   Implementing Fact Sheet Apps   213

6   Implementing Analytical Apps   231

7   Creating OData Services with SAP Gateway   275

PART III   Custom Development and Extension

8   Introduction to SAP Web IDE   325

9   Creating and Extending Transactional Apps   369

10   Creating and Extending Fact Sheet Apps   409

11   Creating and Extending Analytical Apps   457

12   Workflow and SAP Fiori   491

13   Integration with Other SAP Products   525

14   Introduction to SAP Screen Personas   555

Appendices

A   SAP Fiori Client   585

B   Customizing SAP Fiori Launchpad   593

C   The Author   603

	3.1.3	ABAP Front-End Server to ABAP Back-End Server	158
	3.1.4	SAP Web Dispatcher to SAP HANA XS	161
3.2	**Single Sign-On and User Authentication**		163
	3.2.1	Kerberos/SPNEGO	164
	3.2.2	Security Assertion Markup Language 2.0	165
	3.2.3	SAP Logon Tickets	167
	3.2.4	X.509 Certificate	168
3.3	**User Authorizations and Management**		169
	3.3.1	User Management	169
	3.3.2	User Authorization	170
3.4	**Summary**		173

4   Implementing Transactional Apps   175

4.1	**Activating the SAPUI5 Component**		176
4.2	**Activating the OData Services**		179
4.3	**ABAP Front-End Roles**		184
	4.3.1	Copy Business Catalog Role	185
	4.3.2	Start Authorization	186
	4.3.3	Assign Roles to Users	191
4.4	**ABAP Back-End Roles**		192
	4.4.1	Copy the Back-End Role	193
	4.4.2	Assigning Roles to Users	193
4.5	**Running the App**		194
4.6	**Custom Business Catalogs and Roles**		195
	4.6.1	Create a New Launchpad and Application	196
	4.6.2	Create and Assign a Transport Request	199
	4.6.3	Create a New Catalog	201
	4.6.4	Create New Target Mapping	202
	4.6.5	Add a Static Tile	204
	4.6.6	Create the Custom Role and Add the Catalog	206
4.7	**Summary**		211

5   Implementing Fact Sheet Apps   213

5.1   **App Activation Tool** 214

5.2   **Activating the SAPUI5 Component** 218

5.3   **Activating OData Services** 219

5.4   **Assign ABAP Back-End Roles** 220

5.5   **Creating Search Connectors** 221
       5.5.1   Create Connectors Manually 223
       5.5.2   Create Connectors Automatically 225

5.6   **Indexing Search Connectors** 225

5.7   **Running the App** 228

5.8   **Summary** 230

6   Implementing Analytical Apps   231

6.1   **Overview** 232

6.2   **Implementation Prerequisites** 233

6.3   **Analytical Apps with the SAP Smart Business Modeler** 235
       6.3.1   Create the KPI 235
       6.3.2   Create Evaluations for the KPI 238
       6.3.3   Configure the KPI Tile 242
       6.3.4   Configure the KPI Drilldown 246
       6.3.5   Assign Roles to Users to Access SAP HANA Data 254
       6.3.6   Enable the App for Access in SAP Fiori Launchpad 257
       6.3.7   Assign the App Using a Custom Role 261

6.4   **Analytical Apps without the SAP Smart Business Modeler** 270
       6.4.1   Activate the SAPUI5 Application 271
       6.4.2   Assign the SAP HANA Role 271
       6.4.3   Assign the App-Specific Catalog Role 272
       6.4.4   Add the App to SAP Fiori Launchpad 272

6.5   **Summary** 273

7 Creating OData Services with SAP Gateway 275

7.1 Introduction to OData 276
7.1.1 OData Service Basics 276
7.1.2 OData Service Queries 280
7.2 SAP Gateway Service Builder 283
7.3 Modeling an OData Service 288
7.3.1 Importing OData Services 290
7.3.2 Redefining OData Services 309
7.3.3 Include SAP Gateway OData Service 321
7.4 Summary 321

PART III Custom Development and Extension

8 Introduction to SAP Web IDE 325

8.1 SAP Web IDE Overview 325
8.1.1 Architecture 326
8.1.2 Advantages 327
8.2 Setting Up SAP Web IDE with SAP Cloud Platform ... 328
8.3 Development Process Overview 333
8.3.1 Create 334
8.3.2 Develop 340
8.3.3 Preview 348
8.3.4 Deployment 351
8.4 SAP Fiori Elements 356
8.4.1 Overview Page 357
8.4.2 List Report Floorplan 358
8.4.3 Object Page Floorplan 359
8.4.4 Exercise 360
8.5 Summary 367

9 Creating and Extending Transactional Apps 369

9.1 Creating Transactional Apps 369
9.1.1 Create a New Project Using a Template 370
9.1.2 Test the App with Mock Data 373
9.1.3 Deploy the App to the ABAP Back-End Server 375
9.1.4 Publish the App to SAP Fiori Launchpad 376

9.2 Extending Transactional Apps 380
9.2.1 Extend the SAP Business Suite Layer 383
9.2.2 Extend the SAP Gateway Layer 387
9.2.3 Extend the UI Layer 397

9.3 Summary 407

10 Creating and Extending Fact Sheet Apps 409

10.1 Enabling the SAP Web IDE Fact Sheet Editor App 411
10.2 Creating Fact Sheet Apps 412
10.2.1 Create the Search Model 412
10.2.2 Create the UI Layer 418
10.2.3 Deploy the Fact Sheet App 422

10.3 Extending Fact Sheet Apps 427
10.3.1 Extend the Search Model 428
10.3.2 Extend the UI Layer 439
10.3.3 Deploy the Fact Sheet App 454

10.4 Summary 455

11 Creating and Extending Analytical Apps 457

11.1 Introduction to SAP HANA Live 457
11.1.1 SAP HANA Live Views 458
11.1.2 SAP HANA Live Browser 459
11.1.3 Exposing SAP HANA Live Views to Analytical Apps ... 461

11.2 **Creating Analytical Apps** 462

    11.2.1   Create the SAP HANA Live View 462

    11.2.2   Create the OData Service 468

    11.2.3   Configure the KPI 477

11.3 **Extending Analytical Apps** 483

    11.3.1   Extend the SAP HANA Live View 483

    11.3.2   Create the OData Service 490

    11.3.3   Configure the KPI 490

11.4 **Summary** 490

12   Workflow and SAP Fiori   491

12.1 **Workflow Basics** 491

12.2 **Creating Standard and Custom Workflows with the My Inbox App** 492

    12.2.1   Prerequisites 494

    12.2.2   All Items Tile for My Inbox 496

    12.2.3   Scenario-Specific Inbox 506

12.3 **Summary** 523

13   Integration with Other SAP Products   525

13.1 **SAP Jam** 526

    13.1.1   Prerequisites 526

    13.1.2   Configuration 527

    13.1.3   SAP Jam Tiles 534

    13.1.4   Collaboration Components 534

13.2 **SAP BusinessObjects Lumira** 536

    13.2.1   Configuration 536

    13.2.2   SAP BusinessObjects Lumira Tiles 539

    13.2.3   Configure a KPI Tile with a Drilldown to
             SAP BusinessObjects Lumira 543

13.3 **Integrating SAP BusinessObjects BI and SAP Fiori Launchpad** 544

    13.3.1   Configuration 545

    13.3.2   Create an SAP Fiori App 548

13.4 **Summary** 554

14   Introduction to SAP Screen Personas

555

14.1 **SAP Screen Personas 3.0 Architecture and Navigation** 556

14.2 **Creating Your First SAP Screen Personas Project** 560

    14.2.1   Create a Theme 560

    14.2.2   Assign the Theme to a Role and Transaction 562

    14.2.3   Create a Flavor 564

14.3 **Advanced SAP Screen Personas Flavor Concepts** 568

14.4 **SAP Screen Personas Administrative Tasks** 577

14.5 **Deploying SAP Screen Personas Flavors in SAP Fiori Launchpad** 579

14.6 **Summary** 580

Appendices

583

A   **SAP Fiori Client** 585

B   **Customizing SAP Fiori Launchpad** 593

C   **The Author** 603

Index 605

Foreword

The world is changing, and technology is at the center of everything we do. Younger generations are born into a world of rapid technological evolution, and millennials are entering the workforce with the mindset that simplicity is key. We are now a society equipped with mobile devices that allow us instant access to social networks and countless apps. Subsequently, end users are accustomed to a new and improved user experience. Businesses have caught onto this new demand quickly and have realized that enterprise software cannot be an exception. It is unacceptable to show end users the complexity of business software, and it has become imperative to provide a beautiful user experience. Businesses must change with the times if they want to stay relevant, and SAP has emerged as a leader in this evolution.

For the past few years, SAP has been rethinking enterprise software with a focus on end users. Enterprise software is powerful and covers end-to-end business processes. However, the end-to-end cycle is not one-size-fits-all. Depending on your role in an enterprise, you might need to see different data than a counterpart in your organization. For this reason, SAP set out to completely reimagine the end user experience. SAP began by focusing on the most commonly used business transactions, such as vacation requests, time entry, expense reporting, and so on. Then, SAP set out to develop a consistent and holistic user experience for SAP software. Five design guidelines were established to aid in this evolution: role-based, delightful, coherent, simple, and responsive. By keeping a focused alignment with growing end user demands, SAP quickly realized that apps needed to be created per role, allow users to complete their jobs easily, be consistent across offerings, and work intuitively on any device. In May 2013, SAP hit the mark and launched SAP Fiori as the new user experience for SAP.

Today, SAP Fiori consists of over 500 apps, ranging across all lines of business and industries. To support the breadth of business transactions used by customers, SAP developed three supporting SAP Fiori app types: transactional, fact sheet, and analytical apps. Transactional apps support task-based access and support changes, as well as creations and approvals with guided navigation. Fact sheet apps allow you to search and explore essential information about objects and provide contextual navigation between related objects. Analytical apps provide a visual overview of a dedicated topic for further KPI-related analysis. Transactional app types can run on either an AS ABAP or SAP HANA database, but fact sheet and analytical app types require an

SAP HANA database. All these app types are accessed using SAP Fiori launchpad, a web-based entry point for SAP business applications that allows end users to personalize their views.

While SAP worked to simplify business processes and to provide a delightful end user experience, they also realized that customers have individual needs, and out-of-the-box apps might not work for everyone. In recognition of this fact, SAP developed tools to support developers and designers in their implementation of SAP Fiori. Tools such as the SAP Web IDE provide developers everything they need to customize and extend the apps to work for their business, whereas the UI Theme Designer enables companies to easily brand their SAP Fiori launchpads and apps to align with their company brands and color schemes.

SAP Fiori Implementation and Development delivers a comprehensive, end-to-end understanding of SAP Fiori, providing developers and IT professionals with in-depth knowledge of SAP Fiori as the user experience for SAP business applications. With a specific focus dedicated to the deployment and configuration of each of the app types, readers can also expect to learn about technical aspects required for a successful implementation, as well as the security and authentication options vital for their organizations. You will conclude your SAP Fiori learning experience by discovering the underlying technologies and tools that support SAP Fiori, including the creation and extension of OData services within SAP Gateway, the SAP Web IDE for UI extensibility and customizations, business workflows for approval apps, and integration with other SAP technologies.

After reading this book, you will understand not only what SAP Fiori is, but also how you can also leverage its technology to provide your end users with a delightful and consistent user experience. Gone are the days of complexity and focusing only on feature enhancements. SAP has created a new standard of focusing on end users, providing them with a holistic experience centered on tasks relevant to their jobs. The teachings in this book will provide you with the tools to immediately enable SAP Fiori in your organization. With detailed explanations and guidance throughout, *SAP Fiori Implementation and Development* will help simplify your business processes.

Liz Thorburn, SAP
Technology RIG, Development
P&I Technology

Preface

SAP Fiori is a user experience (UX) for SAP software. It applies modern design principles to SAP software and provides a personalized, responsive, and easy-to-use UX. SAP Fiori is a set of applications (HR apps, customer relationship apps, financial apps, and more) that run on SAP ERP and fall into one of three categories based on their general purpose: transactional apps, fact sheet apps, or analytical apps. These apps provide a user interface (UI) from which to use functionality already present in an SAP system.

There are several things a company can do with SAP Fiori applications:

- Implement them
- Customize them
- Create them from scratch

Regardless of what a company does with these apps, any form of implementation or development requires SAP Gateway (the integration technology that connects a front-end SAP Fiori app to the back-end SAP system). In addition, knowledge of SAPUI5 (the programming language on which the UI for SAP Fiori apps is based) is needed to customize or create apps.

It's time to take the first step in your SAP Fiori journey! In this introduction, we'll discuss the book's target audience, lay out its purpose, and provide a structural overview of the topics that lie ahead.

Target Audience

SAP Fiori has a broad appeal, given its wide use in SAP systems and the many apps it offers across industries. However, because of the technical details involved in implementing and developing SAP Fiori apps, this book is primarily focused on the following two audiences:

- Developers and administrators at companies that run SAP ERP
- Consultants hired to implement SAP Fiori for a company running SAP ERP

Again, this casts a wide net in terms of readers for this book. However, each chapter will lay out the general knowledge and prerequisites required for implementing and developing each SAP Fiori app type.

Objective

This book is meant to be a complete guide to implementing and developing SAP Fiori apps; its purpose therefore is to teach you how to implement, customize, and create SAP Fiori applications. You will walk away with a complete understanding of how to accomplish all these tasks thanks to step-by-step instructions, screenshots, and example applications.

Structure of the Book

This book is divided into three parts. Part I, Getting Started, explains the first steps in SAP Fiori: a basic explanation of what it is and instructions on installation and configuration.

Part I includes the following chapters:

- **Chapter 1: Introduction to SAP Fiori**
  To begin your journey, we will look at SAP Fiori's architecture and integration, with a focus on reverse proxy (with SAP Web Dispatcher) and channels of communication. We will then discuss the three SAP Fiori app types and related technologies, such as SAP Gateway, SAPUI5, and SAP HANA.

- **Chapter 2: Installation and Configuration**
  Before any implementation or development can begin, you will need to install and configure your SAP system so that it is ready to deploy SAP Fiori apps. Chapter 2 begins by looking at the three SAP Fiori system landscapes used for implementing the apps: the ABAP environment, the SAP HANA database, and SAP HANA XS. We then move on to the two compatible deployment options: central hub and embedded. The final two sections walk through the installation and configuration processes.

Part II, Implementation, is devoted to the implementation of SAP Fiori apps. It starts by introducing the security measures that should be in place to ensure that the apps are safe. It then explains the step-by-step process for implementing the three different types of SAP Fiori apps: transactional, fact sheet, and analytical. Next, it devotes a chapter to creating OData services in SAP Gateway, which is required in all implementations for the front-end of SAP Fiori to communicate with the back-end of SAP.

Part II includes the following chapters:

- **Chapter 3: SAP Fiori Security**
  It's important to understand the various security mechanisms that can be put in place to prevent the unauthorized and unauthenticated use of SAP Fiori apps. In this chapter, we look at securing the app communication channels and security measures for encryption. We then delve into single sign-on and authenticating app users. Finally, we provide an overview of how to manage users and authorize access.

- **Chapter 4: Implementing Transactional Apps**
  In this first app implementation chapter, we begin by looking at how to implement transactional apps, including activating the SAPUI5 component and OData services. Next, we dive into the ABAP front-end and back-end roles before running the app. We end the chapter with a discussion of creating custom business catalogs and roles.

- **Chapter 5: Implementing Fact Sheet Apps**
  Many ABAP front-end tasks are shared between transactional and fact sheet apps. Chapter 5 focuses on the specific fact sheet app implementation steps that must be completed, including creating search connectors manually and automatically and indexing the search connectors.

- **Chapter 6: Implementing Analytical Apps**
  There are two types of analytical apps: typical analytical apps and analytical apps enabled via the SAP Smart Business modeler. Chapter 6 begins by spelling out the necessary implementation prerequisites before diving deep into the tasks necessary to implement both analytical app types.

- **Chapter 7: Creating OData Services with SAP Gateway**
  SAP Gateway OData services are required to connect SAP Fiori to the SAP back-end system. Chapter 7 offers instructions for how to create OData services. You will use the steps presented here to create OData services when creating SAP Fiori apps in Part III.

Part III, Custom Development and Extension, is devoted to the development tasks related to SAP Fiori, which fall into two categories: new app creation and customization (extension). Both tasks are discussed for each of the three types of SAP Fiori apps. Then, we move on to other important topics that fall under a developer's purview: workflow and integration with other SAP products.

Part III includes the following chapters:

- **Chapter 8: Introduction to SAP Web IDE**
  SAP Web IDE is the environment used to create and extend transactional, fact sheet, and analytical apps. Chapter 8 begins with an overview of the SAP Web IDE environment, including its architecture and advantages, then transitions to the steps for setting up the SAP Web IDE with SAP Cloud Platform. We conclude the chapter by walking through the development process itself, from creation to deployment.

- **Chapter 9: Creating and Extending Transactional Apps**
  SAP Fiori apps can be created from scratch, or you can extend existing apps. In Chapter 9, we look at how to create and extend transactional apps—from creating a new project using a template to extending the UI layer.

- **Chapter 10: Creating and Extending Fact Sheet Apps**
  In Chapter 10, we discuss how to enable the SAP Web IDE fact sheet editor app, which is necessary for the creation and extension process. We will then look at everything from creating the UI layer to extending an existing search model.

- **Chapter 11: Creating and Extending Analytical Apps**
  Analytical apps are developed on query views from SAP HANA Live. Chapter 11 presents an overview of SAP HANA Live, then moves on to the steps to create and extend our example analytical app.

- **Chapter 12: Workflow and SAP Fiori**
  The most common modifications to SAP Fiori apps involve modifying their workflow. Accordingly, Chapter 12 provides an overview of SAP Business Workflow. In addition, we discuss how and when to create a custom workflow, with an example based on the My Inbox app.

- **Chapter 13: Integration with Other SAP Products**
  SAP Fiori apps can be integrated with other SAP products. In Chapter 13, we look at how these apps can be integrated with SAP Jam, SAP BusinessObjects Lumira, and SAP BusinessObjects Design Studio.

- **Chapter 14: Introduction to SAP Screen Personas**
  Chapter 14 introduces the SAP Screen Personas solution. We'll also explain how SAP Screen Personas allows you to transform classic SAP screens into SAP Fiori-inspired designs.

The book then concludes with two appendices on SAP Fiori Client and customizing SAP Fiori launchpad:

- **Appendix A: SAP Fiori Client**
  Appendix A provides a brief introduction to SAP Fiori Client, a native SAP Fiori app for iOS and Android. Information found here includes download and login steps, as well as an overview of SAP Fiori Client functions.

- **Appendix B: Customizing SAP Fiori Launchpad**
  SAP Fiori launchpad provides a platform for accessing all SAP Fiori apps. Using the UI Theme Designer, you can customize SAP Fiori launchpad to your liking. In Appendix B, we walk through how to do so, as well as how to create a custom SAP Fiori launchpad theme.

Our hope is that this book will provide an understanding of the steps involved in installing, implementing, developing, and integrating SAP Fiori apps based on your business requirements.

Acknowledgments

I would like to dedicate this book to my wife Puja and my son Arjun, who supported and encouraged me despite all the endless hours, evenings, and weekends that I took away from them.

I would also like to thank Kelly Grace Weaver for the trust placed in me and for the opportunity to write this book. I would like to extend a heartfelt thanks to the editor, Hareem Shafi, and development editor, Will Jobst, who supported me every step of the way, from the ideas in every chapter of this book to its publication, and for providing advice and help always.

My final—yet very important—thanks goes to the entire SAP PRESS team involved in creating this book.

Anil Bavaraju
March 2017

PART I
Getting Started

Chapter 1
Introduction to SAP Fiori

To begin your SAP Fiori journey, we'll start with the basics: SAP Fiori's architecture, app types, and the related SAP technologies required for implementation.

In today's business environment, users face many challenges in the hunt for timely, up-to-date, and accurate information. In addition, accessibility to this information, anywhere, anytime, is vital to their ability to make faster, smarter decisions. Applications have revolutionized the landscape of "on-demand" business accessibility in addressing the needs of these users.

SAP's answer is *SAP Fiori*. SAP Fiori provides a role-based, personalized user experience (UX) for enterprise-wide engagements across lines of businesses (LOBs) and offers optimal usability on multiple devices for the best business interactions. In this book, we'll discuss the development skills needed to implement, customize, and create SAP Fiori apps.

In this chapter, we'll introduce you to SAP Fiori and all the related concepts you'll come across throughout this book. We'll start with an overview of SAP Fiori and SAP's UX strategy in Section 1.1, then dive into SAP Fiori's architecture and integration technologies in Section 1.2. From there, we'll look at the three main types of SAP Fiori apps—transactional, fact sheet, and analytical—in Section 1.3. Finally, in Section 1.4, we'll discuss related SAP technologies that enable the implementation and use of these apps.

1.1 SAP Fiori and the Evolution of User Experience

Technology requirements are changing. An emphasis on UX now is prevalent in the creation of new and emerging products. Following the popularity of Facebook and Twitter apps, users want a similar UX for their business applications.

At SAP SAPPHIRE 2013, SAP released a new class of SAPUI5-based applications and dubbed them *SAP Fiori*, as part of their revamped UX strategy. The idea: Apply modern design principles for a totally reimagined UX.

The initial release of SAP Fiori had 25 apps, and today (December 2016) the number of SAP Fiori apps has grown rapidly to over 7500, providing consistent and simple UX across multiple devices. The next significant step in the evolution of UX for business applications is SAP Fiori 2.0, a new, award-winning design concept that's now available for both SAP S/4HANA and SAP Business Suite.

Even now, SAP continues to work on new and innovative SAP Fiori apps to add to its portfolio. Up-to-date app information can be found in the SAP Fiori apps reference library: *https://fioriappslibrary.hana.ondemand.com/sap/fix/externalViewer/*. Chapter 2, Section 2.4 provides further information on the apps reference library.

> **Meaning in the Name**
>
> *Fiori* means *flower* in Italian. This is why you'll see pictures of flowers associated with SAP Fiori—such as the cover of this book.

In the sections that follow, we'll provide an overview of SAP's UX strategy, then describe how it's impacted the UX design principles used to develop SAP Fiori apps.

1.1.1   SAP UX Strategy

SAP's UX strategy has four areas of focus:

- **New**
  SAP continues to create new applications with consumer-grade UXs to accomplish customer needs.
- **Renew**
  SAP took all the most frequently used business scenarios and renewed them with SAP Fiori apps by improving the UX.
- **Enable**
  This principle gives SAP customers and partners the ability to improve the UX on their own using various enablement tools. For example, SAP Screen Personas enables customers to optimize or simplify any screen in the graphical user interface (GUI).

- **UX design services**
  This element came about thanks to customers who wanted to transfer their own reality into the SAP UX strategy.

UX design services are at the heart of the SAP UX strategy. Some believe that UX is simply a lot of colors and fancy components, but this simply is not true. Great UX can have a tremendous impact on a business' success. With great UX, you can

- Achieve productivity and work more efficiently
- Increase user adoption and decrease errors
- Save on training costs

To achieve true design innovation, keep the following three concepts in mind:

1. **Business**
   Understanding the business requirements
2. **Technology**
   Exploring and understanding the feasibility of technology
3. **Human values**
   Understanding what usability and desirability mean to your users

As previously mentioned, only once these three components are combined will you achieve design innovation.

In the same vein, in the next section, we'll discuss how SAP's UX design services have been implemented into SAP Fiori UX design principles.

1.1.2   SAP Fiori UX Design Principles

SAP Fiori design principles ensure that all business applications follow the UX design services developed by SAP. The following are five design principles that make up the SAP Fiori UX paradigm. These five design principals together create a beautiful UX that is consistent, regardless of your role in the organization, and delivers the best user experience on any device.

1. **Role-based**
   SAP broke down several SAP transactions and turned them into easy-to-use apps that are task-based and tailored to show only the most relevant information that the user needs.
2. **Responsive**
   SAP ensured that SAP Fiori worked seamlessly to facilitate consistent UX across all

devices, such as phones, tablets, and desktops, and SAP Fiori supports multiple technologies, such as iOS, Android, Windows, and Mac.

3. **Simple**

SAP Fiori is focused on delivering simple, intuitive UX to match consumer demands. SAP used a simple 1-1-3 (one user, one use case, and three screens) philosophy to make SAP Fiori apps easy to use and learn.

4. **Coherent**

SAP ensured that all SAP Fiori apps have a similar look and feel by establishing best practices for design.

5. **Delightful**

SAP Fiori is designed to have a low barrier to adoption and to provide users with apps that enable them to be proactive by providing an assistant.

SAP and Apple Partnership

In May 2016, SAP and Apple announced their partnership, combining Apple's world-renowned UXs with SAP's unparalleled end-to-end business processes and software. All the SAP Fiori for iOS design guidelines are available at *https://experience.sap.com/fiori-design-ios/*.

Clearly defined design principles ensure quality SAP Fiori apps across software environments. Now, let's turn our attention to the architectural components and integration technologies found in SAP Fiori.

1.2   Architecture and Integration

In this section, we'll discuss the high-level architecture that all SAP Fiori apps follow. Figure 1.1 shows different components of the architecture.

From this bird's-eye view, we see that the SAP Fiori system landscape is comprised of a client/browser layer, reverse proxy, ABAP servers, SAP HANA XS, and a back-end database. Each layer has a clearly defined purpose and is bundled with components that help fulfill that purpose. Let's look at each layer:

- **Client/browser**

  The client layer is where the actual consumption of SAP Fiori apps takes place. SAP Fiori launchpad is the entry point for all SAP Fiori apps on mobile, desktop, or tablet (see Section 1.2.1).

- **Reverse proxy**
  A *reverse proxy* is a type of proxy server that typically sits behind the firewall in a private network and directs client requests to the appropriate back-end server. The reverse proxy provides an additional level of security and control to ensure the smooth flow of network traffic between clients and servers. SAP recommends using *SAP Web Dispatcher* as a reverse proxy server (see Section 1.2.2). SAP Web Dispatcher is only required as a reverse proxy for analytical and fact sheet apps.

- **ABAP server**
  The ABAP front-end server is recommended for all app types. The ABAP front-end server contains the UI layer and infrastructure components, as well as SAP Gateway with OData enablement. The ABAP back-end server contains the back-end business logic and search models for fact sheet apps.

- **SAP HANA XS**
  SAP HANA XS is only required for analytical apps; it replicates data from the back-end server and remodels it using virtual data models (VDMs).

- **Back-end server**
  The back-end database can be any database for transactional apps or an SAP HANA database for fact sheet and analytical apps.

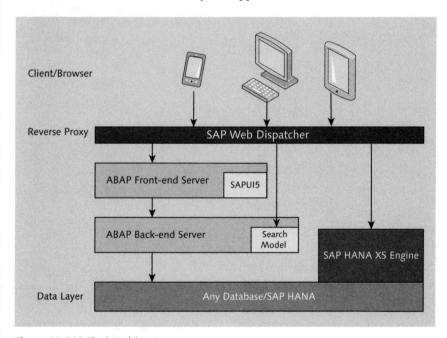

Figure 1.1 SAP Fiori Architecture

Now that you have a general idea of SAP Fiori's architecture and system landscape, we'll look more closely at some of the key architectural features and explore how the different layers of SAP Fiori communicate with one another.

1.2.1   SAP Fiori Launchpad

SAP Fiori launchpad is the entry point for all SAP Fiori applications. It's a role-based, personalized platform with real-time capabilities. The beauty of SAP Fiori launchpad is that it's designed according to a simple and intuitive user experience and doesn't require a lot of training.

Figure 1.2 shows the SAP Fiori 2.0 launchpad homepage, now called the *viewport*, which displays variety of apps; a new panoramic UI with notification and ME areas comes with the new experience. Users can personalize the viewport to keep track of their daily tasks while still keeping track of activities happening in other areas.

Figure 1.2 SAP Fiori Launchpad Homepage

With SAP Fiori launchpad, users can personalize the homepage/viewport views by adding or removing apps or by bundling them into groups. Because apps are controlled by roles, users will have access to only those apps or groups to which content administrators assign them.

When you open the launchpad for the first time, you should see the tiles clustered in groups ❶, and if you have more than one group assigned to you, then you'll see all the groups in the anchor bar ❷ at the top of the page. Click a group in the dropdown list in the anchor bar ❸ to jump directly to that group?

On the top left of the home page is the ME area ❹; clicking the icon slides the ME area into the view. The ME area provides an options bar and lists the most recently used tiles. On the top right of the home page is the notifications area ❺, which helps users keep track of important events without distracting them from their current tasks.

Search ❻ is another key capability of SAP Fiori launchpad. With this feature, users can view recent searches, recent apps used, and any apps found. In addition, users can open a fact sheet app directly. For example, a user can search for a sales order number in SAP Fiori launchpad and open the Sales Order fact sheet app to get answers immediately. In Chapter 5, we'll discuss the implementation of search functionality in fact sheet apps.

SAP Fiori 2.0 now supports the new, award-winning Belize theme; this theme replaces the old Blue Crystal theme. Users can also create their own custom themes using UI Theme Designer, and apply them to SAP Fiori launchpad ❼. In Appendix B, we'll walk through the step-by-step instructions on how to create a custom theme using this tool.

Now, let's explore the ME area. In the options bar of the ME area, you'll see **App Finder**, **Settings**, and **Edit Home Page** (see Figure 1.3).

Figure 1.3 ME Area

1. App Finder is a convenient tool for finding apps that aren't on your home page yet and to add them to the home page. In the catalogs of the App Finder view, you can find apps assigned to your role (see Figure 1.4).

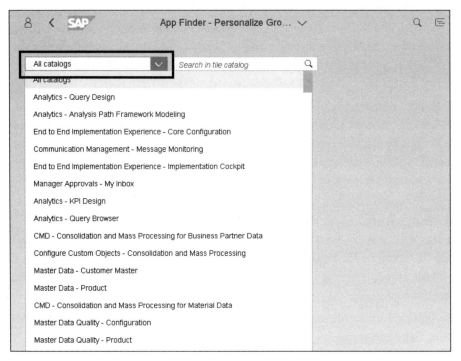

Figure 1.4 App Finder

2. Select **Settings** to set options to display your user account information, change the theme, or change language and user settings. **User Profiling** (see Figure 1.5) lets you record some of your activities to provide personalized results for future searches, and the **Default values** option (see Figure 1.5) option lets you define and launch apps with a set of specific default values.

3. The **Edit home page** option lets you customize your launchpad—by adding or remove or moving tiles/groups.

From the home page of the SAP Fiori Launchpad click ☰ to open the notifications area (see Figure 1.6). This new option in SAP Fiori 2.0 notifies users about important things like approving workflow items from My Inbox; in fact, you can approve or reject workflows right from the notifications area.

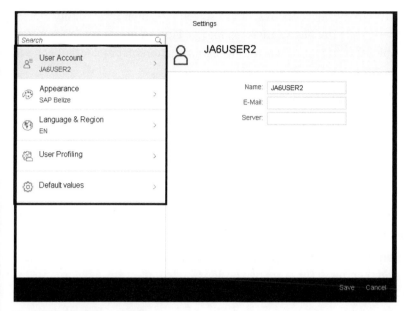

Figure 1.5 ME Area—Settings

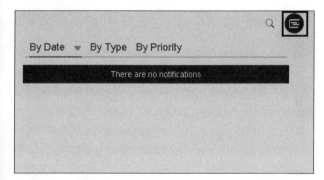

Figure 1.6 Notifications Area

Notifications

SAP Fiori Notifications integration is currently possible only with SAP S/4HANA and not yet available with SAP Business Suite.

Another important aspect of SAP Fiori launchpad is its responsiveness. SAP Fiori launchpad enables cross-device UX for users. This feature makes it so that visual design adapts automatically to the respective screen size, be it for desktop, mobile phones, or tablets. SAP provides a native app for SAP Fiori launchpad called *SAP Fiori Client* that enables this functionality (for more information on SAP Fiori Client, see Appendix A).

Next, let's discuss the different deployment options for SAP Fiori launchpad.

Deployment Options

There are several deployment options available to deploy SAP Fiori launchpad. Depending on your existing landscape and the types of apps you want to implement, you can decide which deployment option is right for you.

As shown in Figure 1.7, you can deploy SAP Fiori launchpad on-premise, in the cloud, or in a hybrid model.

- In an on-premise deployment, a customer buys software from SAP and manages the servers on their own. There are two options:
  - **ABAP front-end server in combination with SAP Gateway**
    This is the traditional implementation and is recommended for customers without an SAP Enterprise Portal implementation. It's the only platform that supports all SAP Fiori app types (transactional, fact sheet, and analytical apps).
  - **SAP Enterprise Portal**
    This deployment is recommended for customers who would want to reuse their existing SAP Enterprise Portal and run SAP Fiori launchpad. Technically, this is just another framework page that enables the use of SAP Fiori launchpad.
- In a cloud deployment, customers rent infrastructure and business software from SAP. Customers can either share a public cloud environment operated by SAP or get a private/managed cloud service (i.e., there's only one customer per cloud; this is managed by SAP as well) or get an enterprise cloud (again, only one customer per cloud, but the customer runs and manages the cloud).
  - **SAP Cloud Platform**
    You can now run SAP Fiori launchpad on SAP Cloud Platform in the software-as-a-service (SaaS) model or on-premise.
- In a hybrid deployment, customers run certain parts of their business on their own servers and use additional services from a cloud provider. This kind of deployment requires powerful integration between on-premise systems and cloud services.

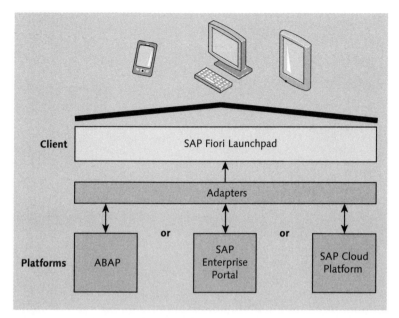

Figure 1.7 SAP Fiori Launchpad Deployments

More Information

For more information on the different SAP Fiori launchpad deployments and on how to implement SAP Fiori launchpad, check out the SAP PRESS E-Bite *Implementing SAP Fiori Launchpad*, by Tamas Szirtes and Aviad Rivlin, available at *www.sap-press.com/3944*.

Features

In this section, we'll walk you through some of the basic features in SAP Fiori launchpad. The following steps walk through the different features and uses of SAP Fiori launchpad. To begin, let's look at adding to, removing from, and personalizing the SAP Fiori Launchpad viewport.

1. Launch SAP Fiori launchpad by entering the following URL in a browser, where <host> is the server name or the IP address of the server, and the <port> is the port number: *https://<host>:<port>/sap/bc/ui5/ui2/ushell/shells/abap/FioriLaunchpad.html*, for example, *https://s4hana.nineboards.com:8001/sap/bc/ui5/ui2/ushell/shells/abap/FioriLaunchpad.html*.

> **Note**
>
> You can launch the SAP Fiori Launchpad by running Transaction /UI2/FLP from the AS ABAP front-end server.

2. Login to SAP Fiori launchpad, navigate to the ME area by clicking 8, and then click **Edit Home Page** (see Figure 1.8).

Figure 1.8 Edit Home Page

3. To remove a tile, click **X** in the upper-right corner of the tile.
4. The tile catalog is where you'll see all the SAP Fiori apps that you have access to. To add a tile from the tile catalog, click **+** (see Figure 1.9).

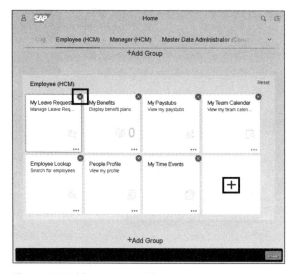

Figure 1.9 Add or Remove Tiles

5. Click **+** on the app and then select the group into which you want to add the app. Click **OK** (see Figure 1.10).

Figure 1.10 Add Tile from Catalog

6. Click 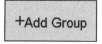 to go back to the workspace area.

Next, let's create a new group and organize the tiles. Proceed with the following steps:

1. From the viewport, click **Add Group** (see Figure 1.11).

+Add Group

Figure 1.11 Add Group

2. Enter a group name and click **Done** (see Figure 1.12).

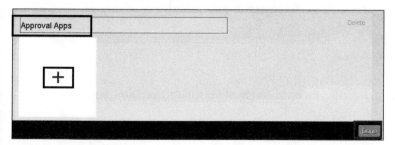

Figure 1.12 Group Name

3. Users can add tiles/apps by dragging and dropping apps from another group (see Figure 1.13) or can add a new app from the catalog by clicking **+** (see Figure 1.12).

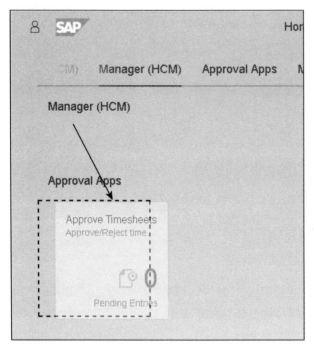

Figure 1.13 Drag and Drop

You can also search for apps or business objects. To do so, proceed as follows:

1. Enter the search term in the search field and click Q (see Figure 1.14).

Figure 1.14 Search

2. Check the search results for apps and business objects, as shown in Figure 1.15.

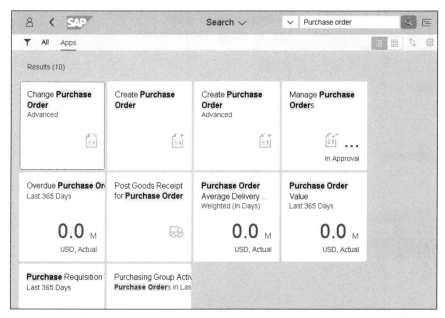

Figure 1.15 Search Output

Users can personalize SAP Fiori launchpad by changing the theme. To do so, perform the following steps:

1. Click 🔲 to open the ME area and select **Settings** (see Figure 1.16).

2. In the pop-up window, click **Appearance** (see Figure 1.16).

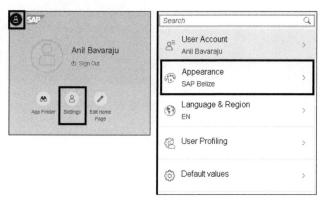

Figure 1.16 Theme Settings

3. Select a theme and click **Save** (see Figure 1.17).

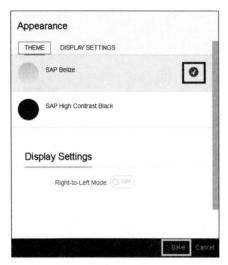

Figure 1.17 Select Theme

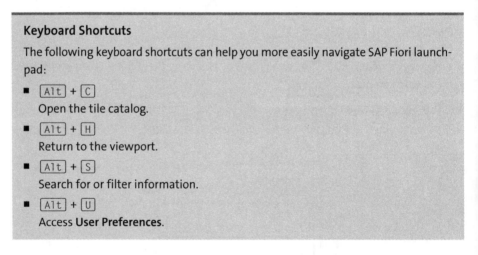

Keyboard Shortcuts

The following keyboard shortcuts can help you more easily navigate SAP Fiori launch-pad:

- ⎡Alt⎤ + ⎡C⎤
  Open the tile catalog.
- ⎡Alt⎤ + ⎡H⎤
  Return to the viewport.
- ⎡Alt⎤ + ⎡S⎤
  Search for or filter information.
- ⎡Alt⎤ + ⎡U⎤
  Access **User Preferences**.

We hope that this quick walkthrough of SAP Fiori launchpad helped you to better understand its features. Next, we'll dive into SAP Web Dispatcher and its role as a reverse proxy.

1.2.2   SAP Web Dispatcher

Depending on the type of SAP Fiori app you're running (transactional, fact sheet, or analytical), queries are directed by the SAP Web Dispatcher from the client/browser to the ABAP front-end or SAP HANA XS. It isn't mandatory to use SAP Web Dispatcher if you're implementing transactional apps, but for analytical apps and fact sheet apps you'll need to configure it.

When a user runs an analytical app, requests are forwarded from the client to the SAP HANA XS engine by SAP Web Dispatcher. Similarly, when a user runs a fact sheet app, requests are forwarded from the client to the ABAP back-end system by SAP Web Dispatcher. SAP Web Dispatcher can either act as a simple forwarding service or actively participate in the exchange between a client and server.

SAP Web Dispatcher is capable of intercepting, inspecting, and interacting with requests and responses. Interacting with requests and responses enables more advanced traffic management services, such as application layer security, web acceleration, page routing, and secure remote access. SAP Web Dispatcher also provides the ability to direct requests based on a wide variety of parameters, such as user device, location, network conditions, and even time of day.

Common uses for SAP Web Dispatcher include the following:

- **Load balancing**
  SAP Web Dispatcher is most commonly used to provide load balancing services for scalability and availability. Increasingly, SAP Web Dispatcher is also used as a strategic point in the network to enforce web application security through web application firewalls, application delivery firewalls, and deep content inspection to mitigate data leaks. SAP Web Dispatcher can also be deployed to offload services from applications to improve performance through acceleration, intelligence, and caching.

- **Web acceleration**
  SAP Web Dispatcher can compress inbound and outbound data and can cache commonly requested content, both of which speed up the flow of traffic between the browser and the ABAP servers or SAP HANA XS. SAP Web Dispatcher can also perform additional tasks such as SSL encryption to take the load off your web servers, thereby boosting their performance.

- **Security and anonymity**
  By intercepting requests headed for your back-end servers, SAP Web Dispatcher protects request identities and acts as an additional defense against security attacks. It also ensures that multiple servers can be accessed from a single record locater or URL, regardless of the structure of your local area network.

1.2.3 Communication Channels

It's vital that different layers of SAP Fiori can communicate with one another. In this section, we'll discuss how data is transferred between the client, ABAP front-end, ABAP back-end, and SAP HANA XS. In doing so, we'll highlight the different communication channels and protocols implemented in the SAP Fiori system landscape. Figure 1.18 shows the high-level SAP Fiori architecture, with the communication channels and protocols included.

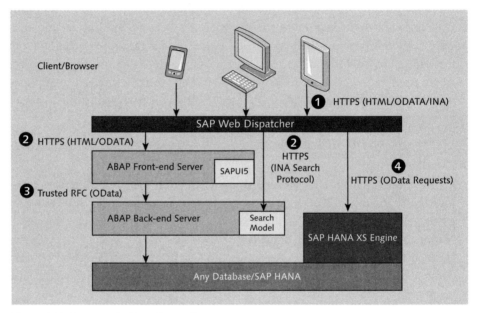

Figure 1.18 Communication Channels

As shown, the communication type between the client and SAP Web Dispatcher ❶ depends on the type of application the user's running in the client/browser or the type of task that the user is performing. For example, when a user runs a fact sheet app, the client sends an INA search request.

The communication between SAP Web Dispatcher and ABAP servers ❷ depends on the type of request SAP Web Dispatcher forwards from the client to the ABAP servers:

- **ABAP front-end server (transactional apps)**
  - HTML requests
  - OData requests

- ABAP back-end server (fact sheet apps only)
  - INA search requests

A trusted RFC connection is established for communication between the ABAP front-end server and the ABAP back-end server ❸. Data and services are provided from the ABAP back-end server to the ABAP front-end server using OData services.

Communication between SAP Web Dispatcher and SAP HANA XS ❹ only happens when a user runs analytical apps. SAP Web Dispatcher forwards the OData request from the client to SAP HANA XS.

Understanding how each of these components speak with one another is useful when errors or issues arise.

1.2.4 SAP Fiori App-Supported Browsers and OS

In this section, we'll list the browsers (Internet Explorer [IE], Google Chrome, Safari, Microsoft Edge, and Mozilla Firefox) and OS versions (Windows, Apple, and Android) that support SAP Fiori apps.

Blackberry
Blackberry OS support ended in October 2016.

Windows Support

Table 1.1 shows the Windows mobile devices and browsers that support SAP Fiori apps.

OS Type	OS Version	SAP Fiori Client	Microsoft Browser
Phone	8.1 GDR1	Latest version	IE 11.x
	10	Latest version	Microsoft Edge

Table 1.1 Windows Mobile

Table 1.2 shows the Windows desktops and browsers that support SAP Fiori apps.

OS Type	OS Version	Microsoft Browser	Google Chrome	Mozilla Firefox
Hybrid (touch-enabled desktops)	8.1	IE 11.x	–	–
	10	Microsoft Edge	–	–
Desktop	8 8.1	IE 10.x IE 11.x	Latest version	Latest rapid release cycle (RRC) Latest extended support release (ESR)
	10	Microsoft Edge	Latest version	Latest RRC Latest ESR
	7	IE 9.x IE 11.x	Latest version	Latest RRC Latest ESR

Table 1.2 Windows Desktop

Internet Explorer 9

IE 9 is not supported for any SAP Fiori apps.

Apple Support

Table 1.3 shows Apple's iOS devices and browsers that support SAP Fiori apps.

OS Type	OS Version	SAP Fiori Client	Apple Safari
iPhone 5 or newer	9.x – 10.x	Latest version	Latest version
iPad Pro, Mini, or Air	9.x – 10.x	Latest version	Latest version

Table 1.3 iOS (iPhone/iPad)

Table 1.4 shows Apple's MacOS X versions and browsers that support SAP Fiori apps.

OS Type	OS Version	SAP Fiori Client	Apple Safari
Desktop	OS X 10.9 OS X 10.10 OS X 10.11	Latest version	Latest Version

Table 1.4 Mac

Android Support

Table 1.5 shows Google's Android devices and browsers that support SAP Fiori apps.

OS Type	OS Version	SAP Fiori Client	Android Browser	Google Chrome
Phone/ Tablet	4.1.3–7.x	Latest version	Latest version	Latest version

Table 1.5 Android Phones/Tablets

Android Devices

The following Android devices have been tested by SAP:

- **Phones**
  Samsung Galaxy S4, S5, S6
- **Tablets**
  Samsung Galaxy Tab Series Pro, Samsung Galaxy Tab Series Pro S, Google Nexus

---

1.2.5   SAP Fiori, Cloud Edition

SAP Fiori, cloud edition is one of the major new releases in SAP Fiori. SAP Fiori, cloud edition provides customers with a simple approach to revolutionize UX by using SAP Fiori apps and services in the cloud, running on SAP Cloud Platform.

With SAP Fiori, cloud edition, customers can connect easily to their on-premise SAP landscape and experience SAP Fiori with literally zero installation and configuration. SAP released a demo cloud edition so that customers can explore SAP Fiori by connecting to their on-premise SAP landscape and can build some prototypes. During SAPPHIRE 2016, SAP released SAP Fiori cloud edition for general availability (GA).

Accessing SAP Fiori, Cloud Edition Trial

You can now access the SAP Fiori, cloud edition trial from the following link: *http:// www.sapfioritrial.com*. Once you open the webpage, click the **See it in Action** button to access the SAP Fiori, cloud edition trial.

SAP Fiori, Cloud Edition Architecture

Figure 1.19 shows the high-level architecture of SAP Fiori, cloud edition. Your on-premise SAP Business Suite is securely connected to SAP Cloud Platform using the SAP Cloud Platform cloud connector. In the SAP Cloud Platform, SAP Fiori launchpad, SAP Fiori apps, UI Theme Designer, and SAP Web IDE run as services consuming data from your on-premise systems.

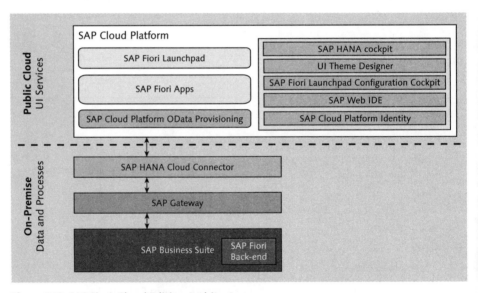

Figure 1.19 SAP Fiori, Cloud Edition Architecture

The best part of the SAP Cloud Platform is that customers can quickly use SAP Fiori launchpad without worrying about software maintenance or updates, and they can seamlessly leverage cloud services to extend and develop SAP Fiori apps.

SAP Fiori On-Premise vs. SAP Fiori Cloud

Now, let's look at some of the key differences between SAP Fiori on-premise and SAP Fiori, cloud edition from both architecture and features perspectives. Figure 1.20 shows the simple, high-level architecture of SAP Fiori, comparing on-premise and cloud versions.

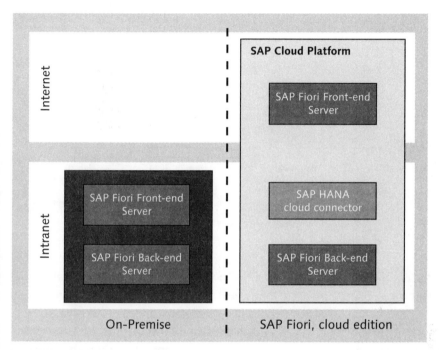

Figure 1.20 SAP Fiori On-Premise vs. SAP Fiori Cloud

Be aware of the following key points:

- SAP Fiori on-premise is managed in your own data center, with full flexibility in installation and configuration. All seven thousand plus apps can be installed and configured.

- SAP Fiori, cloud edition is managed by SAP, and customers can quickly connect SAP Business Suite to it. Only around 70 apps are currently supported on SAP Fiori, cloud edition.

Now that we've looked at SAP Fiori, cloud edition, next we'll begin discussing the different types of SAP Fiori apps.

1.3   Types of SAP Fiori Apps

Whether you want to create or track purchase orders, keep an eye on new business opportunities, or simply display your invoices, SAP Fiori apps help you easily handle business tasks. As of the writing of this book (December 2016), there three types of applications that form the SAP Fiori portfolio: transactional, fact sheet, and analytical apps. Before we jump into the details of each of these app types, we'll illustrate the SAP Fiori journey through individual app developments (see Figure 1.21).

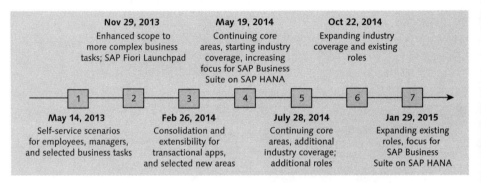

Figure 1.21 SAP Fiori Timeline

It all started in May 2013 (during the SAP SAPPHIRE event). That was when SAP released the first 25 SAP Fiori apps; they were transactional apps that focused on self-service scenarios, Employee Self-Service (ESS) and Manager Self-Service (MSS). From there, SAP began rapidly developing new apps, and in November 2013, SAP introduced two new app types: fact sheet and analytical apps. SAP then continued to expand the scope of apps, from SAP ERP to any database to SAP HANA databases. In May 2014, SAP introduced SAP Fiori apps for different LOBs and industries.

Table 1.6 shows the product shipments, with the release dates and the number of apps SAP delivered during that time. You can see that the SAP Fiori team is releasing more and more apps every quarter.

Shipments	Release Month	No. of Apps (Cumulative)
1	May 2013	25
2	Nov. 2013	226

Table 1.6 SAP Fiori Shipments

Shipments	Release Month	No. of Apps (Cumulative)
3	Feb. 2014	236
4	May 2014	325
5	July 2014	383
6	Oct. 2014	484
7	Jan. 2015	495
8	Dec. 2016	1,139

Table 1.6 SAP Fiori Shipments (Cont.)

As of December 2016, SAP had released 7,671 SAP Fiori apps in total. Table 1.7 shows a breakdown of the SAP Fiori apps by app type. Out of 7,671 apps, 1,139 apps are SAP Fiori apps, and the remaining six thousand plus apps are standard SAP GUI transactions; most of the apps require SAP S/4HANA.

App Types	No. of Apps
Transactional	618
Fact sheet	176
Analytical	345
Total	1,139

Table 1.7 SAP Fiori Wave 8

As SAP Fiori apps continued to be developed, new business requirements arose. Soon, businesses were looking for personalized key performance indicators (KPIs) based on user roles. To address this, SAP developed SAP Fiori apps for different roles—for example, cash managers, transportation managers, marketing executives, MRP controllers, and so on.

This further enhanced SAP's UX strategy and SAP Fiori's customizability. For example, transportation managers could now view transportation costs for the year to date or view the average percentage utilization of weight or volume by transportation orders created to date. Similarly, a marketing manager role enabled marketing managers to plan their yearly budgets using the My Marketing Budget app, and provided them with all initiatives ready for release via the Release Campaigns app.

Table 1.8 shows an overview of the different SAP Fiori user roles across industries and LOBs.

Industries	Cross-LOB
Retail ■ Master data specialist ■ Category manager ■ Promotion specialist ■ Store associate ■ Global trader ■ Assortment planner ■ Allocation manager	■ Manager ■ MDG expert ■ ILM archiving expert ■ Security manager ■ Data aging expert ■ Employee ■ Compliance manager ■ TDMS expert
Oil and gas ■ Hydrocarbon accountant ■ Deferment analyst ■ Field operator	
Insurance ■ Claims specialist	
Higher education ■ Student/applicant	
Public sector ■ Central budget specialist	
Banking ■ Bank account manger ■ Bank mid-office employee ■ Bank back office employee	

Table 1.8 SAP Fiori User Roles for Industries and LOBs

This historical overview provides an outlook of what we can expect for future development trends for SAP Fiori apps. The next three sections will explore the three types of apps.

1.3.1   Transactional Apps

Transactional apps enable users to perform transactional activities such as creating, changing, or approving. These activities are accomplished with guided navigation. Figure 1.22 shows the high-level system landscape for transactional apps.

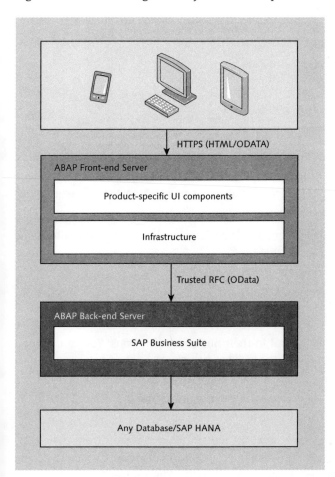

Figure 1.22 Transactional Apps Architecture

When a user launches a transactional app, the launch request is sent from the client/ browser to the ABAP front-end server. Communication between the client and the ABAP front-end server happens via OData HTTP/HTTPS protocols.

The ABAP front-end server contains the UI layers, which house the following components:

- **Product-specific UI components**
  - Governance, Risk, and Compliance (GRC)
  - Customer Relationship Management (CRM)
  - Supply Chain Management (SCM)
  - And more
- **Infrastructure components**
  - Central UI components
  - SAPUI5 control library
  - SAP Fiori launchpad
  - SAP Gateway with OData enablement

Front-end components from the ABAP front-end server connect to the business logic in the ABAP back-end server through a trusted RFC connection. The underlying database for a transactional app can be any database or an SAP HANA database. SAP recommends SAP HANA for the best performance.

In this book, we'll discuss the implementation of transactional apps in Chapter 4 and the creation/extension process in Chapter 9.

1.3.2 Fact Sheet Apps

Fact sheet apps enable users to view essential contextual information or a 360-degree view of specific central objects used in their business operations. You can call fact sheet apps from the search results displayed in SAP Fiori launchpad, from other fact sheets, or from transactional and analytical apps. For example, users can drilldown from a fact sheet app to a related business partner or master data record. Figure 1.23 shows the high-level system landscape for fact sheet apps.

When a user launches a fact sheet app, the launch request is sent from the client/ browser to SAP Web Dispatcher (reverse proxy). Communication between the client and SAP Web Dispatcher occurs via OData HTTP/HTTPS protocols. SAP Web Dispatcher sends INA search protocol requests to the search models in the ABAP back-end server.

The ABAP front-end contains product-specific UI components and infrastructure components. The ABAP back-end server comprises the SAP Business Suite with the business logic, search models, OData services, and model provider. Fact sheet apps run only on an SAP HANA database and require an ABAP stack.

In this book, we'll discuss the implementation of fact sheet apps in Chapter 5 and the creation/extension process in Chapter 10.

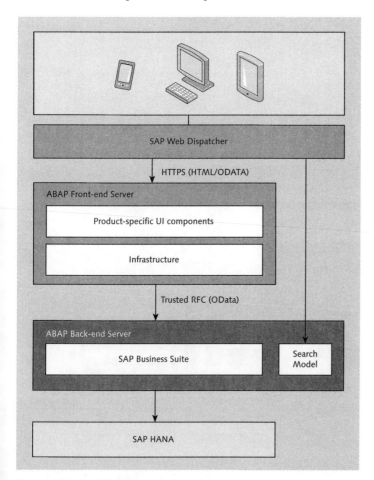

Figure 1.23 Fact Sheet Apps Architecture

1.3.3   Analytical Apps

Analytical apps provide insight into business information, allowing users to analyze and evaluate strategic or operational KPIs in real-time on a large volume of data in a simplified front-end for enterprise control. These types of apps combine the data and analytical power of SAP HANA with the integration and interface components of SAP Business Suite. Figure 1.24 shows the high-level system landscape for analytical apps.

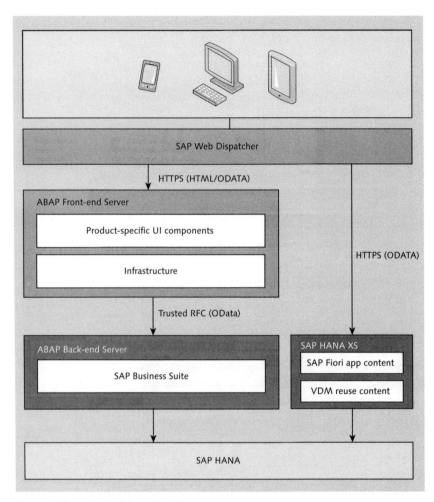

Figure 1.24 Analytical Apps Architecture

When a user launches an analytical app, the launch request is sent from the client/browser to SAP Web Dispatcher, which sends the OData calls to the ABAP front-end server or SAP HANA XS. As with transactional and fact sheet apps, the ABAP front-end for analytical apps contains product-specific UI and infrastructure components. The ABAP back-end server comprises the SAP Business Suite with the business logic. In addition, SAP HANA XS also contains the following:

- SAP Fiori app content for the different SAP Business Suite products
- KPI modeling framework

- A generic drill-down app
- VDM reuse content

Analytical apps run only on an SAP HANA database and use VDMs.

In this book, we'll discuss the implementation of analytical apps in Chapter 6 and the creation/extension process in Chapter 11.

Our focus in this book is to demonstrate how to implement, create, customize, extend, and develop these three app types. In the next section, we'll explore the related SAP technologies that will allow us to perform these functions.

1.4   Related SAP Technologies

In this section, we'll introduce you to all the technologies related to SAP Fiori. These include SAPUI5, SAP Gateway and OData, and SAP HANA XS.

1.4.1   SAPUI5

SAPUI5, a UI development toolkit for HTML5, is a JavaScript UI control library that developers can use to build business applications that run on any device, providing a lightweight programming model for desktop and mobile applications. All SAP Fiori UIs are built using SAPUI5 technology, so it's important to understand the basic concepts of SAPUI5 and the tools that support the development of SAP Fiori apps. The following list highlights the key features of SAPUI5:

- SAPUI5 APIs are designed to be easily consumed and used.
- SAPUI5 supports client-side features based on JavaScript.
- Custom controls or UI components can be easily extended.
- Powerful theming tools allow users to change a theme for custom branding based on CSS.
- SAPUI5 provides AJAX capabilities and can be used with other standard JavaScript libraries.
- It uses the popular jQuery library as a foundation.
- SAPUI5 provides high performance and fully supports SAP product standards.
- The toolkit is based on open standards like OpenAJAX, JavaScript, CSS, HTML5, and so on.

With that overview of SAPUI5's benefits in hand, let's turn our attention to its architecture.

Architecture

Figure 1.25 shows the high-level architecture of SAPUI5 on the right and the SAP Fiori landscape with SAPUI5 on the left. SAPUI5 is primarily comprised of two components: the SAPUI5 library and the SAPUI5 core. The SAPUI5 library contains the themes and controls for both mobile and desktop. The SAPUI5 core includes the following:

- Core, base, and model modules
- Dependency/class loader to load control libraries
- Render manager, which creates HTML strings for the represented controls
- SAP jQuery and jQuery plug-ins

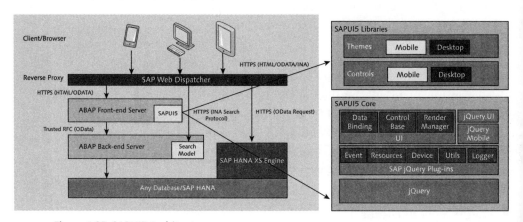

Figure 1.25 SAPUI5 Architecture

Figure 1.26 shows a simplified SAPUI5 architecture with the model-view-controller (MVC) design pattern and the connectivity between the back-end systems and browsers. SAPUI5 now comes automatically with the following systems:

- AS ABAP
- AS Java
- SAP Cloud Platform
- SAP HANA XS engine

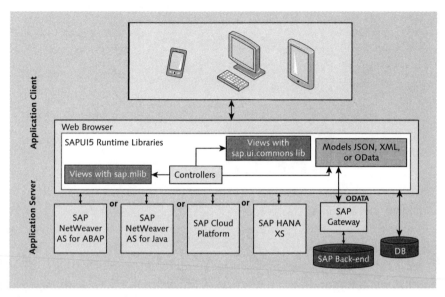

Figure 1.26 SAPUI5 Client Server Architecture

SAPUI5 works best based on OData enriched by metadata exposed via OData annotations. For this reason, SAP recommends SAP Gateway (OData service) to integrate the application layer and SAP back-end systems. You can use JSON or XML format to connect to non-SAP data sources (any database).

Model-View-Controller Concept

Model-view-controller is a fundamental design pattern used to separate UI logic from business logic. It was introduced by Trygve Reenskaug and is one of the first software architectural patterns for implementing UIs.

This concept divides a given software application into three interconnected parts, separating the internal representation of information from the ways that information is accepted from the user. You will see MVC design concepts in most of the SAP Fiori applications when you create or extend an app. Figure 1.27 shows the MVC pattern, which proposes three main components or objects to be used in software development:

1. **Model**

   A *model* represents the underlying, logical structure of data in a software application and the high-level classes associated with it. This object model doesn't contain any information about the UI.

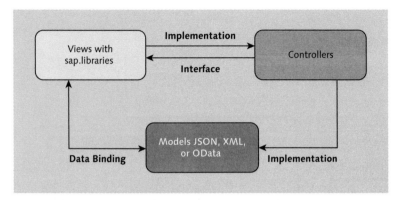

Figure 1.27 MVC Design Concept

2. **View**

    A *view* is a collection of classes representing the different elements in a UI. This is the visual part of your application—that is, all the things a user can see and respond to on the screen, such as buttons, list boxes, and so on. Views can be defined using the following options:

    – XML (`sap.ui.core.mvc.XMLView`)

    – JavaScript (`sap.ui.core.mvc.JSView`)

    – JSON (`sap.ui.core.mvc.JSONView`)

    – Declarative HTML (`sap.ui.core.mvc.HTMLView`)

3. **Controller**

    A *controller* represents the classes connecting the model and the view. When a user clicks a button or selects an item from the list box, an event is triggered. The controller then handles the event and communicates between the classes in the model and view.

In addition to these concepts, SAPUI5 also supports *data binding*. SAPUI5 data binding supports three model implementations: JSON, an XML model, and an OData model. Put simply, SAPUI5 data binding is the process by which the properties in data sources/models are bound to properties in the SAPUI5 control or views. This involves a two-way data binding: Any change in the property values of a model will automatically be reflected in the views, and, similarly, any change in the values of views will automatically be updated in the model.

You can create or extend SAP Fiori apps using SAP Web IDE, and you'll see the MVC design concept while doing so. Next, we'll explain how to set up the SAP Web IDE local version.

Setting Up SAP Web IDE

SAP Web IDE is a cloud-based development environment that enables developers to build new UXs simply with templates, wizards, and WYSIWYG layout editors. We'll be using this tool in Chapter 8 and Chapter 9.

SAP provides SAP Web IDE with full functionalities as part of SAP Cloud Platform. In this section, we'll teach you how to set up SAP Web IDE on SAP Cloud Platform.

1. Create a valid account by registering for an SAP Cloud Platform trial at *https://account.hanatrial.ondemand.com/*.

2. Login to your account once you register.

3. Click **Personal Developer Account** to view the services in the SAP HANA cockpit (Figure 1.28).

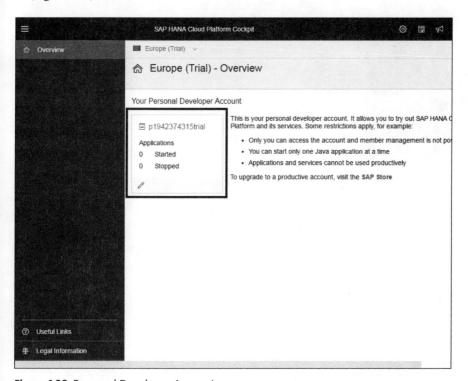

Figure 1.28 Personal Developer Account

4. Select **Services**, then click the **SAP Web IDE, Innovation version** tile (Figure 1.29).

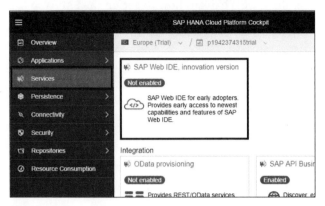

Figure 1.29 Services

Enable SAP Web IDE by clicking **Enable** (Figure 1.30).

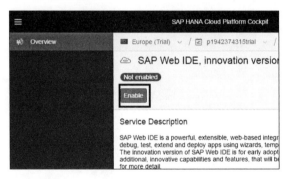

Figure 1.30 Enable SAP Web IDE

5. Once SAP Web IDE is enabled, its status will automatically change to **Enabled** (Figure 1.31).

6. Now, click the **Open SAP Web IDE Innovation** link to start SAP Web IDE (Figure 1.31).

Application Templates

Many best practices are available for free by using SAP Web IDE with application templates.

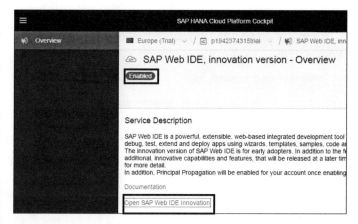

Figure 1.31 Launch SAP Web IDE

You have successfully set up SAP Web IDE on SAP Cloud Platform! Next, we'll launch SAP Web IDE and build our first project. You can call SAP Web IDE directly from a link; in your browser, go to *https://webide-<account ID>.dispatcher.hanatrial.ondemand.com*. You should now see SAP Web IDE (see Figure 1.32).

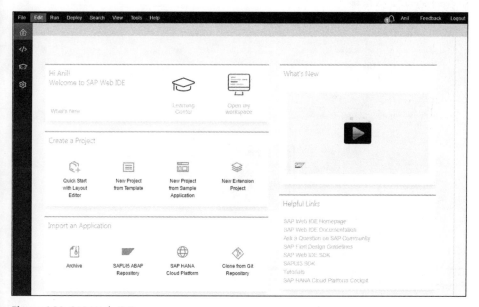

Figure 1.32 SAP Web IDE

Create an SAPUI5 Application

Next, we'll create an SAPUI5 application using SAP Web IDE to show how simple it can be. Proceed with the following steps:

1. Click **New Project from Template** (see Figure 1.33).

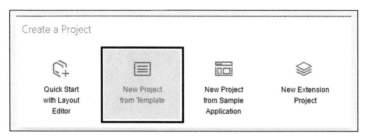

Figure 1.33 New Project

2. Select **SAPUI5 Application** and click **Next** (see Figure 1.34).

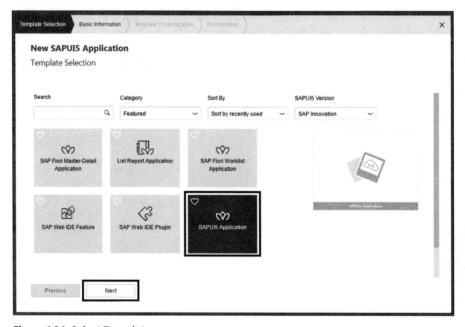

Figure 1.34 Select Template

3. Enter a **Project Name** and click **Next** (see Figure 1.35).

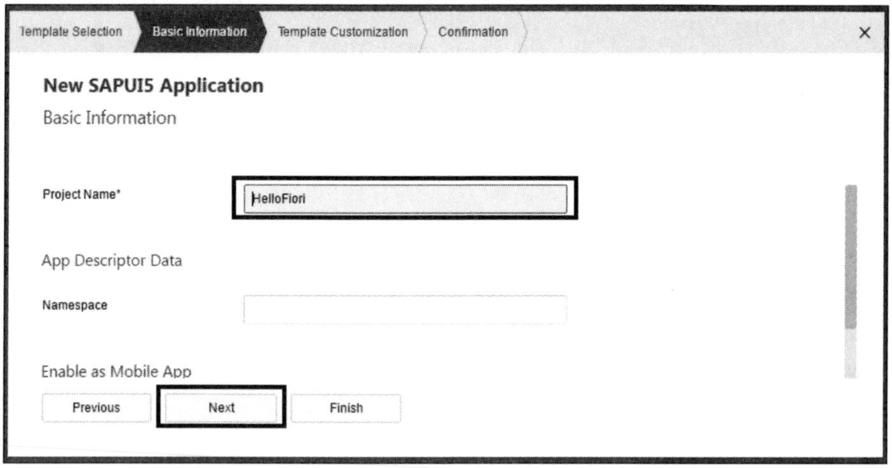

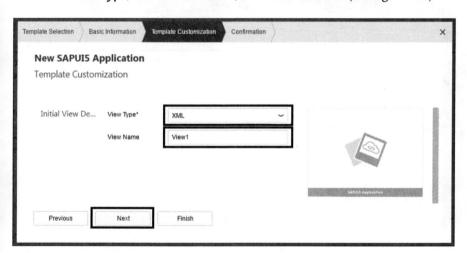

Figure 1.35 Basic Information

4. Select a **View Type**, enter a **View Name**, and then click **Next** (see Figure 1.36).

Figure 1.36 Template Customization

5. Click **Finish** to create the project (see Figure 1.37).

Figure 1.37 Confirmation

6. Expand the new project folder and double-click the **i18n.properties** file.

7. Change the `title` field to "Welcome to the world of SAP Fiori 2.0" (see Figure 1.38).

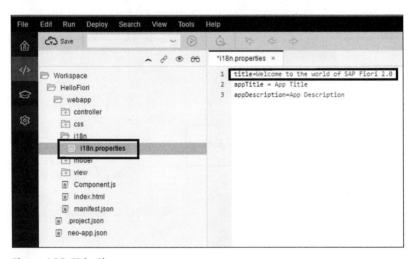

Figure 1.38 Title Change

Before you run this app, we want to highlight some of the code that's automatically generated.

The script tag is where SAPUI5 is bootstrapped. Double-click **Index.html** to view the bootstrap script. The script tag has an ID of `"sap-ui-bootstrapped"`. The following is a list of parameters that can be passed into the script tag (see Figure 1.39):

- **data-sap-ui-libs**
  This contains the libraries that you want to load.

- **data-sap-ui-compatVersion**
  This compatibility version flag allows apps to react to incompatible changes in SAPUI5.

- **data-sap-ui-resourceroots**
  This is the path/location where resources or artifacts can be found.

- **data-sap-ui-theme**
  This is the name of the theme that you want to use.

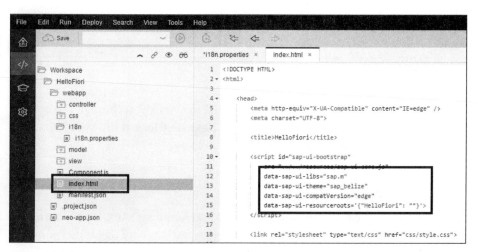

Figure 1.39 Bootstrap

To run the script, click **Save** and then click **Run**. The resulting screen is shown in Figure 1.40.

Congratulations, you've created your very first SAPUI5 app!

> **More Information**
>
> For more information on building applications using SAPUI5, check out the SAP PRESS book *Getting Started with SAPUI5*, by Miroslav Antolovic, available at *www.sap-press.com/3565*.

Welcome to the world of SAP Fiori 2.0

Figure 1.40 Preview

In Chapter 8, we'll dig deeper into SAP Web IDE and walk you through the options available to create or extend an SAP Fiori app. Next, we'll look at the use of OData via SAP Gateway for SAP Fiori apps.

1.4.2   OData and SAP Gateway

Facebook and eBay use it—but what is OData? And how does SAP Gateway harness it for SAP software and applications? In this section, we'll answer these questions and more.

We'll begin by discussing the concepts of OData and REST-based protocols. We'll expand on the benefits of OData and then look at the six constraints used to identify when an application is considered RESTful. Then, we'll walk through how to consume an OData service with a simple example.

Finally, we'll wrap up the section by introducing SAP's solution for harnessing the raw power of OData: SAP Gateway.

OData and REST

Open Data Protocol (*OData*) is a REST-based protocol used to expose and consume data on the web. It was built on web technologies such as HTTP, Atom Publishing protocol (AtomPub), XML, and JSON to provide access to information from a variety of applications. It was originally developed by Microsoft and was designed to provide a

RESTful API accessible by forming an appropriate Uniform Resource Identifier (URI) and assigning it to the corresponding HTTP header. Essentially, anything that's possible with the UI becomes part of the API. Put simply, OData is used to expose, access, and modify information from different sources. The following are some of the advantages of using an OData protocol with SAP Gateway:

- Industry-standard protocols for creating and consuming data APIs
- Builds on core protocols like HTTP
- Lightweight
- Broad adoption by ecosystems
- Main drivers are SAP, Microsoft, and IBM
- Decouple back-end and front-end
- Access by URI
- Multichannel

As we just mentioned, OData is a REST-based protocol, and REST here stands for *representational state transfer*. The concept was first introduced by Roy Thomas Fielding in his 2000 PhD dissertation, *Architectural Styles and the Design of Network-based Software Architectures*. Architectural properties of REST are recognized by applying six constraints. An application is considered RESTful only when all the following constraints are satisfied:

1. **Client server**
   A uniform interface separates clients from servers. This kind of model allows the client and software components on the server to be developed independently or replaced. For example, clients are not concerned about the data storage that remains in the server, and servers are not concerned about the UI or user status, enabling servers to be more scalable.

2. **Stateless**
   Client-server communication is further constrained by no client context being stored on the server between requests; that is, the stateless interface requires the client to send requests with all the necessary information to the server, and a session client is held in the client.

3. **Cacheable**
   Responses from the servers can be cacheable. Therefore, it's important to implicitly or explicitly define whether the responses from the servers are cacheable or

not. Caching partially or completely eliminates client-server interactions and further improves performance and scalability.

4. **Layered system**
A client can't ordinarily distinguish if it's connected directly to an actual end-point server or to an intermediate server. System scalability can be improved by enabling load balancing and by providing shared caches on the intermediate servers.

5. **Code on demand**
This is the only optional constraint of the REST architecture. In this constraint, servers can temporarily extend or customize the functionality of a client through the transfer of executable code at the request of the client—for example, via client-side scripts such as JavaScript and compiled components such as Java applets.

6. **Uniform interface**
This is the core constraint of the REST service. This constraint simplifies and decouples the architecture, enabling each part to evolve independently. There are four subconstraints for this uniform interface:

- *Identification of resources*: Individual resources are identified in requests. For example, when the server sends data from the database in HTML, JSON, or XML format, the server should provide the client with a representation of the resources.

- *Manipulation of create, read, update, delete (CRUD) operations*: Manipulation of resources through these representations must be provided.

- *Self-descriptive messages*: Each response from the server should include messages describing how to process the response.

- *Hypermedia as the engine of application state (HATEOAS)*: State transitions or manipulations of server-side resources may only be performed through actions that are dynamically identified within the hypermedia by the server.

Just to put a face on what we've discussed, next we'll show you how to consume an OData service with a simple example. We'll be using a sample OData service, from *http://services.odata.org/OData/Odata.svc/*.

Proceed with the following steps:

1. View the OData service by going to *http://services.odata.org/OData/Odata.svc/* in your browser (see Figure 1.41). In this data model, on left side you'll see that the product is connected to a supplier and categories.

   The boxes in the visual data model Figure 1.42 are called *entity sets* or *collections*. You can define associations or relationships between the entity sets in the OData service. For example, a product can have zero or one supplier. Similarly, a product can have zero or one category.

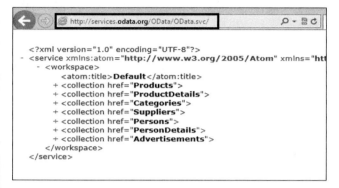

Figure 1.41 Sample Service

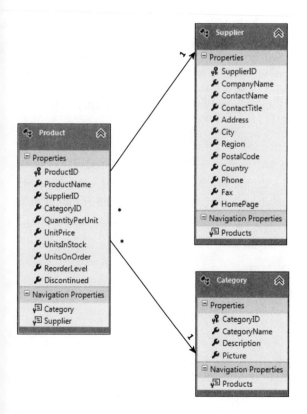

Figure 1.42 Visual Data Model

With an OData service, you have the capability not only to retrieve data from one of the entities but also to navigate from one entity to another. A supplier has exactly one navigation property (called *products*). This property also makes it possible to navigate from suppliers to products; that is, you can view all the products that a particular supplier delivers.

OData services make it easy for the front-end application developer to consume services and build applications. When we say *consume*, that typically implies retrieving data. However, an OData service is bidirectional (it can even update the data back to the database).

2. To continue with our OData example, to view all the suppliers from the back-end database, go to *http://services.odata.org/OData/Odata.svc/Suppliers* in your browser.

3. Now we know that there are two suppliers. Next, we want to find all the products the first supplier delivers. To do so, go to *http://services.odata.org/OData/Odata.svc/Suppliers(0)/Products* in your browser.

4. Similarly, if you want to the view all the products in the food category (which is the first category), go to *http://services.odata.org/OData/Odata.svc/Categories(0)/Products* in your browser.

We hope by now you understand how to consume data from the back-end database using an OData service. Next, we'll look at using SAP Gateway for OData services.

SAP Gateway

To harness the raw power of OData, SAP recommends using SAP Gateway. SAP Gateway is a technology that provides a simple way to connect devices, environments, and platforms to SAP applications, using any programming language or model without the need for SAP knowledge, by leveraging REST services and OData protocols.

SAP Gateway offers the following capabilities:

- Supports any device and any platform
- Multiple object aggregation
- Filtering and adaption based on client application requirements
- Generates structures
- CRUD operations
- Doesn't require coding; well-suited for non-ABAP developers
- No need for SAP knowledge

- Enables rapid prototyping
- Developers can create new SAP Gateway objects from existing SAP Business Warehouse (BW) queries, BAPIs, RFCs, and Web Dynpro screens

SAP Fiori is based on SAP Gateway and OData services for its connectivity to the back-end SAP Business Suite (see Figure 1.43).

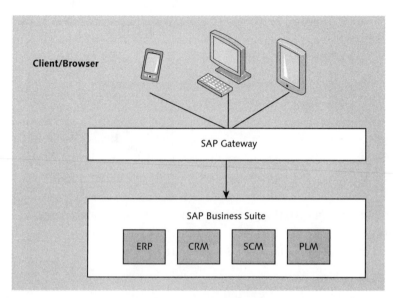

Figure 1.43 SAP Fiori and SAP Gateway Architecture

Figure 1.43 shows the high-level SAP Fiori architecture with SAP Gateway. It consists of three layers:

- **Consumer layer**
  The consumer layer is the entry point to all SAP Fiori apps.
- **SAP Gateway layer**
  This layer holds the major functionalities and tools to create OData services.
- **SAP Business Suite layer**
  This layer holds the back-end business logic and data.

SAP Gateway and OData are important elements of SAP Fiori application development. In Chapter 7, we'll discuss how to create an OData service with SAP Gateway. Next, we'll wrap up our discussion on related SAP Fiori technologies with a look at SAP HANA XS.

1.4.3   SAP HANA XS

SAP HANA XS is a key component of SAP HANA as a platform. SAP HANA XS is a small footprint application and web server. It provides an application development platform inside of SAP HANA, offering improved performance and access to SAP HANA's core features. That said, SAP HANA XS is an extension of the SAP HANA database and not a separate software component installed on the same hardware. SAP HANA XS is tightly integrated into the deepest parts of SAP HANA. With the release of SAP HANA SPS 05, SAP HANA XS became available for customers and partners who want to develop their own SAP HANA-based applications.

> **More Information**
>
> For more information on building applications using SAP HANA XS, check out the SAP PRESS E-Bite *Hands On with SAP HANA XS*, by Craig Cmehil, available at *www.sap-press.com/4068*. This E-Bite can also be used in conjunction with the SAP HANA XS CodeJam.

As previously mentioned, analytical apps only run on an SAP HANA database and use VDMs. SAP HANA XS contains the SAP Fiori app content, KPI modeling framework, generic drilldown, and SAP HANA Live VDMs (see Figure 1.44).

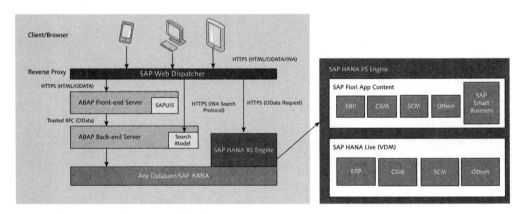

Figure 1.44 SAP HANA XS Engine

SAP HANA Live is a complete set of predefined VDMs that expose SAP Business Suite application data. SAP HANA Live provides different types of views: values help views, private views, reuse views, and query views. We'll discuss SAP HANA Live views further in Chapter 11.

1.5 Summary

In this chapter, we introduced you to SAP Fiori and SAP's UX strategy. From there, we looked at SAP Fiori's architectural components and integration technologies, such as SAP Fiori launchpad and SAP Web Dispatcher, before diving into the different communication channels of SAP Fiori. We then discussed SAP Fiori transactional, fact sheet, and analytical apps, along with their architectures. Finally, we reviewed related technologies used in conjunction with SAP Fiori, including SAPUI5, SAP Gateway and OData services, and SAP HANA XS.

Although this chapter isn't meant to be a comprehensive discussion of SAP Fiori, you should now have a basic understanding of what SAP Fiori is and how it works. In the next chapter, we'll round out Part I of the book with a discussion of the installation and configuration steps needed to use SAP Fiori and its apps.

Chapter 2

Installation and Configuration

This chapter provides an overview of the installation and configuration of the SAP Fiori system so that it's ready to deploy SAP Fiori apps.

This chapter describes the installation and configuration of different components in the SAP Fiori landscape. In Section 2.1, we'll discuss the prerequisites that need to be fulfilled before you install the SAP Fiori system. In Section 2.2, we'll move on to a detailed discussion of the different components in the SAP Fiori system landscape for ABAP, SAP HANA, and SAP HANA XS environments. Then, we'll discuss the different deployment options in Section 2.3, with a look at the pros and cons of each option.

We'll take a quick look at the SAP Fiori apps reference library, in which you can find app-specific installation information, in Section 2.4; then, we'll dive into an installation overview of each component of the architecture in Section 2.5. In Section 2.6, we'll move on to the configuration steps required after you install the components of SAP Fiori.

Let's get started by looking at the prerequisites needed to install each app.

2.1 Prerequisites

Depending on the type of SAP Fiori app (transactional, fact sheet, analytical apps) you're planning to implement, you need to set up the following software:

- **Transactional apps**
  - Any database or SAP HANA, platform edition
  - SAP NetWeaver
  - An SAP Business Suite product

- **Transactional and fact sheet apps**
  - SAP HANA, platform edition
  - SAP NetWeaver
  - An SAP Business Suite product
- **All three app types**
  - SAP HANA, platform edition
  - SAP HANA Live
  - SAP NetWeaver
  - An SAP Business Suite product

In Section 2.5, we'll discuss the required releases and support package stacks (SPS) for each of these software products in greater detail.

2.2   Implementation Options

In Chapter 1, we introduced you to different types of SAP Fiori apps (transactional, analytical, and fact sheets). In this section, we'll discuss the different types of SAP Fiori system landscapes and the SAP Fiori apps they support. Let's start by discussing the ABAP environment.

2.2.1   ABAP Environment

The ABAP environment supports transactional and fact sheet apps (only if the back-end is SAP HANA). The ABAP architecture consists of four layers (see Figure 2.1):

1. **Client**
   This is where the SAP Fiori apps are designed to run, and it serves as the access point. To run SAP Fiori apps, the runtime environment (i.e., either desktop or mobile) must support HTML5.

2. **ABAP front-end server**
   The ABAP front-end server holds SAP Fiori functionalities and components. All the components in this layer are leveraged to generate and run an SAP Fiori app and enable communication among the client, ABAP front-end, and ABAP back-end server. The following elements are found here:

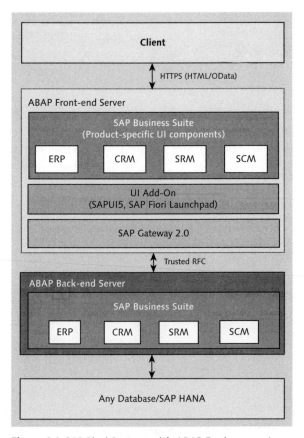

Figure 2.1 SAP Fiori System with ABAP Environment

- *SAP Business Suite (product-specific UI components)*: The product-specific UI add-ons are the specific UIs for the SAP Fiori apps that have been installed on the ABAP front-end server. Products here include SAP ERP, SAP Customer Relationship Management (SAP CRM), SAP Supplier Relationship Management (SAP SRM), and SAP Supply Chain Management (SAP SCM).

- *UI add-on*: The common infrastructure for all SAP Fiori apps is provided by the central UI add-on components. These components contain the SAPUI5 control library and SAP Fiori launchpad.

- *SAP Gateway*: SAP Gateway is the development framework in which you can create and generate OData services; it handles communication between the client and the ABAP back-end server.

> **UI Add-On and SAP Gateway Components**
>
> The UI add-on and SAP Gateway components are usually deployed on the same server.

- **ABAP back-end server**
  The ABAP back-end server contains the installed SAP Business Suite products. These products provide the business logic and back-end data, which includes the users, roles, and authorizations.
- **Back-end database**
  The back-end database can be any database or the SAP HANA database. SAP Fiori apps run best on SAP HANA.

Each layer contains different components that serve a clearly defined purpose.

> **ABAP Front-end and Back-end Components**
>
> ABAP front-end and back-end components are delivered as separate products and must be installed in a system landscape enabled for SAP Fiori.

2.2.2   SAP HANA Database

When using SAP Fiori with the SAP HANA database, the following four layers are implemented: the client, the reverse proxy, the ABAP front-end server, and the ABAP back-end server (see Figure 2.2). This architecture is like what we discussed in the previous section, so we'll only focus on the additional new layers or components. As before, each layer contains different components, each of which has a clearly defined purpose. This type of landscape supports both transactional apps and fact sheet apps.

A *reverse proxy* is needed for fact sheet apps. SAP recommends using SAP Web Dispatcher as a reverse proxy server. SAP Web Dispatcher is an entry point via which connections are accepted or rejected. After a connection is established, SAP Web Dispatcher forwards the OData request to the ABAP back-end server.

In addition to the SAP Business Suite products, the ABAP back-end server contains search models. Data is pulled from SAP HANA through these search models. Therefore, when a user runs a fact sheet app, the client issues an Internet Protocol Network Administrator (INA) request for these search models using HTTPS communication.

SAP HANA is the mandatory back-end database for this type of landscape.

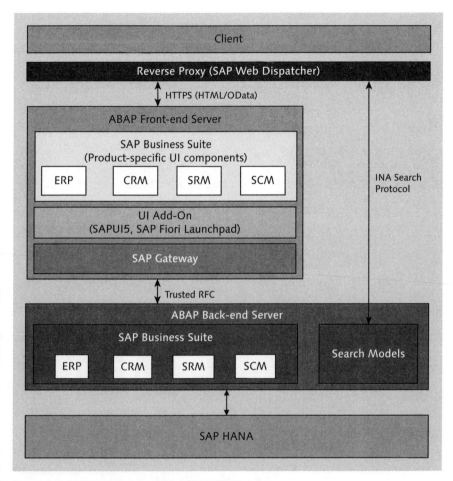

Figure 2.2 SAP Fiori System with SAP HANA Database

2.2.3   SAP HANA XS

SAP HANA XS architecture consists of five layers: the client, the reverse proxy, the ABAP front-end server, the ABAP back-end server, and the SAP HANA XS engine (see Figure 2.3). All three types of apps (transactional, fact sheet, and analytical) are supported in this landscape.

Figure 2.3 shows the integrated scenario, in which both the ABAP back-end server and SAP HANA XS share the same SAP HANA database. Alternatively, you can set up your landscape in a side-by-side scenario (see Figure 2.4), in which the ABAP back-end server is on any database and the SAP HANA XS is on the SAP HANA database. Both underlying databases are connected via data replication.

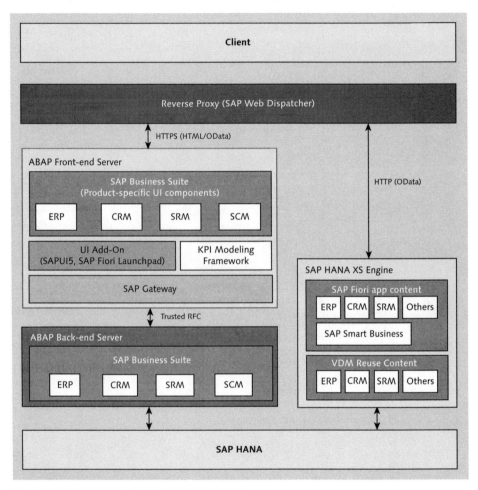

Figure 2.3 SAP Fiori System with SAP HANA XS

Because this type of architecture supports all three types of apps, SAP Web Dispatcher (reverse proxy) is configured to recognize the OData service from the analytical apps. When a user runs an analytical app, SAP Web Dispatcher routes the request to the ABAP front-end server. It then loads the UI, and the call is routed to the SAP HANA XS engine. The queries are routed from the client to the ABAP front-end, ABAP back-end, or SAP HANA XS, depending on the type of app the user is running.

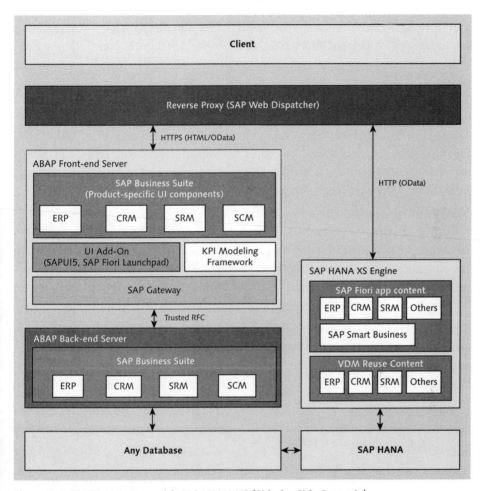

Figure 2.4 SAP Fiori System with SAP HANA XS (Side-by-Side Scenario)

In addition to the product-specific UI add-ons, the central UI add-on, and the SAP Gateway components, the ABAP front-end server also contains a KPI modeling framework, which includes the KPI modeler component, with which you can create and model KPIs, and the generic drilldown component, which provides an infrastructure to view KPI data and to drill down to the detail view.

The SAP HANA XS engine has two components: the SAP HANA Live content, and the SAP Smart Business component. SAP Fiori analytical apps use the SAP HANA XS engine. All content in the SAP HANA XS engine comes from SAP HANA Live views. SAP HANA Live content contains the VDMs. To learn more about SAP HANA XS, refer to Chapter 1. We'll discuss SAP HANA Live in greater detail in Chapter 11.

2.2.4   SAP S/4HANA

SAP S/4HANA is the next-generation business suite that provides customers with extraordinary functionality and superior flexibility, all at the speed of SAP HANA. SAP S/4HANA serves as the nerve center for the enterprise, connecting operations across business units in a single, living structure that provides end users with the information they need in real-time to make better business decisions.

SAP S/4HANA is built on the most modern design principles using the SAP Fiori UX, providing end users with a personalized and coherent UX. SAP Fiori 2.0 is now available with SAP S/4HANA 1610 and the 1608 release of SAP S/4HANA Cloud, so customers can choose either SAP S/4HANA on-premise or SAP S/4HANA Cloud. Customers need SAP Fiori front-end server 3.0 for SAP S/4HANA 1610 with instances based on SAP NetWeaver AS for ABAP 7.50 or 7.51, to have SAP Fiori 2.0 in their landscapes.

Figure 2.5 shows a high-level logical overview of SAP Fiori on SAP S/4HANA; as you can see, the architecture consists of only one archetype for transactional, analytical, and fact sheet. We covered all the components of the architecture in the last two sections; remember that the core OData services (CDS views) access the SAP S/4HANA business data via SAP Gateway.

Recommendation
AS ABAP 7.51 is recommended if you want to consume future innovations.

The SAP HANA database is mandatory to run analytical apps/SAP Smart Business analytical apps. Data is populated from SAP HANA to the analytical apps or SAP Smart Business apps through the SAP HANA XS engine.

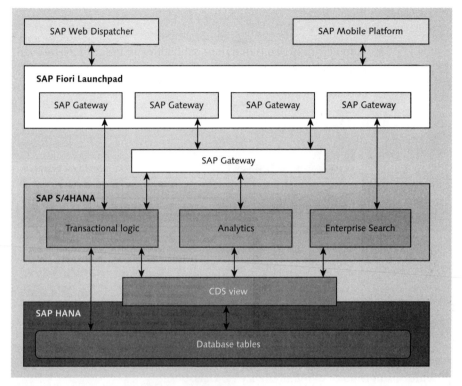

Figure 2.5 SAP Fiori Landscape on SAP S/4HANA

2.3   Deployment Options

In the previous section, we discussed the various landscapes that can be implemented with SAP Fiori. Depending on your SAP Fiori system landscape, you can decide on your deployment options. You have two deployment options in SAP Fiori: a central hub deployment and embedded deployment.

In this section, we'll walk through the advantages and disadvantages of both.

2.3.1   Central Hub Deployment

With this kind of deployment, the SAP Fiori UI add-ons (both central and product-specific) and SAP Gateway components are deployed in the ABAP front-end server. The back-end data and the business logic are deployed on the ABAP back-end server (see Figure 2.6).

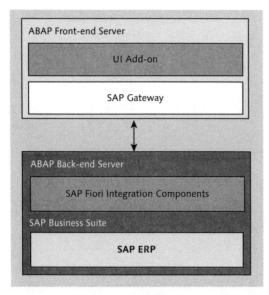

Figure 2.6 Central Hub Deployment

The central hub deployment offers several advantages, including the following:

- A central place is provided for theming and branding SAP Fiori apps, which also provides a single point of maintenance for UI issues.
- Developers can make changes to the UI without worrying about the back-end development authorizations.
- A single point of access is provided to multiple back-end systems; it supports the composition and routing of multiple back-end systems, as well.
- Because there's no direct access to the back-end data, you can benefit from enhanced security.
- The lifecycle of UI applications can be decoupled from the back-end.
- Production scenarios with medium to high loads are supported.

The only disadvantage of this kind of deployment is that it needs an additional server for SAP Gateway.

Important!

SAP recommends separating your back-end business logic and front-end UI components from each other by implementing the central hub deployment option.

2.3.2   Embedded Deployment

Embedded deployment means that SAP Fiori UI add-ons (both central and product-specific) and SAP Gateway are deployed along with the back-end SAP Business Suite (see Figure 2.7).

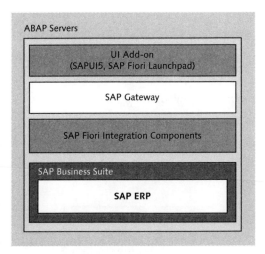

Figure 2.7 Embedded Deployment

The advantages of using an embedded deployment include the following:

- No additional system for SAP Gateway is required.
- Direct access is provided to the business data and business logic.
- Only one remote call to the SAP system is necessary.

Disadvantages of using this deployment option include the following:

- Production use is only suitable for low-load production systems or for proofs of concepts (POCs), not for medium to high loads.
- SAP Gateway must be configured on every system when multiple SAP Business Suite systems are used.
- Components can only be upgraded during system maintenance; especially in large organizations, the SAP Business Suite system is upgraded rarely (i.e., once or twice a year).

You now have a clear understanding of the different deployment options. Whether it's best to choose central hub or embedded deployment depends on each customer's use case.

2.4   Apps Reference Library

The *SAP Fiori apps reference library* lets you explore all SAP Fiori apps, including technical information required to install and configure an SAP Fiori app, which we'll walk through in Section 2.5 and Section 2.6. Before you get started, you should familiarize yourself with the apps reference library.

Because we'll be starting with the implementation of the transactional Create Sales Orders app in Chapter 4, we'll retrieve the technical details of this app from the library as an example:

1. Launch the apps reference library from *http://www.sap.com/fiori-apps-library*.
2. Click **All Apps**.
3. In the **Search by App Name** field, enter "Sales Order", and press ⎡Enter⎤.
4. Select the **Create Sales Orders** app to view the app details on the right side (see Figure 2.8).

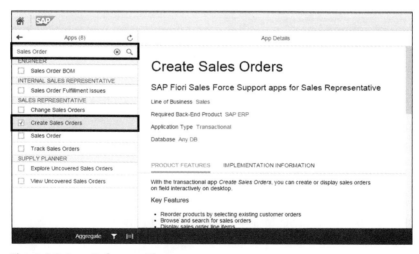

Figure 2.8 Apps Reference Library

5. Select the **Implementation Information** tab, and then select the **Configuration** arrow. This shows all the technical information needed to configure the Create Sales Order app (see Figure 2.9).

In the next section, we'll give you an overview of the installation process.

SAPUI5 Application

The ICF nodes for the following SAPUI5 application must be activated on the front-end server:

Component	Technical Name
SAPUI5 Application	SD_SO_CRE

SAP Fiori Launchpad

You require the following data to give users access to the app in the SAP Fiori launchpad.

Technical Configuration

Technical Catalog	SAP_SD_TC_T_X1
TECHNICAL_PFCG_ROLE	SAP_SD_TCR_T_X1
Semantic Object	SalesOrder
Action	create
LPD_CUST Role	UIX01SD
LPD_CUST Instance	TRANSACTIONAL
SAPUI5 Application	SD_SO_CRE

Business Catalog (Launchpad)	SAP_SD_BC_FIELDSALESREP_X1	Field Sales Representative (SD) - Content
Business Group (Launchpad)	SAP_SD_BCG_FIELDSALESREP_X1	Field Sales Representative (SD
PFCG role for Business Catalog	SAP_SD_BCR_FIELDSALESREP_X1	

Figure 2.9 App-Specific Details

2.5   Installation

Now that we've given you some background about the different landscapes for SAP Fiori and its various deployment options, we'll cover what you need to install to set up an SAP Fiori system and what you should keep in mind when you're installing SAP Fiori-related components. First, we'll give you an installation overview of the components on the ABAP front-end server. We'll then focus on the installation of components on the ABAP back-end server. Next, we'll discuss the installation of SAP Web Dispatcher and the SAP HANA server. This book doesn't include steps to install software such as ABAP AS or to set up the SAP HANA database; we assume that the main software has already been installed.

2.5.1   ABAP Environment

In this section, we'll look at the different ABAP front-end and back-end server components and the steps necessary to install them.

ABAP Front-End Server

The ABAP front-end server component installations depend on the patch level of the SAP NetWeaver version installed on your ABAP front-end server and the SAP Fiori apps that you want to install and configure. SAP highly recommends using the SAP Maintenance Planner to install components. There are three components that you need to check:

- SAP NetWeaver component version
- SAP Gateway component version
- Central UI component version

Use the following list to determine what you need to install, based on your SAP NetWeaver version:

- If the SAP NetWeaver version is 7.31, then you need to install the following:
  - SAP NetWeaver version: 7.31 SPS 5 or higher (SAP recommends SPS 8).
  - SAP Gateway component: SAP Gateway 2.0 SPS 10; this component contains the GW_CORE 200 SP 10, IW_FND 250 SP 10, and WEBCUIF 731 SP 10 components.
  - Central UI components: UI add-on 1.0 for SAP enhancement package (EHP) 3 for SAP NetWeaver 7.0, minimum SPS 12. This component contains UI_INFRA 100 SP 12, UI2_SRVC 100 SP 12, UISAPUI5 100 SP 12, UI2_FND 100 SP 12, UI2_700 100 SP 12, UI2_701 100 SP 12, UI2_702 100 SP 12, and UI2_731 100 SP 12.
- If the SAP NetWeaver version is 7.4, then the SAP Gateway components and the central UI components that are required are included in the SAP NetWeaver installation. All you need to do is verify the product versions and patch levels of each component:
  - SAP NetWeaver version: SPS 4 or higher
  - SAP Gateway component: SAP Gateway Foundation SP 10 (SAP_GWFND) is included in the SAP NetWeaver 7.4 installation. This component replaces the GW_CORE, IW_FND, and IW_BEP components.
  - Central UI components: User Interface Technology 7.40 SP 12 (SAP_UI 740) is included in SAP NetWeaver 7.4 installation.
- To get the new SAP Fiori 2.0 into your system landscape, you need to upgrade the front-end server to SAP front-end server 3.0 with SAP UI 7.51.

If you've already installed the SAP Gateway and central UI components, you can check the versions and the patch levels by following these steps:

1. Log in to ABAP front-end server.
2. Choose **System • Status** (see Figure 2.10).

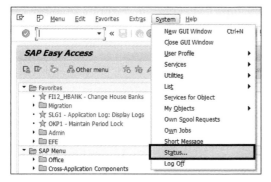

Figure 2.10 Checking System Status

3. Click the **Component information** button ![icon].

4. Go to the **Installed Product Versions** tab.

5. Check the SAP NetWeaver version (see Figure 2.11).

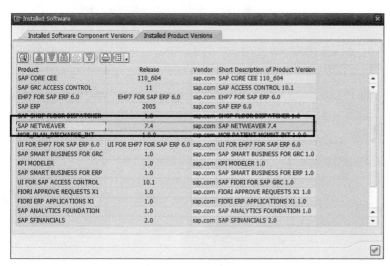

Figure 2.11 Checking SAP NetWeaver Version

6. The SAP NetWeaver version is 7.4, so now you need to verify the component versions. As discussed previously, you need to check the following components:

   – SAP NetWeaver version: SPS 4 or higher

   – SAP_GWFND 740 SP 10

   – SAP_UI 740 SP 12

7. Click on the **Installed Software Component Versions** tab. Figure 2.12 shows the **Component**, **Release**, and **SP-Level**.

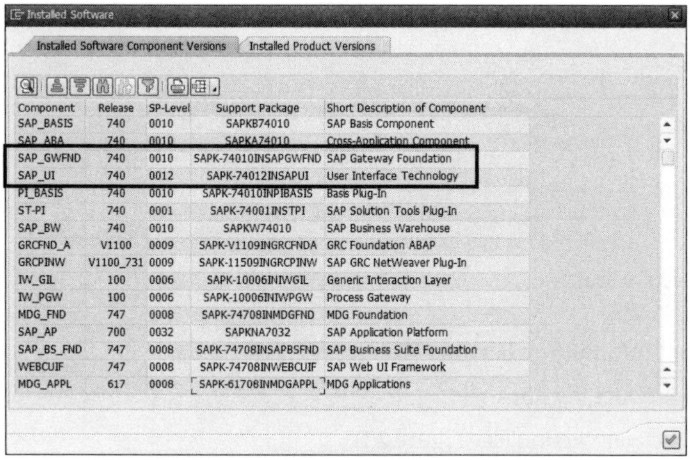

Component	Release	SP-Level	Support Package	Short Description of Component
SAP_BASIS	740	0010	SAPKB74010	SAP Basis Component
SAP_ABA	740	0010	SAPKA74010	Cross-Application Component
SAP_GWFND	740	0010	SAPK-74010INSAPGWFND	SAP Gateway Foundation
SAP_UI	740	0012	SAPK-74012INSAPUI	User Interface Technology
PI_BASIS	740	0010	SAPK-74010INPIBASIS	Basis Plug-In
ST-PI	740	0001	SAPK-74001INSTPI	SAP Solution Tools Plug-In
SAP_BW	740	0010	SAPKW74010	SAP Business Warehouse
GRCFND_A	V1100	0009	SAPK-V1109INGRCFNDA	GRC Foundation ABAP
GRCPINW	V1100_731	0009	SAPK-11509INGRCPINW	SAP GRC NetWeaver Plug-In
IW_GIL	100	0006	SAPK-10006INIWGIL	Generic Interaction Layer
IW_PGW	100	0006	SAPK-10006INIWPGW	Process Gateway
MDG_FND	747	0008	SAPK-74708INMDGFND	MDG Foundation
SAP_AP	700	0032	SAPKNA7032	SAP Application Platform
SAP_BS_FND	747	0008	SAPK-74708INSAPBSFND	SAP Business Suite Foundation
WEBCUIF	747	0008	SAPK-74708INWEBCUIF	SAP Web UI Framework
MDG_APPL	617	0008	SAPK-61708INMDGAPPL	MDG Applications

Figure 2.12 Checking Component Versions

8. Finally, check in SAP Marketplace for new updates or support packages, and then install any new support packages.

Now you know how to update or install components. Note that if you're planning to implement SAP Fiori analytical apps, then you'll have to install the KPI modeler in the ABAP front-end server (see Figure 2.13).

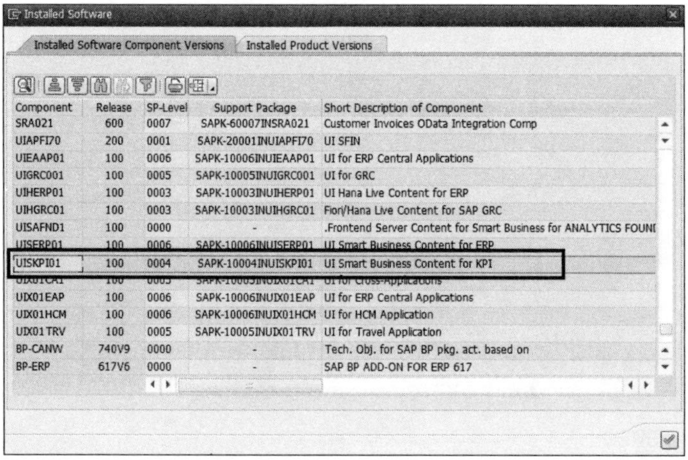

Component	Release	SP-Level	Support Package	Short Description of Component
SRA021	600	0007	SAPK-60007INSRA021	Customer Invoices OData Integration Comp
UIAPFI70	200	0001	SAPK-20001INUIAPFI70	UI SFIN
UIEAAP01	100	0006	SAPK-10006INUIEAAP01	UI for ERP Central Applications
UIGRC001	100	0005	SAPK-10005INUIGRC001	UI for GRC
UIHERP01	100	0003	SAPK-10003INUIHERP01	UI Hana Live Content for ERP
UIHGRC01	100	0003	SAPK-10003INUIHGRC01	Fiori/Hana Live Content for SAP GRC
UISAFND1	100	0000	-	.Frontend Server Content for Smart Business for ANALYTICS FOUNI
UISERP01	100	0006	SAPK-10006INUISERP01	UI Smart Business Content for ERP
UISKPI01	100	0004	SAPK-10004INUISKPI01	UI Smart Business Content for KPI
UIX01CAI	100	0005	SAPK-10005INUIX01CAI	UI for Cross-Applications
UIX01EAP	100	0006	SAPK-10006INUIX01EAP	UI for ERP Central Applications
UIX01HCM	100	0006	SAPK-10006INUIX01HCM	UI for HCM Application
UIX01TRV	100	0005	SAPK-10005INUIX01TRV	UI for Travel Application
BP-CANW	740V9	0000	-	Tech. Obj. for SAP BP pkg. act. based on
BP-ERP	617V6	0000	-	SAP BP ADD-ON FOR ERP 617

Figure 2.13 KPI Modeler Component

ABAP Back-End Server

Installation of the ABAP back-end server components depends on the back-end database and the SAP Business Suite product. To run the SAP Fiori apps, you need to install the instances you need for your SAP Business Suite products on your ABAP back-end servers. As mentioned previously, SAP recommends using SAP Maintenance Planner to install the components. The following are the two main components that you need on the ABAP back-end server:

- **SAP Business Suite products**
  SAP Fiori products are installed on the back-end server as add-ons for specific SAP Business Suite products.

- **SAP NetWeaver component**
  If the back-end database is SAP HANA, then this component should be SAP NetWeaver 7.4 SPS 7. If the back-end database is not SAP HANA (for transactional apps only), then the SAP NetWeaver version depends on the SAP Business Suite product, and you need to refer to the product-specific online help to get the version details.

In this section, we'll explain the components you need to install with a simple example.

If the central application instance of one of the enhancement packages of SAP ERP 6.0 that you're running is EHP 2 to EHP 7, then you need to install Central App INT. If the central application instance of one of the enhancement packages of SAP ERP 6.0 that you're running is EHP 7 (SPS 2 or higher), then you need to install Central App INT NW740.

Similarly, if you're running an SAP ERP Human Capital Management (SAP ERP HCM) application instance for one of the enhancement packages of SAP ERP 6.0 (up to EHP 7), then you need to install HCM INT, and if you're running EHP 7 (SPS 2 or higher), then you need to install HCM INT NW 740.

Figure 2.14 shows the installed product version on the ABAP back-end server and the SAP Fiori principal apps for SAP ERP 1.0 (**FIORI ERP APPLICATIONS X1 1.0**).

Similarly, Figure 2.15 shows the product-specific components on the ABAP back-end server.

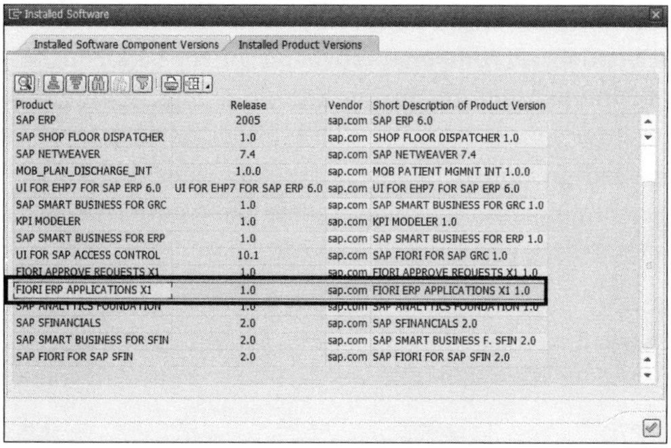

Figure 2.14 SAP Fiori ERP Applications X1

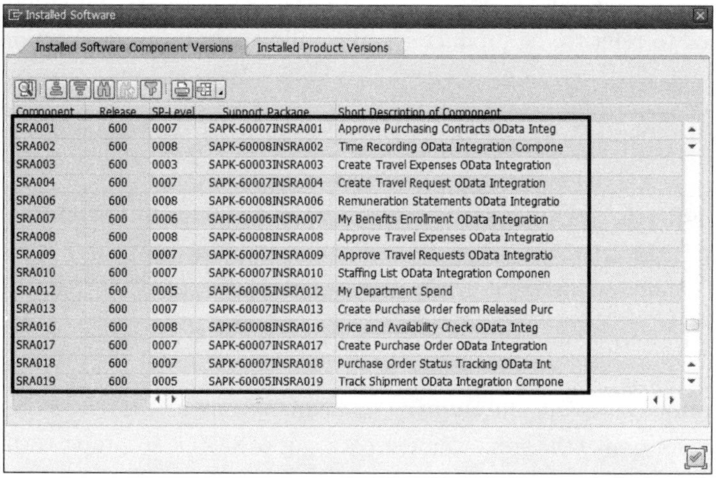

Figure 2.15 ABAP Back-End Components

In the next section, we'll show you how to install the components for the ABAP back-end or ABAP front-end servers.

Installing ABAP Front-End and Back-End Components

In Section 2.2, we explained the different components that are required for setting up the SAP Fiori system. In this section, we'll explore options for how to install the ABAP front-end or back-end components.

SAP Maintenance Planner

SAP recommends using SAP Maintenance Planner to install and update product versions, to make sure all the dependencies are addressed and to ensure that the system remains consistent. SAP Maintenance Planner is the successor of Maintenance Optimizer, Landscape Planner, and SAP Product System Editor, and it's the central point of access for all maintenance activities. Using this tool, you can easily perform system upgrades, support package installations, and enhancement package updates. In addition, you can consolidate critical tasks, such as defining product maintenance dependencies, and so on.

You can launch SAP Maintenance Planner (see Figure 2.16) from *https://apps.support.sap.com/sap/support/mp* (log in with your user ID).

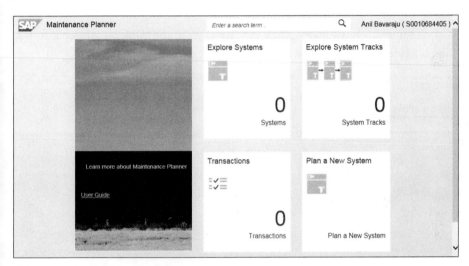

Figure 2.16 SAP Maintenance Planner

As shown in Figure 2.16, SAP Maintenance Planner contains the following four areas:

- **Explore Systems**
  Determines the systems in your landscape.
- **Explore System Tracks**
  Lists groups of technical systems.
- **Transactions**
  Gives you an overview of all the transactions you created.
- **Plan a New System**
  Enables you to add a new system to your landscape.

SAP Fiori apps require front-end and back-end components. These components are delivered in separate products that you need to install in the system landscape. SAP Maintenance Planner addresses the need to install front-end and back-end components delivered in separate products by calculating all the system requirements for an SAP Fiori app installation.

You can choose the apps that you want to install from the SAP Fiori apps reference library and then launch SAP Maintenance Planner from the library to calculate the system requirements to install the apps you selected. Next, we'll highlight some of the steps that will help you get started on this tool, and we'll provide an example based on the My Inbox app. Follow these steps:

1. Launch the SAP Fiori apps reference library via *http://www.sap.com/fiori-apps-library*.

2. Search for and select the **My Inbox** app. Then, go to the **Implementation Information** tab (see Figure 2.17).

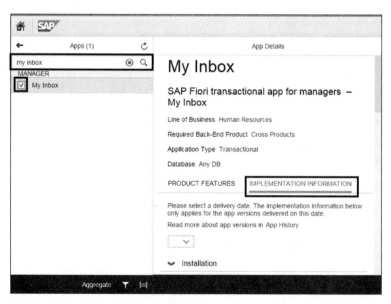

Figure 2.17 SAP Fiori Apps Reference Library

3. Click the **Maintenance Planner** link at the end of the **Installation** section (see Figure 2.18).

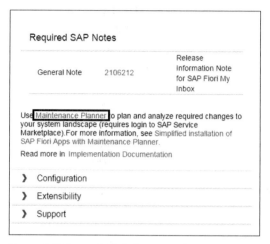

Figure 2.18 Launch Maintenance Planner

This launches SAP Maintenance Planner with the components required to implement the My Inbox app.

4. Log in with your **S-User ID**, and follow the steps in the wizard (see Figure 2.19). SAP Maintenance Planner automatically starts calculating the system requirements based on your current system.

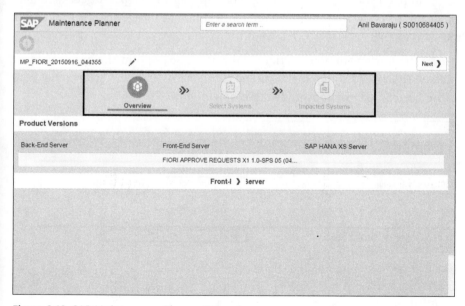

Figure 2.19 SAP Maintenance Planner Wizard

5. At the end of the wizard, you can either select **Push to Download Basket** or **Download Stack XML**.

6. After you've downloaded the archives from SAP Marketplace, you need to use the correct tools to implement the planned landscape changes.

Alternately, you can also download the files from SAP Marketplace and deploy them manually. There are two ways to upload the files to the server: from the front-end server or from the application server.

If the component/file size is too big, we recommend loading the components from the application server. In addition, you can use Transaction SPAM (Support Package Manager) and Transaction SAINT (SAP Add-On Installation Tool) to install or update components. Next, we'll show you how to install a component using Transaction SPAM. You can follow the same procedure to update any ABAP front-end or back-end components.

Update Support Packages

It's important to apply the latest support packages for all components or apps that you're planning to implement.

As an example, if you implement the My Inbox app, the first step is to get the component details from the SAP Fiori apps reference library help page specific to that app. Proceed as follows:

1. Go to the **Implementation** section of the My Inbox app in the apps reference library. Figure 2.20 shows the front-end components and the versions that your system needs to be on for the My Inbox app to work.

Figure 2.20 My Inbox App Front-End Component Versions

2. Check the current version of the components.

3. The minimum patch level for IW PGW 100 should be SP 07 for the My Inbox app to work without any issues, and the IW_PGW component in our example system is on SP 06 (see Figure 2.21).

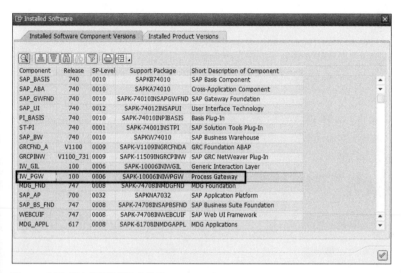

Figure 2.21 IW_PGW (SP 06) Component

In the next section, we'll walk you through how to derive the components that are required on the ABAP back-end or front-end server, as well as how to install components.

> **SAP NetWeaver**
>
> If your SAP NetWeaver version is 7.31, you first must install the software component, then the support packages.

Download the Component Files

Next, you need to download the component files from SAP Marketplace. Follow these steps:

1. Log in to the SAP Software Download Center at *http://support.sap.com/swdc*.

2. Click **Search for Software** (see Figure 2.22).

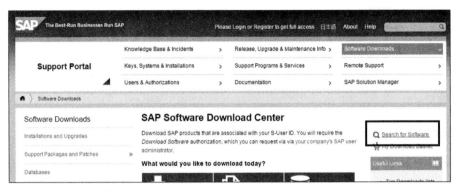

Figure 2.22 Search for Software

3. Enter "IW_PGW" in the **Search Term** field, and click **Search** or press the `Enter` key (see Figure 2.23).

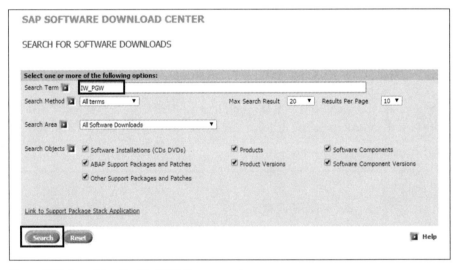

Figure 2.23 Searching for IG_PGW Component

4. Download the latest support package—that is, **SP 0007**, as shown in Figure 2.24.

Support Packages

Support packages aren't cumulative. For example, if your IW_PGW component is on SP 05, and you want to upgrade it to SP 07, then you have to download and install both SP 06 and SP 07.

2

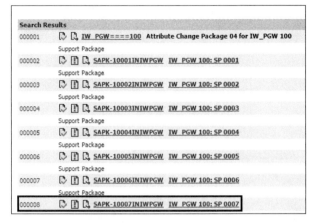

Figure 2.24 Download Support Packages

Upload Support Packages

The next step is to upload the support packages to the ABAP front-end server. Follow these steps:

1. Log in to your ABAP front-end server.

2. Run Transaction SPAM.

3. From the menu bar, go to **Support Package · Load packages · From Front End** (see Figure 2.25).

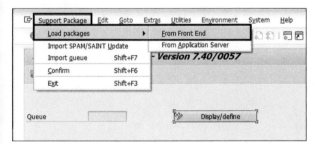

Figure 2.25 Loading Package from Front-End

4. Select the downloaded file.

5. Click **Open** (see Figure 2.26).

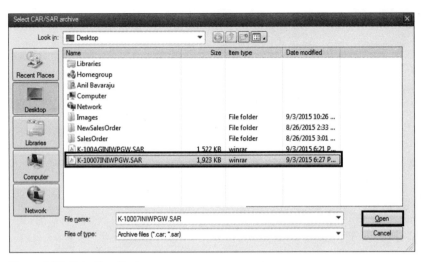

Figure 2.26 Selecting Package

6. Click **Allow**.

7. Click **Decompress** (see Figure 2.27).

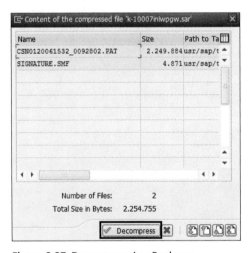

Figure 2.27 Decompressing Package

8. Select the **New Support Packages** radio button, then click **Display** (see Figure 2.28).

Figure 2.28 Displaying Support Packages

9. Select the OCS package, then click **Queue** (see Figure 2.29).

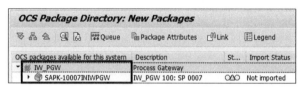

Figure 2.29 Selecting OCS Package

10. Click ✅ in the popup window to confirm the queue.

11. Click **Yes** to add modification adjustments transports to the queue (see Figure 2.30).

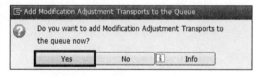

Figure 2.30 Add Transports to Queue

12. You should now see the transport added to the queue; now click the truck icon 🚚 (see Figure 2.31).

Figure 2.31 Import Queue

13. Click **Confirm** to start importing the support packages (see Figure 2.32).

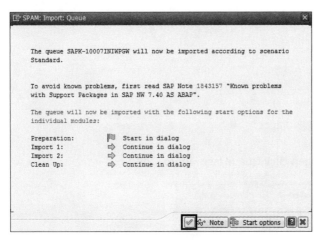

Figure 2.32 Start Importing

14. Click **Confirm** to close the information pop-up window.

15. Confirm the queue by selecting **Support Package • Confirm** (see Figure 2.33).

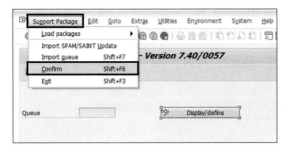

Figure 2.33 Support Package Import Confirmation

16. You should now see the latest support package applied for the IW_PGW component (see Figure 2.34).

We've successfully applied the latest support package for one of the components. You
can follow the same process for any back-end or front-end components. However,
keep in mind that SAP recommends using SAP Maintenance Planner if you do so.

You should now understand how to install the right components depending on the
apps you want to use. In the next section, we'll look at SAP Web Dispatcher.

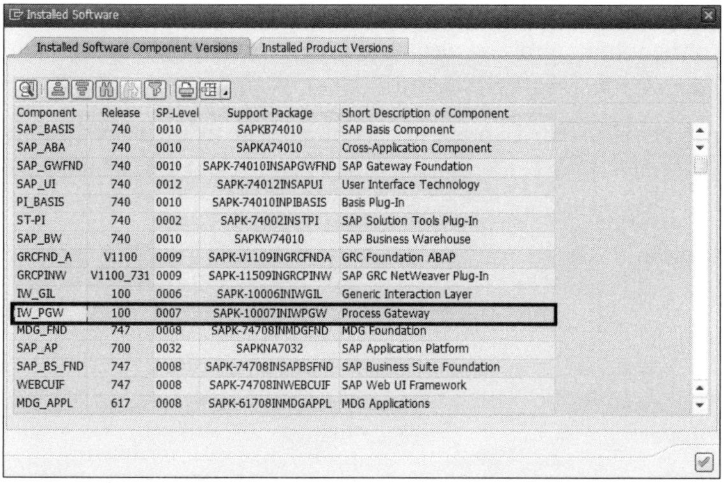

Component	Release	SP-Level	Support Package	Short Description of Component
SAP_BASIS	740	0010	SAPKB74010	SAP Basis Component
SAP_ABA	740	0010	SAPKA74010	Cross-Application Component
SAP_GWFND	740	0010	SAPK-74010INSAPGWFND	SAP Gateway Foundation
SAP_UI	740	0012	SAPK-74012INSAPUI	User Interface Technology
PI_BASIS	740	0010	SAPK-74010INPIBASIS	Basis Plug-In
ST-PI	740	0002	SAPK-74002INSTPI	SAP Solution Tools Plug-In
SAP_BW	740	0010	SAPKW74010	SAP Business Warehouse
GRCFND_A	V1100	0009	SAPK-V1109INGRCFNDA	GRC Foundation ABAP
GRCPINW	V1100_731	0009	SAPK-11509INGRCPINW	SAP GRC NetWeaver Plug-In
IW_GIL	100	0006	SAPK-10006INIWGIL	Generic Interaction Layer
IW_PGW	100	0007	SAPK-10007INIWPGW	Process Gateway
MDG_FND	747	0008	SAPK-74708INMDGFND	MDG Foundation
SAP_AP	700	0032	SAPKNA7032	SAP Application Platform
SAP_BS_FND	747	0008	SAPK-74708INSAPBSFND	SAP Business Suite Foundation
WEBCUIF	747	0008	SAPK-74708INWEBCUIF	SAP Web UI Framework
MDG_APPL	617	0008	SAPK-61708INMDGAPPL	MDG Applications

Figure 2.34 IW_PGW Component

2.5.2 SAP Web Dispatcher

In Chapter 1, we provided a brief introduction to SAP Web Dispatcher; in this section, we'll discuss it in greater detail. To recap, SAP Web Dispatcher enables users to access SAP Gateway servers behind a corporate firewall. SAP Web Dispatcher is the entry point for HTTP or HTTPS requests. The main role of SAP Web Dispatcher is to accept or reject connections from the client/browser. After the connection is accepted, SAP Web Dispatcher diverts queries from the browser to your SAP system.

Depending on the type of app you're running, the queries are directed by SAP Web Dispatcher (reverse proxy) from the browser to the ABAP front-end or the SAP HANA server. For example, when you run an analytical app, SAP Web Dispatcher routes the queries first to the ABAP front-end server and then to the SAP HANA XS engine.

Deploying Transactional Apps

If you're deploying only transactional apps and running them only via an intranet zone, then you don't need to set up a reverse proxy. However, if you want to access the transactional apps via the Internet, then you can use a reverse proxy (SAP Web Dispatcher).

SAP recommends installing SAP Web Dispatcher as the reverse proxy. Follow the installation and configuration process available online at *https://help.sap.com/saphelp_nw74/helpdata/en/48/8fe37933114e6fe10000000a421937/frameset.html*.

After SAP Web Dispatcher is installed, you need to configure the following communication scenarios (we'll cover these configuration topics in further detail when we discuss security setup in Chapter 3):

- HTTP communication
- SSL termination
- SSL reencryption

2.5.3   SAP HANA Server

As previously discussed, analytical apps run only on an SAP HANA database, using VDMs. A VDM is a structured representation of SAP HANA database views, and these VDMs are deployed with SAP HANA Live.

SAP delivers SAP HANA Live packages for several SAP Business Suite application areas. For more information on SAP HANA Live, go to *http://help.sap.com/hba* and select the package you want to install.

Depending on the SAP Fiori apps that you want to implement, you must install the correct SAP Smart Business products on your SAP HANA server. These SAP Smart Business products include the VDMs as well. Table 2.1 provides a list of available SAP Smart Business products.

SAP Business Suite Product	SAP HANA Content Add-On
All products	KPI Modeler 1.0 SPS 02
SAP Customer Relationship Management (SAP CRM)	SAP Smart Business for CRM 1.0 SPS 02
SAP Financial Closing Cockpit (SAP FCC)	SAP Smart Business for FCC 1.0 SPS 02
SAP Enterprise Resource Planning (SAP ERP)	SAP Smart Business for ERP 1.0 SPS 02
SAP Governance, Risk and Compliance (SAP GRC)	SAP Smart Business for GRC 1.0 SPS 02
SAP Event Management (SAP EM)	SAP Smart Business for EM 1.0 SPS 02

Table 2.1 SAP Smart Business Products

SAP Business Suite Product	SAP HANA Content Add-On
SAP Transportation Management (SAP TM)	SAP Smart Business for TM 1.0 SPS 02
SAP Enterprise Warehouse Management (SAP EWM)	SAP Smart Business for EWM 1.0
SAP Foundation (SAP FND)	SAP Smart Business for FND 1.0
SAP Advanced Planning and Optimization (SAP APO)	SAP Smart Business for APO 1.0
SAP Product Lifecycle Management (SAP PLM)	SAP Smart Business for PLM 1.0
SAP S/4HANA Finance	SAP Smart Business for SFIN 1.0 SPS 01

Table 2.1 SAP Smart Business Products (Cont.)

After the SAP HANA Live views are deployed, you'll be able to view the complete list of views using a standard SAP-delivered tool called the *SAP HANA Live Browser* (see Figure 2.35). Using this tool, you can search through, sort, and filter the complete list of available views. You can access this tool at *http://<host>:<port>/sap/hba/explorer/*, where <host> and <port> are the server name and the port.

The SAP Smart Business 1.0 foundation component SPS 4 (SAP Analytics Foundation 1.0) contains an extensive collection of analytic views created within the SAP HANA analytics foundation. The following is a list of components that are automatically installed with the SAP Analytics Foundation 1.0 package:

- HCO_HBA_R_SB_CORE
- HCO_HBA_R_SB_EXT
- HCO_HBA_R_SB_CXO
- HCO_HBA_R_APF_CORE
- HCO_HBA_R_SB_TP

In the next section, we'll look at the postinstallation configuration steps required to set up the SAP Fiori system.

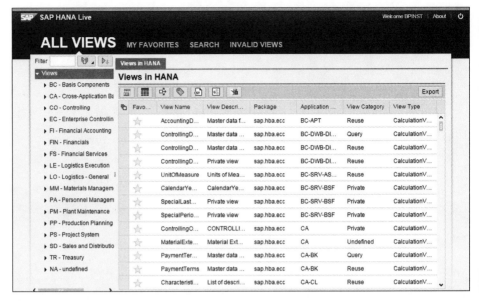

Figure 2.35 SAP HANA Live Views

2.6   Configuration

In this section, we'll walk you through a typical configuration. We'll cover how to perform both manual and automated configuration through predefined tasks.

2.6.1   SAP Fiori Launchpad

SAP Fiori launchpad is the entry point for all SAP Fiori apps. You need to configure SAP Fiori launchpad so that your end users can log in and access the apps. In the sections that follow, we'll walk through the configuration steps needed for SAP Fiori launchpad.

Activate SAP Fiori Launchpad and SAP Fiori Launchpad Designer Services

The first step in the configuration is to activate the OData services for SAP Fiori launchpad and the launchpad designer. Follow these steps:

1. Log on to the ABAP front-end server.

2. Run Transaction /IWFND/MAINT_SERVICE.

3. Click the ⊟ Add Service button.

4. Select the **Input Help** button in the system alias. Select **Local** for the **System Alias**.

5. Enter "page_builder*" for the **External Service Name** (see Figure 2.36).

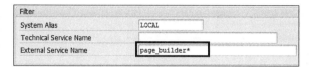

Figure 2.36 External Service Name

6. Click **Get Services**.

7. Select all the following services, as shown in Figure 2.37:

    – **/UI2/PAGE_BUILDER_CONF** (used by SAP Fiori launchpad designer)

    – **/UI2/PAGE_BUILDER_CUST** (used by SAP Fiori launchpad designer)

    – **/UI2/PAGE_BUILDER_PERS** (used by SAP Fiori launchpad)

Figure 2.37 Selecting All Services

8. Click **Add Selected Services**.

9. Select **Local Object**.

10. Click **Continue**, or press ⌷Enter⌷.

11. Repeat steps 6 to 10 to get and add the following services:

    – **/UI2/Interop** (used by both SAP Fiori launchpad and SAP Fiori launchpad designer)

    – **/UI2/TRANSPORT** (used by SAP Fiori launchpad designer)

12. Go back to the **Activate and Maintain Services** screen (Transaction /IWFND/ MAINT_SERVICE). You should now see the activated services in your customer namespace.

13. Select **ZINTEROP** from the **Service Catalog** (see Figure 2.38).

14. Select the **OData** row under **ICF Nodes**, and then click **Call Browser** (see Figure 2.39).

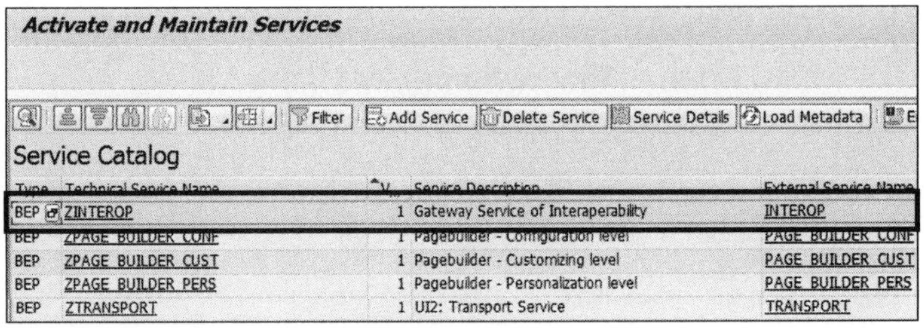

Activate and Maintain Services

🔍 ⬆ ⬇ 🔍 🔄 📋 ⬛ 📊 ⬛ | 🔽 Filter | 📋 Add Service | 🗑 Delete Service | 📊 Service Details | 🔄 Load Metadata | ⬛ E

Service Catalog

Type	Technical Service Name	V	Service Description	External Service Name
BEP	⬛ ZINTEROP	1	Gateway Service of Interaperability	INTEROP
BEP	ZPAGE BUILDER CONF	1	Pagebuilder - Configuration level	PAGE BUILDER CONF
BEP	ZPAGE BUILDER CUST	1	Pagebuilder - Customizing level	PAGE BUILDER CUST
BEP	ZPAGE BUILDER PERS	1	Pagebuilder - Personalization level	PAGE BUILDER PERS
BEP	ZTRANSPORT	1	UI2: Transport Service	TRANSPORT

Figure 2.38 Selecting ZINTEROP

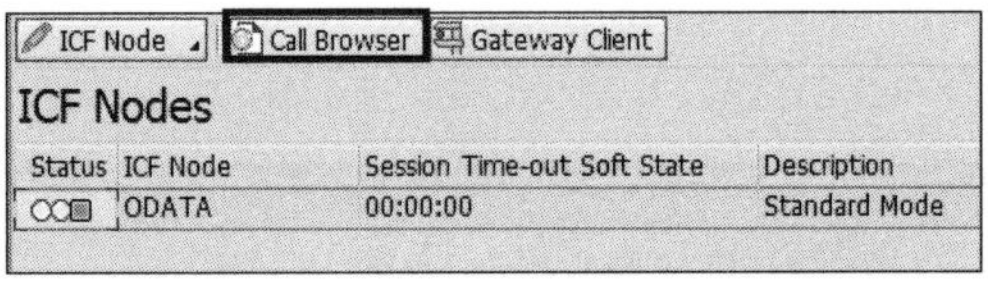

🖊 ICF Node ◢ | 🌐 Call Browser | ⬛ Gateway Client

ICF Nodes

Status	ICF Node	Session Time-out Soft State	Description
∞⬛	ODATA	00:00:00	Standard Mode

Figure 2.39 Clicking Call Browser

You should now see an XML document in the browser without any errors (see Figure 2.40).

```
<?xml version="1.0" encoding="UTF-8"?>
- <app:service xml:lang="en" xmlns:sap="http://www.sap.com/Protocols/SAPData" xmlns:m="http://
  xmlns:atom="http://www.w3.org/2005/Atom" xmlns:app="http://www.w3.org/2007/app" xml:ba
  - <app:workspace>
      <atom:title type="text">Data</atom:title>
    - <app:collection href="Links" sap:content-version="1">
        <atom:title type="text">Links</atom:title>
        <sap:member-title>Link</sap:member-title>
      </app:collection>
    - <app:collection href="SemanticObjects" sap:content-version="1">
        <atom:title type="text">SemanticObjects</atom:title>
        <sap:member-title>SemanticObject</sap:member-title>
      </app:collection>
    - <app:collection href="Messages" sap:content-version="1">
        <atom:title type="text">Messages</atom:title>
        <sap:member-title>Message</sap:member-title>
      </app:collection>
    - <app:collection href="TargetMappings" sap:content-version="1">
        <atom:title type="text">TargetMappings</atom:title>
        <sap:member-title>TargetMapping</sap:member-title>
      </app:collection>
    - <app:collection href="SignatureParameters" sap:content-version="1">
        <atom:title type="text">SignatureParameters</atom:title>
        <sap:member-title>SignatureParameter</sap:member-title>
      </app:collection>
    - <app:collection href="Themes" sap:content-version="1">
        <atom:title type="text">Themes</atom:title>
        <sap:member-title>Theme</sap:member-title>
      </app:collection>
    - <app:collection href="UserProfileProperties" sap:content-version="1">
```

Figure 2.40 XML Document

15. Repeat all the above steps for the remaining four services.

Check the Hash Key

Every time you call an OData service, a hash key is generated in the background. These hash keys are required for the generation of authorizations to assign administrative roles for SAP Fiori launchpad. To check whether the hash key is generated, follow these steps:

1. Return to the SAP GUI (ABAP front-end server), and run Transaction SE16 to view the table contents.

2. Enter "USOBHASH" in the **Table Name** field, and click on the **Table Content** button (see Figure 2.41).

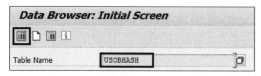

Figure 2.41 Data Browser

3. In the next screen, enter the following details, and click **Execute** (see Figure 2.42):
    - **PGMID**: "R3TR" (program ID)
    - **OBJECT**: "IWSG" (object type)
    - **OBJ_NAME**: "ZINTEROP*" (one of the services activated in the previous steps)

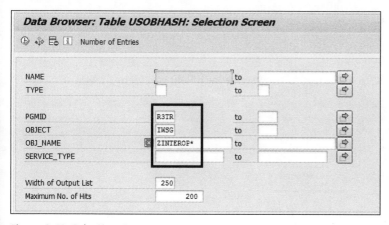

Figure 2.42 Selection Screen

You should receive a table content screen with the hash key details of the **INTEROP** service (see Figure 2.43).

Data Browser: Table USOBHASH Select Entries   1

NAME	TYPE	PGMID	OBJECT	OBJ_NAME	SERVICE_TYPE	SERVICE
4CC78858CF7211088AB530E1E00F95	HT	R3TR	IWSG	ZINTEROP_0001		

Figure 2.43 Hash Key

Activate Internet Communication Framework Nodes

The next step is to activate the Internet Communication Framework (ICF) nodes for SAP Fiori launchpad. The following is a list of services that must be activated:

- /default_host/sap/bc/ui5_ui5/sap/ar_srvc_launch
- /default_host/sap/bc/ui5_ui5/sap/ar_srvc_news
- /default_host/sap/bc/ui5_ui5/sap/arsrvc_upb_admn
- /default_host/sap/bc/ui5_ui5/ui2/ushell
- /default_host/sap/bc/ui2/nwbc
- /default_host/sap/bc/ui2/start_up
- /default_host /sap/public/bc/icf/logoff
- /default_host/sap/public/bc/ui2
- /default_host/sap/public/bc/ui5_ui5

Follow these steps:

1. Run Transaction SICF.

2. Enter "/sap/bc/ui5_ui5/sap" in the **Service Path** field (see Figure 2.44).

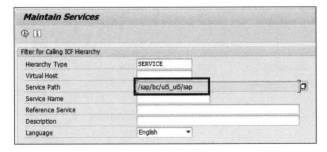

Figure 2.44 Service Path

3. Click [icon].

4. Drill down to **ar_srvc_launch**.

5. Right-click **ar_srvc_launch**, and choose **Activate Service** (see Figure 2.45).

Figure 2.45 Activate Service

6. Click **Yes** with the hierarchy to activate all the child nodes (see Figure 2.46).

Figure 2.46 Activating All with Hierarchy

7. Repeat steps 2 to 6, and activate the remaining services:
   - /default_host/sap/bc/ui5_ui5/sap/ar_srvc_news
   - /default_host/sap/bc/ui5_ui5/sap/arsrvc_upb_admn
   - /default_host/sap/bc/ui5_ui5/ui2/ushell
   - /default_host/sap/bc/ui2/nwbc
   - /default_host/sap/bc/ui2/start_up
   - /default_host /sap/public/bc/icf/logoff
   - /default_host/sap/public/bc/ui2
   - /default_host/sap/public/bc/ui5_ui5

Configure Authorization Roles

In the next step, we'll copy the standard SAP-delivered SAP Fiori launchpad roles and assign them to administrators and end users.

Follow these steps:

1. Run Transaction PFCG.
2. Enter **Role** name "SAP_UI2_ADMIN_700", and click **Copy Role** (see Figure 2.47).

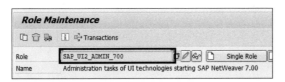

Figure 2.47 Role Maintenance

3. In the **To Role** field, preface the name with the letter "Z".
4. Click **Copy All** (see Figure 2.48).

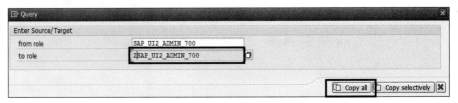

Figure 2.48 Copy Role

5. Edit the new role by clicking the **Change** icon.
6. Select **Authorization Default** under the **Menu** tab (see Figure 2.49).

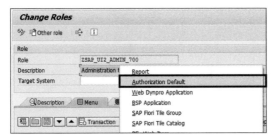

Figure 2.49 Authorization Default

7. Select **TADIR Service** from the dropdown menu.

8. Select **Program ID "R3TR"**.

9. Select **Obj. Type "IWSG"**.

10. Add the services activated in the previous step (see Figure 2.50):

    – **ZINTEROP_0001**

    – **ZPAGE_BUILDER_CONF_0001**

    – **ZPAGE_BUILDER_CUST_0001**

    – **ZPAGE_BUILDER_PERS_0001/**

    – **ZTRANSPORT_0001**

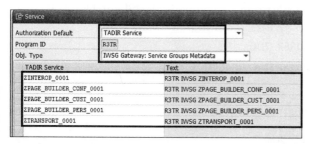

Figure 2.50 Adding Services

11. Click the **Copy** button, then go to the **Authorizations** tab.

12. Click 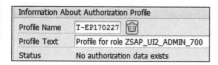 to propose a **Profile Name** (see Figure 2.51).

Information About Authorization Profile	
Profile Name	T-EP170227
Profile Text	Profile for role ZSAP_UI2_ADMIN_700
Status	No authorization data exists

Figure 2.51 Generating Profile Name

13. Click **Change Authorization Data** (see Figure 2.52).

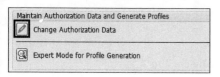

Figure 2.52 Changing Authorization Data

14. Click **Yes** to save the role. You should now see the five services under the copied role.

15. Click **Save**, then click the **Generate** icon (see Figure 2.53).

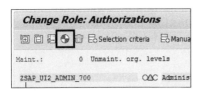

Figure 2.53 Generate

16. We've now copied the SAP standard role for SAP Fiori launchpad administrators. Next, repeat steps 2 to 15 to copy the SAP standard role for SAP Fiori launchpad end users by following these steps:

   – Copy the role **SAP_UI2_USER_700**.
   – Add the following services to the copied role:
      • ZINTEROP_0001
      • ZPAGE_BUILDER_PERS_0001
   – Generate the authorizations.

Assign Generic Roles to User

In this step, we'll assign the generic admin role to a FIORIADMIN ID and the generic user role to a FIORIUSER ID.

Follow these steps:

1. Run Transaction SUO1.
2. Enter the **User Name**, and click **Edit** (see Figure 2.54).

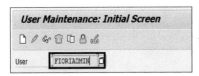

Figure 2.54 User Maintenance

3. Navigate to the **Roles** tab, and add a new row by clicking 🗒.
4. Enter the role name created in the previous step and press [Enter] (see Figure 2.55).
5. Repeat steps 2 to 4, and assign the role ZSAP_UI2_USER_700 to the FIORIADMIN user.

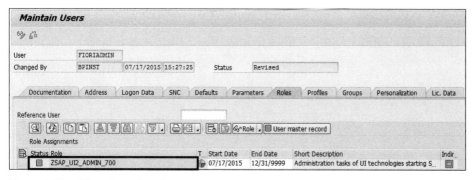

Figure 2.55 Adding Generic Role

Activate Cache Buster

Browsers store resources like JavaScript files, stylesheets, and images in the browser cache; when there's a software upgrade and these resources are changed on the server, you want the browser to load these new resources from the server rather than from the browser cache. With Cache Buster, the resources in the cache are reloaded automatically only when there's a new version available, so the system invalidates the cache only when resources are updated on the server. Follow these steps to activate Cache Buster:

1. In the ABAP front-end server, run Transaction SICF.
2. Enter "/sap/bc/ui2/flp" in the **Service Path** field.
3. Click **Execute** ⊕, or press ⌈F8⌋.
4. Choose **Activate Service** in the context menu.

After activating Cache Buster, SAP Fiori launchpad with Cache Buster can be accessed via any of the following URLs:

- *https://<server>:<port>/sap/bc/ui2/flp/*
- *https://<server>:<port>/sap/bc/ui2/flp/index.html*
- *https://<server>:<port>/sap/bc/ui2/flp/FioriLaunchpad.html*

Configure the SAP Fiori Launchpad Login Screen

The last step is to configure the login screen for SAP Fiori launchpad and SAP Fiori launchpad designer. Follow these steps:

1. In the ABAP front-end server, run Transaction SICF.
2. Enter "/sap/bc/ui5_ui5/ui2/ushell" in the **Service Path** field.

3. Click **Execute** ⊕, or press ⟦F8⟧ (see Figure 2.56).

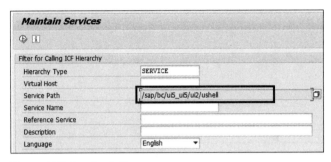

Figure 2.56 Service Path

4. Double-click the **ushell** service.

5. Click the **Error Pages** tab.

6. Select the **System Logon** radio button, then click **Configuration** (see Figure 2.57).

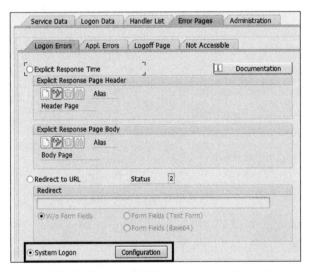

Figure 2.57 Configuring SAP Fiori Launchpad Login Screen

7. Select the **Custom Implementation** radio button.

8. Enter "/UI2/CL_SRA_LOGIN" in the **ABAP Class** field (see Figure 2.58).

9. Click ✅.

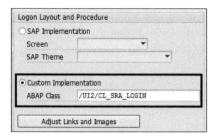

Figure 2.58 Custom ABAP Class

10. Click **Save** on the **Create/Change a Service** screen.

11. Repeat steps 2 to 10 with the /sap/bc/ui5_ui5/sap/arsrvc_upb_admn service to configure the logon for SAP Fiori launchpad designer.

12. Log in to SAP Fiori launchpad with your ID (see Figure 2.59):

    http(s)://<host>:<port>/sap/bc/ui5_ui5/ui2/ushell/shells/abap/FioriLaunch-pad.html?sap-client=<Client>.

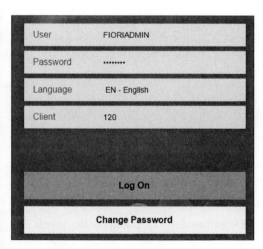

Figure 2.59 SAP Fiori Logon Screen

13. Log in to SAP Fiori launchpad designer with your ID:

    http://<host>:<port>/sap/bc/ui5_ui5/sap/arsrvc_upb_admn/main.html? sap-client=<client>&scope=CUST.

Configure the SAP Fiori Launchpad Logout Screen

After users log out from SAP Fiori launchpad, the browser displays a generic logout screen (see Figure 2.60). However, you can configure a custom HTML page to be displayed as the logout screen.

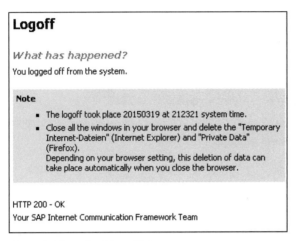

Figure 2.60 Default Logoff Screen

Follow these steps to add a custom logout screen:

1. In the ABAP front-end server, run Transaction SICF.
2. Click **Execute** , or press F8 .
3. Click **External Aliases**.
4. Select the root node of the alias, and choose Create **New External Alias** by clicking .
5. In the **External Alias** field, enter "/default_host/sap/public/bc/icf/logoff".
6. In the **Trg Element** tab, double-click the logoff node: /sap/public/bc/icf/logoff (see Figure 2.61).
7. Navigate to the **Error Pages** tab, then select the **Logoff Page** tab.
8. In **Redirect**, enter the URL of the logout page in HTML format (see Figure 2.62).
9. Save your entries.

2

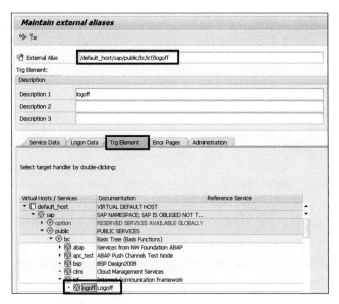

Figure 2.61 Target Element

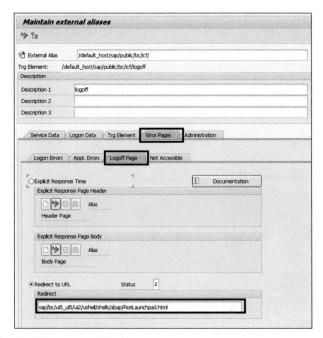

Figure 2.62 Logoff Page

Users should now see the custom logout screen whenever they logout from SAP Fiori launchpad.

If you're running SAP NetWeaver 7.4 SP 06 or higher, you can use the SAP_FIORI_ LAUNCHPAD_INIT_SETUP task list to automatically setup and configure SAP Fiori launchpad and SAP_GATEWAY_ACTIVATE_ODATA_SERV to activate the OData services for SAP Fiori launchpad. We'll cover the task lists in detail in Section 2.6.5.

2.6.2   SAP Gateway

Depending on the deployment option that you've selected, you need to install and configure the SAP Gateway server. As previously discussed, if your SAP NetWeaver version is 7.3, then you must install the SAP Gateway 2.0 SPS 10 component, which is comprised of GW_CORE 200 SP 10, SAP IW_FND 250 SP 10, and SAP WEBUIF 7.31 SP 10.

To install SAP Gateway 2.0, refer to the online help at *http://help.sap.com/nwgateway*, and choose **Installation and Upgrade Information · Installation Guide**.

In SAP NetWeaver 7.4, the GW_CORE, SAP IW_FND, IW_BEP, and IW_HDB components are replaced with the new software component SAP GW_FND (SAP Gateway Foundation SP 10). Therefore, if you're running SAP NetWeaver 7.4, you don't have to install any additional software components; they're already included in SAP NetWeaver 7.4.

Activate SAP Gateway

First, you'll have to activate SAP Gateway services. Follow these steps:

1. Run Transaction SPRO.

2. Click `⬥ SAP Reference IMG` .

3. Drill down to activate or deactivate SAP Gateway, and click ⊕ (see Figure 2.63).

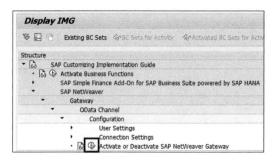

Figure 2.63 Implementation Guide

4. Click **Activate** (see Figure 2.64).

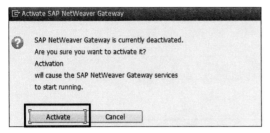

Figure 2.64 Activating SAP Gateway Service

Integrate SAP Gateway and SAP Business Suite

In this step, we'll set up the trusted RFC connection to define a trusted relationship between SAP Gateway on the ABAP front-end server and SAP Business Suite on the ABAP back-end server.

Follow these steps:

1. Log in to your ABAP front-end server.

2. Run Transaction SM59.

3. Click **Create** [□].

4. Set the following configurations on the next screen (see Figure 2.65):
   - **RFC Destination**: Enter "ERPCLNT120" (this is the RFC destination name).
   - **Connection Type**: Enter "3".
   - **Description 1**: Enter "SAP ERP".
   - **Load Balancing**: Select **No**.
   - **Target Host**: Enter the SAP Business Suite server name.
   - **Instance Number**: Enter "00".

5. Click the **Logon and Security** tab, and use the following settings (see Figure 2.66):
   - **Language**: Enter "EN".
   - **Client**: Enter "120".
   - **User**: Select the **Current User** checkbox.
   - **Trust Relationship**: Select **Yes**.

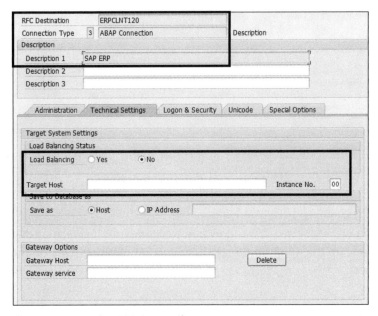

Figure 2.65 Creating RFC Connection

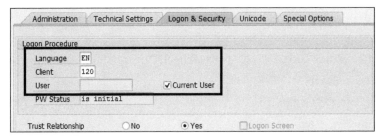

Figure 2.66 Logon and Security

Now, you need to repeat the same steps on your ABAP back-end server, with the target host as your ABAP front-end server. After setting up the RFC destination in the back-end server, you need to run the Creating Trusting Relationships wizard. Follow these steps:

1. Run Transaction SMT1.

2. Click **Create**.

3. Follow the steps in the Creating Trusting Relationships wizard.

4. Save your settings.

Creating the SAP System Alias for Applications

In this step, we'll create the SAP system alias that points to the SAP Business Suite system from the central hub system. We've implemented an embedded deployment, and the system alias should represent the SAP Gateway system itself, so we'll have to create a system alias entry (LOCAL). However, if your landscape has a central hub deployment, then you need to enter the SAP Gateway system details.

Follow these steps:

1. Run Transaction SPRO.

2. Click ✑ SAP Reference IMG .

3. Navigate to **Manage System Aliases,** and click ⊕. Follow the menu path **SAP Net-Weaver · Gateway · OData Channel · Configuration · Connection Settings · SAP NetWeaver Gateway to SAP System · Manage SAP System Aliases** (see Figure 2.67).

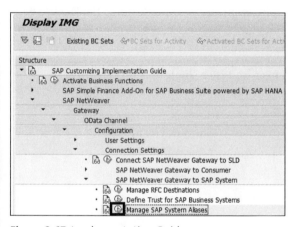

Figure 2.67 Implementation Guide

4. Click **New Entries,** and establish the following settings (see Figure 2.68):

   – **SAP System Alias**: Enter "LOCAL".

   – **Description**: Enter "Local System Alias".

   – **Local GW**: Check this box.

   – **For Local App**: Do not check this box.

   – **RFC Destination**: Enter "NONE".

   – **Software Version:** Select **DEFAULT** from the available software versions by clicking 🔍 in the field.

  – **System ID**: Leave blank.

  – **Client**: Leave blank.

  – **WS Provider System**: Leave blank.

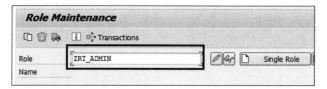

Figure 2.68 System Aliases

Assign a Role Template to an Admin User

In this step, we need to assign the role template /IWFND/RT_ADMIN to the FIORIADMIN user. Follow these steps:

1. Run Transaction PFCG.

2. Enter "ZRT_ADMIN" in the **Role** field, and click **Single Role** (see Figure 2.69).

Figure 2.69 Role Maintenance

3. Select the **Authorizations** tab, then click **Save** (if there's a pop-up message).

4. Click **Change Authorization Data** (see Figure 2.70).

```
Maintain Authorization Data and Generate Profiles
   Change Authorization Data
```

Figure 2.70 Generating Profiles

5. Choose the **/IWFND/RT_ADMIN** template, and click **Adopt reference** (see Figure 2.71).

6. Click the **Generate** icon (see Figure 2.72).

7. Click **Save**.

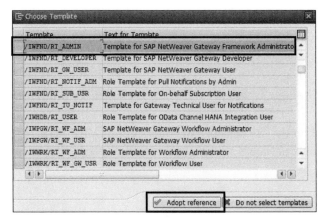

Figure 2.71 Adopting Reference, Template

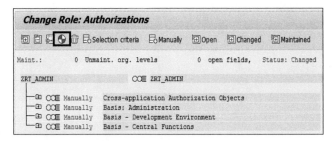

Figure 2.72 Generate

8. Click the **Back** button, and select the **User** tab.

9. Enter "FIORIADMIN" in the **User ID** field and press [Enter] (see Figure 2.73).

Figure 2.73 Adding Administrator to Role

10. Click **Save**.

Specify the Default Language and Logon Language

You need to make sure that the default language in both SAP Gateway and the back-end system are the same, because the SAP Gateway system supports only those languages that are the same in the connected SAP Business Suite back-end systems. If they aren't the same, then you need to verify whether the back-end language is a subset of the languages in the SAP Gateway system.

The logon language is based on the user settings in Transaction SU01. If nothing is defined there, then the default language is automatically used (see Figure 2.74).

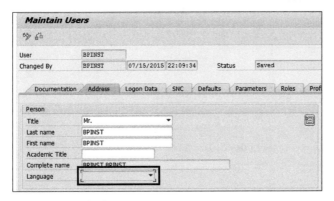

Figure 2.74 Default Language

If a service in Transaction SICF is activated with the **Required with Logon Data** indicator, then the system uses the language defined in the **Language** field (see Figure 2.75).

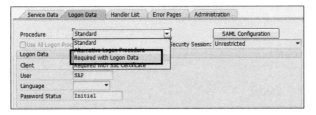

Figure 2.75 Request with Logon Data

2.6.3   Embedded Search

Search functionality lets users search apps and central business objects, as well as view lists of recently used apps. The search toolbar is in the top-right corner of SAP Fiori launchpad (see Figure 2.76).

Figure 2.76 Search Toolbar

SAP Fiori fact sheet apps are called using this search functionality. As a prerequisite for the fact sheet apps, you need to set up SAP Search.

If your SAP NetWeaver version is 7.4 SPS 06 or higher, you can use the predefined tasks to automatically set up and configure the communication channels among the client, front-end servers, and back-end servers. Using the predefined tasks list, you can configure the initial system setup, SAP Gateway, SAP Fiori Launchpad, and so on. In this section, we'll focus on the predefined tasks for setting up embedded search.

On the front-end server, you need to set up communication between SAP Web Dispatcher and the ABAP front-end servers, which we did in the previous sections. On the back-end server, you must set up embedded search.

Activating Embedded Search User Interface Services

In this step, we'll activate the central UI services related to the embedded search. In Section 2.6.1, we described how to activate services; follow the same process to activate the following services in the ABAP back-end server:

- `default_host/sap/es/cockpit`
- `default_host/sap/es/saplink`
- `default_host/sap/es/search`
- `default_host/sap/es/ina`
- `default_host/sap/bc/webdynpro/sap/ESH_ADMIN_UI_COMPONENT`
- `default_host/sap/bc/webdynpro/sap/esh_eng_modelling`
- `default_host/sap/bc/webdynpro/sap/esh_eng_wizard`
- `default_host/sap/bc/webdynpro/sap/esh_search_results_ui`
- `default_host/sap/bc/webdynpro/sap/wdhc_help_center`

Assign Authorizations for Embedded Search

In this step, we'll assign authorizations to the FIORIADMIN user to manage embedded search. Follow these steps:

1. Run Transaction SUO1.

2. Enter "FIORIADMIN" in the **User** field.

3. Click [pencil icon].

4. Enter "SAP_ESH_CR_ADMIN" and "SAP_ESH_BOS_ADMIN" in the **Role** field and press [Enter] (see Figure 2.77).

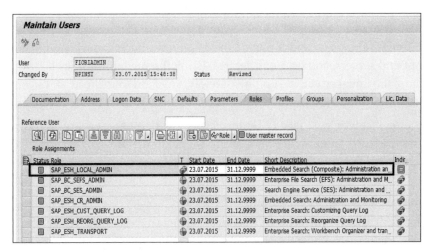

Figure 2.77 Embedded Search–Related Roles

5. Click **Save**.

The FIORIADMIN user will now have access to control the embedded search.

Check Business Functions

In this step, we need to check whether some of the business functions related to embedded search are activated in the back-end server. Follow these steps in your ABAP back-end server:

1. Run Transaction SFW5.

2. Click **Continue**.

3. On the next screen, open the **Enterprise Business Functions** folder.

4. Search for the following functions, and check if they're activated (you'll see a light-bulb next to their names if they are; see Figure 2.78):

   – **BSCBN_HANA_NAV**

   – **BSESH_HANA_SEARCH**

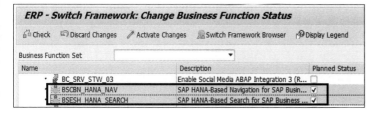

Figure 2.78 Business Functions

5. If these functions aren't activated, then select the **Planned Status** checkbox and click **Activate Changes**.

Set Up Embedded Search Using Task List (Client 000)

Fact sheets are shown in the results lists of embedded search. In this step, we'll show you how to perform the initial setup of embedded search using the task list. Proceed as follows:

1. Login to the ABAP back-end server using client 000.

2. Run Transaction STC01.

3. Enter "SAP_ESH_INITIAL_SETUP_000_CLIENT" in the **Task List** field (Figure 2.79), and click ⊕ to generate the task list. This task prepares the ESH-specific tables in client 000 and then copies the tables to the target client.

Figure 2.79 Task List

4. Click **Confirm** (Figure 2.80).

Figure 2.80 Task List Documentation

5. The ⚇ icon indicates that there are manual activities you must **Precheck** before running the task (Figure 2.81).

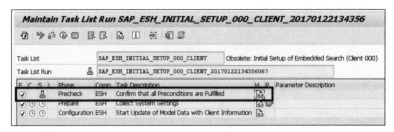

Figure 2.81 Precheck

6. Click ⚇ to confirm that all the preconditions are fulfilled (Figure 2.82).

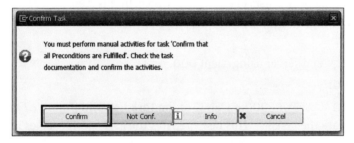

Figure 2.82 Confirm Task

7. Click **Confirm** to confirm that all preconditions are met.

8. Make sure the checkboxes next to all the tasks are checked (Figure 2.83), then click 🔲 to run the task list in the background.

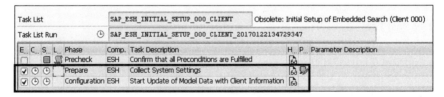

Figure 2.83 Tasks

9. After the task list is executed, you can check the log by running Transaction STC02.

Set Up Embedded Search Using Task List (Working Client)

In the previous section, we set up embedded search for client 000; now, we'll follow the same steps to set up embedded search in the working client:

1. Login to the ABAP back-end server using the working client.

2. Run the SAP_ESH_INITIAL_SETUP_WRK_CLIENT task list from Transaction STC01. This task list activates ICF services. Set TREX/HANA destination/connection.

3. Confirm that all the preconditions are fulfilled (Figure 2.84).

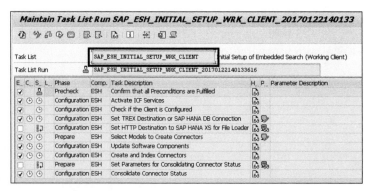

Figure 2.84 Task List Items

4. Because this task takes a long time to run, we recommend running it in the background. Click 🔲 to do so.

Configuration Check: Search User Interface (Fact Sheet Apps Only)

To check that SAP Fiori search has been installed correctly, run Transaction ESH_SEARCH in the back-end system; the Web Dynpro UI for the search should appear (see Figure 2.85).

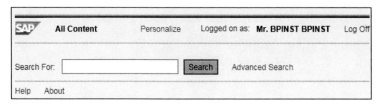

Figure 2.85 Web Dynpro UI

2.6.4   SAP HANA

In this section, we'll look at some of the generic configuration steps required for analytical apps to work on the SAP HANA database.

Assign SAP Smart Business Modeler Roles

In this step, you need to assign roles to the user to use the SAP Smart Business modeler. Follow these steps:

1. Log in to the SAP HANA server from SAP HANA Studio.

2. Open the **Security** folder, then open the **Users** folder.

3. Double-click the **FIORIADMIN** user name to open the user's profile (see Figure 2.86).

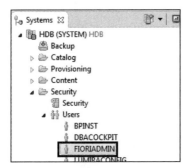

Figure 2.86 User Maintenance

4. Click the **Granted Roles** tab.

5. Enter the following role, then click **OK** (see Figure 2.87): "sap.hba.r.sb. core.roles:: SAP_SMART_BUSINESS_MODELER".

6. Repeat the steps to add the remaining roles:

    – sap.hba.r.sb.core.roles::SAP_SMART_BUSINESS_RUNTIME

    – sap.hba.apps.kpi.s.roles::SAP_SMART_BUSINESS_MODELER

    – sap.hba.apps.kpi.s.roles::SAP_SMART_BUSINESS_RUNTIME

    – sap.hba.apps.ps.s.roles::SAP_SMART_BUSINESS_PROJECT_MANAGER

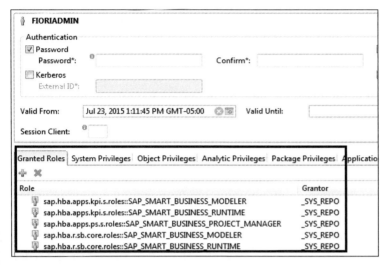

Figure 2.87 Adding Roles

Assign the KPI Modeler and KPI Framework Roles

In this step, we'll assign the KPI modeler roles to the administrative user and end user using Transaction PFCG in the ABAP front-end server. Follow these steps:

1. Follow the same steps from the previous section, and assign the roles **/UI2/SAP_ KPIFRW5_TCR_S** and **/UI2/SAP_KPIMOD_TCR_S** to the SAP Fiori administrator user—for example, **FIORIADMIN** user (see Figure 2.88).

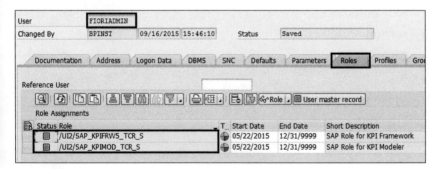

Figure 2.88 KPI Modeler and KPI Framework Roles

2. Similarly, assign **/UI2/SAP_KPIFRW5_TCR_S** to an end user—for example, **FIORI-USER** (see Figure 2.89).

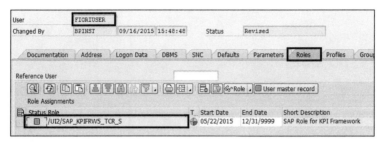

Figure 2.89 KPI Framework Role

Activate SAP Smart Business Modeler Service

In this step, you need to activate a service in the ABAP front-end server. In Section 2.6.1, we showed you how to activate services. Here, you need to follow the same process and activate the following service in the ABAP front-end server: default_host/sap/bc/ui5_ui5/sap/CA_KPI.

Configuration Check

After you've configured the KPI modeler framework, you should see the following KPI modeler apps in the **KPI Modeler** catalog in SAP Fiori launchpad (see Figure 2.90):

- **KPI Workspace**
- **Configure KPI Drill-Down**
- **Manage KPI Authorizations**
- **Manage KPI Associations**
- **Create KPI**
- **Create Evaluation**
- **Configure KPI Tiles**
- **Migration Tool**

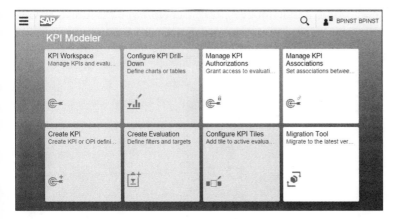

Figure 2.90 KPI Modeler Apps

2.6.5 Configuration Using the Task List

In section Section 2.6.1, we walked you step-by-step through how to configure the SAP Fiori launchpad manually; in this section, we'll introduce the predefined task list, with which you can configure your ABAP system automatically. We'll walk you through an example based on the SAP Fiori launchpad configuration. This predefined task list is available in SAP NetWeaver 7.4 SP 06 or higher. SAP_FIORI_LAUNCHPAD_ INIT_SETUP is the task list you need to run to set up SAP Fiori launchpad.

Requirements

Your server must be on SAP NetWeaver 7.4 SPS 08 or higher to use all the available task lists for configuring SAP Fiori.

Follow these steps:

1. Run Transaction STCO1.

2. Enter the task name in the **Task List** field, then click the **Display Task List** icon 𝒢 to view the tasks (Figure 2.91).

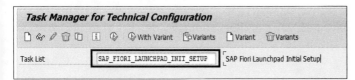

Figure 2.91 Task Manager

3. Be sure to review documentation for every task list before you execute it. To view the documentation, click **Goto** · **Documentation** · **Display** (see Figure 2.92).

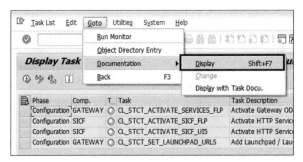

Figure 2.92 Task List Documentation

4. After you review the documentation, press F8 or click ⊕ to generate the task list.

5. Make sure the checkboxes next to all the tasks are checked, then click ⊕ to run the task list (see Figure 2.93).

Figure 2.93 Task List Final Check

Important!

Some tasks will take a long time to run, so we recommend running those task lists in the background.

---

6. After the task list is executed, you can check the log by running Transaction STC02 (see Figure 2.94).

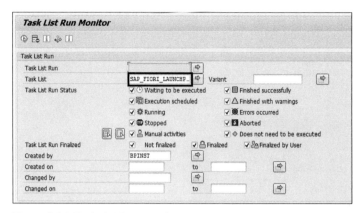

Figure 2.94 Task List Run Monitor

After the task list is successfully completed, the initial set up of SAP Fiori launchpad is done. We performed the same process manually in Section 2.6.1.

Table 2.2 presents a selection of tasks and their task lists.

Task	Task List
SAP Gateway—Basic Configuration	SAP_GATEWAY_BASIC_CONFIG
SAP Fiori Launchpad Initial Setup	SAP_FIORI_LAUNCHPAD_INIT_SETUP
Create Trusted Connection from SAP System to SAP Gateway	SAP_SAP2GATEWAY_TRUSTED_CONFIG
Enable Embedded Search	SAP_ESH_INITIAL_SETUP_000_CLIENT
SAP Gateway—Add Back-end System	SAP_GATEWAY_ADD_SYSTEM
SAP Gateway—Maintain System Alias	SAP_GATEWAY_ADD_SYSTEM_ALIAS
SAP Gateway—Activate OData Services	SAP_GATEWAY_ACTIVATE_ODATA_SERV
SAP Basis—Activate HTTP Services (SICF)	SAP_BASIS_ACTIVATE_ICF_NODES

Table 2.2 Configuration Task Lists

SAP Cloud Platform

SAP Cloud Platform is a platform-as-a-service (PaaS) for the cloud application. With SAP Cloud Platform, customers can build new cloud apps quickly, extend existing

SAP Fiori apps, and easily integrate apps with SAP and non-SAP systems. There are many tools available in SAP Cloud Platform, such as SAP Fiori, cloud edition and SAP Web IDE (see Figure 2.95). Customers can easily integrate SAP Fiori, cloud edition account into their on-premise SAP landscapes to customize and run apps in SAP Fiori launchpad on the cloud.

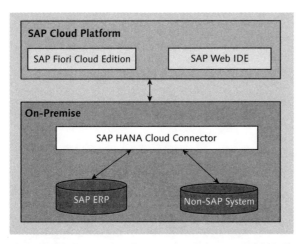

Figure 2.95 Connecting On-Premise Systems and SAP Cloud Platform

In this section, we'll show you how to connect an on-premise system to SAP Cloud Platform. The first step is to install and configure SAP Cloud Platform cloud connector, which serves as the link between SAP Fiori, cloud edition and on-premise SAP landscapes.

Install the Cloud Connector

There two versions of the cloud connector. The portable version of the cloud connector can be installed on Windows and Linux, and the installer version of the cloud connector can be installed on Windows, Linux, and macOS.

Prerequisites:

- *Memory*: Minimum 1 GB RAM; 4 GB recommended
- *Hard disk space*: Minimum 1 GB; 20 GB recommended
- *CPU*: Minimum single-core 3 GHz; dual core 2 GHz recommended; x86–64 architecture compatible
- *Java developer kit*: Version 7 or 8 needs to be installed; most recent version is available via *https://tools.hana.ondemand.com/#cloud*

Now let's explore the steps to install the cloud connector. Follow these steps:

1. Download SAP Cloud Platform cloud connector 2.x via *https://tools.hana.onde-mand.com/#cloud.*

2. Run the setup file to install the cloud connector, click **Next** in the setup wizard (Figure 2.96).

Figure 2.96 SAP Cloud Platform Cloud Connector Installation

3. Follow the simple steps in the wizard to complete the installation. Close the installer window once the installation is complete.

You should now see two icons added to your desktop, one to start and one to stop the SAP Cloud Platform cloud connector.

Set Up SAP Cloud Platform Cloud Connector

Once the cloud connector is installed, you need to log in and perform its initial setup, as follows:

1. Launch the cloud connector via *https://localhost:8443/.*

2. Login with the initial admin credentials; enter "administrator" for **User Name** and "manage" for **Password** (Figure 2.97).

3. Change the initial password and click **Save** (Figure 2.98).

Figure 2.97 Cloud Connector Login

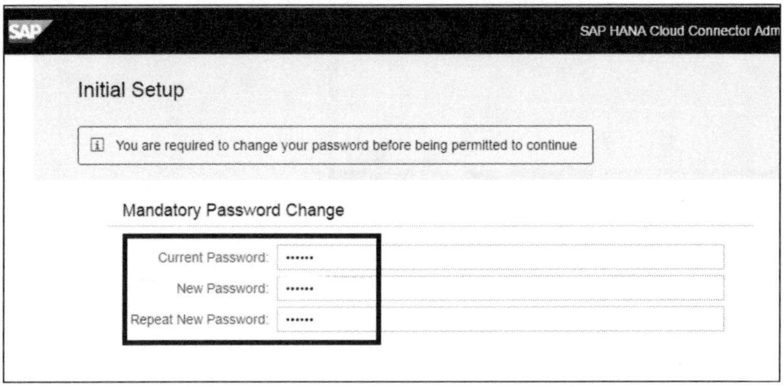

Figure 2.98 Initial Password

Before we move on to the next step, you need to register at *https://account.hanat-rial.ondemand.com/register* to create a trial account for SAP Cloud Platform. Once you create an account, we'll create a trust between SAP Cloud Platform cloud connector and SAP Cloud Platform, as follows:

In the SAP HANA Cloud Connector admin cockpit, add the trial account details and click **Save** (Figure 2.99).

We've now successfully installed the cloud connector, created an account with SAP Cloud Platform, and connected the two.

Figure 2.99 SAP Cloud Platform Account

Next, we need to create a mapping between SAP Cloud Platform and the on-premise systems using the cloud connector, as follows:

1. Click **Cloud To On-Premise** in the cloud connector (Figure 2.100).

Figure 2.100 Cloud to On-Premise

2. Click **+** to add the on-premise system (Figure 2.101).

Figure 2.101 Add Internal System

3. Select the **back-end type of on-premise system** (Figure 2.102), and click **Next**.

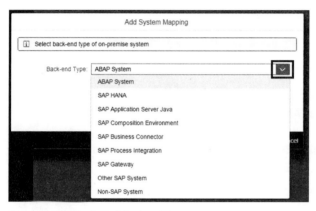

Figure 2.102 Back-End System Type

4. Select the **Protocol** (i.e., HTTP/HTTPS, etc.), and click **Next** (Figure 2.103).

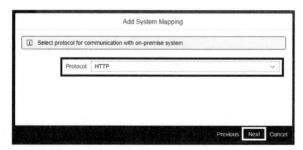

Figure 2.103 System Protocol

5. Enter the **Host** and the **Port** name of the on-premise system (Figure 2.104).

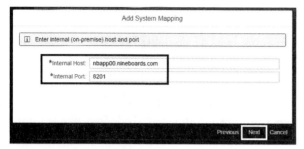

Figure 2.104 Host and Port

6. Select a **Principal Type** (Figure 2.105).

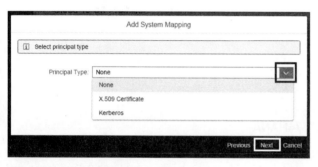

Figure 2.105 Principal Type

7. Enter a **Description** and click **Finish** to add the system (Figure 2.106).

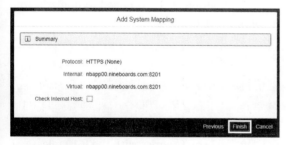

Figure 2.106 System Summary

By now, you should have all the pieces in place to start using the SAP Fiori system.

2.7   Upgrading to SAP Fiori 2.0

In this section, we'll highlight the requirements for upgrading SAP Business Suite and SAP S/4HANA systems to SAP Fiori 2.0. Before you start preparing for the upgrade, let's explore a few crucial points regarding SAP Fiori 2.0:

- SAP Fiori 2.0 is available for the SAP S/4HANA 1610 release and for the SAP Business Suite powered by SAP HANA or AnyDB. SAP Fiori 2.0 is not available for the previous SAP S/4HANA release 1511.
- SAP Fiori 2.0 is available for the 1608 release for SAP S/4HANA Cloud.
- SAP Fiori 2.0 is mandatory for SAP S/4HANA 1610 and higher.
- Systems based on SAP NetWeaver Application Server (AS) for ABAP 7.4 or SAP NetWeaver AS for ABAP 7.5 can only enable the basic notification capability of SAP Fiori 2.0.

Now, let's look at the component that needs to be upgraded to implement SAP Fiori 2.0.

2.7.1   SAP Fiori 2.0 for SAP S/4HANA

If you are currently running SAP Fiori on SAP S/4HANA, and would like to upgrade to SAP Fiori 2.0, you must upgrade SAP Fiori front-end server 2.0 to SAP Fiori front-end server 3.0, and upgrade SAP S/4HANA 1511 to SAP S/4HANA 1610.

SAP Fiori front-end server 3.0 is the key add-on component for SAP NetWeaver AS for ABAP for providing the SAP Fiori 2.0 user experience, so you need to upgrade your SAP Fiori front-end server 2.0 to version 3.0 with SAP UI 7.51.

> **Note**
>
> For SAP S/4HANA 1610, SAP Fiori front-end server 3.0 can also be installed on instances based on the SAP NetWeaver AS for ABAP 7.50 SP04.

For SAP S/4HANA, SAP Fiori 2.0 is only available on premise with the 1610 release, so you will also need to upgrade your back-end system to SAP S/4HANA 1610.

> **Important**
>
> SAP S/4HANA 1511 does not support SAP Fiori front-end server 3.0, so it continues to run version 2.0.

Once the front-end server is upgraded to version 3.0 and the back-end server to SAP S/4HANA 1610 (see Figure 2.107) your system will be running SAP Fiori 2.0.

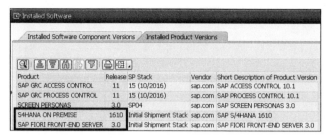

Figure 2.107 Installed Product versions

2.7.2   SAP Fiori 2.0 for SAP Business Suite Powered by SAP HANA or AnyDB

For SAP Business Suite powered by SAP HANA or AnyDB, all you have to do is to upgrade the front-end server from version 2.0 to version 3.0, including SAP UI 7.51 to upgrade to SAP Fiori 2.0 in your landscape.

> **Note**
>
> SAP Fiori front-end server 3.0 for SAP NetWeaver 7.5 and 7.4 is particularly designed and offered for customers using SAP Business Suite powered by SAP HANA. SAP recommends implementing the latest released support packages for the SAP Fiori front-end server 3.0.

2.8   Summary

This chapter provided an overview of the SAP Fiori system landscape and how to connect it with the ABAP environment, SAP HANA, and SAP HANA XS. We've discussed the many steps and tasks needed to install and configure SAP Fiori. There are certainly many SAP Fiori apps (7,000+), and your choice of SAP Fiori landscape depends on the types of SAP Fiori apps you'll use.

Now that you understand how to set up SAP Fiori and what's needed to install different components in the landscape, we'll discuss securing different layers of the SAP Fiori system using authentication methods or SSO procedures in the next chapter.

PART II

Implementation

Chapter 3
SAP Fiori Security

This chapter discusses the various security mechanisms that can be put in place to prevent the unauthorized and unauthenticated use of SAP Fiori apps.

When configuring SAP Fiori apps, it's important that you keep in mind security measures that will ensure the right users are given proper access to assigned apps. Also, you must ensure that your data and processes support your business needs without allowing unauthorized access to critical information.

In this chapter, we'll introduce you to security measures for SAP Fiori and the various single sign-on procedures that are supported. We'll even look at the concepts related to securing the various layers of SAP Fiori. We'll begin in Section 3.1 by reviewing some key concepts that will crop up throughout the chapter, such as data flow between different layers of the SAP Fiori landscape, what the different network and communication channels are, and how to secure each of these channels. After we walk you through the basic concepts, in Section 3.2 we'll provide an overview of the various authentication methods or SSO procedures, such as Kerberos, Security Assertion Markup Language (SAML), and SAP logon tickets, and discuss the flow/processes of these authentication methods.

Finally, we'll conclude with a discussion of user authorizations required for different types of apps in Section 3.3. We'll look at authorizations a user needs to have in SAP Fiori launchpad, SAP Gateway, and the ABAP front-end and back-end systems to run apps in SAP Fiori launchpad.

> **Scope**
>
> This book doesn't discuss how to secure the ABAP stack or the SAP HANA platform, because those are huge topics. However, we've added links where appropriate that point to online help pages.

3.1   Communication Channel Security and Encryption

As we discussed in Chapter 1, Section 1.2, SAP Fiori architecture crosses different network layers (see Figure 3.1).

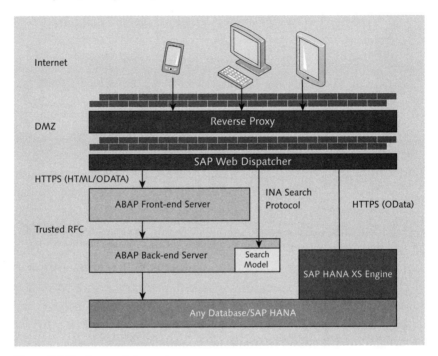

Figure 3.1 Deployment Scenario

The first point of defense in your SAP Fiori system should be to secure the lines of communication among these layers. As Chapter 1 explained, communication among the client, reverse proxy, and servers must be established by using different communication channels and protocols to transfer data securely within your SAP Fiori system landscape.

When a user launches an SAP Fiori application, the launch request is sent from the client to the SAP Gateway server via SAP Fiori Launchpad. During that launch, the SAP Gateway server (or ABAP front-end server) authenticates the user by using one of the authentication and SSO mechanisms.

For example, if you're implementing a transactional app in an Internet-facing scenario (i.e., the external-facing scenario), a common security measure is to put a reverse proxy—that is, either SAP Web Dispatcher or a third-party reverse proxy, such as from Apache—in the demilitarized zone (DMZ). SAP also recommends deploying SAP Web Dispatcher in your Internet-facing deployment scenario (see Figure 3.1) because the security features aren't very strong in SAP Web Dispatcher; for example, it can't scan incoming POST bodies.

Table 3.1 shows the communication paths used by SAP Fiori applications and the protocol that is used for each connection. The application and security credentials types of data are transferred among all these communication paths.

Communication Path	Protocol	Application Type
Web browser to SAP Web Dispatcher	OData HTTP/HTTPS	Fact sheet and analytical apps
SAP Web Dispatcher to ABAP front-end server	OData HTTP/HTTPS	All
SAP Web Dispatcher to SAP HANA XS	OData HTTP/HTTPS	Analytical apps
SAP Web Dispatcher to ABAP back-end server	INA HTTP/HTTPS	Fact sheet apps
ABAP front-end server to ABAP back-end server	RFC	Transactional apps and fact sheet apps
ABAP back-end server to SAP HANA/any database	SQL	Analytical apps

Table 3.1 Communication Paths

To avoid third parties intercepting communications between two layers, a system needs to be in place that isn't susceptible to eavesdropping. Securing communication means monitoring which users have access to their company's sensitive data on SAP Fiori launchpad, in addition to ensuring that third parties that weren't provided access can't intercept anything. Communications take place over different layers of the SAP Fiori landscape, and there is an increasing awareness of the importance of interception issues. In this section, we'll discuss a couple of ways to secure your communication channels.

Encryption makes data hard to read by unauthorized parties. There are two important steps you can take to ensure that your data is safe:

1. HTTP connections can be protected using Transport Layer Security (TLS) or Secure Sockets Layer (SSL).

2. RFC connections can be protected by using Secure Network Communications (SNC).

Now, let's dig deep into the layers of these communication channels and discuss how to secure them. By now, you should be familiar with the SAP Fiori landscape. Figure 3.2 shows the high-level system landscape from the communication channel and apps perspective.

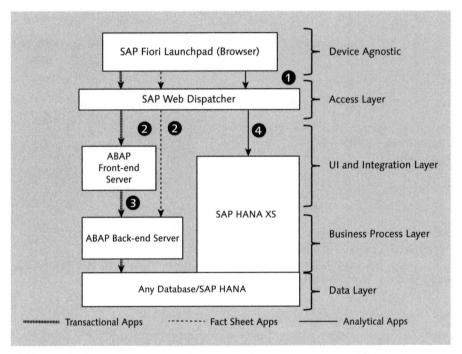

Figure 3.2 SAP Fiori System Landscape from Communication Channel/Apps Perspective

The following elements are shown in Figure 3.2:

1. Communication between the client and SAP Web Dispatcher

2. Communication between SAP Web Dispatcher and ABAP servers

3. Communication between the ABAP front-end server and the ABAP back-end server

4. Communication between SAP Web Dispatcher and SAP HANA XS

Figure 3.2 also shows what layers each of these app types pass through in the SAP Fiori landscape. All communication channels discussed earlier should be encrypted to ensure integrity and confidentiality of data. In the next section, we'll show you how to secure the communication channels of your SAP Fiori system.

3.1.1   Client to SAP Web Dispatcher

Starting from the top, to simplify communication between the browser and the different systems in the SAP Fiori system landscape, we use a reverse proxy to ensure queries from the browser are routed correctly (i.e., to the ABAP front-end, ABAP back-end, or SAP HANA XS engine). Depending on the type of app users run from SAP Fiori launchpad, a client issues the request to SAP Web Dispatcher. To secure this communication channel, you need to enable SAP Web Dispatcher to use HTTPS communication. The client sends the HTTPS-encrypted data to SAP Web Dispatcher, and then SAP Web Dispatcher decrypts the data and sends the unencrypted data to the ABAP servers.

3.1.2   SAP Web Dispatcher to ABAP Servers

The next level in securing the SAP Fiori landscape is configuring the connection between SAP Web Dispatcher and the ABAP servers. SAP Fiori transactional apps route calls from SAP Web Dispatcher to the ABAP front-end server, and SAP Fiori search and fact sheet apps route calls from SAP Web Dispatcher to the ABAP back-end server. To secure these communication channels, you need to configure the components discussed in the following two sections.

Enable ABAP Front-End and ABAP Back-End Servers to Use HTTPS

The following are the high-level steps for how to configure the ABAP front-end and back-end servers to use HTTPS. Because both servers are based on SAP NetWeaver, they have the same configuration steps.

Make sure SAP Web Dispatcher is installed. Next, you'll configure it as an SSL client in the system landscape by following these steps:

1. Log in to the OS of SAP Web Dispatcher, and edit the **WDP_W<Instance Number>_<hostname>** instance profile.

2. Enable **HTTPS** for SAP Web Dispatcher. Enter the following details in the **WDP_W<Instance Number>_<hostname>** instance profile:

- DIR_INSTANCE = <SECUDIR_Directory>
- ssl/ssl_lib = <Location of SAP Cryptographic Library>
- ssl/server_pse = <Location of SSL server PSE>
- ssl/client_pse = < Location of SSL client PSE >
- wdisp/ssl_encrypt = 1
- wdisp/ssl_auth = 2
- wdisp/add_client_protocol_header = 1
- wdisp/ping_protocol = https
- icm/HTTPS/verify_client = 0

The following is an example of how we set the SAP Web Dispatcher parameters in our system landscape:

- DIR_INSTANCE=C:\dispatcher\
- ssl/ssl_lib=C:\ dispatcher \sapcrypto.dll
- ssl/server_pse=C:\ dispatcher \sec\SAPSSLS.pse
- ssl/client_pse=C:\ dispatcher \sec\SAPSSLC.pse
- wdisp/ssl_encrypt = 1
- wdisp/ssl_auth = 2
- wdisp/add_client_protocol_header = 1
- wdisp/ping_protocol = https
- icm/HTTPS/verify_client = 0

3. For Internet Communication Manager (ICM) ports, enter the following profile parameters:

   icm/server_port_0 = PROT=HTTPS,PORT=<Web Dispatcher Port>,TIMEOUT=<Mins>

   The following is an example of how we set the ICM ports in our system landscape:

   cm/server_port_0 = PROT=HTTPS, PORT=443, TIMEOUT=120

4. Define the routing rules for the SAP Web Dispatcher by entering the following profile parameters:

   - wdisp/system_0 = SID=<Front-end SID>, MSHOST=<Front-End Hostname>, MSPORT=<Front-end Messaging Port>, SRCSRV=*:<Web Dispatcher Port>, SRCURL=/sap/opu/; /sap/public/;/sap/bc/;/sap/saml2/;/ui2/nwbc/, CLIENT=<Front-end client>

- wdisp/system_1 – SID=<Back-end SID>, MSHOST=<Back-end Hostname>, MSPORT= <Back-end Messaging Port>, SRCSRV=*:<Web Dispatcher Port>, SRCURL=/sap/es/, CLIENT= <Back-end client>

- wdisp/system_2 = SID=<HANA SID>, EXTSRV=<HANA XS URL>, SRCSRV=*:<Web Dispatcher Port>, SRCURL=/sap/hba/;/sap/hana/;/sap/bi/;/sap/viz/;/sap/vi/;/sap/ui5/

The following is an example of how we defined routing rules in our system landscape:

- wdisp/system_0 = SID=ABA, MSHOST= sapaba02.cloud.sap-nb.com, MSPORT=8101, SRCSRV=*:443, SRCURL=/sap/opu/;/sap/bc/; /sap/public/bc/;/sap/saml2/;/ui2/ nwbc/,CLIENT=120

- wdisp/system_1 = SID=ERP, MSHOST= saperp02.cloud.sap-nb.com, MSPORT=8101, SRCSRV=*:443, SRCURL=/sap/es/, CLIENT=180

- wdisp/system_2 = SID=HDB, EXTSRV=https://saphdb02.cloud.sap-nb:4302, SRCSRV=*:443, SRCURL=/sap/hba/;/sap/hana /;/sap/bi/

5. Save the **WDP_W<Instance Number>_<hostname>** instance profile.

6. Restart the SAP Web Dispatcher process.

You've now successfully enabled HTTPS for the ABAP servers.

Enable SSL between SAP Web Dispatcher and the ABAP Front-End Server

SSL is one of the standard security technologies for establishing an encrypted link between a server and client. SSL allows sensitive information to be transmitted securely. Typically, data is sent between the browser/client and the ABAP servers in plain text, leaving you exposed to eavesdropping. The most important part of SSL is the digitally signed certificate authority (CA); when a user tries to connect to the ABAP servers, the client will only trust certificates coming from the organizations on its list of trusted CAs. In this section, we'll provide the high-level steps for securing communications between SAP Web Dispatcher and the ABAP front-end server using SSL. Follow these steps:

1. Extract the SAP Cryptographic Library package, and install it on SAP Web Dispatcher.

2. Create an SAP Web Dispatcher's Personal Security Environment (PSE) and the certificate requests using the SAPGENPSE configuration tool.

> **SAPGENPSE**
>
> For those without an SAP Basis background, the cryptography tool SAPGENPSE is used to generate a keystore in which you can store a certificate.

3. After the certificate request is created, send the contents of each of the certificate requests to a CA to be signed.

4. After you've received the certificate request response from your CA, import it into SAP Web Dispatcher's corresponding PSE using either the trust manager or the SAPGENPSE tool.

5. Create credentials for SAP Web Dispatcher to access the PSEs during runtime.

6. Set the SSL profile parameters for SAP Web Dispatcher.

7. Restart SAP Web Dispatcher, and test the connection.

3.1.3   ABAP Front-End Server to ABAP Back-End Server

In the previous section, we discussed SSL, which is used to secure the communications between the client and the ABAP server. Similarly, there is a software layer in the SAP NetWeaver system called *Secure Network Communications*, which enables stronger authentication, encryption, and SSO mechanisms from server to server. Using SNC, you can enable end-to-end application-level security. In addition, you can implement security features, such as SSO functions that SAP doesn't provide directly.

In SAP Fiori, transactional apps and fact sheet apps transfer data from the ABAP back-end to the ABAP front-end server using OData services. We'll look at how to secure these ABAP layers using SNC next.

Enabling Secure Network Communications for the ABAP Front-End and Back-End Servers

First, enable SNC on both ABAP servers by following these steps:

1. Log in to the ABAP back-end server.

2. Run Transaction RZ10.

3. Select an **Instance Profile**.

4. Select **Extended maintenance**, and click **Change** (see Figure 3.3).

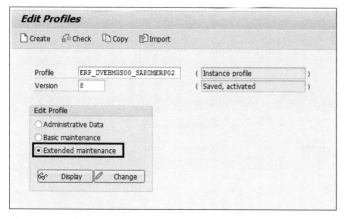

Figure 3.3 Editing Profile

5. Click the **Create** button.

6. Enter the parameters shown in Table 3.2.

Parameter	Definition	Value (Example)
snc/enable	Activate SNC	1
snc/gssapi_lib	Full path and file name of the shared library sapcrypto lib	D:/usr/sap/ERP/SYS/exe/uc/ANC443/libsap-crypto.so
snc/identity/as	SNC name of the application server	p/secude: CN=ERP, O=SAP-NB, C=CA
snc/r3int_rfc_secure	Internal RFC connections aren't SNC-protected	0

Table 3.2 Parameters for Enabling SNC

7. Restart the system.

Securing RFC Connections with Secure Network Communications

Next, you need to secure the RFC connections. The following steps show how to secure RFC connections between SAP Gateway and the ABAP back-end using SNC:

1. Log in to the ABAP back-end server, and run Transaction SM59.

2. Select the connection under **RFC Connections**, and click 🖉 (see Figure 3.4).

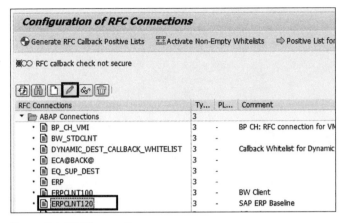

Figure 3.4 RFC Connection

3. Click the **Logon & Security** tab, and click the **SNC** button under **Status of Secure Protocol**.

4. Enter "8" in the **QOP (Quality of Protection)** field.

5. Enter the **SNC Name**, which we defined in Table 3.2, and click **Save**.

6. Activate the SNC by selecting the **Activate** radio button under **Status of Secure Protocol**, and click **Save**.

7. Select the **SNC Connection** and click **Connection Test**.

SNC

If the SNC isn't activated globally, then you need to repeat these steps on the ABAP front-end server as well.

The following are some recommendations for how to protect these communication channels in the SAP Fiori landscape:

- **OData and HTTP methods**
  Because SAP Fiori apps use OData to access data, the reverse proxy must be configured to allow certain HTTP methods to be made available. As part of the SAP Web Dispatcher configuration, you saw how to enable SAP Web Dispatcher (reverse proxy) to use HTTPS. Similarly, you need to enable the ABAP front-end server and SAP HANA XS to use HTTPS methods.

- **URL rewriting**
  You should configure the URL rewrite rules at the reverse proxy level, because when the OData services are accessed through reverse proxy these URLs may be invalid or might disclose protocols, host names, or port numbers.

- **ICF security**
  SAP Fiori applications consist of OData services and SAPUI5-based content, which are managed by the ICF. For security reasons, these are disabled initially. Therefore, you need to activate these services during the configuration.

- **Security session protection**
  We recommend that you activate HTTP security session management using Transaction SICF_SESSIONS for SAP NetWeaver version 7.0 and higher. For extra protection for security-related cookies, we also recommend that you activate the following:

  - **HttpOnly** flag: This instructs the browser to deny access to a cookie through a client-side script. Therefore, even if a user accidently accesses a link that exploits the cross-site scripting (XSS) flaw, the browser won't reveal the cookie to a third party.

  - **Secure** flag: To protect cookies from being passed via unencrypted requests, the **Secure** flag tells the browser to send cookies only if the request is sent through a secured channel, such as HTTPS.

Now that we've looked at the security measures in place to protect communications between layers, let's discuss the authentication and supported SSO methods.

3.1.4 SAP Web Dispatcher to SAP HANA XS

SAP Web Dispatcher should allow only those requests that will be routed to the general ICF services. If you're using SAP Fiori analytical apps, then the queries are routed from SAP Web Dispatcher to SAP HANA XS. To transfer the data securely between these two components, see the following sections.

Enable SAP HANA XS to Use HTTPS

The SAP HANA XS engine is a lightweight web application, and SAP HANA uses SAP Web Dispatcher as a reverse proxy. In this section, we'll provide high-level steps for how to enable the SAP HANA XS engine to use HTTPS.

Follow these steps:

1. Log in to the OS of the SAP HANA server, and edit the instance profile of the SAP Web Dispatcher at */usr/sap/<SID>/HDB<instance_nr>/<hostname>/wdisp.*

2. Add the following parameters:
   - `wdisp/shm_attach_mode = 6`
   - `wdisp/ssl_encrypt = 0`
   - `wdisp/add_client_protocol_header = true`
   - `ssl/ssl_lib = /usr/sap/<SID>/SYS/global/security/libsapcrypto.so`
   - `ssl/server_pse`
   - `/usr/sap/<SID>/HDB<instance_nr>/<hostname>/sec/SAPSSL.pse icm/HTTPS/verify_client = 0`

3. Download and install SAP Cryptographic Library on the SAP HANA server, and copy libsapcrypto.so to */usr/sap/<SID>/SYS/global/security/lib/.*

4. Copy SAPNetCA.cer to */usr/sap/<SID>/HDB<instance_nr>/<hostname>/sec.*

5. Run the following command to set the SECUDIR environment variable:
   `export:SECUDIR="/usr/sap/<SID>/HDB<instance_nr>/<hostname>/sec"`

6. Create a certificate request and SSL key pair using the SAPGENPSE tool.

7. Download SAPNetCA.cer, and save it to */usr/sap/<SID>/HDB<instance_nr>/<hostname>/sec.*

8. Import the signed certificate using the following command:
   `/sapgenpse import_own_cert -c SAPSSL.cer -p SAPSSL.pse -x <PIN> -r SAPNetCA.cer.`

9. Create a credential file for SAP Web Dispatcher to access the PSEs during runtime.

10. Import the signed certificate to the SAP Web Dispatcher server.

11. Restart SAP Web Dispatcher.

You've successfully enabled HTTPS communication between SAP Web Dispatcher and SAP HANA XS. You can test the configuration by running the following URL: *https://<host_name>:<port>/sap/hana/xs/admin.*

3.2   Single Sign-On and User Authentication

Now that we've covered some of the basic concepts of security in the SAP Fiori system, we can dive into some advanced security concepts of the authentication strategies that are supported in the SAP Fiori landscape. In this section, we'll give you an overview of various advanced security-related system components based on Kerberos/SPNEGO, Security Assertion Markup Language (SAML) 2.0, SAP logon tickets, and X.509 certificate authentication configuration.

The SAP Fiori system needs to know the identity of a user. Knowing a user's identity allows the SAP Fiori system to provide a customized experience and grant the user permissions to access the data from the back-end servers. The authentication concept for SAP Fiori apps includes initial user authentication on the ABAP front-end server, followed by the authentication of all requests to the back-end systems. Table 3.3 shows different types of SAP Fiori apps that support different authentication methods for SSO.

Authentication is a process in which the credentials provided by a user from the client/browser are compared to those on file in a database of authorized users. After the user is authenticated, system then creates a security session between the client and the SAP Gateway server for that specific user.

Authentication Method for SSO	Transactional Apps	Fact Sheet Apps	Analytical Apps (via SAP HANA XS)	Search (Fact Sheet) Apps
User name/ password	Yes	Yes	Yes	Yes
SPNEGO/ Kerberos (with SAP NetWeaver SSO)	Yes	Yes	No	No
SAML 2.0	Yes	Yes	No	No
SAP logon tickets	Yes	Yes	Yes	Yes
X.509	Yes	Yes	Yes	Yes

Table 3.3 Authentication for Requests in Front-End Server

Important!

Setting up security and authentication is a huge topic, so we recommend that you always refer to the documentation provided at *http://help.sap.com* for an in-depth understanding and the most up-to-date information on this topic.

3.2.1   Kerberos/SPNEGO

Kerberos/SPNEGO is a network authentication protocol developed by MIT, and it's a robust protocol that protects from any form of attack. In a nutshell, Kerberos offers the following advantages:

- A protocol for authentication
- Use of tickets to authenticate
- Able to avoid storing passwords locally or send them over the Internet
- A trusted third party
- Built on symmetric key cryptography

If you've already implemented Kerberos/SPNEGO (e.g., Active Directory), then this authentication mode is recommended. You can enable Kerberos/SPNEGO authentication for the ABAP front-end server to access the SAP Fiori apps in your corporate network. Because the Active Directory system is typically located in your corporate network, Kerberos/SPNEGO authentication can't be used outside your corporate network. To enable SSO outside your corporate network, you might have to set up a virtual private network (VPN) connection.

Configuring Kerberos/SPNEGO

The complete detailed steps for configuring Kerberos/SPNEGO authentication are documented in the IMG on the SAP Help Portal at *http://help.sap.com/sapsso*.

The following are some of the advantages of using Kerberos/SPNEGO authentication:

- It simplifies the logon process to the ABAP front-end server by using the user's Windows logon data.
- A separate logon to the ABAP front-end server isn't required.

- SSO setup within your system landscape will be simplified by using Kerberos for both SAP GUI and HTTP.
- It's supported by most mobile device vendors.

Important!

The configuration of the Kerberos/SPNEGO authentication requires significant involvement from your Active Directory administration team.

3.2.2   Security Assertion Markup Language 2.0

SAML is an XML-based standard for communicating identity information between organizations and service providers. It's used for enabling the secure transmittal of authentication tokens and other user attributes across domains.

If you've already implemented SAML version 2.0 as the method of SSO, you can configure the ABAP front-end server for use with SAML 2.0 in conjunction with identity provider (IDP) software such as SAP IDP, Ping Federate, or Microsoft's Active Directory Federation Services (ADFS). In comparison with Kerberos authentication, SAML 2.0 authentication is relatively easy to configure. To enable SSO outside your corporate network (Internet-facing), you must make sure that the SAML IDP is securely accessible from outside your corporate network.

The following are some of the advantages of using SAML 2.0:

- Works well in scenarios in which trust configuration can be complicated
- Enables end users to login to SAP Fiori with their Win Active Directory accounts
- Enables you to map SAP users based on user name attributes or a user's e-mail address
- Works well for scenarios with multiple user domains

Important!

In the SAP Fiori system landscape, SAML 2.0 is supported only for communication with the ABAP front-end server—not for SAP HANA.

Let's take a closer look at SAML authentication flow. The most basic SAML architecture involves three main objects: a user, an IDP, and a service provider (see Figure 3.5).

Users will need to authenticate themselves in a process known as *service provider-based authentication*.

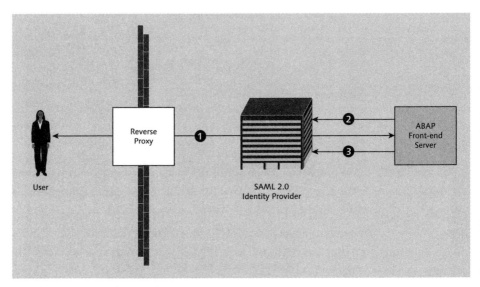

Figure 3.5 SAML Authentication

Figure 3.5 illustrates the following steps for service provider-based authentication:

1. First, the user attempts to access the application (i.e., the client sends a request to SAP Gateway server via a proxy server).

2. The federated identity software running on the IDP kicks into action, and the SAML 2.0 IDP server validates the user credentials, allowing the user to be properly authenticated.

3. The IDP then constructs and sends a specially formatted message containing information about that user (SAML artifact) back to the SAP Gateway server. SAP Gateway then determines that the message came from a known IDP and creates a session for that specific user in SAP Gateway, allowing the user direct access to that application.

Note

The whole process of the SAML message being created and the operation between the IDP and SAP Gateway is completely hidden to users. All they see is SAP Fiori launchpad after clicking on the URL or app.

The complete detailed steps for configuring SAML 2.0 authentication are documented in the IMG on the SAP Help Portal at *http://help.sap.com/nw74*. Once there, choose **Application Help · Function-Oriented View · Security · User Authentication and Single Sign-On · Integration in Single Sign-On (SSO) Environments · Single Sign-On for Web-Based Access · Using SAML 2.0 · Configuring AS ABAP as a Service Provider.**

3.2.3   SAP Logon Tickets

SAP logon tickets are the cookies of a session and are stored in the client's browser. For SAP logon tickets, you have two options: Either use the existing system, such as a portal that already issues logon tickets, or configure the ABAP front-end server to issue logon tickets. You must also configure the required back-end systems (ABAP or SAP HANA) to accept logon tickets. SSO then provides access to the SAP HANA database (or any database) from any front-end application without needing to log in. The SAP HANA trust store contains the root CA used to sign the trusted certificates required for SSO authentication.

> **Important!**
>
> User mapping isn't supported, so you must ensure that users in the ABAP system have the same user names as the database users in SAP HANA. If a customer uses all three types of SAP Fiori apps, make sure the user name complies with the stricter restriction rules from SAP HANA.

As we explained in Chapter 2, Section 2.6.5, from SAP NetWeaver 7.4 SP 06, you can even perform system configuration tasks automatically by using predefined task lists. You can use the SAP_SAP2GATEWAY_TRUSTED_CONFIG task list to create a trusted connection from an SAP system to an SAP Gateway system. Follow the process from Chapter 2, Section 2.6.5, and the system will guide you through the configuration of the tasks when you execute a task list (see Figure 3.6).

The complete detailed steps for configuring the SAP logon token authentication are documented in the IMG on the SAP Help Portal at *http://help.sap.com/nw74*. Once there, choose **Application Help · Function-Oriented View · Security · User Authentication and Single Sign-On · Integration in Single Sign-On (SSO) Environments · Single Sign-On for Web-Based Access · Using Logon Tickets · Using Logon Tickets with AS ABAP · Configuring AS ABAP to Accept Logon Tickets.**

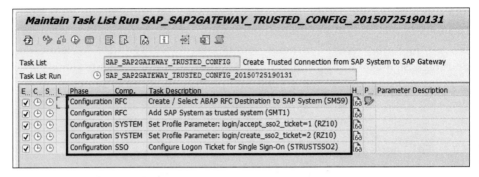

Figure 3.6 Predefined Task List

After the configuration is completed, the ABAP front-end server acts as a ticket-issuing system, and the ABAP back-end system acts as a ticket-accepting system. The following are the authentication flow steps between the ABAP front-end and ABAP back-end servers:

1. The user logs in with his user name and password to the ABAP front-end server.

2. The ABAP front-end verifies the user name and password. After the authentication is successful, the user is logged on to the system and issued a logon ticket.

3. The user's web browser then stores the logon ticket and uses that ticket for authentication on the ABAP back-end system.

4. The web browser then sends the issued logon ticket with the user logon ticket to the ABAP back-end server.

5. The ABAP back-end server verifies the tickets.

6. If the tickets are valid, then the ABAP servers provide access to the user.

> **SAP Logon Tickets**
>
> SAP logon tickets are transferred as web browser cookies; therefore, you can only use this authentication if all the systems in your landscape are located within the same DSN.

3.2.4   X.509 Certificate

If your customer has implemented a public key infrastructure (PKI) for user authentication, you can use X.509 certificates by configuring the required back-end systems (ABAP or SAP HANA) to accept them.

The following are some advantages of using X.509 certificates:

- X.509 certificates work well in Internet-facing scenarios because they don't require an issuing system during logon.
- Using X.509 certificates for both SAP GUI and HTTP will simplify SSO setup within your system landscape.

To run SAP Fiori apps on desktops and mobile devices, X.509 certificates must be distributed to them. For mobile devices, X.509 certificates are distributed by mobile management software.

To minimize security risks, SAP recommends implementing a method to revoke X.509 certificates, because they remain valid for a relatively long time.

3.3   User Authorizations and Management

Two primary processes are involved in providing access in SAP Fiori:

1. **Authentication process**
   Proves that users are allowed to access the servers.

2. **Authorization process**
   Determines whether the person who is logged in has access to a specific app or to perform a specific action.

In this section, we'll look at the various user authorization steps for SAP Fiori launchpad, SAP Gateway, and different SAP Fiori apps.

But before we begin our discussion of authorizations, let's review user management.

3.3.1   User Management

A couple of user management tools are provided for both AS Java and AS ABAP. You'll use the following transaction codes while working with user management in SAP Fiori:

- Transaction SU01: User Maintenance (user management for AS ABAP)
- Transaction PFCG: Profile Generator (to create roles and assign authorizations to users)

There are a couple of important considerations to note from a user management perspective:

- The user must exist in the following systems:
  - SAP Gateway front-end server for all app types
  - SAP Business Suite ABAP back-end server for all app types
  - SAP HANA database for fact sheet and analytical apps
- User names must be the same in both the ABAP system and the SAP HANA database. If you're planning to implement all three types of apps, make sure the user name complies with the stricter restriction rules from SAP HANA.
- If your deployment is embedded, it isn't necessary to create users in an additional system.
- You can use Central User Administration (CUA) to synchronize users in the back-end and the front-end systems to ensure user names in both systems match.

3.3.2   User Authorization

With a better understanding of how users are managed, let's look at the different user authorizations required.

SAP Fiori Launchpad

SAP Fiori launchpad is the entry point for all SAP Fiori apps. After users are authenticated, they can see and access those SAP Fiori apps that have been assigned by an administrator to the catalog designed for the user's role.

SAP delivers business roles for users of SAP Fiori apps. Every business role provides access to a sample of apps relevant for specific business users. For example, the PFCG role for the business catalog of the My Quotations app gives the user access to the My Quotations app (see Figure 3.7). Therefore, for a user to see this app in SAP Fiori launchpad, the administrator must assign the business catalog role to that user. In Chapter 4, Section 4.4, we'll discuss these roles and authorizations in greater detail. The SAP Fiori launchpad catalog and the UI PFCG roles bundle all front-end privileges required for the execution of the apps.

Figure 3.7 shows an app-specific (My Quotation app) implementation help page from the SAP Fiori apps reference library.

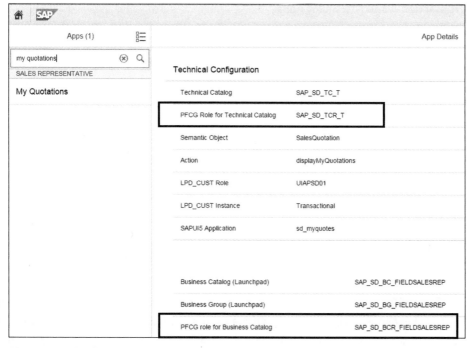

Figure 3.7 Roles for My Quotations App

SAP Gateway

After the user is authorized to see an app in SAP Fiori launchpad, the next step is to give authorizations to run/start OData services. The SAP Gateway-level authorization is used to set up authorizations to start OData services to run an app. Figure 3.8 shows start authorizations for one of the services.

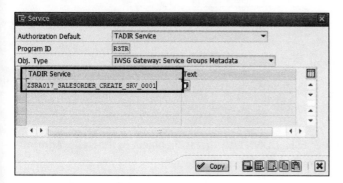

Figure 3.8 Adding OData Service Permissions

171

Transactional and Fact Sheet Apps

Like the front-end PFCG role for the business catalog covered previously, SAP delivers back-end PFCG roles for every transactional app and fact sheet app; for example, the My Quotations app (refer to Figure 3.7) is delivered with a back-end authorization role (PFCG) for the technical catalog. These roles include references to the corresponding OData services, which are required to run the apps.

Transactional App Roles

Roles for the transactional apps don't comprise authorizations for business data to be displayed in the app. These authorizations are provided by the customer.

For the user to access this transactional app, the administrator must assign both the back-end and front-end roles to the user. We'll discuss this topic further in Chapter 4, Section 4.3 and Section 4.4.

Fact Sheet Apps

For fact sheet apps, in addition to the OData service authorization, you need to authorize users' access to the underlying search models. You can find the search model entries in the **Authorizations** tab of Transaction PFCG (Role Maintenance). Follow these steps:

1. From your ABAP back-end server, run Transaction PFCG.
2. Enter a role name—for example, "SAP_SD_SALESORDER_APP"—and click 🖉.
3. Go to the **Authorization** tab, and click 🖉. You should now see the screen shown in Figure 3.9.

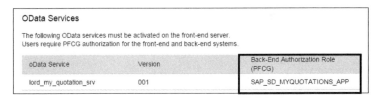

Figure 3.9 Fact Sheet Authorizations

You must add entries to the **S_ESH_CONN** authorization object in the **Basis: Administration** subtree. Fill in the following fields (see Figure 3.9):

- **Request of Search Connector**
  This value is the request for which a user receives search results.

- **Search Connector ID**
  This is the ID of the search connectors that the user will be allowed to explore.

- **System ID**
  This is the system ID that the user will be allowed to explore.

- **Client**
  This is the client taken into account during the search.

We'll discuss this in further detail in Chapter 4, Section 4.3.2.

Analytical Apps

For a user to read KPI data, an SAP Fiori analytical app needs to be granted to app-specific roles in the SAP HANA server. For example, Figure 3.10 shows the role for a cash position app that is assigned to a user.

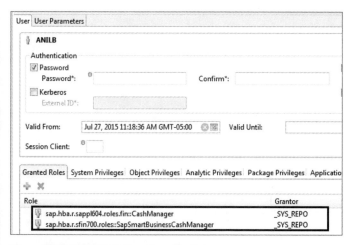

Figure 3.10 SAP HANA App-Specific Roles

3.4 Summary

This chapter offered a foundation in the technologies and processes needed to configure access control in SAP Fiori. Although this is a complex and involved topic with many third-party technologies, the introduction provided here should kick-start configuring your solution. We've provided you with an overview of how communication happens at different layers and how to secure the communication channels. At this point, you should have a solid understanding of the different authentication methods supported in the SAP Fiori landscape and how to configure them in the front-end and back-end servers. These roles and authorization concepts will be discussed throughout the rest of the book.

We can now examine the SAP Fiori apps implementation process. We'll cover how to implement SAP Fiori transactional apps in detail in Chapter 4.

Chapter 4

Implementing Transactional Apps

In this chapter, we'll look at implementing transactional apps—from activating the SAPUI5 component to running the app.

As you've learned from the previous chapters, SAP Fiori transactional apps can be implemented on an SAP HANA database or any database. Therefore, no matter what the SAP Fiori system landscape may be (AS ABAP, SAP HANA database, or SAP HANA XS), the major tasks for implementing transactional apps remain the same in all environments. The ABAP front-end server infrastructure is comprised of the central UI component with an SAPUI5 control library, SAP Fiori launchpad, and SAP Gateway with OData enablement. We've installed and configured all these components in the previous chapters. The ABAP back-end server contains the business logic, with the front-end components accessing the back-end server through a trusted RFC connection.

> **Prerequisites**
>
> Before you proceed with the next steps, make sure the front-end and back-end components for your app are already available in your system landscape (refer to Chapter 2, Section 2.5.1).

We'll begin with the ABAP front-end server tasks. The front-end server (ABAP) contains the UI layer with the product-specific UI components for the products and the infrastructure components. We already activated the central UI add-on ICF services in Chapter 2. We'll now work on the central services relevant to this specific app. In this section, we'll use the Create Sales Order transactional app as an example.

The following is an overview of the configuration tasks for transactional apps:

- Activate the SAPUI5 component.
- Activate OData services for the SAPUI5 applications in SAP Gateway.
- Set up the front-end roles, which involves the following subtasks:
  - Copy the business catalog role that provides access to the relevant catalog in SAP Fiori launchpad.
  - Add start authorizations for the required OData service to the business role.
  - Assign front-end roles to users.
- Set up the back-end roles, which involves the following subtasks:
  - Copy the back-end authorization role that provides access to the back-end data.
  - Assign back-end roles to users.

The following sections look in detail at these tasks for configuring the front-end and back-end servers when implementing transactional apps.

4.1   Activating the SAPUI5 Component

During front-end configuration, the first step is to activate the ICF service via Transaction SICF (Activate and Maintain SAP Web Services). Transaction SICF is used to maintain services for HTTP communication in the SAP system using the ICM and the ICF. This is a software layer in the application server that provides an ABAP interface for HTTP, HTTPS, and SMTP requests.

For security reasons, all ICF services are made available in an inactive state. When you first install your new SAP system, standard SAP services may not be active, so you'll have to use Transaction SICF to activate them. Also, when you create a new web service, you may have to activate it before it can be executed; otherwise, you may get an error.

Now that you know what Transaction SICF is and what it does, you need to know which service to activate to enable the Create Sales Order transactional app. For that, you need to go to the app-specific page in the apps reference library. Follow the steps in Chapter 2, Section 2.4 to get the SAPUI5 application name for the Create Sales Order app (see Figure 4.1); copy the name.

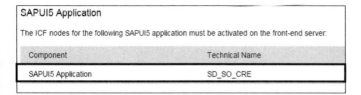

Figure 4.1 SAPUI5 Application

The first task is to activate the SAPUI5 application service on the ABAP front-end server. To do so, follow these steps:

1. Run Transaction SICF (Maintain Services) on the front-end server, and press Enter.

2. Enter the **Service Name** (i.e., the technical name you copied in the previous step). Press F8 on the keyboard, or click the **Execute** icon (see Figure 4.2).

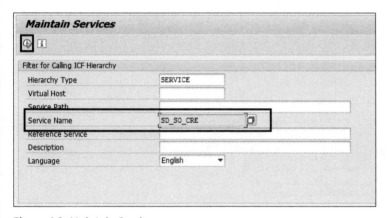

Figure 4.2 Maintain Services

> **Note**
>
> If you can't find the service on the SAP Gateway server (ABAP front-end), you haven't installed the SAP Fiori app UI components. Go back to Chapter 2, Section 2.5 for instructions on installing the UI component.

3. Navigate to the path **default_host · sap · bc · ui5_ui5 · sap**.

4. Under this node, navigate to the SAPUI5 application for the Create Sales Order app: **sd_so_cre** (see Figure 4.3).

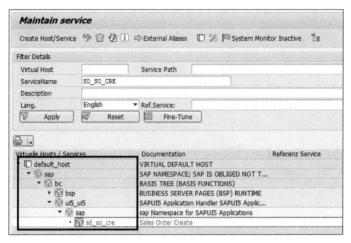

Figure 4.3 SD_SO_CRE Service

5. To activate the service (SAPUI5 application), right-click it and select **Activate Service** (see Figure 4.4).

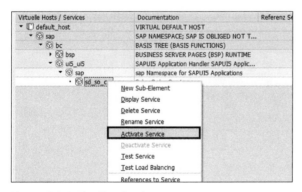

Figure 4.4 Activating Service

6. In the dialog box that appears, click **Yes** with the hierarchy icon (see Figure 4.5).

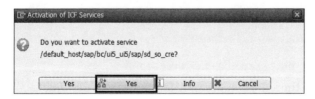

Figure 4.5 Activating with Hierarchy

We've successfully activated the ICF service. Now, let's move on to activating the OData service.

4.2   Activating the OData Services

In Chapter 3, we discussed how the SAP Fiori client, ABAP front-end, and ABAP back-end communicate, and how apps send OData requests through the ABAP front-end server to the ABAP back-end server securely by a trusted RFC. In this section, we'll discuss how to activate the OData service. For those who are new to OData services, we'll discuss it in greater detail in Chapter 7. To keep it simple, *OData* is a standardized protocol built over existing HTTP and REST protocols to support CRUD operations for creating and consuming data APIs.

To begin activating the OData services for your app, follow these steps:

1. From the app-specific page (**Create Sales Order**) in the apps reference library, copy the technical name of the OData service from the **oData Service** section (see Figure 4.6).

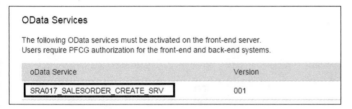

OData Services

The following OData services must be activated on the front-end server.
Users require PFCG authorization for the front-end and back-end systems.

oData Service	Version
SRA017_SALESORDER_CREATE_SRV	001

Figure 4.6 OData Service for Create Sales Order App

2. Run Transaction /IWFND/MAINT_SERVICE to activate and maintain services on the front-end server, and press `Enter`.

3. On the **Activate and Maintain Services** page, click **Add Service** (see Figure 4.7).

Activate and Maintain Services

Refresh Catalog | OAuth | Soft State
Service Catalog

| Type | Technical Service Name | ^V | Service Description |

Figure 4.7 Adding Service

4. Enter the **System Alias** of your back-end system.

5. In the **External Service Name** field, enter the information shown in Figure 4.8. Then, enter the **Technical Service Name** of the OData service for your app. (In this example, it's the technical name that you copied in Step 1.) Click **Get Services**.

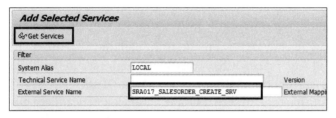

Figure 4.8 Get Services

6. Select the service name in the **Select Back-end Services** section. From here, click **Add Selected Services** (see Figure 4.9).

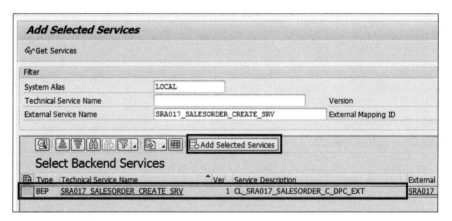

Figure 4.9 Adding Selected Service

7. Enter the **Technical Service Name** for the service in your customer namespace.

8. Assign a package, or click **Local Object** (see Figure 4.10).

9. Click **Execute** to save the service.

10. After the service is activated, you should receive a pop-up message, which you can confirm (click the green checkmark; see Figure 4.11).

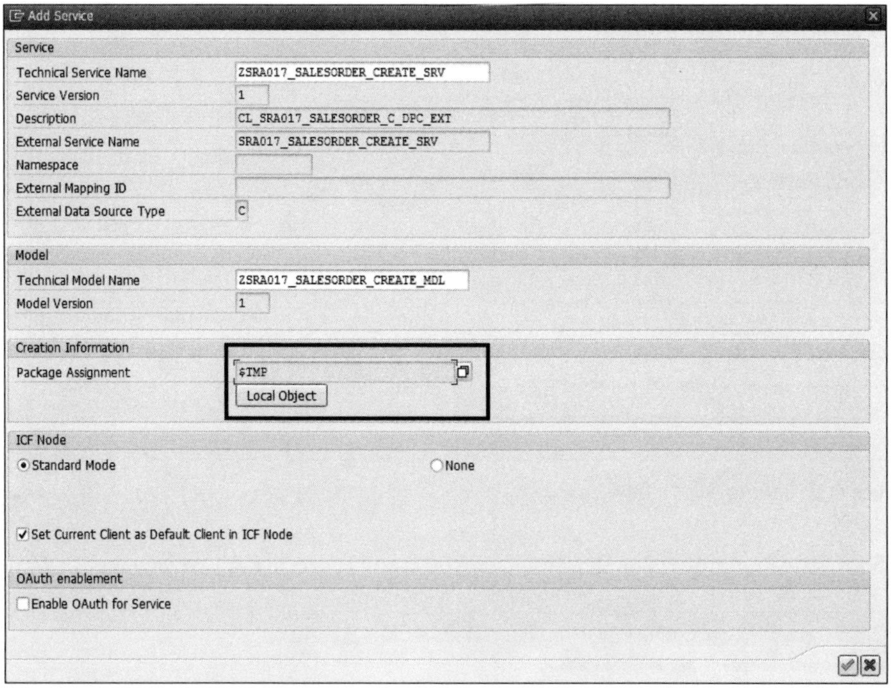

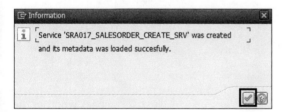

Figure 4.10 Assigning Package

Figure 4.11 Activation Confirmation

The service is now added and activated successfully!

Now, let's check whether this service is responding by running it in a browser. To do so, follow these steps:

1. Click the ✏ button to go back to the **Activate and Maintain Services** screen.

2. Check whether the **SAP System Alias** is maintained correctly. If not, delete the alias and add the correct one.

3. Select the **ODATA** node, and click **Call Browser** (see Figure 4.12).

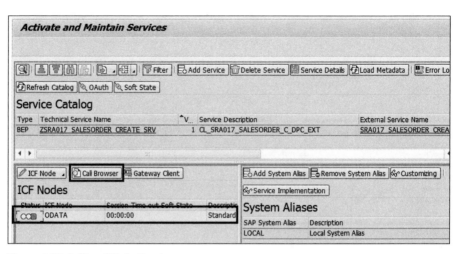

Figure 4.12 Calling OData Service

4. Select the **Remember My Decision** checkbox, and then click **Allow** (see Figure 4.13).

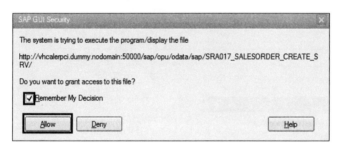

Figure 4.13 Allowing Access

You've now tested the service, and it works like a charm. Next, let's check whether the hash key is generated. A *hash key* is generated whenever you call a service. This key is required for the generation of an authorization profile. You can restrict access to the system on the system level.

You can verify the hash key generation in the hash key table. To do so, follow these steps:

1. Return to SAP GUI (front-end server), and run Transaction SE16 to view the table contents.

2. Enter "USOBHASH" in **Table Name**, and click on the **Table Content** button (see Figure 4.14).

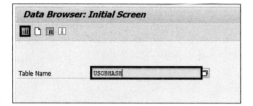

Figure 4.14 Hash Key Table

3. On the next screen, enter the following details, and click **Execute** (see Figure 4.15):
   - **PGMID**: "r3tr" (program ID)
   - **OBJECT**: "IWSG" (object type)
   - **OBJ_NAME**: "ZSRA017*" (service name activated in the previous steps)

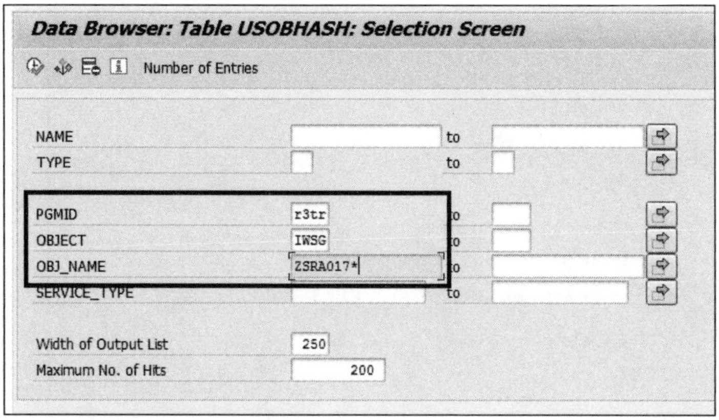

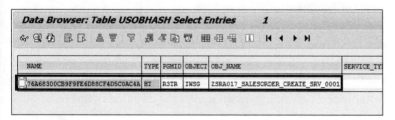

Figure 4.15 Selection Screen

You should see a table content screen, like the one in Figure 4.16.

NAME	TYPE	PGMID	OBJECT	OBJ_NAME	SERVICE_TY
76A68300CB9F9FE6D88CF4D5C0AC4A	HT	R3TR	IWSG	ZSRA017_SALESORDER_CREATE_SRV_0001	

Figure 4.16 Hash Key

You've now activated the ICF and OData service successfully. The next step is to set up the roles and authorizations for users to access this app.

4.3 ABAP Front-End Roles

This is the most important step in the app implementation process. SAP Fiori launchpad is the entry point for SAP Fiori apps. For users to access apps, certain business user rights need to be assigned to those users.

SAP delivers standard technical content for every specific app; you can get the details from the apps reference library (see Figure 4.17). For now, we'll focus on just the PFCG role for the business catalog, because that's what we need in this step; all the other components will be covered in subsequent chapters.

Technical Configuration		
Technical Catalog	SAP_SD_TC_T_X1	
TECHNICAL_PFCG_ROLE	SAP_SD_TCR_T_X1	
Semantic Object	SalesOrder	
Action	create	
LPD_CUST Role	UIX01SD	
LPD_CUST Instance	TRANSACTIONAL	
SAPUI5 Application	SD_SO_CRE	
Business Catalog (Launchpad)	SAP_SD_BC_FIELDSALESREP_X1	Field Sales Representative (SD) - Content
Business Group (Launchpad)	SAP_SD_BCG_FIELDSALESREP_X1	Field Sales Representative (SD
PFCG role for Business Catalog	SAP_SD_BCR_FIELDSALESREP_X1	

Figure 4.17 Technical Configuration

You need to understand this simple standard flow before you work with this content. As shown in Figure 4.18, apps/tiles are assigned to catalogs, and these catalogs and users are assigned to roles. Therefore, when a user logs in to SAP Fiori launchpad, it will show only certain apps, depending on what roles the user is assigned to.

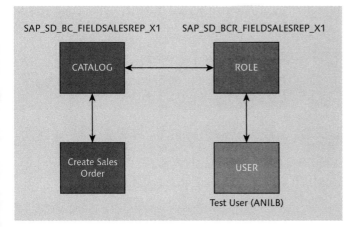

Figure 4.18 Assigning Catalog and Users to Role

The PFCG role for the business catalog provides access to a sample of apps relevant for specific business users. In our example, we'll enable the Create Sales Order app for sales representatives. Any user who has access to business role SAP_SD_BCR_FIELDSA-LESREP_X1 will have access to the following apps as well in SAP Fiori launchpad:

- Create Sales Orders
- Change Sales Order
- Customer Invoices
- Track Sales Order
- Check Price and Availability

In the sections that follow, we'll copy the business role and assign users to that role. After roles are assigned to a user, SAP Fiori launchpad will display the apps included in the catalog.

4.3.1   Copy Business Catalog Role

The first step in this process is to copy the template business role. The authorization for the Create Sales Order app is included in the PFCG role for the business catalog for SAP_SD_BCR_FIELDSALESREP_X1.

Follow these steps:

1. Run Transaction PFCG (Role Maintenance).
2. Enter the role name in the **Role** field.

3. Copy the business role to your customer namespace by clicking the **Copy** icon on the top left (see Figure 4.19).

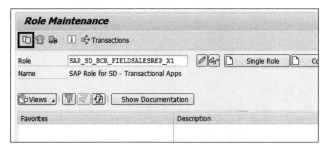

Figure 4.19 Copying Roles

4. Enter the new role name, and click **Copy all** in the pop-up window (see Figure 4.20).

Figure 4.20 Copying All Contents of Role

5. You'll see a ☑ Role copied notification on the bottom left after the role is copied.

4.3.2   Start Authorization

You've successfully copied the role, so now you need to add the start authorizations for the activated OData services to launch the app. To do so, you need to assign the start authorization to the business catalog role you copied in the previous section.

> **App-Specific OData Service**
>
> You must call the app-specific OData service at least once before you can assign start authorizations for it (refer to Section 4.2).

Follow these steps to add OData start authorizations to the copied role on the front-end server:

1. Edit the business role by clicking the **Pencil** icon 🖉 (see Figure 4.21).

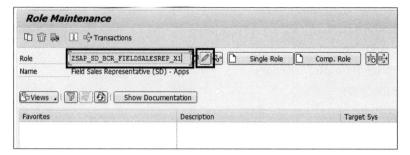

Figure 4.21 Editing Copied Role

2. Navigate to the **Menu** tab, and click the dropdown next to the **Transaction** button (see Figure 4.22).

Figure 4.22 Inserting Node

3. Select the **Authorization Default** object from the dropdown (see Figure 4.23).

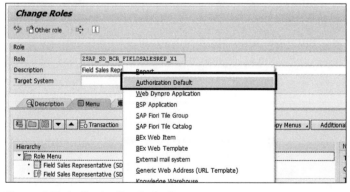

Figure 4.23 Authorization Default

4. Select and fill the fields in the **Service** pop-up window, and search for the OData service that you activated in the previous section. Enter the following relevant information (see Figure 4.24):

   - **Authorization Default**: TADIR Service
   - **Program ID**: "R3TR"
   - **Obj. Type**: IWSG
   - **TADIR Service**: "ZSRA017*"

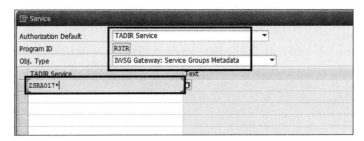

Figure 4.24 Search Service

5. Select the OData service from the search results, and click **Execute** (see Figure 4.25).

Figure 4.25 Selecting Service

6. Click **Copy**; you'll see a notification at the bottom left after the entry is created (see Figure 4.26).

Table TADIR

Table TADIR is the standard table in SAP used to store a directory of repository object information.

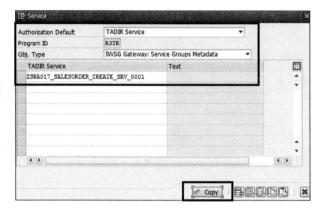

Figure 4.26 Adding Service

You should now see the service added to the role (see Figure 4.27).

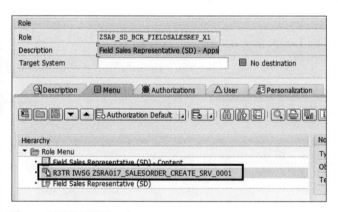

Figure 4.27 TADIR Service

7. Navigate to the **Authorization** tab, and click the button next to the **Profile Name** field to generate the authorization profile/propose profile name (see Figure 4.28).

8. Click the **Pencil** icon next to **Change Authorization Data**.

9. Click **Yes** to save the role (see Figure 4.29).

10. Generate the role by clicking the **Generate** button on the next screen (see Figure 4.30).

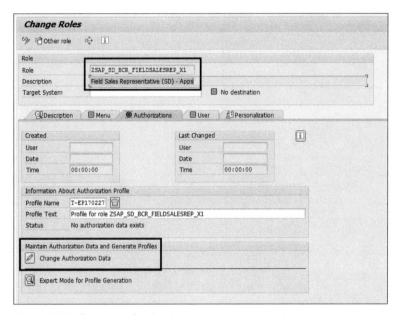

Figure 4.28 Change Authorization

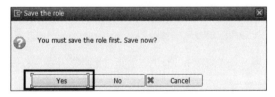

Figure 4.29 Saving Role

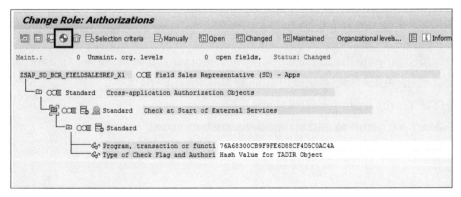

Figure 4.30 Generating Role

11. Check whether the role has generated correctly by double-clicking the last node in the hierarchy (see Figure 4.31).

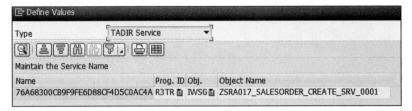

Figure 4.31 Service Name

You've successfully added the activated OData service to the business role, which you copied from the SAP standard business role.

4.3.3   Assign Roles to Users

In the next step, we'll assign this business catalog role to a user. After the user is assigned to this role, he can view the Create Sales Orders app in SAP Fiori launchpad.

Follow these steps:

1. Run Transaction PFCG.

2. Enter the role name that you created in the previous section, and click 🖉 (see Figure 4.32).

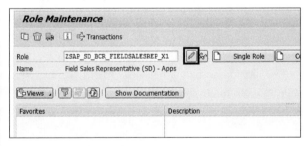

Figure 4.32 Editing Role

3. Navigate to the **User** tab, and add a new row (see Figure 4.33).

4. Enter the appropriate information in the **User ID** field, and press ⌷Enter⌷.

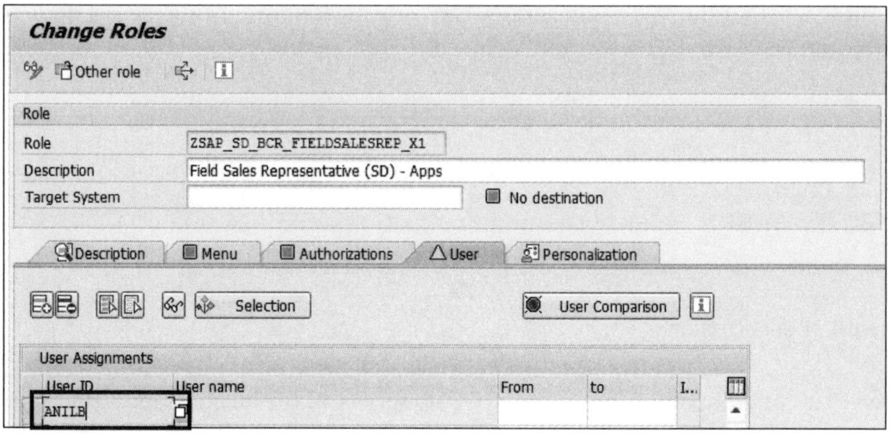

Figure 4.33 User Name

5. After the user is added, click **Save** 🖫.

You've now successfully granted access to the Create Sales Order app to a user. To recap, you first activated the ICF service of the SAPUI5 application, which activates the UI layer of the app, and then you activated the OData service, which is responsible for retrieving the data from the back-end. You then copied the standard catalog role and assigned it to a user, which will grant access to view the app in SAP Fiori launchpad. Now that you've completed the front-end tasks, let's complete the back-end tasks to enable the user to view the data in the app.

> **Standard Roles**
>
> You can in fact assign the standard SAP_SD_BCR_FIELDSALESREP_X1 role to users to give them access to the Sales Rep catalog and its apps/tiles. In this section, we showed you how to copy the standard role and to create your own role because you'll encounter this task a lot in the real world.

4.4   ABAP Back-End Roles

SAP delivers back-end roles for every app. These roles include references to the corresponding OData services required to run the apps. In this section, we'll copy the back-end role and assign roles to users.

4.4.1   Copy the Back-End Role

To copy the back-end role, you'll follow the same steps as for the front-end server (i.e., to copy the front-end role; refer to Section 4.3). In this situation, you'll be working with a different role (i.e., back-end role) on the back-end server. You'll copy the back-end authorization shown in Figure 4.34.

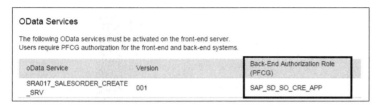

Figure 4.34 ABAP Back-End Role

Now, follow these steps:

1. Log in to the ABAP back-end server.
2. Run Transaction PFCG (Role Maintenance).
3. Enter the role name, and click **Copy** on the top left.
4. Enter the new role name, and click **Copy all** in the **Query** pop-up window (see Figure 4.35).

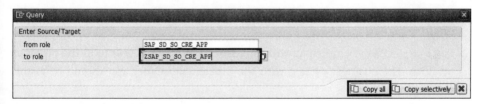

Figure 4.35 Copying Back-End Role Name

4.4.2   Assigning Roles to Users

Now, assign the custom role to a user by following these steps:

1. Log in to the ABAP back-end server.
2. Run Transaction PFCG.
3. Edit the role that you copied in the previous steps by clicking 🖉.
4. Navigate to the **User** tab, and add a new row.
5. Enter the user ID in the **User ID** field, press ⏎Enter⏎, then click **Save** (see Figure 4.36).

193

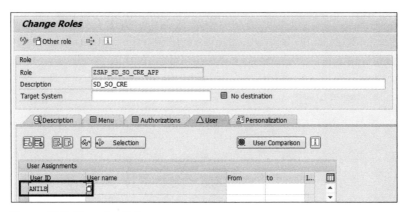

Figure 4.36 Changing Role

You've successfully provided a user with access to the back-end data for the Create Sales Order app. In the next section, you'll test and run your new app.

4.5   Running the App

Now that you've configured both the ABAP back-end and front-end components, you're ready to run and view the data. Follow these steps:

1. Run SAP Fiori launchpad via *http://<host>:<port>/sap/bc/ui5_ui5/ui2/ushell/shells/abap/FioriLaunchpad.html*.

2. Log in to SAP Fiori launchpad with the **User ID** you gave access to in the previous sections. The business catalog with the Create Sales Order app should be visible (see Figure 4.37).

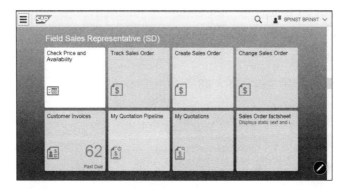

Figure 4.37 SAP Fiori Launchpad

3. Run the app by clicking the **Create Sales Order** tile; you should now be able to launch the app (see Figure 4.38).

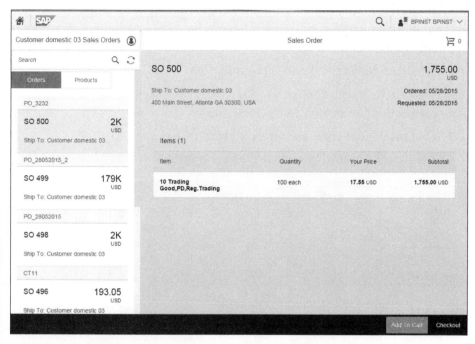

Figure 4.38 Create Sales Order App

You've successfully enabled the Create Sales Order app, with standard SAP roles, next we'll look at enabling the same Create Sales Order app with the custom role and custom catalog.

4.6   Custom Business Catalogs and Roles

In the previous section, we discussed how to enable the Create Sales Order transactional app using the standard SAP business role (SAP_SD_BCR_FIELDSALESREP_X1) and the standard SAP business catalog (SAP_SD_BC_FIELDSALESREP_X1). However, in a real-world scenario, you might have to create your own catalogs and roles.

To demonstrate how to do this, let's look at an example. User A is supposed to only have access to the Create Sales Order transactional app. User B is supposed to only have access to the Change Sales Order transactional app. However, both the apps are part of the same standard catalog (SAP_SD_BC_FIELDSALESREP_X1), so if you assign the standard SAP business role to both users, then they both will be able to use the apps. To address such scenarios, you must create custom business catalogs and custom roles. In this exercise, we'll show you how to do so.

4.6.1   Create a New Launchpad and Application

In this section, we'll walk through how to create a new launchpad and application for your custom business catalog. Follow these steps:

1. Log in to your ABAP front-end server, and run Transaction LPD_CUST.

2. Create a new launchpad by clicking the **New Launchpad** button (see Figure 4.39).

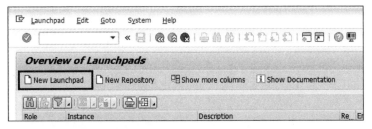

Figure 4.39 New Launchpad

3. Enter the field values shown in Figure 4.40.

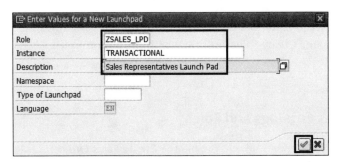

Figure 4.40 Launchpad Role

4. Click **Yes** to ignore the namespace (see Figure 4.41).

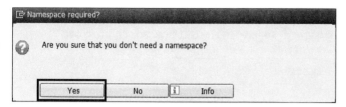

Figure 4.41 Ignoring Namespace

5. Create a new application by clicking **New Application** (see Figure 4.42).

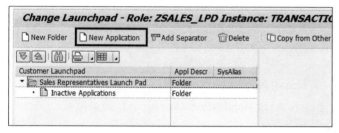

Figure 4.42 New Application

6. Enter "Create Sales Order" in the **Link Text** field. From the **Application Type** drop-down, select **URL** (see Figure 4.43).

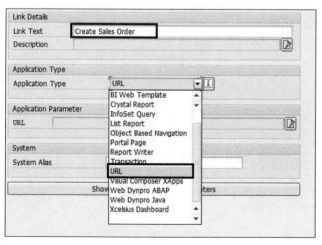

Figure 4.43 Application Type

7. Click the **Edit** button 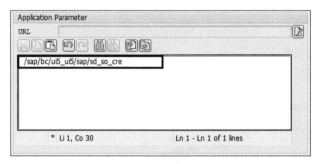 next to the **URL** input box.

8. Enter "/sap/bc/ui5_ui5/sap/sd_so_cre" in the **URL** box (see Figure 4.44).

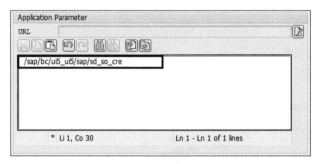

Figure 4.44 Application Parameter

9. Click **Show Advanced (Optional) Parameters**.

10. Click the **Edit** button 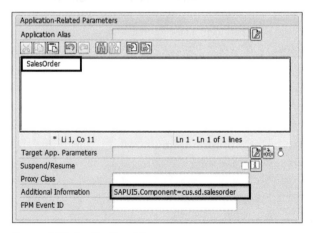 next to the **Application Alias** input box.

11. Enter "SalesOrder" in the box.

12. Enter "SAPUI5.Component=cus.sd.salesorder" in the **Additional Information** box, then click **Save** (see Figure 4.45).

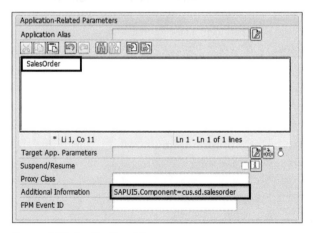

Figure 4.45 Application Alias

4.6.2   Create and Assign a Transport Request

Before we move to the next step, let's discuss the transportation concepts in SAP Fiori launchpad designer. You can launch SAP Fiori launchpad designer in two scopes:

- **Customization scope**
  http://hostname:port/sap/bc/_ui5/sap/arsrvc_upb_admn/main.html20? sap-client=120&scope=CUST

- **Configuration scope**
  http://hostname:port/sap/bc/ui5_ui5/sap/arsrvc_upb_admn/main.html20? sap-client=120&scope=CONF

When you create, update, or delete a catalog or tile, all these actions must be captured. If you launch the SAP Fiori launchpad designer in a customization scope, these actions are captured under the Customizing request. Similarly, when you launch it in the configuration mode, the actions are captured in the workbench request. For testing, the customization scope can be used, and then the content can be transported through the Customizing request. Next, we'll show you how to create and assign a request via SAP Fiori launchpad designer.

Follow these steps:

1. Log in to your ABAP server, and run Transaction SEO1.

2. Create a new request by clicking 🗅.

3. Select **Customizing request,** and click ✔ (see Figure 4.46).

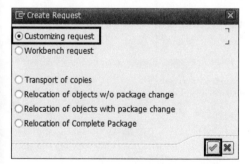

Figure 4.46 Creating New Transport Request

4. Enter a **Short Description**, then click 🖫 (see Figure 4.47).

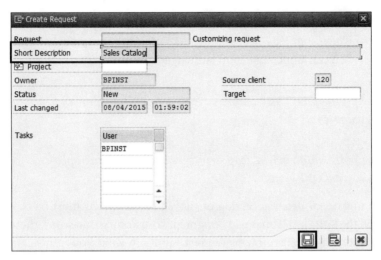

Figure 4.47 Saving Request

You should now see the request, as shown in Figure 4.48.

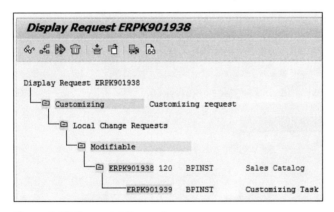

Figure 4.48 Transport Request

5. Log in to SAP Fiori launchpad designer at *http://hostname:port/sap/bc/ui5_ui5/ sap/arsrvc_upb_admn/main.html2O?sap-client=12O&scope=CUST*.

6. Click ⚙ at the top-right corner.

7. Uncheck the **None (Local Object)** checkbox, then select the **Customizing Request** from the dropdown box. Click **OK** (see Figure 4.49).

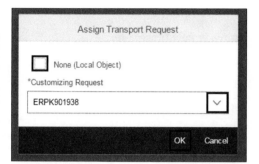

Figure 4.49 Assigning Transport Request

4.6.3   Create a New Catalog

Now you're all set to create, update, or delete catalogs or tiles, with all the actions captured in the transport requests. To create a new catalog, follow these steps:

1. From the SAP Fiori launchpad designer screen, click **Catalogs** (see Figure 4.50).

Figure 4.50 Selecting Catalogs

2. Create a new catalog by clicking **+**.

3. Select the **Standard** catalog, enter the details shown in Figure 4.51, and click **Save**.

Figure 4.51 Creating Catalog

4.6.4   Create New Target Mapping

Next, you need to create a new target mapping. Follow these steps:

1. Select the catalog which you created in the previous step.

2. Click the **Target Mapping** icon ⬆, then click **Create Target Mapping** (see Figure 4.52).

Figure 4.52 Creating Target Mapping

3. *Intent* is a mechanism that allows end users to perform actions on semantic objects. In the **Intent** section, select the semantic object by clicking 🗗, then manually enter the action. Enter the information in the fields, as shown in Figure 4.53.

Figure 4.53 Intent Section

4. To configure the target, select **SAP Fiori App using LPD_CUST** from the dropdown list, then enter the details shown in Figure 4.54. Click **Save**.

5. In the **General** section, configure the following fields (see Figure 4.55):

   – **Information**
     In this field, you can enter any important information or comments.

- **Device Types**
  Select all the devices; tiles will only be displayed for the devices selected here.
- **Parameters**
  Define optional or mandatory parameters of the target mapping.
- **Allow additional parameters**
  Allows passing additional parameters that aren't defined in the parameters table.

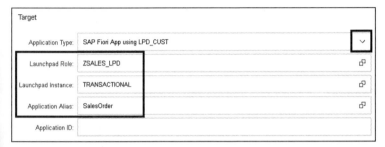

Figure 4.54 Target Section

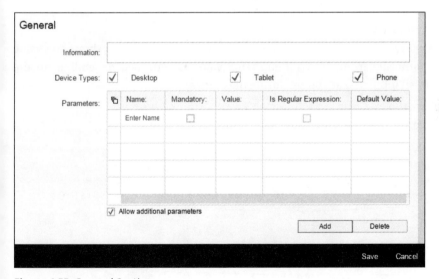

Figure 4.55 General Section

6. Click **Save**.
7. Save the changes by clicking **OK**.

4.6.5 Add a Static Tile

Next, you'll add a new tile. Follow these steps:

1. Click the **Tiles** icon, then click **+** to add a tile (see Figure 4.56).

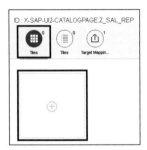

Figure 4.56 Adding Tile

There are three type of tiles, and each shows information differently (see Figure 4.57):

– **Static tile**
Displays static information, such as the title, subtitle, logo, and information.

– **Dynamic tile**
Displays all the information that the static tile displays, and shows the value dynamically from the back-end. This value is refreshed depending on the refresh interval that you set during tile creation.

– **News tile**
Streams a live news feed directly in your SAP Fiori launchpad.

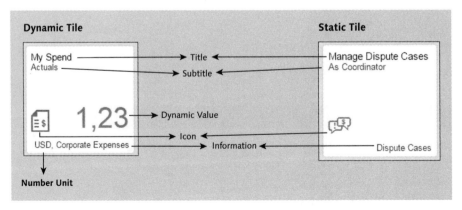

Figure 4.57 Dynamic Tile and Static Tile

2. Select the **App Launcher—Static** tile (see Figure 4.58).

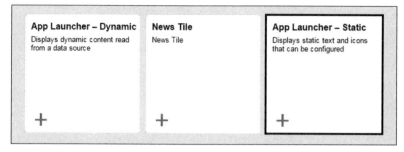

App Launcher – Dynamic

Displays dynamic content read from a data source

News Tile

News Tile

App Launcher – Static

Displays static text and icons that can be configured

+   +   +

Figure 4.58 Adding Static App Launcher

3. Enter "Create Sales Order" in the **Title** field, and select an icon from the **Icon** field (see Figure 4.59).

General

Title:	Create Sales Order
Subtitle:	|
Keywords:	
Icon:	sap-icon://inbox
Information:	
Number Unit:	

Figure 4.59 General Section

4. Enter the following details in the **Navigation** section and click **Save** (see Figure 4.60):

   - **Semantic Object**: "SalesOrder"
   - **Action**: "create"

5. Click **OK** to confirm the changes.

Figure 4.60 Navigation Section

4.6.6   Create the Custom Role and Add the Catalog

The next step is to add the catalog to a custom role, so first, let's create a custom role by following these steps:

1. Log in to your ABAP front-end server, and run Transaction PFCG (Role Mainte-nance).

2. Enter the role name "Z_SAL_REP_ROLE", and click **Single Role** (see Figure 4.61).

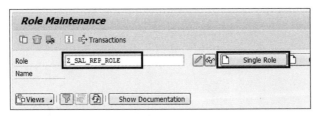

Figure 4.61 Role Maintenance

3. Click **Save**.

4. Enter a meaningful description in the **Description** field (see Figure 4.62).

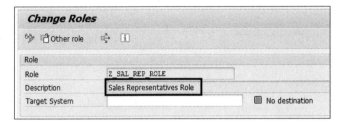

Figure 4.62 Changing Role

5. Click the **Menu** tab, then click ⬛ to insert the node (see Figure 4.63).

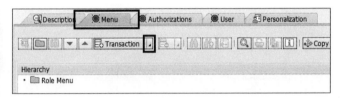

Figure 4.63 Inserting Node

6. Select **SAP Fiori Tile Catalog** from the menu (see Figure 4.64).

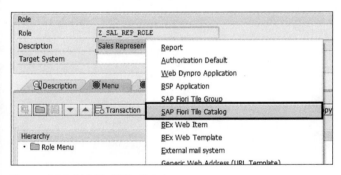

Figure 4.64 SAP Fiori Tile Catalog

7.   Enter "Z_SAL_REP" in the **Catalog ID** field, then click ✅ (see Figure 4.65).

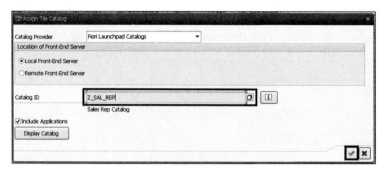

Figure 4.65 Assigning Tile Catalog

8. Navigate to the **User** tab, enter the **User ID**, and click ▣ (see Figure 4.66).

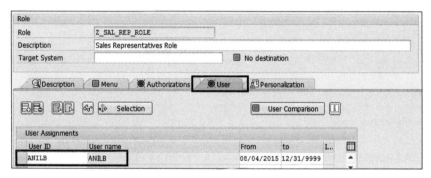

Figure 4.66 Assigning User

9. Log in to SAP Fiori launchpad, and click 🔒 to open the ME area.

10. Click on **App Finder** (see Figure 4.67).

Figure 4.67 App Finder

11. From the **Catalogs** dropdown box, select the **Sales Rep Catalog** (see Figure 4.68).

Figure 4.68 Selecting Custom Catalog

12. Click **+** to add the tile to a group.

13. Select the **My Home** checkbox, then click **OK** (see Figure 4.69).

Figure 4.69 Adding Tile to My Home Group

14. Click 🏠 to go back to the main page. You should now see the **Create Sales Order** tile under the **My Home** group (see Figure 4.70).

Figure 4.70 My Home Group

15.   Click the tile to run the app (see Figure 4.71).

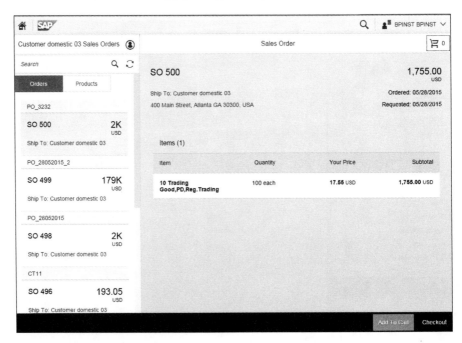

Figure 4.71 Create Sales Order App

Congratulations, you've successfully completed the exercise!

4.7   Summary

In this chapter, we walked through the steps needed to implement a transactional app. We first looked at the tasks to activate the SAPUI5 component and OData services. We then looked at the ABAP front-end and back-end roles before running our transactional app. Finally, we discussed how to create custom business catalogs and roles.

In the next chapter, we'll look at implementing fact sheet apps, which involves many of the same steps as those for transactional apps.

Chapter 5
Implementing Fact Sheet Apps

This chapter walks through the implementation of fact sheet apps, including information on ABAP back-end roles and search connectors.

SAP Fiori fact sheet apps display contextual information and key facts about central objects used in business operations. Fact sheets can be called from SAP Fiori launchpad or from other fact sheet, transactional, or analytical apps.

Although many of the ABAP front-end tasks for transactional and fact sheet apps are similar, it's important to understand where their differences lie in terms of implementation. From an architectural perspective, when compared to transactional apps, the following points are true for fact sheet applications:

- Fact sheet apps *must* run only on an SAP HANA database system.
- Fact sheet apps require a reverse proxy.
- Fact sheet apps directly access search engines on the back-end server via the INA search protocol.
- Fact sheet apps display data from the SAP HANA database through search models.

In this chapter, we'll show you how to implement the Sales Order fact sheet app. The following is an overview of the configuration tasks for fact sheet apps:

- Activate the SAPUI5 component.
- Activate OData services for the SAPUI5 applications in SAP Gateway.
- Assign an ABAP back-end role to the user.
- Create search connectors.
- Index search connectors.

5.1   App Activation Tool

SAP released an SAP Fiori app to configure and activate SAP Fiori applications for SAP Fiori launchpad. This SAP Fiori App Activation tool simplifies the activation of OData and UI services for transactional apps and fact sheet apps by replacing the manual activation process for OData services from Transaction SICF and the activation of UI services from Transaction /IWFND/MAINT_SERVICE. Follow these steps to enable the App Activation tool:

1. Install the SAPUIFT component on your SAP front-end server (Figure 5.1; see Chapter 2, Section 2.5.1 for instructions about how to install a component).

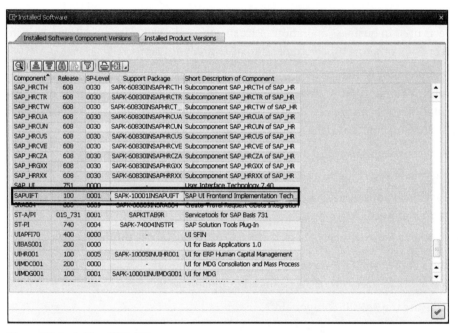

Figure 5.1 Installing SAPUIFT

2. Run Transaction VSCANPROFILE and set the **/UI2/FT_CONF_UI/BOM_UPLOAD** virus scan profile to **Active** (Figure 5.2).

3. Run Transaction /IWFND/MAINT_SERVICE and activate the /UI2/FT_CONFIG_UI OData service (Figure 5.3; see Chapter 2, Section 2.6.1 for a refresher on how to activate OData services).

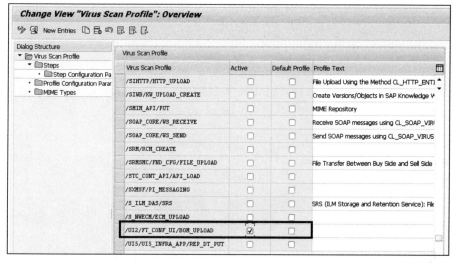

Figure 5.2 Activating Virus Scan Profile

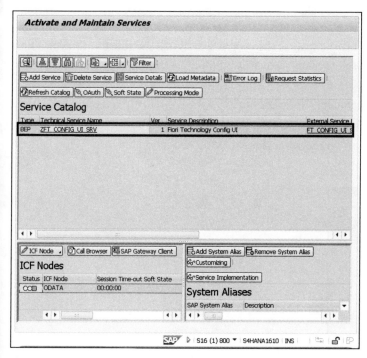

Figure 5.3 Activate Config UI Service

4. Run Transaction SICF and activate the following UI services (see Chapter 4, Section 4.1):
   - /SAP/BC/UI2/BOM_UPLOAD
   - /SAP/BC/UI5_UI5/UI2/SAPCONFLP

5. Run Transaction PFCG and assign the SAP_FIORITECH_ADMIN role to the user who needs access to the App Activation tool (see Figure 5.4).

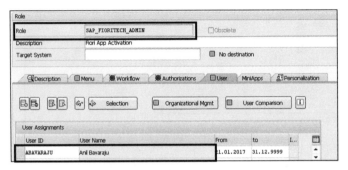

Figure 5.4 Assigning User to Role

6. Log in to SAP Fiori launchpad as the user you assigned the role to in the previous step. You should see the **App Activation** tile under the **SAP Fiori Administration** group.

7. Download the metadata file from *https://fioriappslibrary.hana.ondemand.com/ sap/fix/externalViewer/services/downloads/downloadServiceList.xsjs*.

8. Run the App Activation tool by clicking the **App Activation** tile in SAP Fiori launchpad (see Figure 5.5).

Figure 5.5 App Activation Tile

9. Click the **Update Reference Library** button.

10. Click **Browse** and select the services list XML file (Figure 5.6), which you down-
    loaded in Step 7.

Figure 5.6 Uploading Reference Library

11. Click **Upload**. Once the upload is completed, click **OK**.

12. Search for the catalog that you would like to enable in the SAP Fiori Launchpad
    (see Figure 5.7).

13. Choose the back-end system you want to connect to (see Figure 5.7).

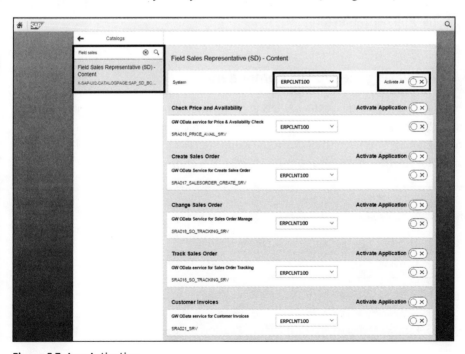

Figure 5.7 App Activation

14. Select the apps you want to activate by clicking the **Activate** button next to each app, or you can activate all the apps in the catalog by clicking **Activate All** (see Figure 5.7).

15. Change the **Service Names** to meet your requirements; assign a **Package** and the required transport requests.

16. Once the apps are activated, a success message will appear in the catalog view.

Transactional Apps

You can use the App Activation tool to activate OData and UI services for transactional apps as well.

You've now activated OData and UI services that are required for the Sales Order fact sheet app with the App Activation tool!

You can also activate the same OData and UI services manually, so for your reference we'll walk you through how to do so in the next two sections. However, you can choose to skip Section 5.2 and Section 5.3 if you've already activated a fact sheet app using the App Activation tool.

5.2 Activating the SAPUI5 Component

The first step is to activate the SAPUI5 application for the Sales Order fact sheet app. Figure 5.8 shows the SAPUI5 component details, which you can get from the apps reference library. You need to perform the same steps as those to activate the UI application for the transactional apps (see Chapter 4, Section 4.1).

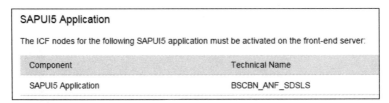

SAPUI5 Application	
The ICF nodes for the following SAPUI5 application must be activated on the front-end server:	
Component	Technical Name
SAPUI5 Application	BSCBN_ANF_SDSLS

Figure 5.8 SAPUI5 Component (Apps Reference Library)

Figure 5.9 shows the activated SAPUI5 application for the Sales Order fact sheet app.

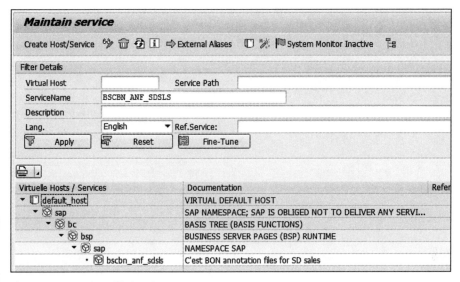

Figure 5.9 App-Specific Services

5.3   Activating OData Services

In this section, we'll activate OData services in the front-end server. You need to perform the same steps as in Chapter 4, Section 4.2. Figure 5.10 shows app-specific OData service details from the apps reference library.

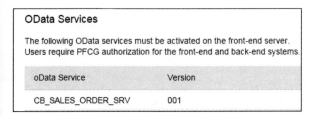

Figure 5.10 OData Service (Apps Reference Library)

Figure 5.11 shows the activated OData service for the Sales Order fact sheet app.

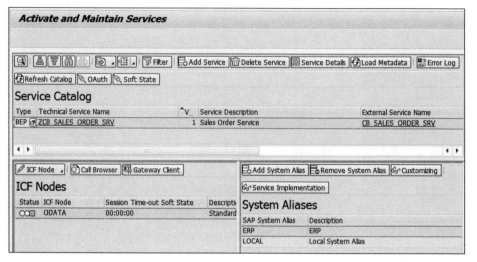

Figure 5.11 App-Specific OData Service

5.4   Assign ABAP Back-End Roles

In this part of the implementation, we'll assign a role to a user in the ABAP back-end server, which will grant the user access to the search models in the ABAP back-end server. In Chapter 4, Section 4.4.2, we showed you how to assign roles to a user. You can follow the same process to assign the SAP_SD_SALESORDER_APP role to a user. Figure 5.12 shows the role details from the apps reference library.

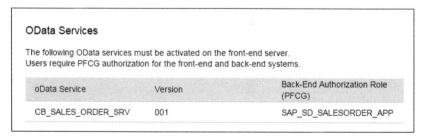

Figure 5.12 ABAP Back-End Role

Figure 5.13 shows the app-specific role assigned to an end user.

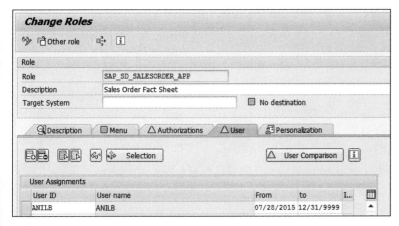

Figure 5.13 Assigned Back-End Role

5.5   Creating Search Connectors

SAP Fiori fact sheet apps are based on search models. To enable the use of fact sheet apps, search connectors must be created for the underlying search models.

A *connector* is a runtime object corresponding to a search model. It's a system-specific and client-specific object that's created in Transaction ESH_COCKPIT. Most of the data displayed in fact sheet apps comes from *search models*, which are transferred to the front-end server using OData services.

To enable the use of a specific fact sheet app, the underlying search models must be activated. When activating a search model, a search connector is created. The search models that need to be activated for your app are listed in the app-specific implementation information in SAP Help at *http://help.sap.com/fiori*.

> **SAP Fiori Search**
>
> Before you work on the back-end changes, make sure you've set up SAP Fiori search (see Chapter 2).

Fact sheet apps read business data via search connectors from the database. The creation of search connectors is therefore a prerequisite to using fact sheet apps.

To create search connectors, you need the following authorizations (see Figure 5.14):

- SAP_ESH_BOS_SEARCH
- SAP_ESH_CR_ADMIN

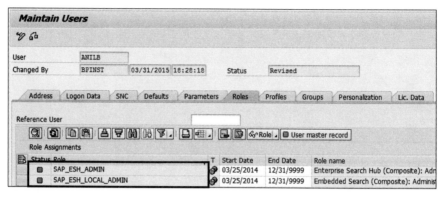

Figure 5.14 Roles to Create Search Connectors

The SAP HANA–enabled search models for the search software component SAPAP-PLH may only be used in SAP Fiori search. Figure 5.15 shows information from the apps reference library for the search connectors and search models information of a Sales Order fact sheet app.

Search Connector		
The following search connectors need to be activated in the back-end system:		
Search Component (Software Component)	Application Component	Search Model
EAAPPLH	SD-BIL	CUSTOMER_BILL_DOC_H
SAPAPPLH	LO-MD-BP-CM	CUSTOMER_H
	SD-SLS	CUST_QUOTATION_H
	LE-SHP	OUTBOUND_DELIVERY_H
	SD-SLS	SALES_ORDER_H
	BC-EIM-ESH	USER_H

Figure 5.15 Search Connectors for Sales Order Fact Sheet App

Search Models

All the delivered search models can be found in SAP Note 1861013 in the SAP Business Suite at *http://service.sap.com/sap/support/notes/1999463.*

5.5.1 Create Connectors Manually

You must activate the underlying search models by creating connectors to be able to use a fact sheet app. We'll go over the steps to create connectors for CUSTOMER_BILL_DOC_H, and then you'll need to repeat the steps to create connectors manually for all the search models listed under the **Search Connector** section (see Figure 5.15).

The *Connector Administrator cockpit* is the central point from which to monitor and manage search object connectors and to access monitoring and administration tools. To create connectors manually, follow these steps:

1. Launch the Embedded Search Administration cockpit in the browser via *http://<host_name>:<port_number>/sap/es/cockpit.*

Note

The *<host_name>* placeholder variable stands for the host and *<port_number>* stands for the port that you use to reach the ABAP system.

You can also launch the Connector Administration cockpit using Transaction ESH_COCKPIT.

2. Click **Create** (see Figure 5.16).

   Note: If the models are grayed out, the search connectors are already created, and you can skip this step.

Figure 5.16 Connector Administration Cockpit

3. Choose the software component that provides the required models (see Figure 5.17).

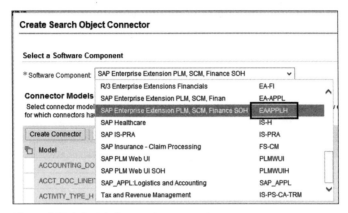

Figure 5.17 Select Software Component

4. In the list, select the required models you want to use with embedded search, then click **Create Connector**.

5. Next, a background job is created to create the search connector. You can monitor the job in Transaction SM37, where you'll notice a job with the name ESH_<your client>_C_<unique code> (see Figure 5.18).

Figure 5.18 Search Connector Job

Models

Models can reference other models. If this is the case, the system creates more than one connector in the Embedded Search Administration cockpit, although you only chose one connector model.

If you're using the SAP HANA–based variant of embedded search, all connectors with database support can be used directly for the search. For models that don't provide database support, you must start or schedule indexing.

5.5.2   Create Connectors Automatically

Instead of creating the connectors manually, you can generate them automatically by using Transaction STC01 (ABAP Task Manager). The SAP_ESH_CREATE_INDEX_SC task list is available for this purpose; use this task list to create the connectors automatically and then index them immediately (Figure 5.19).

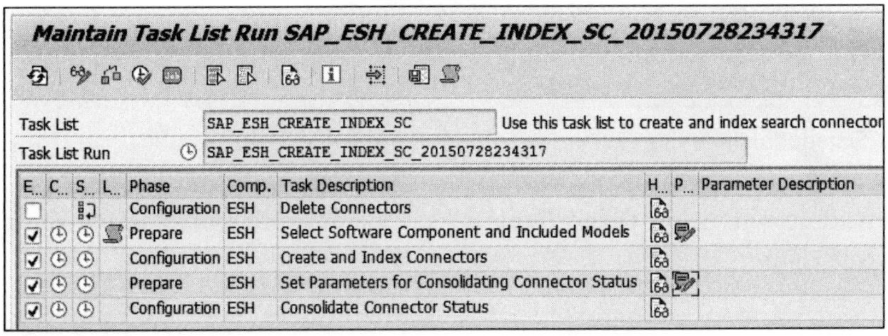

Figure 5.19 Search Connector Task List

5.6   Indexing Search Connectors

In the previous section, you created a connector, but to make the objects in the connector available in the search, you must schedule indexing for that connector.

In the SAP HANA–based variant, indexing runs either as *full indexing* or as *delta indexing*. This depends on whether the underlying model supports delta transfers and on the settings you define for indexing.

Follow these steps to index the connector previously created:

1. In the Connector Administration cockpit (Figure 5.20), choose the connectors you want to schedule indexing for, then select **Actions · Schedule Indexing.**

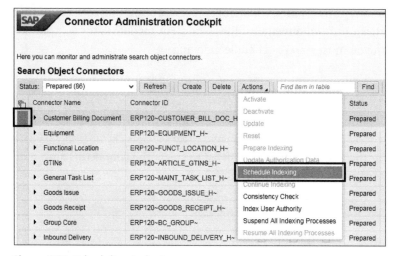

Figure 5.20 Scheduling Indexing

2. On the next screen, below **Object Type**, select one or more search and analysis models (see Figure 5.21).

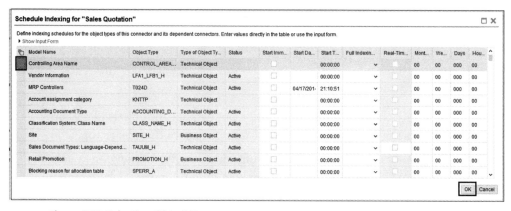

Figure 5.21 Selecting Object Type

Entry Screen

The entry screen allows you to make settings for more than one model at the same time.

3. To trigger indexing immediately, select the **Start Immediately** checkbox. Alternatively, you can schedule indexing to run later. To do so, specify a start time.

   In addition, you can select multiple objects and schedule indexes for all at the same time using the input form (see Figure 5.22).

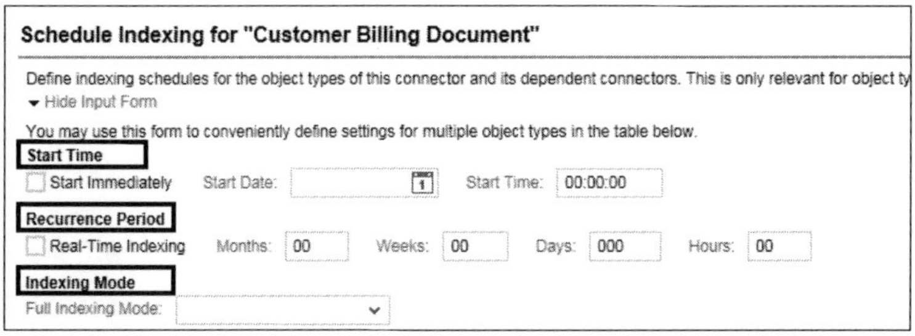

Schedule Indexing for "Customer Billing Document"

Define indexing schedules for the object types of this connector and its dependent connectors. This is only relevant for object ty
▾ Hide Input Form

You may use this form to conveniently define settings for multiple object types in the table below.

Start Time
☐ Start Immediately   Start Date: [   ] [📅1]   Start Time: [00:00:00]

Recurrence Period
☐ Real-Time Indexing   Months: [00]   Weeks: [00]   Days: [000]   Hours: [00]

Indexing Mode
Full Indexing Mode: [▾]

Figure 5.22 Input Form

4. Choose to schedule indexing immediately, or you can start it at a specific date and time.

5. You can choose to index data in real time by checking the box next to **Real-Time Indexing** under the **Recurrence Period** section. Here, you need to define the recurrence period as well (i.e., months, weeks, days, or hours).

6. If you want to perform a full indexing run, click the **Full Indexing Mode** dropdown option, and select either **Keep Index Content** or **Clear Index Content**.

The **Keep Index Content** mode will retain the existing index. The **Clear Index Content** mode will delete the index completely and recreate it. If you don't choose a mode, the system will perform delta indexing.

You've now completed all the configuration steps required to enable a fact sheet app. Before you run the app, let's test the search connector via Web Dynpro:

Note

SAP blacklisted the ESH_SEARCH transaction from SAP S/4HANA 1511, so you can ignore this step if your system landscape is on SAP S/4HANA 1511 or higher.

1. Run Transaction ESH_SEARCH.

2. Enter "Sales Order" in the **Search For** field (see Figure 5.23). You should see the search results for the Sales Order app.

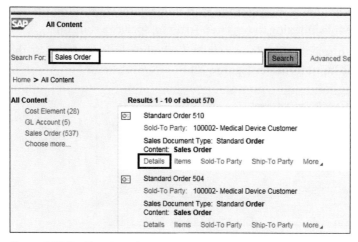

Figure 5.23 Testing Search

3. Click **Details** to see the details of the entity type.

Now, you're all set to run the app on SAP Fiori launchpad!

5.7   Running the App

Fact sheet apps can be called from the results of an SAP Fiori search, or from the drop-down box next to the search window. To access the Sales Order fact sheet app, follow these steps:

1. Log in to SAP Fiori launchpad.
2. Use the SAP Fiori search in SAP Fiori launchpad to narrow down the search results to Sales Order business objects. Enter the term "sales order" in the **Search** field and press ⌈Enter⌉. You'll see search results based on **Sales Order** (see Figure 5.24).
3. From the search results, you should be able to open the Sales Order fact sheet app by clicking one of the result sets (see Figure 5.25).

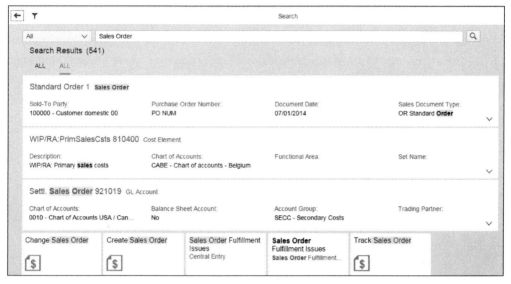

Figure 5.24 Search Sales Orders

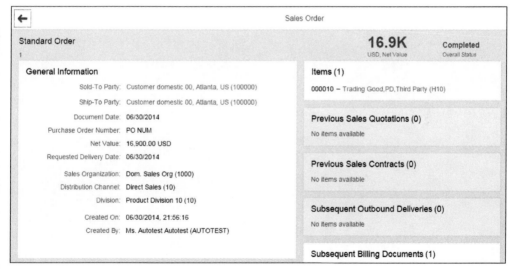

Figure 5.25 Sales Order Fact Sheet

5.8   Summary

In this chapter, we looked at the implementation steps for fact sheet apps. Many of the steps are like those for transactional apps; however, there are still some fact sheet-specific steps that needed to be covered, such as specific ABAP back-end roles, creating search connectors, and indexing search connectors. In the next chapter, we'll look at implementing the last of the three SAP Fiori app types: analytical apps.

Chapter 6
Implementing Analytical Apps

This chapter walks through implementing analytical apps with and without the SAP Smart Business modeler.

In Chapter 1, we discussed the architecture and communication channels among different layers for analytical apps. In this chapter, we'll provide step-by-step instructions for implementing analytical apps run on an SAP HANA database, which use VDMs. We'll use examples based on the Days Sales Outstanding app and the Profit Analysis app, but these steps apply to most analytical app implementations.

In Section 6.1, we'll begin with an overview of standard analytical apps and analytical apps created using SAP Smart Business modeler; the latter are enriched analytical apps with real-time KPI data and are designed for specific business roles. We'll include in our discussion the SAP Fiori roles for different LOBs. We'll then look at the prerequisites that need to be covered prior to implementing the Days Sales Outstanding app in Section 6.2 before we dive into the KPI modeling steps.

In Section 6.3, we'll discuss the SAP Smart Business modeler and model a KPI using an example based on the Days Sales Outstanding app. In addition, we'll cover the technical aspects of the SAP Smart Business modeler and show you how to leverage them in conjunction with an analytical app. You'll then learn how to create a generic drill-down application using the SAP Smart Business modeler. At the end of this section, we'll show you how to create your own catalogs and groups to enable the app.

In Section 6.4, we'll introduce you to analytical apps that don't require the SAP Smart Business modeler to implement them. We'll use an example based on the Profit Analysis app and provide high-level steps for how to implement them. As previously mentioned, these steps apply to most analytical apps that don't use the SAP Smart Business modeler.

6.1   Overview

SAP Fiori analytical apps are the new UX for SAP Business Suite powered by SAP HANA and are developed using SAPUI5. These apps allow real-time insights into your business by displaying KPIs, allowing you to make faster, better decisions. In this chapter, we'll show you how to configure both analytical app types with examples based on the Days Sales Outstanding app and the Profit Analysis app, respectively.

There are two types of apps under the analytical umbrella:

1. **Analytical apps (nonsmart apps)**
   These apps provide real-time information about large volumes of data.

2. **Analytical apps designed using SAP Smart Business modeler**
   These apps closely monitor the most important KPIs. SAP Smart Business apps are analytical apps that offer drilldown capabilities based on the SAP Smart Business framework.

In Chapter 1, we discussed SAP Fiori roles for different LOBs. For example, in the SAP UX for the finance LOB, you have accounts payable, accountant, cash manager, and GL accountant roles. Certain apps can be configured for each of these roles. Figure 6.1 shows an SAP Smart Business product called SAP Smart Business for SAP S/4HANA Finance (formerly SAP Smart Business for SAP Simple Finance). This product contains one or more analytical apps. Similarly, for each LOB, there are different SAP Smart Business products.

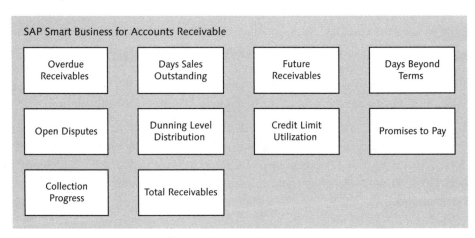

Figure 6.1 SAP Smart Business for SAP S/4HANA Finance

These apps provide real-time insight into your business. For example, Figure 6.1 shows your company's collection progress, days sales outstanding, and other KPIs. You'll be able to further drill down from this KPI or an operational performance indicator (OPI) to a detailed analysis. In the next section, we'll show you how to model a KPI or OPI and how to drill down from that KPI tile.

What Are KPIs and OPIs?

Both KPIs and OPIs relate to the vital metrics of an aspect of your business, approaching them from different perspectives that are crucial to the success of your business. KPIs look at broad categories, such as the sales of a particular region, and OPIs focus on a specific measure of a specific function or operation—for example, orders processed per shift.

The following are some of the key benefits of analytical apps designed using the SAP Smart Business modeler (smart apps):

- They offer role-based access to all relevant information, such as KPIs, OPIs, newsfeeds, specific tasks, trends, and alerts.
- You can easily build your own KPIs with threshold values and color-coded visualizations.
- You can create a drilldown from one application to another, to an SAP BusinessObjects Lumira storyboard, or to an SAP BusinessObjects Design Studio application.
- They provide end-to-end insight into action scenarios, including simulation and forecasting.

We've now covered some of the basic concepts of analytical apps. Before you enable and implement the two types of analytical apps, let's review some of the prerequisites.

6.2   Implementation Prerequisites

Several prerequisites need to be fulfilled prior to implementation to configure analytical apps. In Chapter 2, Section 2.5.3, we covered all the components that must be installed on SAP HANA and the ABAP front-end and back-end servers.

The following is a quick checklist of components that should be installed and configured in your system:

- Install the KPI framework on the ABAP front-end server.
- Enable the KPI framework on the SAP HANA server.
- Install SAP Gateway on the ABAP front-end server.
- Install the central UI components.
- Install the following SAP Smart Business products on the ABAP front-end server:
  - SAP Smart Business for CRM 1.0
  - SAP Smart Business for FCC 1.0
  - SAP Smart Business for ERP 1.0
  - SAP Smart Business for GRC 1.0
  - SAP Smart Business for EM 1.0
  - SAP Smart Business for TM 1.0
- Configure SAP Web Dispatcher.
- Install the SAP HANA Application Lifecycle Manager (HALM).
- Enable SAP HANA authentication and SSO.
- Assign the PFCG role `/UI2/SAP_KPIMOD_TCR_S` to your front-end user.
- Assign the `sap.hba.r.sb.core.roles::SAP_SMART_BUSINESS_MODELER` role to your SAP HANA user to access the SAP Smart Business modeler.

> **Important!**
>
> You must implement the SAP Notes required for each specific app. Refer to the app-specific online help at *http://help.sap.com/fiori*.

By now, you know that analytical apps run on an SAP HANA database that houses KPI data. For users to access the data from the SAP HANA database, you need to provide access to SAP HANA from the ABAP front-end server. For that, you need to enable user access to the KPI data (see Chapter 3, Section 3.2 and Section 3.3).

There are two ways to implement analytical apps, and the implementation differs according to the type of app that you want to use:

- **Analytical apps launched using the KPI tile**
  For these types of apps, you can either model your KPI or use predefined KPIs with the SAP Smart Business modeler apps. In addition, you can even configure a

generic drilldown using a predefined template or a custom drilldown. We'll cover this implementation method in Section 6.3.

- **Analytical app that uses the app launcher tile**
  App-specific content is provided for these types of apps. This content defines what to display and how to display it in SAP Fiori launchpad. You can't adapt or configure the information displayed by these apps. We'll cover this implementation method in Section 6.4.

We'll begin by implementing analytical apps using the SAP Smart Business modeler.

6.3   Analytical Apps with the SAP Smart Business Modeler

The SAP Smart Business Modeler is a tool delivered as part of the SAP Smart Business suite. This tool allows you to model KPIs and report tiles that enable targeted monitoring of key business data using SAP Fiori launchpad.

You can define KPIs and reports in the SAP Smart Business modeler to which you can apply different evaluations so that you can respond to the ever-changing business landscape. You can even add additional perspectives on the relevant data with drilldown views that are accessed through the KPI tile.

Analytical apps using the SAP Smart Business modeler are launched via KPI tiles. The Days Sales Outstanding app allows users to filter and drill down by various dimensions, then check the days sales outstanding data by customer country and company code. As you did in Chapters 4 and 5 for transactional and fact sheet apps, refer to the SAP Fiori apps reference library for information about the app that you'll be implementing in the next section.

Now, we'll show you step-by-step instructions for how to create a Days Sales Outstanding analytical app using the SAP Smart Business modeler and how to add a drilldown from the KPI tile. The first step is to create a KPI.

6.3.1   Create the KPI

Create a KPI by following these steps:

1. Log in to SAP Fiori launchpad.
2. Click the **Create KPI** app under the **KPI Design** group (see Figure 6.2).

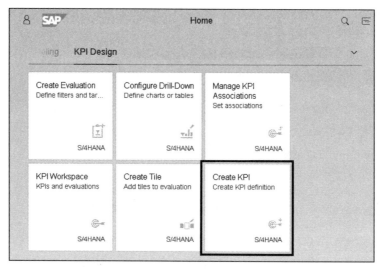

Figure 6.2 Create KPI

KPI Design Group

If you don't see the **KPI Design** group in SAP Fiori launchpad, refer to Chapter 2, Section 2.6.4, and grant user access to KPI Design.

---

3. In the next screen, you need to fill in the following mandatory details about the KPI (see Figure 6.3):

   – **Title**: Enter a meaningful name, which will appear in the tile header at runtime. Here, we entered "Days Sales Outstanding (KPI)".

   – **Additional Languages** (optional): To create a KPI tile in different language, select a language from the list.

   – **Description** (optional): Enter "Total Days Sales Outstanding for the last 12 months".

   – **Goal Type**: This indicates which kind of KPI value is meaningful for the application. Choose from three options:

     – **Maximizing (Higher is better)**: The higher, the better—for example, profit-related KPI values.

     – **Minimizing (Lower is better)**: The lower, the better—for example, cost-related KPI values.

- **Target (Closer to target is better)**: The closer value is to the target, the better—for example, attrition rate.

   Here, we chose **Minimum (Lower is better)**.

- **Tags** (optional): Enter these to search more easily for your KPI.

- **Owner Name** (optional): Enter the name of the person responsible for executing the KPI.

- **Owner ID And Email** (optional): Enter the details of the owner.

Figure 6.3 KPI Parameters

4. Scroll down to the next section, and select the values by clicking ⟝ (see Figure 6.4).

5. The following fields are displayed in Figure 6.4:

   - **CDS View:** This is the source for this Days Sales Outstanding app. Select **C_DaysSalesOutstanding**.

   - **OData Service**: This is the path of the OData service responsible for aggregating the data. Enter "/sap/opu/odata/sap/C_DAYSSALESOUTSTANDING_CDS".

   - **Entity Set**: This provides the metadata of the OData service of the SAP HANA calculation view. Enter "C_DAYSSALESOUTSTANDINGResults".

   - **Value Measure**: Select only one value from this dropdown. Again, select **DaysSalesOutstanding**.

- **Additional Information** (optional): You can enter additional information about the data source in this field.
- **Semantic Object/Action** (optional): You can leave this blank, because you're using the default drilldown feature of SAP Smart Business apps.

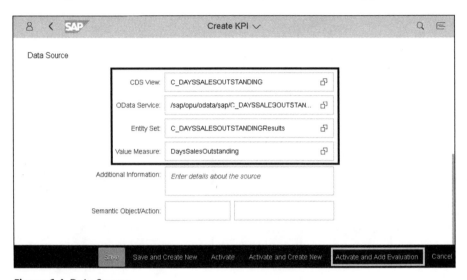

Figure 6.4 Data Source

6. After the fields have been filled, click **Activate and Add Evaluation.**

7. In the next screen you can either assign the changes to a transport, or save it as a **Local Object**.

6.3.2   Create Evaluations for the KPI

An *evaluation* defines what information about the KPI or report is visible to the user at runtime. It's a combination of variants/filters, thresholds, parameters, trends, and authorizations that are applied to a KPI or a report. You can create and activate evaluations for KPIs or OPIs, and several different evaluations can be applied to a single KPI or report.

Let's now create evaluations for the KPIs. Follow these steps:

1. Enter the values shown in Figure 6.5 in the **Parameters** section.

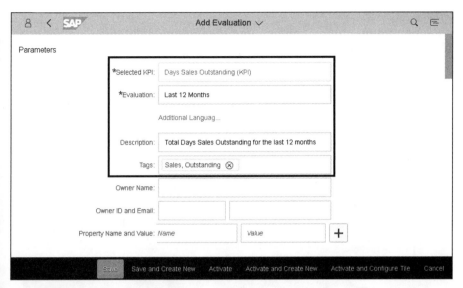

Figure 6.5 Evaluation Parameters

2. Scroll down and verify the **Data Source** fields. In this section, you have additional options (see Figure 6.6):

   - **Scaling Factor**: You can select the scaling factor based on the value that you're expecting:

     - **Auto**: Value is scaled to the available space. (We selected this option.)
     - **Kilo**: Value is displayed in multiples of one thousand.
     - **Million**: Value is displayed in multiples of one million.
     - **Billion**: Value is displayed in multiples of one billion.
     - **Percent**: Value is displayed as a percentage.

   - **Decimal Precision**: You can choose appropriate decimal formats as well. Here, we selected **Auto**.

   All the values that are configured in tiles, drilldowns, and tables for all measures of the selected evaluation are formatted by **Decimal Precision**. Only two decimal places are displayed to the right of the decimal point when the measure represents currency.

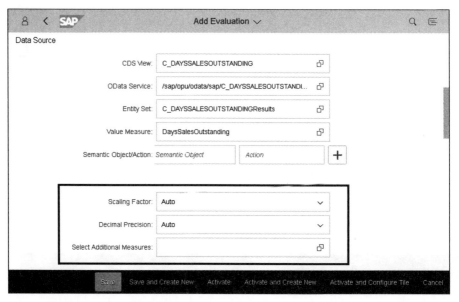

Figure 6.6 Evaluation Data Source

3. Next, you need to add variants/input parameters. A *variant* is a set of filter settings and input parameters that you define to achieve a particular perspective on a KPI or a report. Variants can be created without reference to a specific KPI or report because they're global in nature.

4. Scroll down to the **Input Parameters and Filters** section. Add the input parameters expected in the calculation view (see Figure 6.7):

   – **Display Currency Equal to (=) USD**
   – **Exchange Rate Type Equal to (=) M**
   – **Months for Calculation of Rolling Average for Receivables Equal to (=) 1**
   – **Months for Calculation of Rolling Average for Revenue Equal to (=) 1**

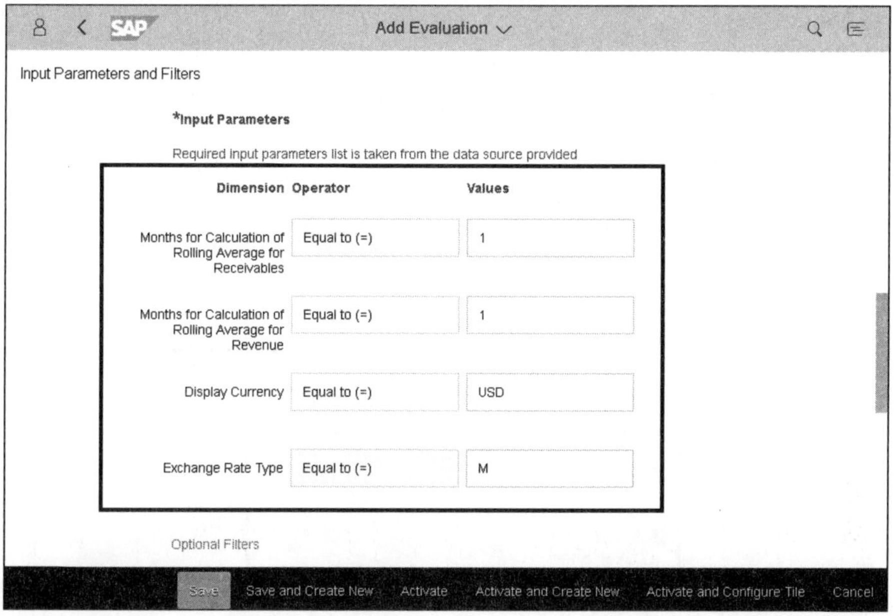

Figure 6.7 Input Parameters and Filters

5. Next, you need to add the **Target, Thresholds, and Trend** values. The thresholds defined for the KPI evaluation are determined by the **Goal Type** you selected for the KPI earlier in Figure 6.3:
   - **Critical**: Enter "100"
   - **Warning**: Enter "30"
   - **Target**: Enter "10"

   Critical, Warning, and **Target** values are the threshold values of a KPI. These depend on the goal type selected previously. For example, if you select **Lower is Better**, then your **Critical** and **Warning** values should be high. Therefore, when the KPI value is above 100, the KPI value color turns red, and when the KPI value is below 29, the KPI value color turns green. When the color is yellow, this indicates that the KPI has a value between 30 and 99 (see Figure 6.8).

6. Click **Activate and Configure Tile**.

You've now successfully created the KPI with the evaluation and activated the evaluation. In the next step, you'll configure the KPI tile.

Figure 6.8 Target, Thresholds, and Trend

6.3.3   Configure the KPI Tile

A *KPI tile* is the graphical representation of the evaluation of the KPI, which is visible to the user at runtime. The KPI is displayed in a tile. When you click the tile in SAP Fiori launchpad, you'll be able to drill down into the details. There are six types of KPI tiles:

1. **Numeric tile**
   The aggregated value of the KPI measure of the evaluation that you created in Section 6.3.2 is displayed in the tile. In this tile, data is displayed in numeric format. The color of the value displayed depends on the threshold values, which you created with critical and warning values (see Figure 6.9).

Figure 6.9 Numeric Tile

2. **Deviation tile**

In this tile, data is displayed graphically in the form of a bullet chart that shows the current value of the KPI in relation to the target value and its thresholds (see Figure 6.10).

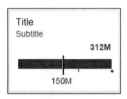

Figure 6.10 Deviation Tile

3. **Trend tile**

For this title, data is displayed graphically in the form of a line chart showing the trend over time. You must enter a time dimension representing a duration to visualize this tile (see Figure 6.11).

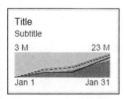

Figure 6.11 Trend Tile

4. **Comparison tile**

With this tile, you select a dimension to show the top KPI values in comparison to each other. For example, if you select **Country** as a dimension, you'll see a comparison of the values for the countries contributing to this KPI (see Figure 6.12).

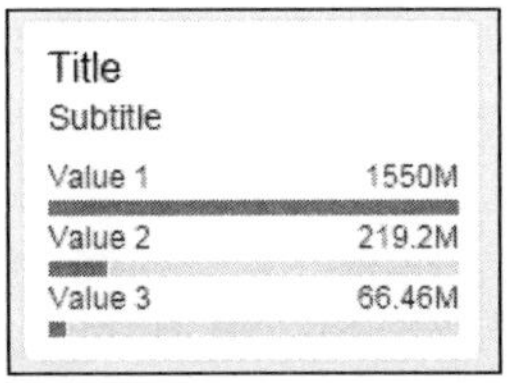

Title
Subtitle
Value 1
1550M
Value 2
219.2M
Value 3
66.46M

Figure 6.12 Comparison Tile

5. **Comparison tile, multiple measures**
   This tile is like the comparison tile, but instead of comparing dimensions, you compare different measures. You can select a maximum of three measures and must select at least two measures for this tile (see Figure 6.13).

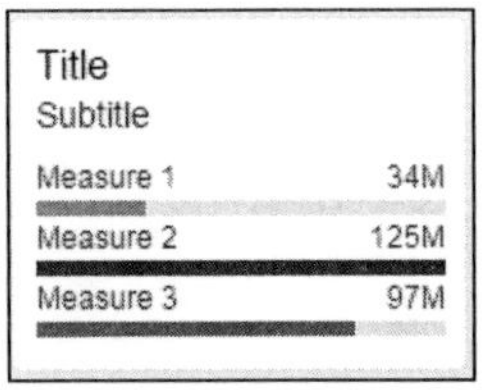

Title
Subtitle
Measure 1
34M
Measure 2
125M
Measure 3
97M

Figure 6.13 Comparison Tile, Multiple Measures

6. **Dual tile**
   This tile shows two tile types in a single tile. The left part of this tile always displays the numeric tile; on the right side, you can select any chart that's supported (see Figure 6.14).

Title
Subtitle
0.0 M
USD, Actual
Value 1
1550M
Value 2
219.2M
Value 3
66.46M

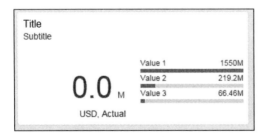

Figure 6.14 Dual Tile

Let's now look at how to configure a KPI tile, using the numeric tile as an example:

1. After clicking **Activate and Configure Tile** in the previous steps, you should see the screen shown in Figure 6.15.

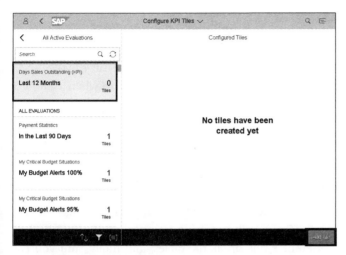

Figure 6.15 Configuring Tile

2. Enter the following details, as shown in Figure 6.16:
   - **Tile Format:** Select **Numeric Tile** from the dropdown list.
   - **Title:** Enter "Days Sales Outstanding (KPI)".
   - **Catalog:** Enter "/UI2/SAP_KPIFRW5_TC_S".
   - **Select Drill-Down:** Choose **Generic**.

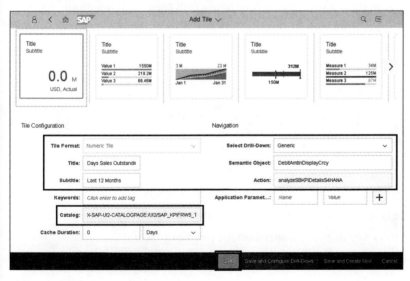

Figure 6.16 Tile Parameters

3. Click **Save**.

4. Return to the home screen by clicking [⌂].

That's it! You've successfully created a KPI tile. Now users will see this KPI tile in SAP Fiori launchpad. The next step is to create a generic drilldown so that when users click on the tile they will see the detail level. A drilldown can be a generic drilldown application, which we'll be covering in the next section, or it can even be a drilldown to another application, such as SAP Lumira or a custom application.

6.3.4   Configure the KPI Drilldown

When you click on a KPI tile, it will take you to a drilldown application. This functionality is configured using the **Configure Drill-Down** app. You can create your own drill-down applications with different kinds of charts, tables, and filters, and you can customize them with different colors as well. A drilldown application contains views with tables and charts. In this section, we'll look at configuring the KPI drilldown by creating views, configuring the KPI header, and creating filters.

Create Views

In this section, we'll show you how to create views using the dimensions and measures from the KPI evaluation. Follow these steps:

1. From SAP Fiori launchpad, click the **Configure Drill-Down** app (see Figure 6.17).

Figure 6.17 Configure Drill-Down App

2. Select the evaluation, and click **Configure** (see Figure 6.18).

3. Follow the below steps to add the first view, **Last 12 Months by Customer Country**.

4. Select **Country Key** from the **Dimension** list (see Figure 6.19).

5. Click the **Measures** tab, select **Days Sales Outstanding**, and click **OK** (see Figure 6.19).

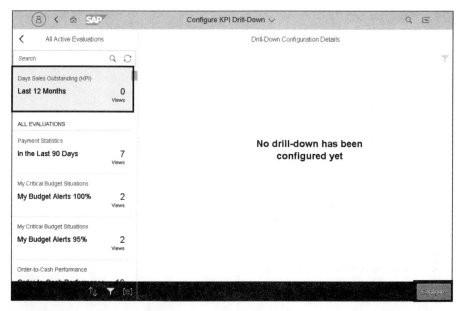

Figure 6.18 Configuring Drilldown

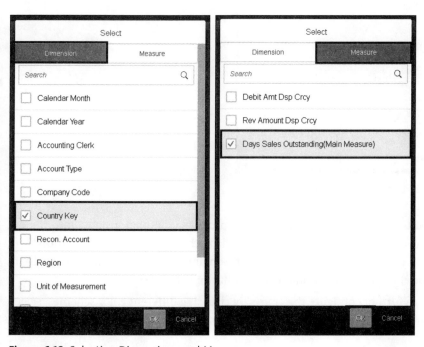

Figure 6.19 Selecting Dimensions and Measures

You should now see the dimension and the measure that you selected, as shown in Figure 6.20.

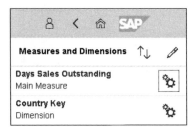

Figure 6.20 Selected Measures and Dimensions

6. You can sort the dimensions by clicking the **Sort Order** dropdown list (see Figure 6.21).

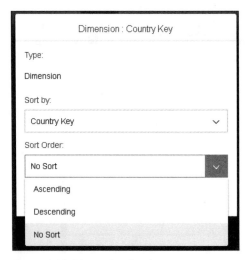

Figure 6.21 Dimension Settings

7. In addition, you can configure views to provide additional insights into the KPI data. You can add a chart, add a table, or add both. The available visualization types are **Bar** chart, **Column** chart, **Line** chart, **Columns and Lines** combination chart, **Bubble** chart, **Table**, and **Donut** chart, as shown in Figure 6.22.

8. You can further configure the charts by choosing different color schemes, selecting single or dual axis, and formatting the value displayed in the chart (see Figure 6.23).

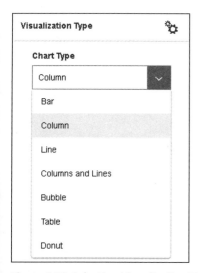

Figure 6.22 Selecting Visualization Type

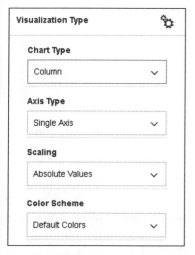

Figure 6.23 Additional Visualization Properties

9. As shown in Figure 6.24, enter or select the following fields:
   - **Visualization Type**: Select the type of visualization that you want to add to the view. Here, we selected **Column**.
   - **View Title**: Enter "Last 12 Months by Customer Country".

- **View Title**: This view name will be visible to the user during runtime. Select **Last 12 Months by Customer Country**.

- **Set Data Limit** (optional): You can set the maximum number of records that can be retrieved during runtime.

- **Data**: You can develop a view with the dummy data as well. Select **Actual Back-end Data**.

Figure 6.24 First View

10. Click **OK**.

Drilldown Application

You don't need to activate the drilldown application; changes are available immediately, as soon as you save the application.

We've successfully created the Last 12 Months by Customer Company view. You can create several views and switch between different views during runtime.

Let's add one more view: Days Sales Outstanding by Company Code. Follow these steps:

1. Click ➕ , as shown in Figure 6.25.

Figure 6.25 Adding View

2. Select the **Company Code** from the **Dimension** list, and click **OK** (see Figure 6.26).

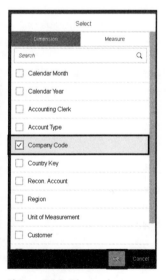

Figure 6.26 Dimensions

3. Select or enter the following details, as shown in Figure 6.27:
   - **Visualization Type**: Choose **Column**.
   - **View Title:** Enter "Last 12 Months by Company Code".

Figure 6.27 View Details

4. Click **Ok.**

With these views, you can analyze data in several formats and with different selection criteria to allow for better insight into the business processes from different perspectives.

Configure the KPI Header

In the previous section, you created two views in the drilldown app. The next step in this process is to configure the *KPI header*, the header area of the KPI drilldown app. You can add mini charts in the header section, and these mini charts can be created on multiple measures. To configure the header, follow these steps:

1. Click **+** from the **Header** section, as shown in Figure 6.28.

Figure 6.28 Adding KPI Header

2. Select a **Mini Chart**; in this example, we selected **Actual Vs. Target** (see Figure 6.29).

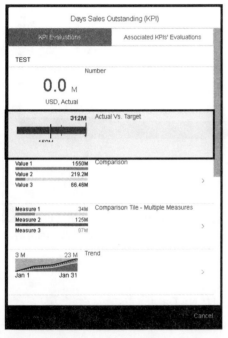

Figure 6.29 Selecting Mini Chart

Create Filters

The next available option is to create filters. You can specify up to five filters that allow you to look at the drilldown data from different perspectives. Follow these steps:

1. Click ![filter icon] to add filters.

2. Select the **Display Currency, Customer,** and **Region** filters, and click **OK** (see Figure 6.30).

Figure 6.30 Selecting Filters

3. Click **Save Configuration**.

You've now successfully created a numeric KPI tile with an evaluation and created a drilldown with two views. The KPI tile is now ready to be made available to users on SAP Fiori launchpad.

6.3.5   Assign Roles to Users to Access SAP HANA Data

Users launch analytical apps from SAP Fiori launchpad, then SAP Web Dispatcher directs the OData request from the client to SAP HANA XS. Both the data and the KPI definitions are stored in the SAP HANA system. Therefore, for users to access the data and the KPI definitions from the SAP HANA system, you need to ensure that they're given the correct access rights.

In Chapter 2, we gave you an overview of the SAP Fiori architecture with the SAP HANA XS landscape. SAP HANA XS contains the SAP Fiori app content, KPI modeling framework, generic drilldown, and VDM reuse content. SAP HANA XS reads data from the SAP HANA database. Using the OData services that require authorizations (i.e.,

SAP HANA privileges), these privileges are grouped together in roles, and these roles are assigned to SAP HANA database users.

There are certain generic roles that must be assigned to all users. In Chapter 2, we discussed these roles in greater detail. In addition to generic roles, SAP delivers a role for each analytical app, which includes all app-specific privileges as well. For users who need access to a specific app, you need to assign the correct app-specific role to the user.

SAP HANA Role

For more information on the SAP HANA role for a specific app, refer to the app-specific documentation.

Figure 6.31 shows the Days Sales Outstanding app-specific role that has to be assigned to a user for the user to read the KPI data from the SAP HANA system.

Technical Configuration

Technical Catalog	/UI2/SAP_KPIFRW5_TC_S
TECHNICAL_PFCG_ROLE	/UI2/SAP_KPIFRW5_TCR_S
Semantic Object	*
Action	AnalyzeKPIDetails

OData Services

oData Service	Package
/sap/hba/r/sfin700/odata/ar/kpi.xsodata	sap.hba.r.sfin700.db

SAP HANA Roles

Role	Package
sap.hba.r.sfin700.roles::SapSmartBusinessReceivablesManager	sap.hba.r.sfin700.roles

Figure 6.31 App-Specific Configuration Details

To assign this role to a specific user in the SAP HANA system, follow these steps:

1. Log in to SAP HANA Studio.

2. Under the SAP HANA system (**HDB SYSTEM**), choose **Security · Users**.

255

3. Double-click the user name (see Figure 6.32).

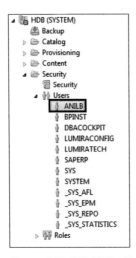

Figure 6.32 SAP HANA Users

4. Click the **+** button on the **Granted Roles** tab (see Figure 6.33).

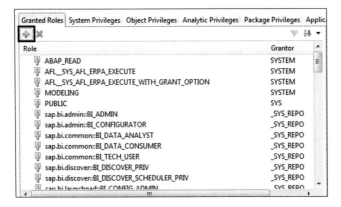

Figure 6.33 Granted Roles

5. Search for and then select the **sap.hba.r.sfin700.roles::SapSmartBusinessRe-ceivablesManager** role, then click **OK** (see Figure 6.34).

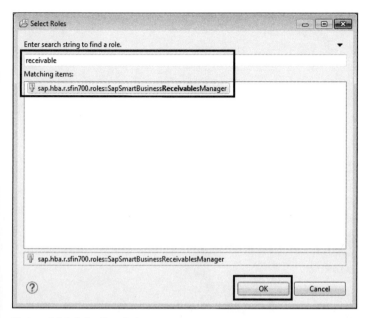

Figure 6.34 Selecting Role

6. Click the **Deploy** icon ⚙ to save the changes.

You've successfully enabled the user to access data from the SAP HANA database.

6.3.6   Enable the App for Access in SAP Fiori Launchpad

After the ICF service is activated, the next step is to assign authorizations to the user to access the SAP KPI catalog in SAP Fiori launchpad. By now, you know that SAP Fiori launchpad is the entry point for SAP Fiori apps. For users, SAP Fiori launchpad displays the apps that have been assigned to the catalog designated for a user's role. Therefore, users who have the role SAP_KPIFRW5_TCR_S assigned to their user IDs will have access to the KPI's catalog.

Via Transaction PFCG (Role Maintenance), you can grant access to a user to the role SAP_KPIFRW5_TCR_S. This role allows the user to view all the analytical apps that are activated using the SAP Smart Business modeler. Refer back to Chapter 4, Section 4.3.3 for a refresher on how to assign roles to a user. Figure 6.35 shows the role assigned to an end user using Transaction PFCG.

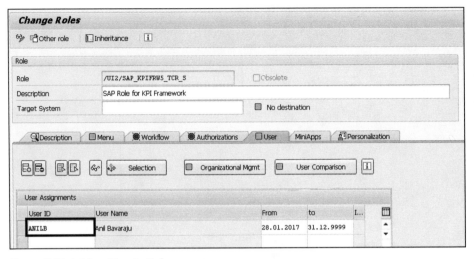

Figure 6.35 Adding User to Role

You've successfully assigned the SAP standard role to a user, who now has access to all the analytical apps. You created the Days Sales Outstanding app with the SAP Smart Business modeler, and all the analytical apps that are created using the SAP Smart Business modeler are automatically added to the predefined KPI catalog in SAP Fiori launchpad. After you activate the app in the SAP Smart Business modeler, it's automatically added to the **KPI Catalog** category.

Follow these steps to add the app to SAP Fiori launchpad:

1. Log in to SAP Fiori launchpad with the **User ID** you accessed in the previous steps (see Figure 6.35).
2. Navigate to the ME area by clicking 🔏, and click **App Finder**
3. Select **SAP: KPIs** from the catalog dropdown list, as shown in Figure 6.36.

Figure 6.36 SAP KPIs

You should now see the app that you created and activated in earlier steps (see Figure 6.37).

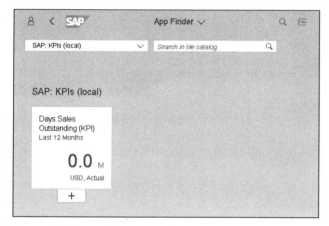

Figure 6.37 Days Sales Outstanding Custom App

4. Click the **+** button, add the app to your **My Home** group by checking the corresponding box, and then click **OK** (see Figure 6.38).

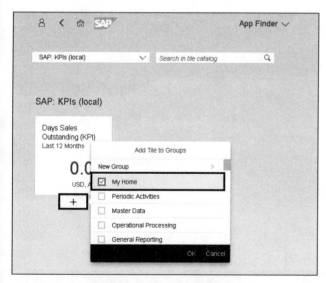

Figure 6.38 Adding App to My Home Group

5. Return to the home screen by clicking the 🏠 button.

6. You should now see the **Days Sales Outstanding** app under the **My Home** group, as shown in Figure 6.39.

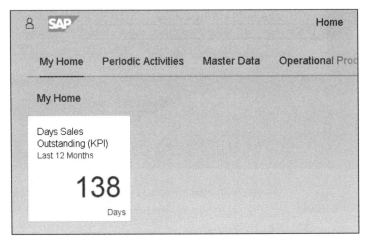

Figure 6.39 My Home Group

7. Click the app to see the two views you created previously (see Figure 6.40).

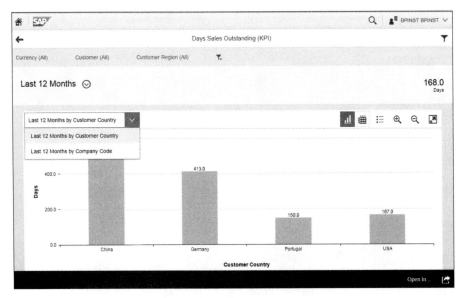

Figure 6.40 Days Sales Outstanding App with Custom Views

8. Toggle between the table view and the chart view by clicking the buttons above the chart. In addition, you can zoom in, zoom out, or view the app full screen by using the buttons shown in Figure 6.41.

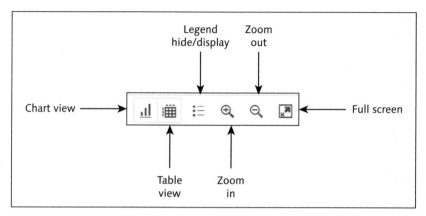

Figure 6.41 View Features

You should now understand the basics of creating an analytical app with the SAP Smart Business modeler and how to grant access to users. In the next section, we'll discuss a more advanced topic: assigning an app using a custom role.

6.3.7   Assign the App Using a Custom Role

In a real-world scenario, you wouldn't want to give access to all analytical apps to your users (i.e., any user assigned to the SAP_KPIFRW5_TCR_S role will have access to all the apps). In this section, we'll show you how to create a custom catalog and role to give access to specific analytical apps in SAP Fiori launchpad.

In Chapter 4, Section 4.6, we discussed how to create a custom catalog and custom role for a transactional app. You'll be following a similar process for nonsmart analytical apps.

To enable your app with custom roles and catalogs, you must complete the following steps:

1. Log in to your ABAP front-end server, and run Transaction LPD_CUST.
2. Create a new launchpad by clicking the **New Launchpad** button.
3. Enter the fields as shown in Figure 6.42, and click **Confirm.**

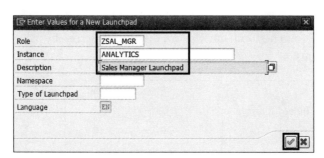

Figure 6.42 New Launchpad

4. Click **Yes** to ignore the namespace.

5. Create a new application by clicking **New Application.**

6. Enter "Days Sales Outstanding (KPI)" in the **Link Text** field. From the **Application Type** dropdown list, select **URL**. Click the **Edit** button next to the **URL** input box. Enter "/sap/bc/ui5_ui5/sap/ca_kpi/drilldown/" in the **URL** box (see Figure 6.43).

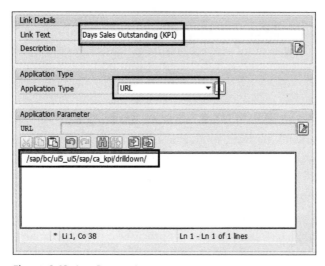

Figure 6.43 App Parameters

7. Click **Show Advanced (Optional) Parameters**.

8. Click the **Edit** button next to the **Application Alias** input box. Enter "analyzeKPIDetails" in the box. Enter "SAPUI5.Component=drilldown" in the **Additional Information** box (see Figure 6.44).

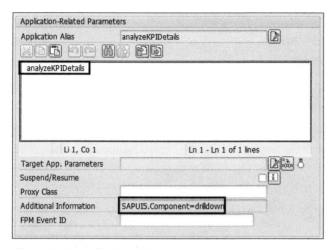

Figure 6.44 Application-Related Parameters

9. Click **Save**.

10. Log in to the SAP Fiori launchpad designer at *http://hostname:port/sap/bc/ui5_ui5/sap/arsrvc_upb_admn/main.html20?sap-client=120&scope=CUST*.

11. Click **Catalogs.**

12. Create a new catalog by clicking **+** at the bottom of the screen.

13. Enter the **Title** and the catalog **ID** shown in Figure 6.45.

Figure 6.45 Create Catalog

14. Click **Save.**

15. Select the catalog you created in the previous step.

16. Click the **Target Mapping** icon 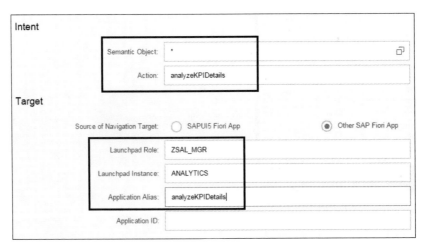.

17. Click **Create Target Mapping.**

In the next steps, you'll define the target mapping, but before that, let's explore some of the components of target mapping.

An *intent* allows users to perform actions on semantic objects. In this example, we choose *, which means we want to navigate to all the analytical apps and analyze all the details. The **Intent** area of the screen lets you perform actions without worrying about the technical part of the navigational target.

Intent has the following components (see Figure 6.46):

- **Semantic Object**
  Represents business entities, such as a product or sales order. You can bundle apps that reflect a specific scenario. In this exercise, we're specifying a generic semantic object, which allows you to analyze all the semantic objects in a standardized way.

- **Action**
  Defines which operations are performed on the semantic object—for example, displaying a purchase order. Here, display is the action, and the purchase order is the semantic object.

Follow these steps:

1. Enter the details in the **Intent** section as shown in Figure 6.46.

Figure 6.46 Intent and Target

2. In the **Target** section, enter the details of the custom launchpad you created previously.

3. Click **Save.**

4. Select the **Group** tab in the SAP Fiori launchpad designer, and then create a new group by clicking ⊕ at the bottom of the screen.

5. Enter the group **Title** and the group **ID** shown in Figure 6.47, and click **Save.**

Figure 6.47 Create Group

You should now see the new group created in the SAP Fiori launchpad designer.

6. Add a tile by clicking on the tile with the **+** sign (see Figure 6.48).

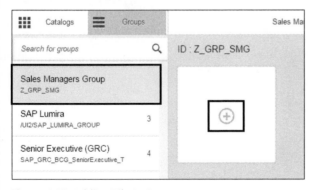

Figure 6.48 Adding Tile to Group

7. Click the **Search** icon to search the catalog.

8. Select the **SAP: KPIs** catalog from the list, as shown in Figure 6.49.

Figure 6.49 SAP KPIs Catalog

9. You'll now see all the KPI tiles that have been modeled using the SAP Smart Business modeler. Select the **Days Sales Outstanding (KPI)** app by clicking **+** at the bottom of the tile, as shown in Figure 6.50.

Figure 6.50 Adding App to Group

You should now see the Days Sales Outstanding app added to your group in the SAP Fiori launchpad designer.

You've successfully created a custom catalog, created a custom group, and assigned the Days Sales Outstanding app to the group. The next step is to create a custom role and add the category and group to the role. Follow these steps:

1. Log in to your ABAP front-end server, and run Transaction PFCG.

2. Enter the **Role** name "Z_ROLE_SM", and click **Single Role** (see Figure 6.51).

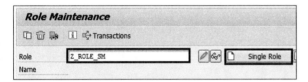

Figure 6.51 Create Custom Role

3. Enter the **Description**, and click **Save**.

4. Click the **Menu** tab, then select **Catalog** from the **Transaction** button dropdown menu (see Figure 6.52).

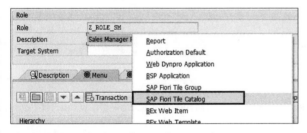

Figure 6.52 Assigning Tile Catalog to Role

5. Enter "Z_SMGR_CATALOG" in the **Catalog ID** field, and click **Confirm** (see Figure 6.53). This is the ID of the catalog you created previously.

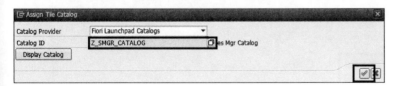

Figure 6.53 Catalog ID

6. Add a group you created by selecting **SAP Fiori Tile Group** from the dropdown menu (see Figure 6.54).

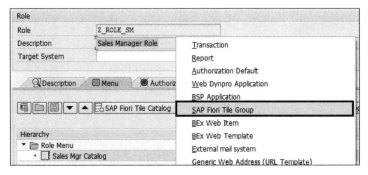

Figure 6.54 Assigning Group Catalog to Role

7. To search for your group, click the **Search** button next to the **Group ID**.
8. Select the **Z_GRP_CM1** group from the pop-up window (see Figure 6.55). Click **Execute.**

Figure 6.55 Group ID

You've successfully created the custom role. Your role should now show both the category and group (see Figure 6.56).

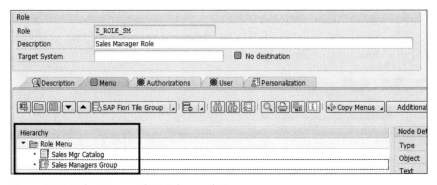

Figure 6.56 Role Menu with Catalog and Group

The last step in this process is to assign the custom role to the user. Follow these steps:

1. Select the **User** tab.

2. Enter the **User ID**, and click **Save** (see Figure 6.57).

Role	
Role	Z_ROLE_SM
Description	Sales Manager Role
Target System	☐ No destination

🔍Description ☐ Menu ◉ Authorizations ☐ User 📇 Personalization

☒☒ ☒☒ ✂ ◄► Selection   ☐ User Comparison ℹ

User Assignments

User ID	User name	From	to	I...	🗓
ANILB	ANILB	08/07/2015	12/31/9999		▲

Figure 6.57 Assigning User

> **Important!**
>
> All users must be assigned to the generic KPI framework role /UI2/SAP_KPIFRW5_TCR_ S. For more information, refer to Chapter 2, Section 2.6.4.

3. Log in to SAP Fiori launchpad with the user ID that you assigned to the role, and you should see the **Days Sales Outstanding (KPI)** app under the **Sales Managers Group** (see Figure 6.58)

Figure 6.58 Days Sales Outstanding (KPI) App

In this section, we explored how to provide user access to analytical apps using both an SAP standard role and a custom role. You've successfully created a KPI tile, completed the front-end tasks, and created user authorizations.

6.4 Analytical Apps without the SAP Smart Business Modeler

In the previous section, you created an analytical app using the SAP Smart Business modeler. In this section, we'll show you how to enable an analytical app without using the SAP Smart Business modeler; we'll use an example based on the Profit Analysis analytical app.

First, let's get the app-specific configuration details from the SAP Fiori apps reference library. Figure 6.59 shows the configuration details of the Profit Analysis app.

SAPUI5 Application

The ICF nodes for the following SAPUI5 application must be activated on the front-end server:

Component	Technical Name
SAPUI5 Application	FIN_PRFTANLYS

SAP Fiori Launchpad

You require the following data to give users access to the app in the SAP Fiori launchpad.

Technical Configuration

Technical Catalog	SAP_SFIN_TC_A
TECHNICAL_PFCG_ROLE	SAP_SFIN_TCR_A
Semantic Object	ControllingDocument
Action	analyzeProfit
LPD_CUST Role	UIHSFIN1
LPD_CUST Instance	ANALYTICS
SAPUI5 Application	FIN_PRFTANLYS
Business Catalog (Launchpad)	SAP_SFIN_BC_SALESMANAGER
Business Group (Launchpad)	SAP_SFIN_BCG_SALESMANAGER
PFCG role for Business Catalog	SAP_SFIN_BCR_SALESMANAGER

Figure 6.59 App-Specific Configuration

In the sections that follow, we'll walk through the necessary tasks to complete this implementation.

6.4.1   Activate the SAPUI5 Application

The first step in implementing an analytical app without the SAP Smart Business modeler is to activate the SAPUI5 application. We discussed these steps in detail in Chapter 4, Section 4.1. You can follow along with the same steps to activate the FIN_ PRFTANLYS service (see Figure 6.60).

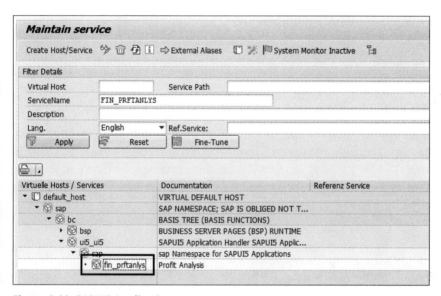

Figure 6.60 SAPUI5 Application

6.4.2   Assign the SAP HANA Role

In this section, we'll assign a product-specific SAP HANA role to the user. This role enables users to access KPI data (i.e., the SAP HANA Live views and the OData service of the specific app). Follow the steps we covered in Section 6.3.5, and grant access to the user for the sap.hba.apps.sfin.s.roles::fiori_sfin role (see Figure 6.61).

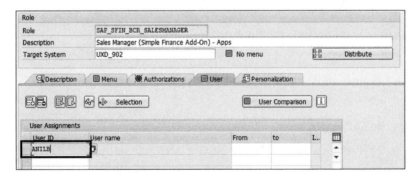

Figure 6.61 SAP HANA Role

6.4.3   Assign the App-Specific Catalog Role

The next step is to assign the app-specific PFCG role for the business catalog to the user. After this is enabled, the user will have access to the catalog in SAP Fiori launchpad. Assign the SAP_SFIN_BCR_SALESMANAGER business catalog role to an end user (see Figure 6.62). Refer to Chapter 4, Section 4.3.3 if you need to review how to assign roles to users.

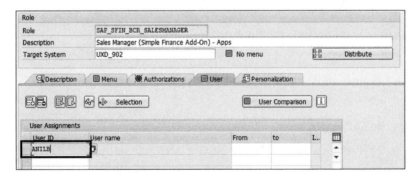

Figure 6.62 Assigning User

6.4.4   Add the App to SAP Fiori Launchpad

After you've completed all the preceding steps, the last step is to add the app to a group. Follow the same steps you performed in Chapter 4, Section 4.6.6 to add the **Profit Analysis** app to the **Sales Manager** group (see Figure 6.63).

Figure 6.63 Profit Analysis App in Sales Manager Group

Sales Order Fulfillment App

Typically, all SAP Smart Business apps drill down from one analytical app to another analytical app. However, there is one hybrid app, the Sales Order Fulfillment app, that drills down from an analytical app to a transactional app.

The Sales Order Fulfillment app is the only hybrid app that uses SAP Gateway (ABAP front-end server) and SAP HANA XS as well. It needs SAP Gateway because it sends requests to the back-end server. After you configure the Sales Order Fulfilment app, it will be added as an analytical app tile in SAP Fiori launchpad. When a user opens the app, a transactional app is opened. Hence, this is the only hybrid app that has a tile for an analytical app and launches with the features of a transactional app.

6.5   Summary

In this chapter, we provided step-by-step instructions for how to create an analytical app using the SAP Smart Business modeler for the Days Sales Outstanding app. We discussed everything from how to create a KPI to providing authorization to the user to access an app and its drilldown views. In addition, we showed you how to enable an app with custom groups and catalogs. We then provided an overview of how to enable analytical apps that don't use a KPI tile to launch (non-smart analytical apps).

In the next chapter, we'll explore OData services in depth. Understanding OData services is very important, as you'll be using this concept a lot during the extension or creation of transactional, fact sheet, and analytical apps, which we cover in the third part of this book.

Chapter 7

Creating OData Services with SAP Gateway

OData services are required to connect SAP Fiori to the back-end SAP system. This chapter gives you an overview of service-generation methods and offers step-by-step instructions for generating OData services using SAP Gateway Service Builder.

Before we begin creating and extending SAP Fiori apps, we need to make clear some basic concepts about OData services and SAP Gateway Service Builder. The main objective of this chapter is to give you an in-depth look at OData services and SAP Gateway Service Builder, as well as the process of creating an OData service. We'll walk you through service-generation methods using SAP Gateway Service Builder, and at the end of this chapter, we'll work through a couple of simple exercises to explain the three main steps in service creation: data model definition, service implementation, and service maintenance.

In Chapter 1, we introduced the REST protocol, OData protocol, and SAP Gateway. SAP Gateway and OData service creation is a big topic. Our intent is to discuss certain scenarios or methods of service generation that will enable you to better understand the processes when creating or extending SAP Fiori apps in the next chapters. In this chapter, you'll learn three different ways to create data models and generate OData services using SAP Gateway Service Builder.

We start with an overview of OData concepts by exploring the documents with an example in Section 7.1 and then guide you through the various terms in SAP Gateway Service Builder in Section 7.2. In Section 7.3, we'll first introduce you to import functions to build a data model, use an example of Sales Order Header data from the Business Object Repository (BOR), and show you how to build a data model and generate an OData service (Section 7.3.1). Then, we'll provide an overview of the second method to generate data models and OData services by redefining services (Section 7.3.2).

Finally, we finish Section 7.3 by showing you how to create an OData service on top of an SAP Business Explorer (BEx) query (Section 7.3.3).

7.1   Introduction to OData

By now, you know that OData is the open standard that provides standard platform-agnostic interoperability and access to data sources via websites. OData was built on web technologies such as HTTP, AtomPub, XML, and JavaScript Object Notation (JSON) to provide access to information from a variety of applications. It was designed to provide a RESTful API that is accessible by forming an appropriate URI and assigning it to the corresponding HTTP header. The biggest advantage of OData services is that they're multichannel and developed to serve many applications. Put simply, OData is used to expose, access, and modify information from different sources.

In the following sections, we'll discuss the basics of an OData service and OData queries.

7.1.1   OData Service Basics

In this section, we'll cover the basic structure of an OData service. Let's start with simple operations that can be performed using the OData protocol.

We'll use the standard OData service of a Create Sales Order app, which you activated in Chapter 4, Section 4.2, to understand the concepts of an OData service. Follow these steps to view the OData service of the app:

1. Log in to your ABAP front-end server.

2. Run Transaction IWFND/MAINT_SERVICE.

3. Filter **External Service Name** for "SRA017_SALESORDER*", then press ⌈Enter⌋ (see Figure 7.1).

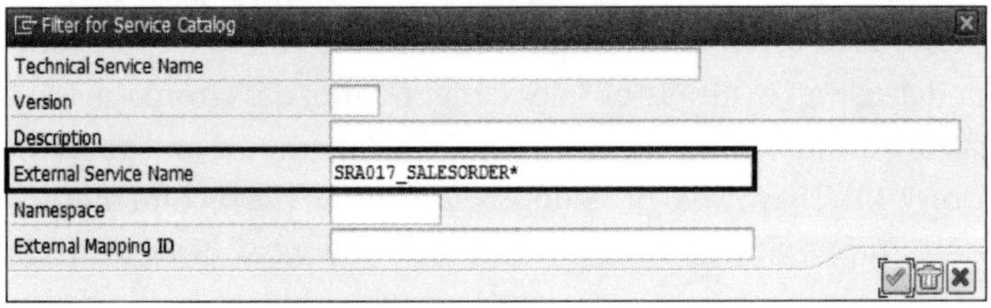

Figure 7.1 Service Name

4. Select the service, then click **Gateway Client** (see Figure 7.2).

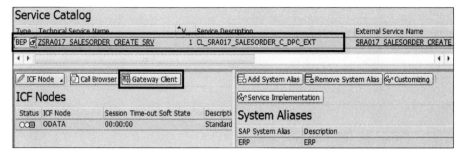

Figure 7.2 Gateway Client Button

5. Click **Execute** (see Figure 7.3).

Figure 7.3 Executing Service

An OData service is a logical data model that depicts how users perceive the model behind the UI. Essentially, anything that's possible with the UI becomes part of the API, and each OData service is represented with a service root URI. There are two types of documents accompanying each OData service:

1. **Service document**
   This shows the details about the *entity set*. Figure 7.4 shows the service document with seven entities: Customers, Products, Product Images, Sales Orders, Product Attributes, Order Items, and Partner Addresses.

2. **Service metadata document**
   This gives you the structure of an OData service. It describes the *Entity Data Model* (EDM) of the source. In the service metadata document, the data is described in EDM terms, using XML for describing models called the *Conceptual Schema Definition Language* (CSDL). An EDM describes the organization and the relationships

between different data resources with models and entity types within a particular business scenario. Figure 7.5 shows an example of what the OData feed looks like from SAP. Run the following URL in your browser to view the service metadata document of the Create Sales Order service:

http://<host>:<port>/sap/opu/odata/sap/SRA017_SALESORDER_CREATE_SRV/ $metadata

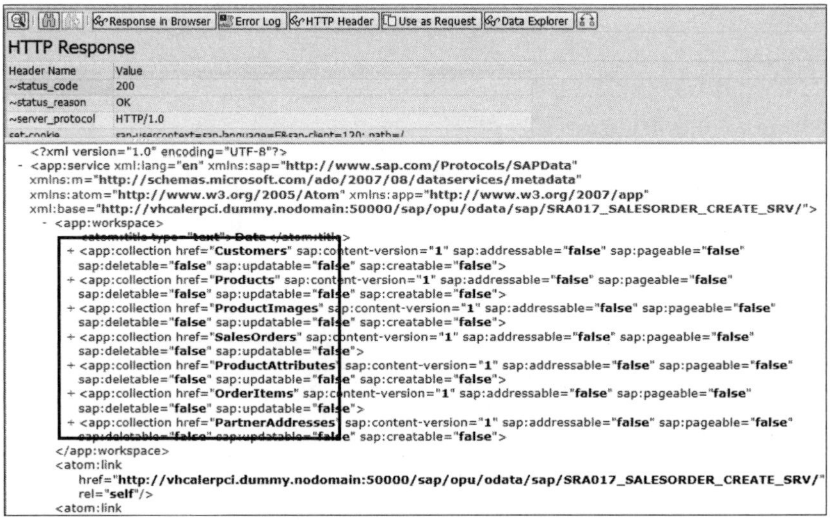

Figure 7.4 Service Document

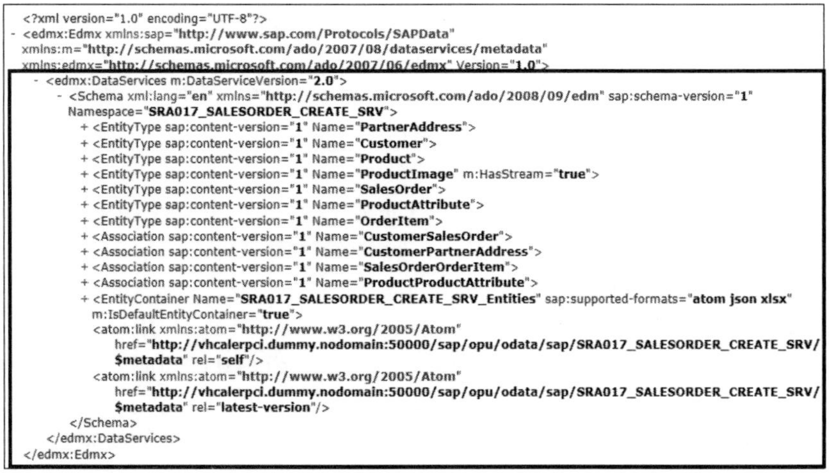

Figure 7.5 Service Metadata Document

Let's now dive deep into the EDM and the corresponding parts of the service metadata document. We'll explain each element as we work through the Create Sales Order OData service.

In the service metadata document, expand EntityContainer, where the service metadata document defines EntitySets belonging to one service. EntitySets listed in the service document and the service metadata document are exactly the same (see Figure 7.6).

```
- <EntityContainer Name="SRA017_SALESORDER_CREATE_SRV_Entities" sap:supported-formats="atom json xlsx"
  m:IsDefaultEntityContainer="true">
    <EntitySet sap:content-version="1" sap:addressable="false" sap:pageable="false" sap:deletable="false"
      sap:updatable="false" sap:creatable="false" Name="Customers"
      EntityType="SRA017_SALESORDER_CREATE_SRV.Customer"/>
    <EntitySet sap:content-version="1" sap:addressable="false" sap:pageable="false" sap:deletable="false"
      sap:updatable="false" sap:creatable="false" Name="Products"
      EntityType="SRA017_SALESORDER_CREATE_SRV.Product"/>
    <EntitySet sap:content-version="1" sap:addressable="false" sap:pageable="false" sap:deletable="false"
      sap:updatable="false" sap:creatable="false" Name="ProductImages"
      EntityType="SRA017_SALESORDER_CREATE_SRV.ProductImage"/>
    <EntitySet sap:content-version="1" sap:addressable="false" sap:pageable="false" sap:deletable="false"
      sap:updatable="false" Name="SalesOrders"
      EntityType="SRA017_SALESORDER_CREATE_SRV.SalesOrder"/>
    <EntitySet sap:content-version="1" sap:addressable="false" sap:pageable="false" sap:deletable="false"
      sap:updatable="false" sap:creatable="false" Name="ProductAttributes"
      EntityType="SRA017_SALESORDER_CREATE_SRV.ProductAttribute"/>
    <EntitySet sap:content-version="1" sap:addressable="false" sap:pageable="false" sap:deletable="false"
      sap:updatable="false" Name="OrderItems"
      EntityType="SRA017_SALESORDER_CREATE_SRV.OrderItem"/>
    <EntitySet sap:content-version="1" sap:addressable="false" sap:pageable="false" sap:deletable="false"
      sap:updatable="false" sap:creatable="false" Name="PartnerAddresses"
      EntityType="SRA017_SALESORDER_CREATE_SRV.PartnerAddress"/>
  + <AssociationSet sap:content-version="1" sap:deletable="false" sap:updatable="false" sap:creatable="false"
    Name="CustomerPartnerAddressSet"
    Association="SRA017_SALESORDER_CREATE_SRV.CustomerPartnerAddress">
  + <AssociationSet sap:content-version="1" sap:deletable="false" sap:updatable="false" sap:creatable="false"
    Name="ProductProductAttributeSet"
    Association="SRA017_SALESORDER_CREATE_SRV.ProductProductAttribute">
  + <AssociationSet sap:content-version="1" sap:deletable="false" sap:updatable="false" sap:creatable="false"
    Name="SalesOrderOrderItemSet" Association="SRA017_SALESORDER_CREATE_SRV.SalesOrderOrderItem">
```

Figure 7.6 EntitySet

Entity sets group entities, and all the entities of one entity set are of the same entity type. For example, a Customer entity set is a set of Customer instances (see Figure 7.7), and all Customer instances are of the Customer entity type.

```
<?xml version="1.0" encoding="UTF-8"?>
- <edmx:Edmx xmlns:sap="http://www.sap.com/Protocols/SAPData"
  xmlns:m="http://schemas.microsoft.com/ado/2007/08/dataservices/metada
  xmlns:edmx="http://schemas.microsoft.com/ado/2007/06/edmx" Version="1.
  - <edmx:DataServices m:DataServiceVersion="2.0">
    - <Schema xml:lang="en" xmlns="http://schemas.microsoft.com/ado/20(
      Namespace="SRA017_SALESORDER_CREATE_SRV">
      + <EntityType sap:content-version="1" Name="PartnerAddress">
      - <EntityType sap:content-version="1" Name="Customer">
        - <Key>
            <PropertyRef Name="CustomerID"/>
            <PropertyRef Name="SalesOrganization"/>
            <PropertyRef Name="DistributionChannel"/>
            <PropertyRef Name="Division"/>
          </Key>
```

Figure 7.7 EntityType

Entities are structured as records with a key, under the entity types. For example, expand the Customer entity type, and you'll notice the keys (Customer ID, Division, etc.).

An *association* defines the relationship between two entity types, and every association includes two association ends (entity types). An association end states the entity type elements, the roles of each of the entity type elements, and the cardinality rules for each association end. For example, expand the CustomerSalesOrder association in the service metadata document (see Figure 7.8), and you'll see that the end types are Customers and Sales Order, and the cardinality is one to many (i.e., one customer can have many products).

```
- <Association sap:content-version="1" Name="CustomerSalesOrder">
    <End Type="SRA017_SALESORDER_CREATE_SRV.Customer" Role="FromRole_CustomerSalesOrder"
        Multiplicity="1"/>
    <End Type="SRA017_SALESORDER_CREATE_SRV.SalesOrder" Role="ToRole_CustomerSalesOrder"
        Multiplicity="*"/>
  - <ReferentialConstraint>
      - <Principal Role="FromRole_CustomerSalesOrder">
          <PropertyRef Name="Division"/>
          <PropertyRef Name="DistributionChannel"/>
          <PropertyRef Name="SalesOrganization"/>
          <PropertyRef Name="CustomerID"/>
        </Principal>
      - <Dependent Role="ToRole_CustomerSalesOrder">
          <PropertyRef Name="Division"/>
          <PropertyRef Name="DistributionChannel"/>
          <PropertyRef Name="SalesOrganization"/>
          <PropertyRef Name="CustomerID"/>
        </Dependent>
    </ReferentialConstraint>
  </Association>
```

Figure 7.8 Association

For example, to read the list of customers from an OData service, replace $metadata with customers at the end of the service URL. Initially you might find this very confusing, but eventually you'll get used to all these terms, and you'll be able to understand an OData service very easily.

7.1.2   OData Service Queries

Now that you understand how to read a service, let's move on to the most important operations—that is, the CRUD operations. OData uses the existing HTTP verbs (POST, GET, PUT, and DELETE) against addressable resource identifiers in the URI. Figure 7.9 shows the HTTP methods in SAP Gateway client.

Figure 7.9 HTTP Methods

The following list describes the different requests used for entities:

- To read a single entity, use a GET request.
- To create an entity, use a POST request.
- To modify a single entity, use a PUT request.
- To modify the whole entity, use a PATCH request.
- To merge a subset of entity properties, use a MERGE request.
- To delete an entity, use the DELETE command.

OData specifies a simple query language that allows the client to request random filters, sorts, or pages. Table 7.1 shows some of the most important query options.

Operation	Query Option
Filtering	$filter
Projecting	$select
Sorting	$orderby
Paging	$page
Inlining	$expand

Table 7.1 OData Query Options

The following are some examples of OData service queries:

- To read all sales orders using the sales order OData service, enter the following URI in the **Request URI** field and click **Execute** (see Figure 7.10): "/sap/opu/odata/sap/CB_SALES_ORDER_SRV/SalesOrders?".

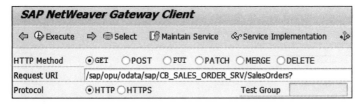

Figure 7.10 Sales Order Service

- Similarly, to read a single sales order, enter the following **Request URI** and click **Execute** (see Figure 7.11): "/sap/opu/odata/sap/CB_SALES_ORDER_SRV/SalesOrders('499')?".

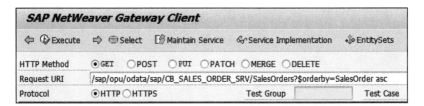

Figure 7.11 Example 2

- To sort the sales orders in ascending order, enter the following **Request URI** and click **Execute** (see Figure 7.12): "/sap/opu/odata/sap/CB_SALES_ORDER_SRV/SalesOrders?orderby=SalesOrder asc".

SAP NetWeaver Gateway Client

| ⇐ ⊕ Execute | ⇨ ⊜ Select | 🖳 Maintain Service | ⅙ Service Implementation | ⋰ EntitySets |

HTTP Method	⦿ GET ◯ POST ◯ PUT ◯ PATCH ◯ MERGE ◯ DELETE
Request URI	/sap/opu/odata/sap/CB_SALES_ORDER_SRV/SalesOrders?$orderby=SalesOrder asc
Protocol	⦿ HTTP ◯ HTTPS Test Group [ ] Test Case

Figure 7.12 Example 3

In this section, you learned about the two OData service documents in detail, as well as what entity, entity set, entity container, and different query options are. You'll see a lot of these in subsequent chapters, especially when we create or extend existing apps.

Now, let's discuss how to build an OData service using SAP Gateway Service Builder.

7.2   SAP Gateway Service Builder

SAP Gateway translates complex data structures into easy-to-consume OData services. SAP Gateway Service Builder is the central interface of SAP Gateway (accessed via Transaction SEGW); it includes both code-based development of OData services for experienced developers and non-code-based generation of services for less experienced developers. We'll cover only the non-code-based development services in this book.

SAP Gateway Service Builder contains all relevant functions for the modeling and development of OData services in SAP Gateway, and supports the entire development lifecycle of an OData service in SAP Gateway. SAP Gateway Service Builder's main objective is to provide comprehensive support for building OData services in a declarative way or for reusing existing business objects in the SAP Business Suite system. Later, you'll see a data model in SAP Gateway Service Builder. This modeling environment follows a project-based approach, and all relevant data is consolidated in these projects.

Now that you understand the terms *entities*, *entity types*, *entity sets*, *associations*, and so on from the service document and service metadata document, let's explore these concepts in the SAP Gateway Service Builder. To begin, first navigate to SAP Gateway Service Builder by following these steps:

1. Log in to the SAP Gateway server.
2. Open SAP Gateway Service Builder by running Transaction SEGW.
3. Open a project by clicking 📂.
4. Enter the Create Sales Order project details; that is, enter "SRAO17_SALESORDER_CREATE" in the **Project** field and press ⏎ (see Figure 7.13).

Figure 7.13 Create Sales Order Project

You should now see the **Sales Order Creation** project (see Figure 7.14).

Figure 7.14 SAP Gateway Service Builder

From the screen shown in Figure 7.14, note the following details:

- **Entity Types**
  Each entity type can have a data dictionary binding to an existing ABAP Data Dictionary (DDIC) structure element. Expand the **Customer** entity type shown in Figure 7.14, and double-click **Properties**. Figure 7.15 shows the **Customer** entity type with the entities.

- **Navigation Properties**: Each entity type contains one or more navigation properties. These properties contain links representing an association; for example, Figure 7.16 shows the navigation properties of the **Customer** entity type; **PartnerAddressSet** is the link from the **Customer** entity to the **PartnerAddress** entity.

- **Associations**
  Associations are relationships between two or more entities; for example, Figure 7.17 shows the relationship between **CustomerPartnerAddress** with the one to many cardinality. With SAP Gateway Service Builder, you can create or edit an association.

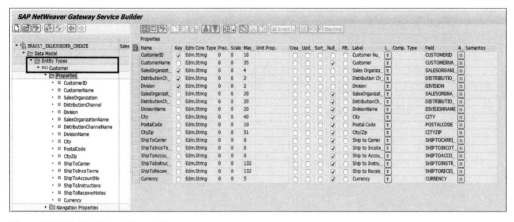

Figure 7.15 Entity Type Properties

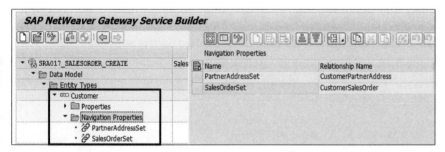

Figure 7.16 Navigation Properties

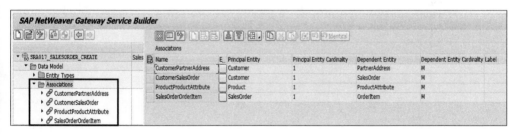

Figure 7.17 Associations

- **Entity Sets**

  As previously mentioned, entities (e.g., customers, order items, etc.) are grouped in entity sets, and these entities are instances of the entity types (e.g., customer ID, customer name, etc.; see Figure 7.18).

285

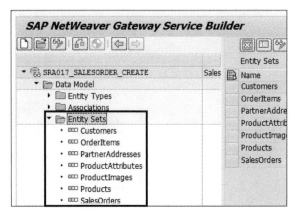

Figure 7.18 Entity Sets

- **Service Implementation**

  This folder contains references to the operations and methods of a service. Based on the OData model, the services are implemented under the **Service Implementation** folder after the project is generated. Under each individual entity set, the following operations can be found: **Create**, **Delete**, **GetEntity**, **GetEntitySet**, and **Update** (see Figure 7.19).

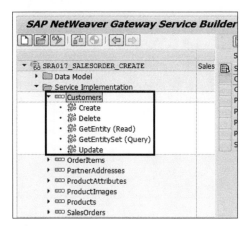

Figure 7.19 Service Implementation

- **Runtime Artifacts**

  When you generate an OData service, SAP Gateway Service Builder automatically generates the code (i.e., it generates the runtime artifacts) and registers the OData

286

service to the SAP Gateway server. The following are important runtime artifacts (see Figure 7.20):

– *Data Provider Base Class (suffix _DPC)*: This is an ABAP class. DPC provides all the methods required to handle OData requests; for example, it's used to code your create, read, update, and delete a query (CRUD) methods and function import methods.

– *Data Provider Extension Class (suffix _DPC_EXT)*: You can define all your back-end logic in redefined methods of the DPC extension class.

– *Model Provider Base Class (suffix _MPC)*: This is a base ABAP class. MPC is used to define the EDM of your service. Typically, developers don't touch this class unless there's some feature that isn't available in the SAP Gateway tool and they want to build the service with that feature.

– *Model Provider Extension Class (suffix _MPC_EXT)*: This is the implementation class that inherits the base class. Developers can modify and add features to this class.

– *Registered Model (suffix _MDL)*: This is the technical name of the OData service model—for example, SALESORDER_MDL.

– *Registered Service (suffix _SRV)*: This is the technical name of the OData service—for example, SALESORDER_SRV.

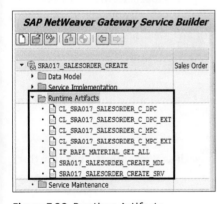

Figure 7.20 Runtime Artifacts

- **Service Maintenance**
  During the runtime artifacts generation, the ABAP classes are registered to the SAP Business Suite back-end system, and then the technical service names are registered with the SAP Gateway hub system (see Figure 7.21).

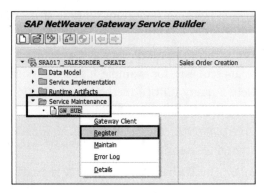

Figure 7.21 Service Maintenance

So far, we've reviewed the basic OData concepts and SAP Gateway Service Builder components via an example based on the Create Sales Order OData service. Now, let's look at the most important part of SAP Gateway Service Builder: modeling an OData service.

7.3 Modeling an OData Service

OData model creation is at the heart of application development in SAP Gateway. In this section, we'll give you an overview of the OData service modeling methods and discuss in detail the different modeling phases for an OData service.

There are two ways to create OData services with SAP Gateway:

1. **Service development**
   This is a code-based option and is very flexible for developing highly efficient and specialized services.

2. **Service generation**
   This is a quicker approach to building a service with a lot less effort. There are three options to generate SAP Gateway services with this approach, which you can choose from (see Figure 7.22):

   – *Option 1—RFC generation*: Service is generated using a tool called the *RFC/BOR Generator*.

   – *Option 2—Redefinition*: Allows you to define a service based on an existing data source or an existing SAP Gateway service.

– *Option 3—Model composition*: Allows you to mash up multiple existing services.

In the service-creation process, there are three main phases (see Figure 7.22):

- **Phase 1: Data model definition**
  In this phase, you define your model (i.e., define the entity types, entity sets, and associations your service will use).

- **Phase 2: Service implementation**
  In this phase, you implement the operations supported by the service. If you're using the RFC/BOR Generator, then the implementation takes place by mapping the OData model to the methods of the RFC function module or a BOR object.

- **Phase 3: Service maintenance**
  In this last phase, you publish the service. This is usually a one-time activity (i.e., you don't have to revisit this step, even if you update the model or implementation).

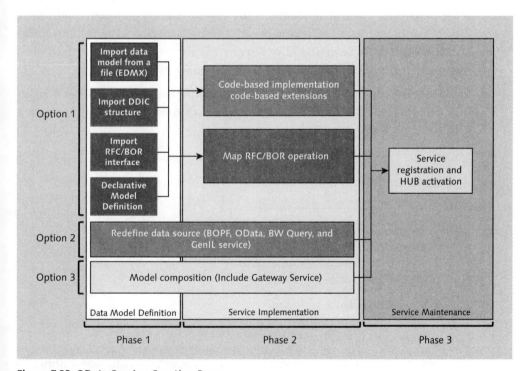

Figure 7.22 OData Service-Creation Process

Application developers can then create services in several ways and implement them by binding to the existing data sources or new data sources.

We covered the basic concepts of OData and SAP Gateway Service Builder in the previous sections. In the next sections, we'll look at the different steps for the service development and service-generation processes.

7.3.1   Importing OData Services

To reduce the time required to create entity types and complex types in your data model, SAP Gateway Service Builder provides various import options, used for both the service-development and service-generation processes. In this section, we'll look at the options for importing OData services. Under the **Data Model** folder (shown in Figure 7.23), you'll see different entries in which you can create different OData entities.

The first step to model an OData service is to create entity types and assign them some properties. You can create the entity types manually, you can import them (from the context menu, under **Import**, choose **Data Model from File**, **DDIC Structure**, **RFC/BOR Interface**, or **Search Help**), or you can redefine the services (from the context menu, under **Redefine**, choose **BOPF**, **OData**, **BW Query**, or **GenIL**).

In the sections that follow, we'll walk through the different functions shown in Figure 7.23 that can be used to import a data model: **Data Model from File**, **DDIC Structure**, **RFC/BOR Interface**, and **Search Help**.

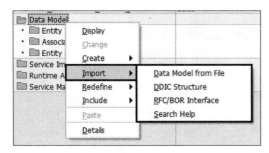

Figure 7.23 Import Functions

Data Model from File

The **Data Model from File** function allows you to import the data model from files such as EDMX files (created using Microsoft Visual Studio) or XML files (metadata files). An EDMX file is an XML file that defines the conceptual model, a storage model, and the mapping between these models. To import the EDMX file, right-click **Data Model** and choose **Import · Data Model from File**. This opens the **File Import** wizard.

Follow these steps to use the wizard:

1. Click **Browse** to import the data model file (see Figure 7.24).

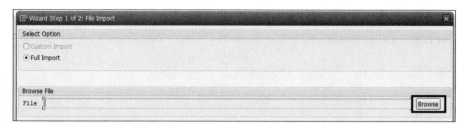

Figure 7.24 Importing File

2. Select the data model file, then click **Open** (see Figure 7.25). Click **Next**.

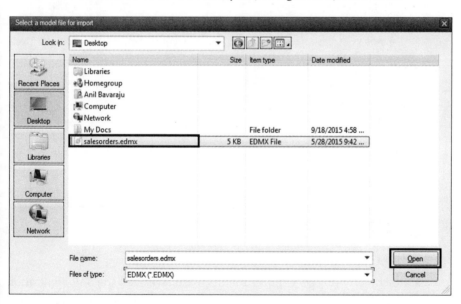

Figure 7.25 Selecting EDMX File

3. Click **Allow** to grant access to the file (see Figure 7.26).

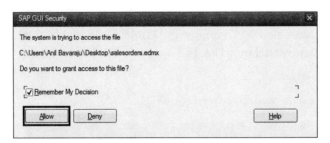

Figure 7.26 Granting Access

4. Click **Finish,** and you'll see the data model imported into the project (see Figure 7.27).

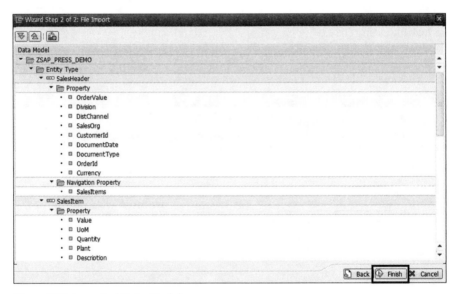

Figure 7.27 Imported Data Model

DDIC Structure

These data dictionary objects connect the database layer and the SAP application layer. For every transparent table, there is a physical table on the database. When a table is activated, a physical table definition is created in the database that the table definition stores in the ABAP Data Dictionary (DDIC). You can import views, database tables, or structures using the DDIC structure import method. You can then reuse the structure to develop new entity types and complex types easily, reducing the development time significantly.

To use this option, follow these steps:

1. Right-click **Data Model**, then choose **Import** · **DDIC Structure** to open the **DDIC Structure Import** wizard.

2. Enter the **Name**, and select an **ABAP Structure**. Click **Next** (see Figure 7.28).

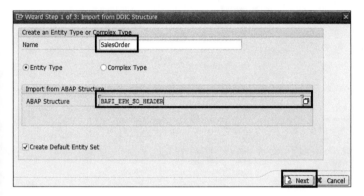

Figure 7.28 Importing DDIC Structure

3. Select the parameters/fields and click **Next** (see Figure 7.29).

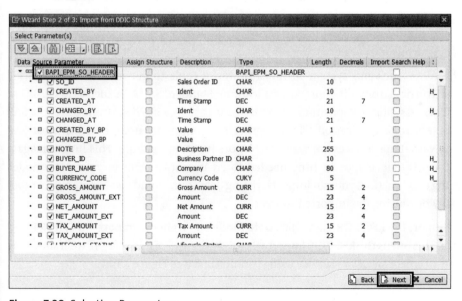

Figure 7.29 Selecting Parameters

4. Click **Finish**, and you'll see the data model imported into the project (see Figure 7.30).

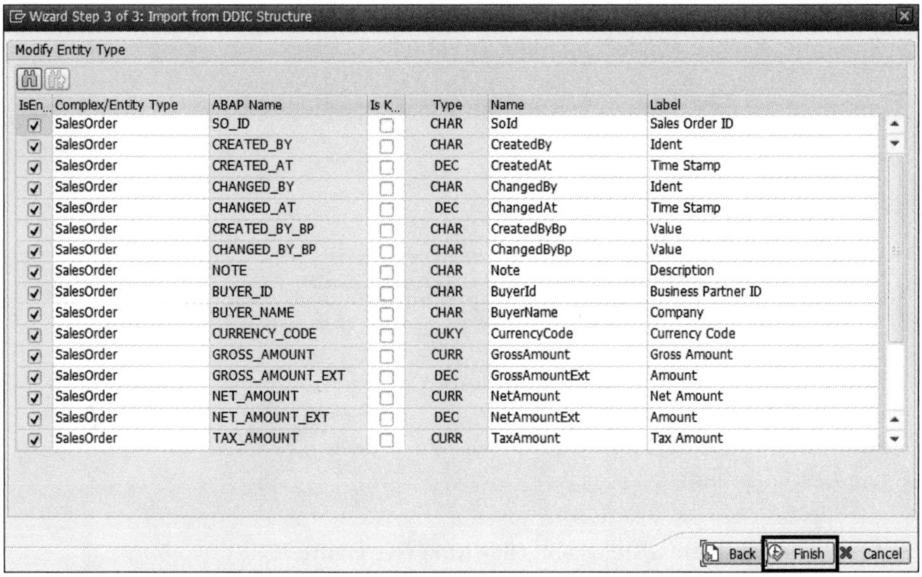

IsEn...	Complex/Entity Type	ABAP Name	Is K...	Type	Name	Label	
☑	SalesOrder	SO_ID	☐	CHAR	SoId	Sales Order ID	▲
☑	SalesOrder	CREATED_BY	☐	CHAR	CreatedBy	Ident	▼
☑	SalesOrder	CREATED_AT	☐	DEC	CreatedAt	Time Stamp	
☑	SalesOrder	CHANGED_BY	☐	CHAR	ChangedBy	Ident	
☑	SalesOrder	CHANGED_AT	☐	DEC	ChangedAt	Time Stamp	
☑	SalesOrder	CREATED_BY_BP	☐	CHAR	CreatedByBp	Value	
☑	SalesOrder	CHANGED_BY_BP	☐	CHAR	ChangedByBp	Value	
☑	SalesOrder	NOTE	☐	CHAR	Note	Description	
☑	SalesOrder	BUYER_ID	☐	CHAR	BuyerId	Business Partner ID	
☑	SalesOrder	BUYER_NAME	☐	CHAR	BuyerName	Company	
☑	SalesOrder	CURRENCY_CODE	☐	CUKY	CurrencyCode	Currency Code	
☑	SalesOrder	GROSS_AMOUNT	☐	CURR	GrossAmount	Gross Amount	
☑	SalesOrder	GROSS_AMOUNT_EXT	☐	DEC	GrossAmountExt	Amount	
☑	SalesOrder	NET_AMOUNT	☐	CURR	NetAmount	Net Amount	
☑	SalesOrder	NET_AMOUNT_EXT	☐	DEC	NetAmountExt	Amount	▲
☑	SalesOrder	TAX_AMOUNT	☐	CURR	TaxAmount	Tax Amount	▼

Figure 7.30 Imported DDIC Structure

RFC/BOR Interface

The ABAP back-end system includes powerful tools to generate services quickly based on data from different SAP applications. Standard SAP APIs such as RFCs, BAPIs, or Business Object Repository (BOR) make it easier to get data from different SAP Business Suite applications. This approach is commonly used, because most SAP Gateway OData services are based on remote function modules. This function again reduces the development time needed to create entity types in your data model. Using this function, you can import existing data sources and create new entity types easily by reusing the imported sources.

To import the RFC/BOR, right-click **Data Model**, then choose **Import · RFC/BOR Interface**. This opens the **RFC/BOR Import** wizard. At the end of this section, we'll show you how to create an OData service using this method (see Figure 7.31).

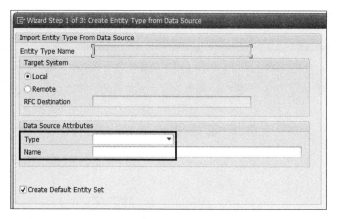

Figure 7.31 Importing RFC/BOR Interface

Search Help

The **Search Help** function allows you to import and reuse an existing search help from the system to create a new entity type. To enable the import of search help, follow these steps:

1. Right-click **Data Model**, then choose **Import • Search Help**. This opens the **Import from Search Help** wizard.

2. Enter the **Entity Type Name**, then select the **Import Search Help** field. Click **Next** (see Figure 7.32).

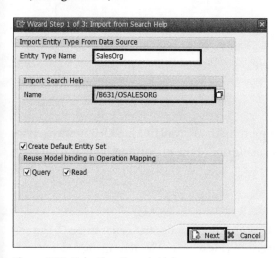

Figure 7.32 Selecting Search Help

3. Select the parameters and click **Next** (see Figure 7.33).

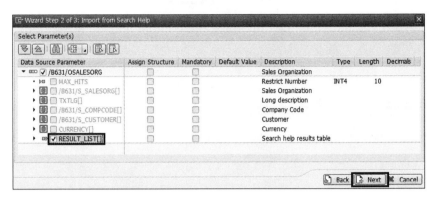

Figure 7.33 Selecting Parameters

4. Click **Finish**, and you'll see the search help imported into the project (see Figure 7.34).

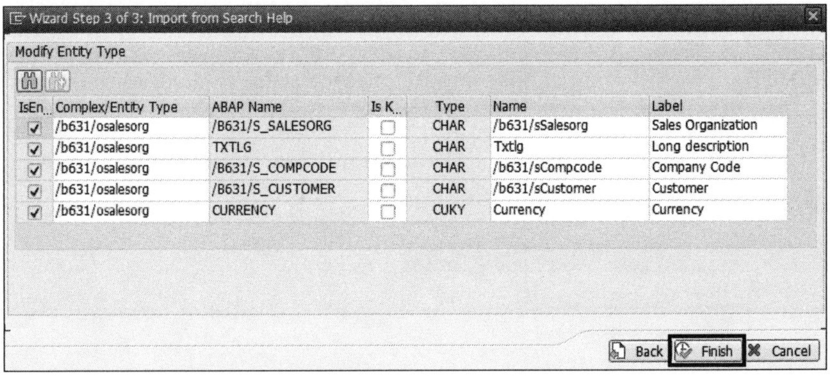

Figure 7.34 Imported Search Help

So far, we've reviewed the different import methods available in SAP Gateway Service Builder. Next, let's build a data model using one of the import methods and generate an OData service.

Exercise

In this exercise, we'll show you how to create a data model and generate an OData service by importing the RFC/BOR interface. In this scenario, we'll be using a Sales Order Header data (BOR) example.

Create a Project

The first step is to create a project by following these steps:

1. Log in to the ABAP back-end server, and run Transaction SEGW.

2. Create a new project by clicking 🗋.

3. Enter the **Project** name and **Description**, then click **Local Object** (see Figure 7.35).

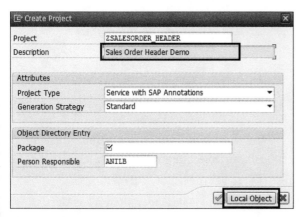

Figure 7.35 New Project

Import the BOR Interface to Create the Entity Types

Next, you need to import the BOR interface. Follow these steps:

1. Right-click on **Data Model**, select **Import**, then click **RFC/BOR Interface** (see Figure 7.36).

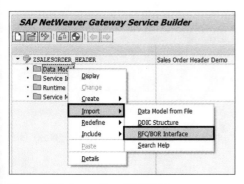

Figure 7.36 Importing RFC/BOR

2. As shown in Figure 7.37, enter the **Entity Type Name**.

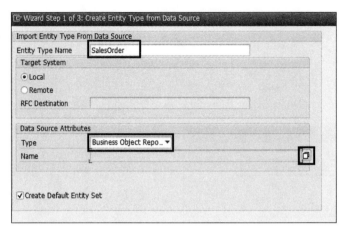

Figure 7.37 Selecting BOR

3. From the **Type** dropdown, select **Business Object Repository**.

4. Click on the **Name** field and press F4 to get the list of BOR methods.

5. From the list shown in Figure 7.38, expand **EpmSalesOrder**, then select **GetList**.

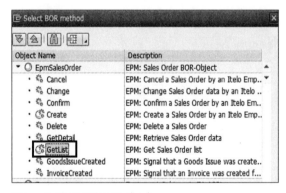

Figure 7.38 GetList Method

6. Click **Continue** ✅.

7. You should now see the selected BOR method in the **Name** field. Click **Next** (see Figure 7.39).

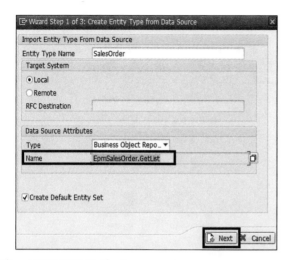

Figure 7.39 BOR Method

8. Select **Soheaderdata()**, then click **Next** (see Figure 7.40).

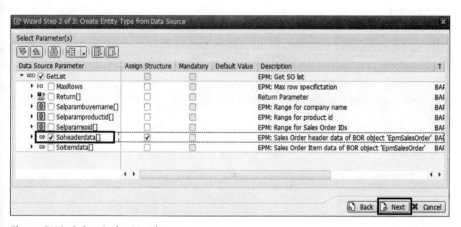

Figure 7.40 Sales Order Header

9. In the next screen, you'll see all the entities of **Soheaderdata**; Sales Order ID (**SO_ ID**) is automatically selected as a **Key**. Click **Finish**, and make sure there are no errors (see Figure 7.41).

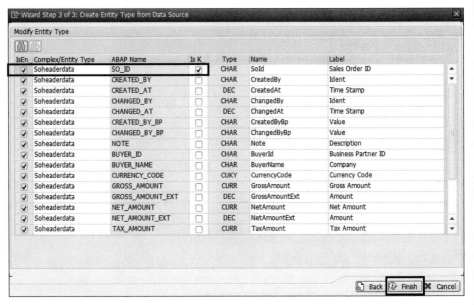

Figure 7.41 Sales Order ID

The **Entity Sets** and the **Service Implementation** are automatically created, as shown in Figure 7.42.

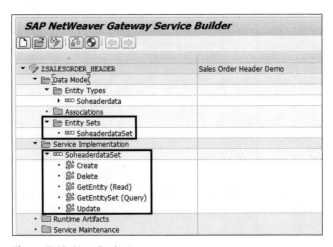

Figure 7.42 New Project

10. Save your project by clicking ▣.

Map to Data Source

In this step, you map the parameters of the data source with the properties of the entity set. Follow these steps:

1. Right-click **GetEntitySet(Query)**, then select **Map to Data Source** (see Figure 7.43).

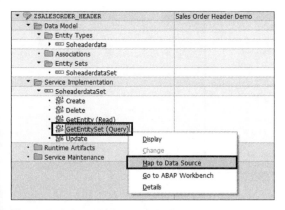

Figure 7.43 Map Entity to Data Source

2. As shown in Figure 7.44, from the **Type** dropdown list, select **Business Objects Repository**.

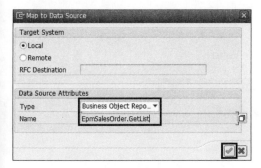

Figure 7.44 Data Source Attributes

3. Enter "EmpSalesOrder.GetList" in the **Name** field.

4. Click **Continue** ✅.

5. Click on the **Propose Mapping** button to map the fields, and you're automatically provided with the mapping proposal between entity sets and the data source. SAP Gateway Service Builder automatically performs certain checks to verify the mapping (see Figure 7.45).

Mapping of Operation GetEntitySet (Query) for SoheaderdataSet					
P	Entity Set property	Constant	Map dir	Data Source Parameter	Set Range
	SoId		⇐	Soheaderdata\SO_ID	
□	CreatedBy		⇐	Soheaderdata\CREATED_BY	
□	CreatedAt		⇐	Soheaderdata\CREATED_AT	
□	ChangedBy		⇐	Soheaderdata\CHANGED_BY	
□	ChangedAt		⇐	Soheaderdata\CHANGED_AT	
□	CreatedByBp		⇐	Soheaderdata\CREATED_BY_BP	
□	ChangedByBp		⇐	Soheaderdata\CHANGED_BY_BP	
□	Note		⇐	Soheaderdata\NOTE	
□	BuyerId		⇐	Soheaderdata\BUYER_ID	
□	BuyerName		⇐	Soheaderdata\BUYER_NAME	
□	CurrencyCode		⇐	Soheaderdata\CURRENCY_CODE	
□	GrossAmount		⇐	Soheaderdata\GROSS_AMOUNT	
□	GrossAmountExt		⇐	Soheaderdata\GROSS_AMOUNT_EXT	
□	NetAmount		⇐	Soheaderdata\NET_AMOUNT	
□	NetAmountExt		⇐	Soheaderdata\NET_AMOUNT_EXT	
□	TaxAmount		⇐	Soheaderdata\TAX_AMOUNT	
□	TaxAmountExt		⇐	Soheaderdata\TAX_AMOUNT_EXT	
□	LifecycleStatus		⇐	Soheaderdata\LIFECYCLE_STATUS	
□	BillingStatus		⇐	Soheaderdata\BILLING_STATUS	
□	DeliveryStatus		⇐	Soheaderdata\DELIVERY_STATUS	

Figure 7.45 Propose Mapping

6. Save your project by clicking 🖫.

Generate Runtime Objects

The next step is to generate runtime objects:

1. Select the project, and then click **Generate** 🌐. On the next screen, you'll see the model and service definition details.

2. Click **Continue** ✅, or press ⌜Enter⌟ (see Figure 7.46).

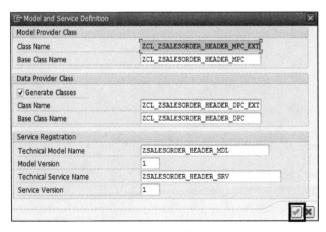

Figure 7.46 Generating Runtime Objects

3. On the **Create Object Directory Entry** screen, click **Local Object** (see Figure 7.47).

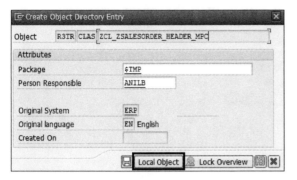

Figure 7.47 Saving Local Object

You should now be able to see the generated MPC, DPC, and service registration details under the **Runtime Artifacts** folder (see Figure 7.48).

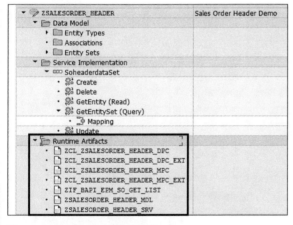

Figure 7.48 Runtime Artifacts

Register the OData Service

In this step, you'll register the service to the SAP Gateway hub. If the SAP Gateway deployment is a hub deployment, then you must register the technical detail service with the SAP Gateway system. The following are the steps to register a service with the system. If your deployment is an embedded deployment (i.e., SAP Gateway components are deployed in the SAP Business Suite), then you can skip this step because the technical details will be registered automatically.

Follow these steps:

1. Right-click the SAP Gateway hub system under the **Service Maintenance** folder, and select **Register** (see Figure 7.49).

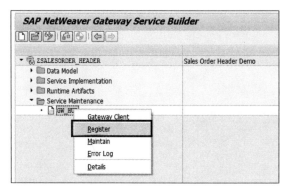

Figure 7.49 Registering Service

2. Press ⌐F4⌐ to select the system, select the SAP Gateway system, and click **Continue** ☑.

3. Select **Local Object**, then click **Continue** ☑ (see Figure 7.50).

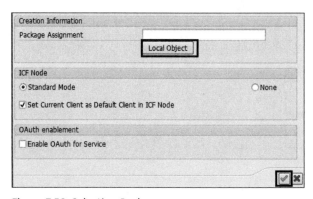

Figure 7.50 Selecting Package

Activate the OData Service

Now that you've registered the service, it's time to activate it in the SAP Gateway server. Follow these steps:

1. Run Transaction IWFND/MAINT_SERVICE.

2. Click the **Add Selected Services** button.

3. Enter "LOCAL" in the **System Alias** field.

4. Enter "ZSALES*" as the **External Service Name** and press ⌈Enter⌉.

5. Select **ZSALESORDER_HEADER_SRV**, then click the **Add Selected Services** button (see Figure 7.51).

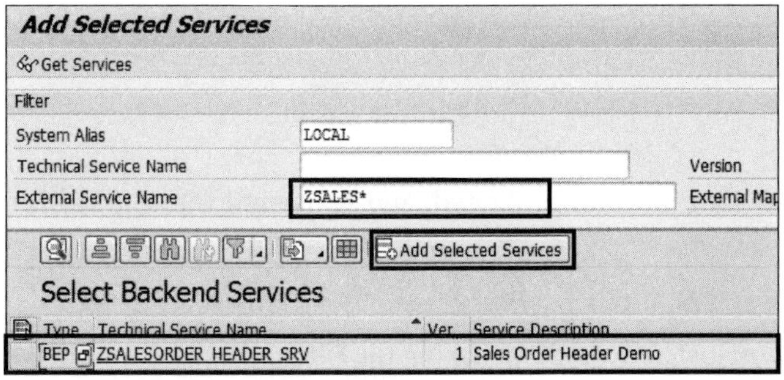

Figure 7.51 Adding Selected Service

6. Select **Local Object**, then click **Continue** ☑ (see Figure 7.52).

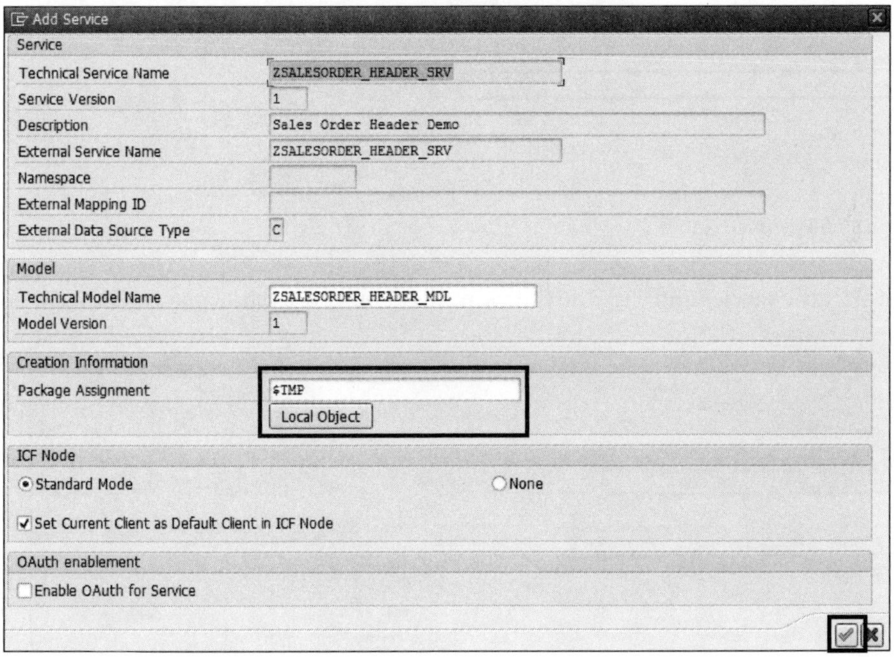

Figure 7.52 Adding Service

7. In the pop-up that appears, click **Continue** ☑ (see Figure 7.53).

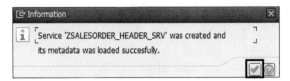

Figure 7.53 Information Pop-up

Test the OData Service

Now that you've successfully modeled, generated, and registered the service, you need to test it. Follow these steps:

1. Go back to the **Activate and Maintain Services** screen by clicking ⊛.

2. Filter the service that you just activated by clicking the **Filter** button.

3. On the **Filter for Service Catalog** screen, enter "ZSALESORDER_HEADER_SRV" in the **External Service Name** field, then click **Continue** ☑ (see Figure 7.54).

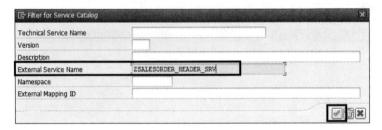

Figure 7.54 Service Name

4. Select the service and click the **Gateway Client** button, as shown in Figure 7.55.

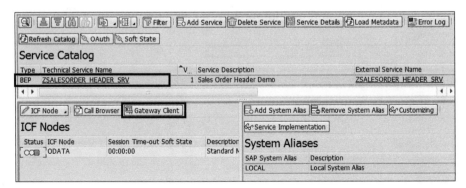

Figure 7.55 Service Catalog

5. The SAP Gateway client opens with the Sales Order Header service. Click the **Execute** button (see Figure 7.56).

Figure 7.56 Testing Service

You should now receive the HTTP response with the status code **200** (see Figure 7.57).

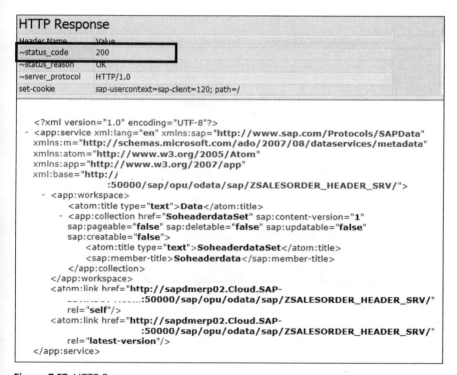

Figure 7.57 HTTP Response

6. To view the sales order data, add **SoheaderdataSet** to the following **Request URI**: **/sap/opu/odata/sap/ZSALESORDER_HEADER_SRV/** (see Figure 7.58). Click **Execute**.

Figure 7.58 Request URI

In the **HTTP Response** area, you'll see the sales order header information with the status code **200** (see Figure 7.59).

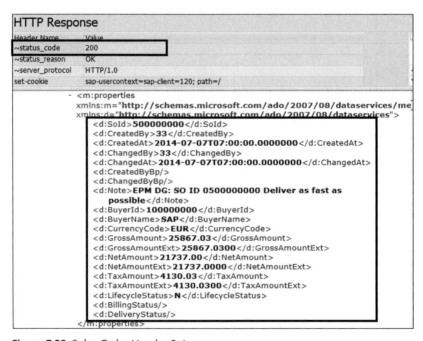

Figure 7.59 Sales Order Header Set

In this section, you learned how to create a data model by using import methods. In the next section, we'll show you a different way to generate an OData model, by redefining an existing service.

7.3.2   Redefining OData Services

Using SAP Gateway Service Builder, you can redefine a service from an existing OData service that was created using SAP Gateway and from the external services developed using different back-end frameworks (SAP BW query service, GenIL Service). In this section, we'll give an overview of each of these functions. Figure 7.60 shows the dropdown to access the **Redefine** option.

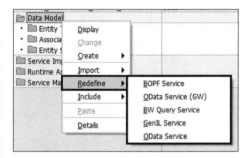

Figure 7.60 Redefine Functions

You use redefining techniques when you want to extend an existing data model by adding new entities, adding a new property to an existing entity, or adding an association or navigation property. Using these redefining methods, you can quickly and easily build a data model and extend it in SAP Gateway Service Builder. After the extended data model is generated, SAP Gateway Service Builder generates a new OData service with the new changes you added in the data model.

In the sections that follow, we'll go through the options shown in Figure 7.60.

BOPF Service

The BOPF service allows you to consume business objects in the Business Object Processing Framework (BOPF) by using SAP Gateway BOPF Integration (GBI). This framework is based on object-oriented ABAP, which provides a set of generic services and functionalities to speed up and modularize development. To use this option, follow these steps:

1. Right-click **Data Model** and choose **Redefine • BOPF Service**. This opens the **BOPF Configuration** wizard.
2. Select the **Business Object** and the **Default Query**, then click **Next** (see Figure 7.61).

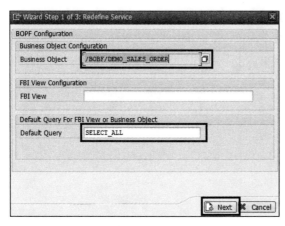

Figure 7.61 BOPF Configuration

3. In the **Service Registration** area, enter descriptions in the **Description** fields for the **Model Name** and the **Service Name**. Click **Next** (see Figure 7.62).

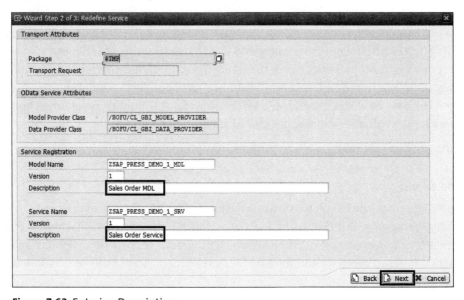

Figure 7.62 Entering Descriptions

4. Select the fields and click **Finish**. You should now see the fields from the business objects added to your project (see Figure 7.63).

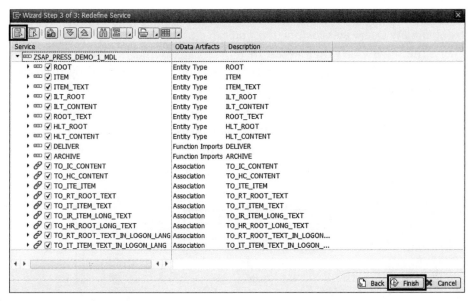

Figure 7.63 Redefining BOPF

OData Service (GW)

Using the OData Service (GW) function, you can extend an existing OData service created in an SAP Gateway OData service. You can not only extend the existing OData service but also overwrite an existing one by using this function in SAP Gateway Service Builder. In Chapter 9, Section 9.2, we'll explain the step-by-step process of how to extend a transactional app by redefining it using this method.

To access this option, right-click **Data Model** and choose **Redefine · OData Service (GW)**. This opens the **OData Service** wizard (see Figure 7.64).

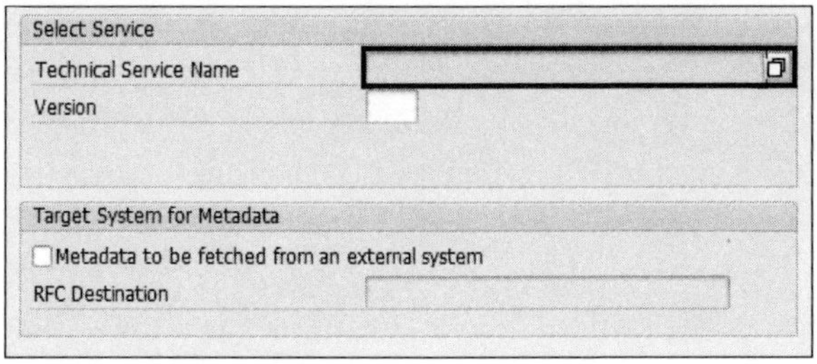

Figure 7.64 OData Service

BW Query Service

Using the BW Query Service function, you can create SAP Fiori apps on an SAP BW query. The SAP BW Easy Queries feature provides an external interface for accessing analytic queries in SAP BW. At the end of this section, we'll show you how to create a data model and how to generate an OData service using this function.

To use this option, right-click **Data Model** and choose **Redefine · BW Query Service**. This opens the **Service Generator for BW Query Service** wizard (Figure 7.65). The **Query Name** field is where you enter the name of the SAP BW query. We'll discuss this method in greater detail in an exercise at the end of this section.

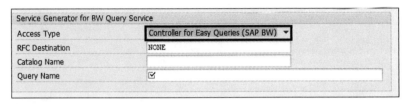

Figure 7.65 SAP BW Query Service

GenIL Service

Generic Interaction Layer (GenIL) is the connection between the Business Object Layer (BOL) and the back-end business engine. This layer handles the data transfer from the BOL to the APIs of the business engine. By using this function in SAP Gateway Service Builder, you can create a data model from this framework.

To access this option, right-click **Data Model** and choose **Redefine · GenIL Service**. Using the input help will list all the GenIL objects that are available (see Figure 7.66). A plug-in in SAP Gateway Service Builder provides a wizard that will guide you through the steps to create a service using this framework.

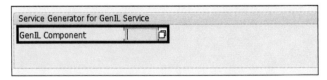

Figure 7.66 GenIL Service

OData Service

This function lets you create a data model on an existing OData service. This function is different from the OData Service (GW) option, because the latter will let you redefine an OData service generated using SAP Gateway. In this function, you define the **HTTP Destination** and the **Service Namespace**.

To use this function, follow these steps:

1. Right-click **Data Model** and choose **Redefine · OData Service**. This opens the **External Service** wizard.

2. Enter the **HTTP Destination**, **Service Namespace**, and **Service Name**. Click **Next** (see Figure 7.67).

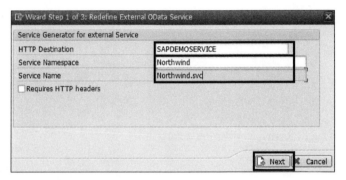

Figure 7.67 Service Name

OData Service Example

We used an example OData service: *http://services.odata.org/Northwind/Northwind.svc.* You need to define this RFC destination using Transaction SM59.

---

3. Enter descriptions in the **Description** fields for the model and service, then click **Next** (see Figure 7.68).

4. Select the fields and click **Finish** on the last screen to create a data model in the project.

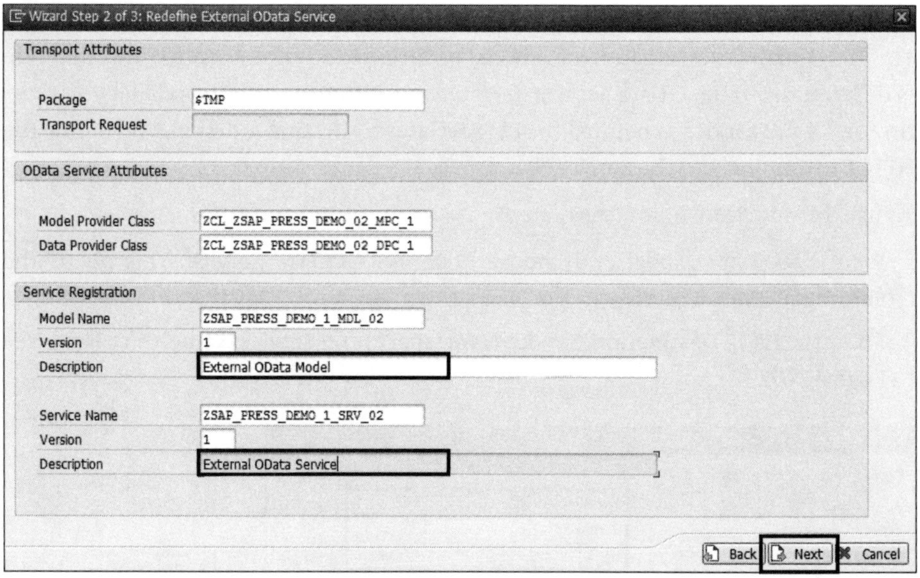

Figure 7.68 Service Registration Details

Next, we'll round out this section with an example exercise.

Exercise

Let's look at a use case in which a customer needs a custom SAP Fiori app on an SAP BEx query. To achieve this, you first need to understand how to generate an OData service based on an SAP BEx query, which we'll explain next. We made a copy of the OFIN_PA_T10_Q0001 query and saved it as ZOFIN_PA_T10_Q0001. We'll be using this query in the remainder of this section.

The following sections walk through the individual steps.

Enable External Access to an SAP BEx Query

The first step is to enable the SAP BW query for external access:

1. Open the SAP BEx query ZOFIN_PA_T10_Q0001 in the SAP BEx query designer.

2. Go to the **Extended** tab in the **Properties** of the query.

3. Check the **By Easy Query** box, then save the query (see Figure 7.69).

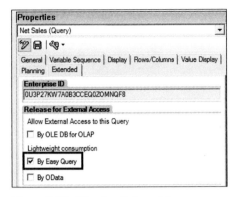

Figure 7.69 Allowing External Access

Generate OData Service

In this step, you'll generate an OData service on top of an SAP BEx query:

1. Log in to the front-end server, and run Transaction SEGW.

2. Create a new project by clicking [🗋].

3. Enter the project technical name and description, then click **Continue** [✓] (see Figure 7.70).

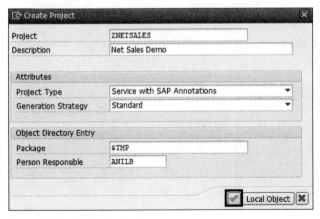

Figure 7.70 Create Project

4. Right-click the **Data Model** folder and choose **Redefine · BW Query Service** (see Figure 7.71).

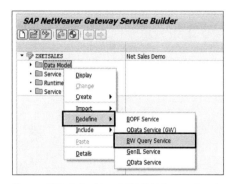

Figure 7.71 Selecting SAP BW Query Service

5. Select **Controller for Easy Queries (SAP BW)** from the **Access Type** dropdown.

6. Click ⬚ to open the list of queries (see Figure 7.72).

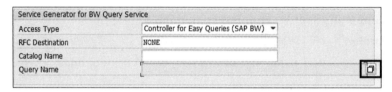

Figure 7.72 Query Name

7. You should now see the query for which you set the easy query property, as shown in Figure 7.73.

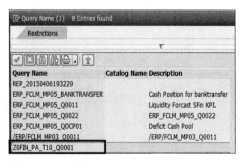

Figure 7.73 Selecting SAP BW Query

8. Click **Continue** ✓.

9. You should now see the SAP BEx query in the **Query Name** field. Click the **Next** button.

10. Enter descriptions for the model name and service name, then click **Next** (see Figure 7.74).

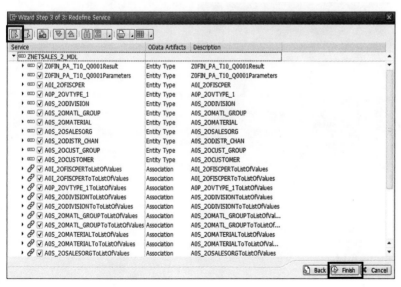

Figure 7.74 Entering Description

11. Select all services by clicking , then click **Finish** (see Figure 7.75).

Figure 7.75 Selecting All Objects

You should now see the data model with the **Entity Types**, **Associations**, **Entity Sets**, and so on (see Figure 7.76).

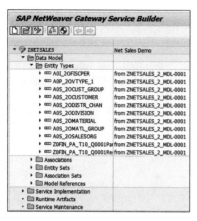

Figure 7.76 Redefined Data Model

12. Generate the runtime objects by selecting the project folder and clicking **Generate** 🌐.

13. You'll see the technical details of the MOD, DPC, and service. Click **Continue** ✅ (see Figure 7.77).

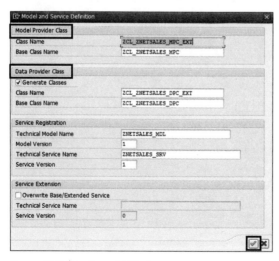

Figure 7.77 Runtime Artifacts

14. Select **Local Object**.

Add the Service to SAP Gateway

In this section, you'll add the service to SAP Gateway. Follow these steps:

1. Run Transaction IWFND/MAINT_SERVICE.

2. Click **Add Service**.

3. Search for the external service named "ZNETSALES_SRV".

4. Select **ZNETSALES_SRV**, then click the **Add Selected Services** button (see Figure 7.78).

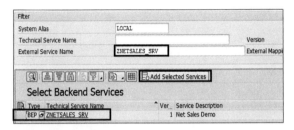

Figure 7.78 Adding Selected Service

5. Click **Continue** ✅ (see Figure 7.79).

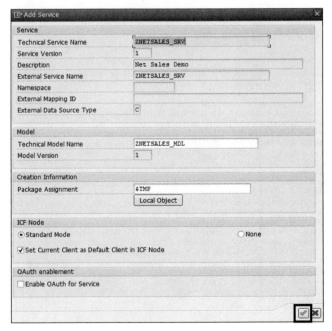

Figure 7.79 Adding Service

6. Click **Continue** ☑ again to close the information pop-up.

Test the Service

In this section, you'll finally test the service. Follow these steps:

1. Click **Back** to return to the **Activate and Maintain** screen.

2. Filter **Service Catalog** for "ZNETSALES_SRV".

3. Select the service, then click **Gateway Client** (see Figure 7.80).

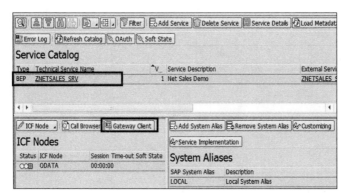

Figure 7.80 Testing Service

4. Click **Execute** to test the service (see Figure 7.81).

Figure 7.81 SAP BW Query Elements

7.3.3   Include SAP Gateway OData Service

The methods we discussed in Section 7.3.1 and Section 7.3.2 are limited to the scope of the underlying data source. The third way to create an OData service is through mashups. The **Include** function is used when you want to combine your existing data model with a different data model; for example, you can mash up two or more services to form a completely new service without changing the existing service. You can access the **Include Service Creation** wizard by right-clicking **Data Model** and choosing **Include · OData Service (GW)** (see Figure 7.82).

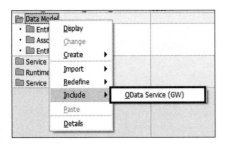

Figure 7.82 Include Services

Enter the **Technical Service Name** and **Version**, then click **Continue** ☑ (see Figure 7.83).

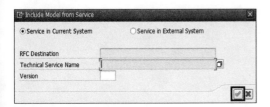

Figure 7.83 Technical Service Name

7.4   Summary

This chapter provided an overview of OData services and the SAP Gateway Service Builder. We discussed basic OData concepts via an example Create Sales Order service. We then covered SAP Gateway Service Builder, discussing details about data model elements such as entity types, associations, entity sets, service implementation, and service maintenance. Next, we provided an overview of OData modeling and the different methods to create a data model. We also provided step-by-step instructions for generating an OData service by importing an RFC/BOR interface.

We then covered how to create the OData service using redefining methods in SAP Gateway Service Builder. Finally, we walked you through the steps for creating a data model and an OData service using an SAP BEx query as a data source.

In Chapter 8, we'll introduce you to the SAP Web IDE tool and the process of developing SAP Fiori apps using an OData service.

PART III

Custom Development and Extension

Chapter 8
Introduction to SAP Web IDE

This chapter provides an overview of SAP Web IDE and how it can be used to create or extend SAP Fiori apps.

SAP Web IDE is the environment used to create and extend SAP Fiori apps. In this chapter, we'll take a deep dive into SAP Web IDE to see how it works. We'll begin in Section 8.1 with an overview of SAP Web IDE and how to leverage this tool in conjunction with developing and extending SAP Fiori applications. In Section 8.2, we'll show you how to set up SAP Web IDE with SAP Cloud Platform.

In Section 8.3, we'll turn our attention to the technical aspects of this tool and look at the different phases of the end-to-end SAP Fiori application development process, from designing the application to developing it to previewing the app with the simulator to finally deploying the app into different application landscapes.

We'll also discuss the various templates and the WYSIWYG layout editor capabilities for nonprogrammers. After each phase of the development process, we'll include steps to show you how to create a Master Detail transactional app using an EDMX file. We'll then demonstrate how to create mock data to test the app, and then deploy it.

Version

During the writing of this chapter, we used SAP Web IDE – March 2017 version.

8.1 SAP Web IDE Overview

SAP Web IDE is a browser-based tool that enables developers to build new UXs. It's designed to shorten the end-to-end application development lifecycle, from prototyping to developing to instantly previewing to deploying SAP Fiori applications.

SAP Web IDE accelerates building modern applications for mobile and desktop using the latest UI technologies. It's a flexible tool with robust code editors for developers who want to develop applications quickly and efficiently. In addition, this tool also empowers nonprogrammers to build applications using wizards and templates.

In this section, we'll look at the architecture of SAP Web IDE, then provide an outline of its advantages over technologies such as the Eclipse IDE.

8.1.1   Architecture

From a bird's-eye view, Figure 8.1 shows the position of SAP Web IDE in the SAP Cloud Platform architecture, in which the full functionality is available.

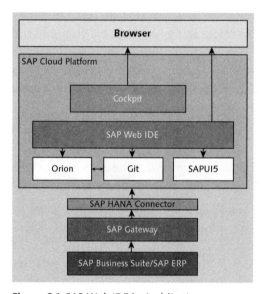

Figure 8.1 SAP Web IDE in Architecture

The following elements are found in the SAP Web IDE architecture:

- **SAP Cloud Platform**
  This is a PaaS via which users can build, deploy, run, and manage applications in the cloud.

- **SAP HANA cockpit**
  This is a central managing cockpit via which users manage all the key information about applications and activities through a web-based interface.

- **SAP Web IDE**
  This is where all the development takes place.

- **Orion**

  Orion provides a workspace where the projects or files are located and enables users to work on their projects that are stored in the workspace.

- **Git**

  This is a repository that manages the versions of your applications, controlling your source code versioning.

- **SAPUI5**

  This is the technology used to build your applications.

- **SAP Cloud Platform cloud connector**

  This is the connector that integrates SAP Web IDE and SAP Cloud Platform securely.

- **SAP Gateway**

  This is the connector that connects SAP Web IDE to your SAP system, with access to OData functionality.

8.1.2 Advantages

Although some developers continue to use an Eclipse IDE for their application development projects, there are several advantages to using SAP Web IDE.

Figure 8.2 shows today's method and process for developing an application: You start by installing the IDE, plug-ins, and libraries, then code the application from scratch, then finally wait for reviews.

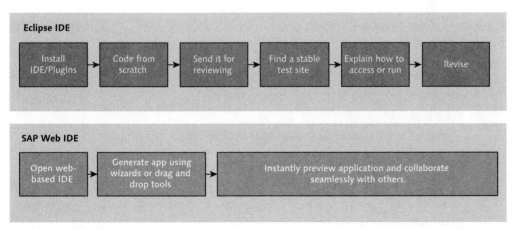

Figure 8.2 SAP Web IDE vs. Eclipse IDE

8

As shown in Figure 8.2, SAP Web IDE has one particularly visible advantage over Eclipse IDEs: the speed at which it allows developers to deliver applications. This is because SAP Web IDE has the advantage of ready-made templates for SAP Fiori apps. Therefore, you have the option either to develop an application using the templates and run the app with mock data or to start development by directly importing the service from the SAP Gateway server.

In addition, installing and updating the Eclipse IDE for developers isn't an easy task. Making sure that all developers are on the same version is an even bigger challenge, because Eclipse has multiple versions, such as Juno and Kepler. SAP Web IDE, on the other hand, just requires subscribing to the IDE service and running SAP Web IDE; it's that simple.

When it comes to developing applications, SAP Web IDE is the next-generation cloud-based development environment. It provides real-time code review and testing in the modern pipeline—allowing more than one person to code in real time by connecting to the same shared repository—and instantly previews applications. These features allow developers to collaborate with business experts and designers to fulfill end-user requirements and expectations more effectively.

8.2   Setting Up SAP Web IDE with SAP Cloud Platform

In this section, we'll show you how to set up a development environment with SAP Web IDE on SAP Cloud Platform. Currently, SAP Cloud Platform is available for productive use in the following locations:

- **Australia**
  https://account.ap1.hana.ondemand.com/cockpit
- **Europe**
  https://account.hana.ondemand.com/cockpit
- **US East**
  https://account.us1.hana.ondemand.com/cockpit
- **US West**
  https://account.us2.hana.ondemand.com/cockpit

In addition, SAP is offering SAP HANA cockpit for trial use at *https://account.hanatrial.ondemand.com/cockpit*.

To set up the development environment with SAP Web IDE on SAP Cloud Platform, follow these steps:

1. Start the SAP HANA cockpit at *https://account.hanatrial.ondemand.com/cockpit*.
2. Enter your login credentials, and click **Log On.** If you don't have an account, you can register by clicking the **Register** button.
3. After you're logged on, your screen should look like Figure 8.3.
4. Click **Services**.

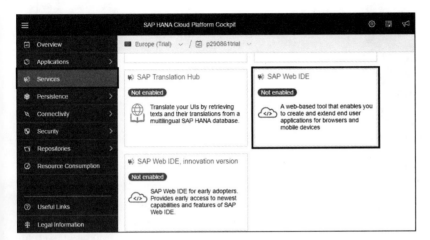

Figure 8.3 SAP HANA Cockpit

5. Click the **SAP Web IDE** tile.
6. Click **Enable**, then click **Save** (see Figure 8.4).

Figure 8.4 Enable

329

7. Click **Open SAP Web IDE** under the **Service Description** area to launch SAP Web IDE (see Figure 8.5).

Figure 8.5 SAP Web IDE

You've now successfully enabled and launched SAP Web IDE. Next, you need to create a connection to the back-end system. Then, we'll show you how to create a destination for multiusage. The destination setup depends on where the back-end server exists (i.e., if it's available publicly via the Internet or exists behind a firewall).

The following steps will configure the destination if the ABAP back-end server is publicly accessible on the Internet:

1. Go to the homepage of the SAP HANA cockpit and click **Destinations**. Click **New Destination** (see Figure 8.6).

2. Enter or select the following information (see Figure 8.7):
   - **Name**: Enter "Connection1".
   - **Type**: Choose **HTTP**.
   - **Description**: Enter "Connection 1" (description will be visible in SAP Web IDE during app creation).
   - **URL**: Enter "<protocol>://<host>:<port>".
   - **Proxy Type**: Choose **Internet**.
   - **Cloud Connector Version**: Choose **2**.
   - **Authentication**: Choose **NoAuthentication.**

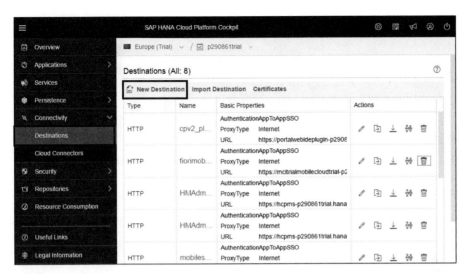

Figure 8.6 New Destination

Destination Configuration

* Name:	NineBoards-Fiori
Type:	HTTP
Description:	NineBoards-Fiori
* URL:	https://nineboards01.nineboards.com:8201
Proxy Type:	OnPremise
Authentication:	NoAuthentication

Additional Properties   New Property

No additional properties defined

Save   Cancel

Figure 8.7 Destination Properties

SAP Cloud Platform Cloud Connector

If your back-end server resides behind a firewall, then you need to set up the SAP Cloud Platform cloud connector. The cloud connector integrates SAP Cloud Platform with existing on-premise systems. There are two versions of the cloud connector: the developer version, which can be installed on your system easily without administrator rights, and the productive version, which requires administrator access to install.

Installation of the SAP Cloud Platform cloud connector is simple and straightforward. Download the developer version from *https://tools.hana.ondemand.com/#cloud*, and follow the instructions from the online help. After you add the back-end system to the cloud connector, you need to add the destination in SAP Web IDE with the following details (refer to the previous step):

- **URL**: "<protocol>://<virtual host>:<virtual port>"
- **Proxy Type: OnPremise**

3. Click **New Property** under the **Additional Properties** section, then enter the following values:
   - **WebIDEUsage**: This property defines access to the URL paths:
     - **odata_abap** grants access to the OData functionality of SAP Gateway.
     - **odata_gen** grants access to the generic OData functionality.
     - **ui5_execute_abap** grants access to execute SAPUI5 applications from the SAPUI5 ABAP Repository.
     - **dev_abap** grants access to develop apps or deploy apps to the SAPUI5 ABAP Repository.
     - **bsp_execute_abap** grants access to work with fact sheet apps.
     - **plugin_repository** grants access to the optional plugins.
     - **odata_xs grants** access to SAP HANA XS OData services.
   - **sap-client: 120** (the SAP client from the ABAP system)
   - **WebIDEEnabled: true**
   - **WebIDESystem: ERP** (**WebIDESystem** is the SAP system ID)
4. After you've entered the values, your screen should look like Figure 8.8.
5. Click **Save** to save the connection.

You're now set up to use SAP Web IDE to develop SAP Fiori apps. In Chapter 9 and the remainder of this book, we'll be using this connection to create or extend SAP Fiori apps.

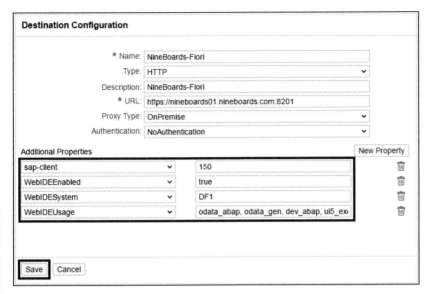

Figure 8.8 Additional Destination Properties

8.3 Development Process Overview

Before we start developing applications or discussing the development process, let's take a moment to explore SAP Web IDE's features. After you log in to SAP Web IDE, you should see the development page (see Figure 8.9).

As shown in Figure 8.9, the menu bar ❶ gives access to all the functions and features available in SAP Web IDE. Below the menu bar is the toolbar ❷, which provides access to some of the most commonly used features, such as **Save**, **Delete**, **Run**, and so on. On the left side of the screen are the **Welcome** page and the **Development** preferences ❸. When you click the **Development** button, you'll open a screen area next to it, which shows the list of projects and files within a project ❹. You can open a file and see its contents on the right-hand side in the code editor area ❺. If you open several files, then those files will be shown as tabs. On the right side of the screen, you'll find features such as **Search**, **Git Pane**, **Git History**, and the **Collaboration** pane, with features such as SAP Jam, API Reference, and Outline ❻.

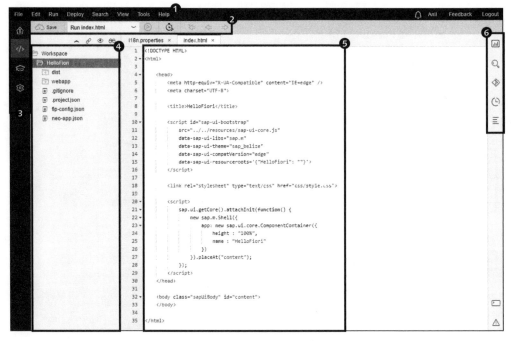

Figure 8.9 SAP Web IDE Interface

To further understand SAP Web IDE, we need to examine each of the phases in the development process. The sections that follow walk through each phase of the development process—from creation to deployment.

8.3.1   Create

During the create phase of the SAP Web IDE development process, you can start by either creating a new project or importing an application. Various methods exist for creating new projects in SAP Web IDE, and each of these methods depends on the kind of application you want to create and the data source for your app.

There are three methods for creating new projects using SAP Web IDE, as shown in Figure 8.10:

- **New Project from Template**
- **New Project from Sample Application**
- **New Extension Project**

Figure 8.10 Creating New Project in SAP Web IDE

Alternatively, you can create a new project from the menu bar as well by going to **File · New**. The same new project options are available there.

Next, we'll look at these three options in closer detail.

New Project from Template

Choose **New Project from Template** if you want to create an application using standard templates provided by SAP. SAP Web IDE is more than just a tool to build SAP Fiori apps; currently, there are 15 templates (see Figure 8.11), which you can use to build a Basic SAPUI5 Project, use for Plugin Development, use to build SAP Fiori Applications, or use to build SAPUI5 Mobile Applications.

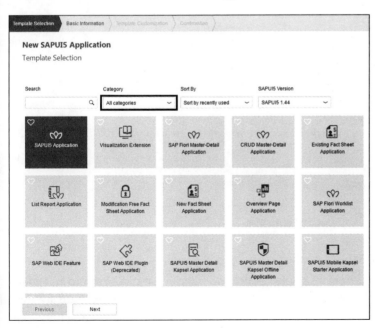

Figure 8.11 All Templates

We'll be focusing only on the templates for SAP Fiori apps. The following is a list of templates use specifically for developing SAP Fiori apps. With these eight templates, you can develop transactional apps and fact sheet apps (Figure 8.12):

1. **SAP Fiori Master-Detail Application** (transactional apps)

2. **CRUD Master Detail Application** (transactional apps)

3. **SAP Fiori Worklist Application** (transactional apps)

4. **Transactional App for SAP Event Management** (transactional apps)

5. **Existing Fact Sheet Application** (fact sheet apps)

6. **Modification Free Fact Sheet Application** (fact sheet apps)

7. **New Fact Sheet Application** (fact sheet apps)

8. **SAPUI5 Application**

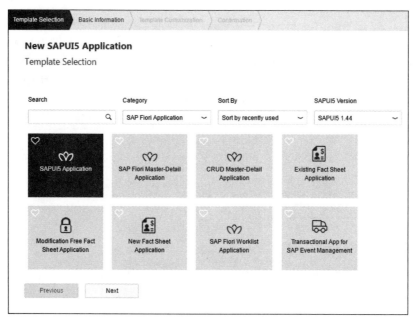

Figure 8.12 SAP Fiori Application Templates

New Project from Sample Application

Choose **New Project from a Sample Application** when you want to refer to an application to build your own SAP Fiori application based on it. Currently, there are three sample applications, and all three samples are specifically for transactional app development (see Figure 8.13):

- **Shop**

  This is a full-screen app that shows a shopping scenario on the Enterprise Performance Model (EPM).

- **Manage Products**

  This is a Master Detail app that shows creation and maintenance of product entities for EPM.

- **Approve Purchase Orders**

  This is a Master Detail app that shows the approval process based on EPM.

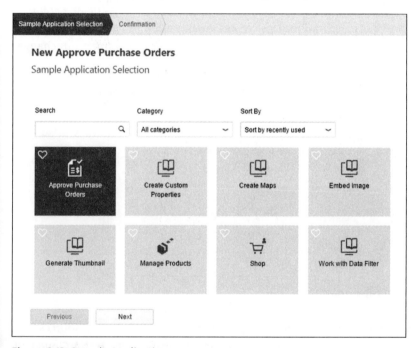

Figure 8.13 Sample Applications

- **Create Custom Properties**

  This is a sample application to create your own property and integrate it with SAP Lumira property editor.

- **Create Maps**

  This is a sample Google Heatmap extension showing how to use the Google map service.

- **Embed Image**

  This sample application shows how to use image files in the extensions.

- **Generate Thumbnail**
  With this sample app you can create a thumbnail view in SAP Lumira by adding custom code in exportToSVGString().
- **Work with Data Filter**
  This is an SAP Lumira visualization extension that demonstrates the filters/excludes/drill context menu options of SAP BusinessObjects Lumira.

New Extension Project

Choose **New Extension Project** if you want to alter the functionality or appearance of an original SAP Fiori application. This creates an extension project; the changes are added only to the extension project, so the original application remains unchanged (see Figure 8.14).

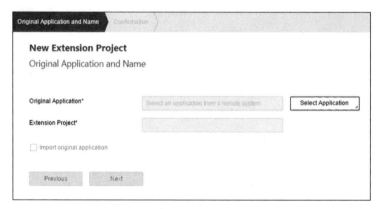

Figure 8.14 Extension Project

You can also begin a project by importing an existing application and resources from one of four places—choose **Archive, SAPUI5 ABAP Repository, SAP HANA Cloud Platform**, or **Clone from Git Repository**—into the SAP Web IDE workspace, as shown in Figure 8.15.

Figure 8.15 Importing Applications into SAP Web IDE

Alternatively, you can import an application from the menu bar as well by choosing **File · Import**. To clone a Git repository, go to **File · Git**.

Exercise

In the previous chapter, we discussed the EDMX file in detail and the terms of an EDM. Next, you'll use an EDMX file as a source and develop your first SAP Fiori application in SAP Web IDE. In the create phase, you'll open SAP Web IDE and create a project from a template. Follow these steps:

1. Log in to the SAP HANA cockpit, and start SAP Web IDE by clicking the **SAP Web IDE** application from your services.

2. Click on the **Open SAP Web IDE** URL to launch SAP Web IDE

3. Create a new project by clicking **New Project from Template** (see Figure 8.16).

Figure 8.16 New Project from Template

4. Select **SAP Fiori Master-Detail Application** and click **Next** (see Figure 8.17).

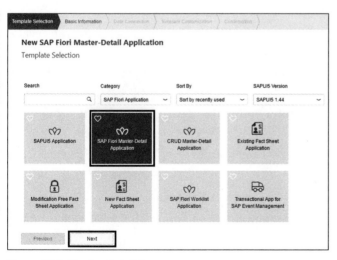

Figure 8.17 Master-Detail App

339

8.3.2   Develop

We've explored the different options for creating a project, so now let's turn our attention to the development phase. You have many different options to develop an application, and your options depend on whether you're a programmer or a nonprogrammer.

If you have programming experience, you can use the source code editor, which has features such as code completion, dynamic API references, and so on, to start coding your app.

Alternatively, you can use the templates: Wizards will guide you through the coding process step-by-step and will automatically generate the files and the code for your app. You can use the what you see is what you get (WYSIWYG) layout editor as well to design your UI. The standard templates provided by SAP Web IDE were shown earlier in Figure 8.12. In addition, you can create your own templates and manage those custom templates from the same location. For extensibility projects, you can use the visual extensibility support to take existing SAP Fiori applications and extend, modify, or replace elements of your app.

The following is a list of advantages you'll notice in SAP Web IDE while you're in the development phase:

- You can collaborate directly with other developers via the integrated collaboration features, such as SAP Jam.
- With dynamic interactive features such as code completion and API reference, you can accelerate your coding and testing process.
- You can build your app without connecting to any system; that is, you can develop with mock data and preview the app as well.
- Using WYSIWYG editors, templates, and wizards, you can build SAP Fiori apps very quickly.
- You can share the same repository with other developers, with virtually no setup required.
- You can extend the SAP-delivered applications using SAP Web IDE's extensibility framework.

Continuing with the exercise, next we'll use an EDMX file to create a master-detail app. Before you start the exercise, download the sample EDMX file, which we provided along with this book:

1. Enter "MyContacts" in **Project Name** and click **Next** (see Figure 8.18).

Figure 8.18 Project Name

2. Select **File System** as the source.

3. Browse for the EDMX file that you downloaded before starting this exercise (see Figure 8.19).

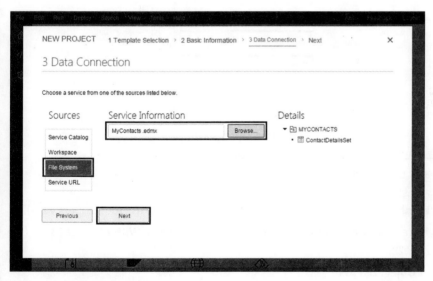

Figure 8.19 EDMX File

4. Click **Next**.

5. Enter the details shown in Figure 8.20 for **Master Section**.

Figure 8.20 Master Section

6. Enter the details as shown in **Detail Section** and click **Next** (see Figure 8.21).

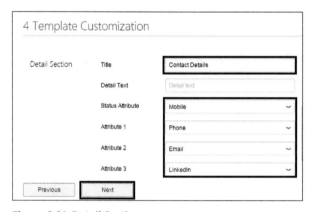

Figure 8.21 Detail Section

7. Click **Finish**. This will automatically take you to SAP Web IDE (developers view).

8. Navigate to **Master.view.xml**, right-click, and select **Open With • Layout Editor** (see Figure 8.22).

9. Select **Object List Item**.

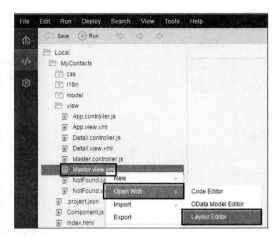

Figure 8.22 Master View

10. Select the **Company** field in the **Intro** section from the list by clicking 🖉 (see Figure 8.23).

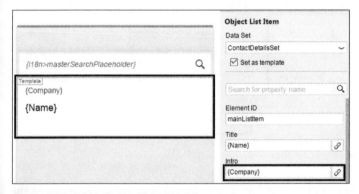

Figure 8.23 Add Intro to Object List Item

11. Click **Save**.

We successfully changed the master view; next, let's change the detail view:

1. Navigate to **Detail.view.xml**, right-click, and select **Open With • Layout Editor** (see Figure 8.24).

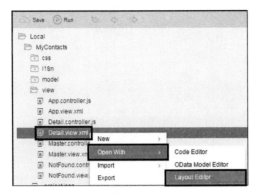

Figure 8.24 Detail View

2. Select **Object Header**. Then, select the **Company** field in the **Intro** section from the list by clicking [⌀] (see Figure 8.25).

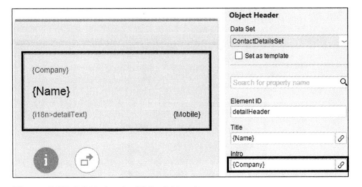

Figure 8.25 Add Intro to Object Header

3. Search for the **Image** control, then drag and drop the image component to the object header area (see Figure 8.26).

4. Click the **Image** field, and select the image in the source file by clicking [⌀].

5. Set the **Height** and **Width** of the image to "50px" (see Figure 8.27).

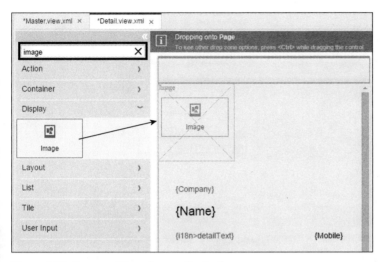

Figure 8.26 Drag and Drop Image Control

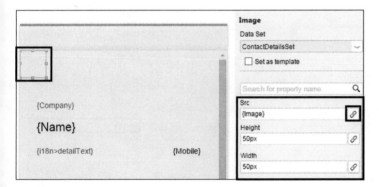

Figure 8.27 Set Source, Height, and Width of Image

6. Next, let's change the icons. Select the icon and set the value in the **Icon** field to *sap-icon://contacts*, or select the icon from the value help by clicking 🗗 (see Figure 8.28).

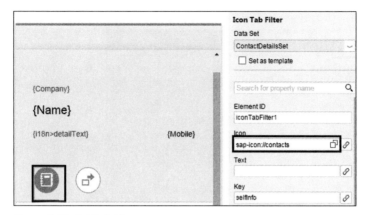

Figure 8.28 Set Tab 1 Icon

7. Similarly, click the second icon and change the icon to *sap-icon://map*.

8. In the second tab, select the label and set the text to **Address** (see Figure 8.29).

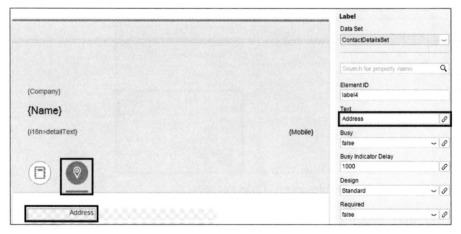

Figure 8.29 Set Tab 2 Icon and Label

9. Select the second text box, then select the **Address** field from the value help by clicking ⌀ (see Figure 8.30).

10. Click **Save**.

11. Next, we'll import the sample data models. Right-click the **Model** folder and select **Import • From File System** (see Figure 8.31).

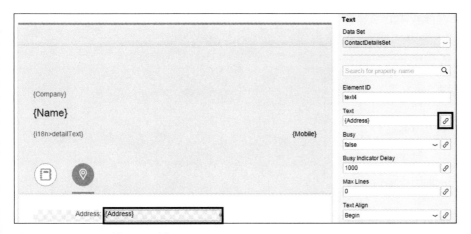

Figure 8.30 Map Address Field to Text

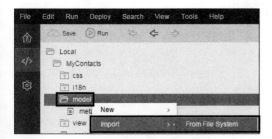

Figure 8.31 Import Models

12. Click **Browse** (see Figure 8.32).

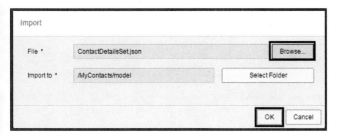

Figure 8.32 Browse File

13. Select the ContactDetailsSet.json file from the source file you downloaded prior to this exercise.

14. Repeat steps 1, 2, and 3, and add the KM.jpg, KS.jpg, and RR.jpg files to the **model** folder (see Figure 8.33).

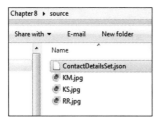

Figure 8.33 Select Files

15. After you complete the previous steps, your **model** folder should look like Figure 8.34.

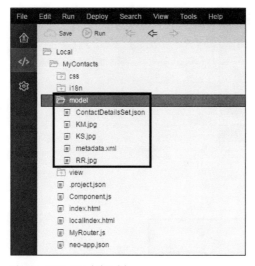

Figure 8.34 Model Folder

16. Click **Save**.

8.3.3   Preview

Now that we've explored the options available for creating and developing applications, we can discuss previewing the finished product. In the preview phase, you can test your application by previewing it on different device screen sizes, such as a desktop, tablet, smartphone, or smartwatch, to see exactly what it would look like. You can also preview applications using simulators. The beauty of SAP Web IDE is that you can test your app with random mock data generated by SAP Web IDE.

When running an application with mock data, you can either let the mock service generate the sample data for you, or edit the mock data to have more meaning. You can even provide the data in a JSON file format.

To edit and run the mock data, follow these steps:

1. Right-click **metadata.xml** and select **Edit Mock Data** (see Figure 8.35).

Figure 8.35 Edit Mock Data

2. Figure 8.36 shows the mock data we loaded in the previous step.

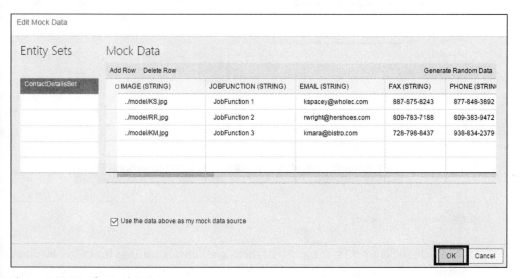

Figure 8.36 Verify Mock Data

3. To run the app with mock data, click the project folder, and then from the menu bar go to **Run • Run with Mock Data** (see Figure 8.37).

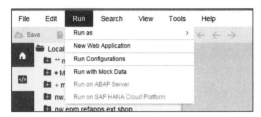

Figure 8.37 SAP Web IDE Application, Run with Mock Data

You should now see the My Contacts app in the simulator.

Now, let's look at the simulator in Figure 8.38. In the preview phase of the application, this feature lets you choose different types of devices.

Figure 8.38 Simulator

As shown in Figure 8.38, at the top of the page there are settings for **Large, Medium, Small,** and **Custom ❶**; pick the size of the screen that you want to test your application on. After you make changes to the code of your application, you can see the changes instantly by clicking the **Refresh** button ❷. You can change the orientation of the application to landscape or portrait by clicking the **Orientation** button ❸. You can also select different languages from the language dropdown ❹; however, this requires the language property files to be part of your application project. You can generate a QR code for your application ❺, and you can then test the application directly on your mobile device by scanning the QR code.

8.3.4   Deployment

The last phase in the development process is to deploy your application from SAP Web IDE to your server. You can deploy your application to the following areas/platforms:

- SAP Cloud Platform
- ABAP Repository
- Register to SAP Fiori launchpad

All these options are integrated with Git for your source code management needs.

In this final phase of the development process, let's deploy the app to SAP Cloud Platform and then register it with SAP Fiori launchpad:

1. Right-click the project folder, then choose **Deploy • Deploy to SAP HANA Cloud Platform** (see Figure 8.39).

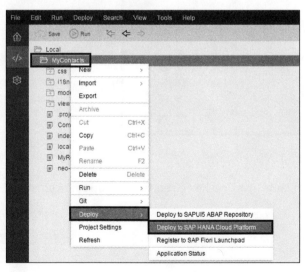

Figure 8.39 Deploy to SAP Cloud Platform

2. Log in to SAP Cloud Platform (see Figure 8.40).

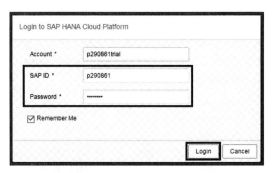

Figure 8.40 Logging in to SAP Cloud Platform

3. Enter an **Application Name** and the **Version** number (see Figure 8.41).

4. Click **Deploy** (see Figure 8.41).

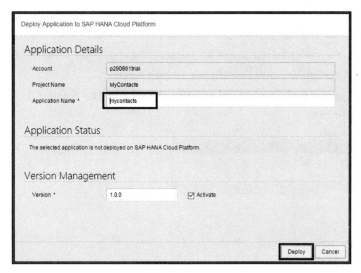

Figure 8.41 Application Name

5. To run this app on SAP Fiori launchpad, click **Register to SAP Fiori Launchpad** (see Figure 8.42).

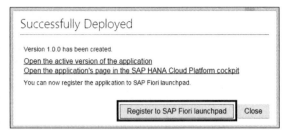

Figure 8.42 Registering to SAP Fiori Launchpad

6. Enter the **Application Name** and **Description** and click **Next** (see Figure 8.43).

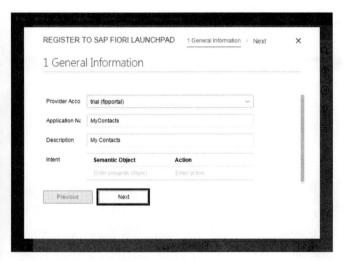

Figure 8.43 General App Information

7. Configure the tile by selecting the app **Type**, **Title**, **Subtitle**, and **Icon** (see Figure 8.44), and then click **Next**.

8. Assign the app to a **Category** and a **Content Package** and click **Next** (see Figure 8.45).

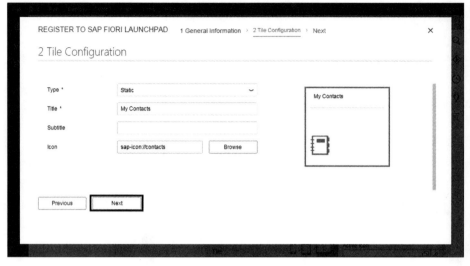

Figure 8.44 Tile Configuration

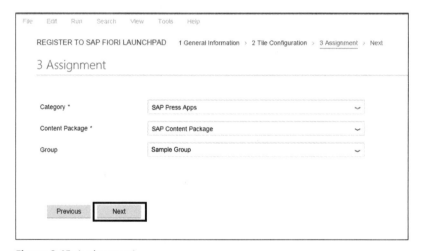

Figure 8.45 Assignment

9. Click **Finish** to confirm that the app is registered to SAP Fiori launchpad (see Figure 8.46).

10. After the app is registered, you should receive a pop-up confirmation message. Click **OK** to open SAP Fiori launchpad (see Figure 8.47).

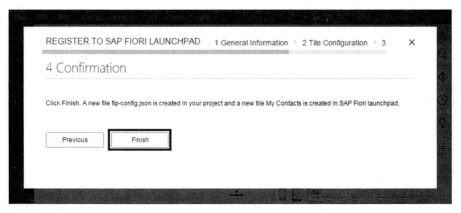

Figure 8.46 Confirmation Step

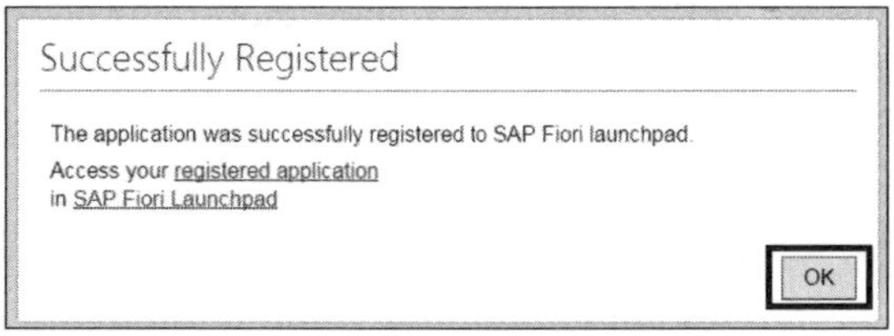

Figure 8.47 App Registration Notification

11. In SAP Fiori launchpad, you should see the **My Contacts** app in the catalog. Add the app to the **My Home** group by clicking **+** below the tile (see Figure 8.48).

Figure 8.48 SAP Fiori Catalog

You should now see the **My Contacts** app in SAP Fiori launchpad. Clicking the tile will open the app created in this exercise (see Figure 8.49).

Figure 8.49 SAP Fiori Launchpad

8.4   SAP Fiori Elements

To reduce the amount of front-end code while developing an SAP Fiori app and to keep the design consistent, SAP introduced a framework to generate UIs; it's called *SAP Fiori elements*.

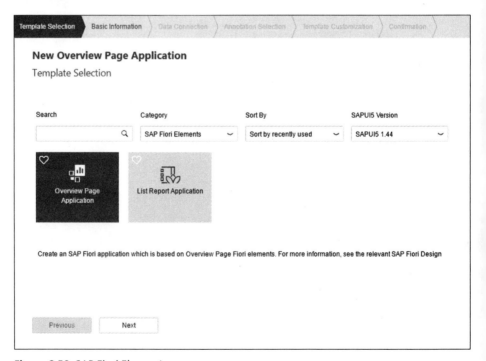

Figure 8.50 SAP Fiori Elements

SAP Fiori elements uses metadata annotations and predefined templates to generate an SAP Fiori app. With the latest release of SAPUI5 (version 1.44), the floorplans shown in Figure 8.50 are available with SAP Fiori elements.

8.4.1 Overview Page

The SAP Fiori overview page application is a type of floor plan with a UI framework that provides quick access to vital business information at a glance in the form of actionable cards on a single page, enabling users to make faster decisions and focus on their most important tasks (see Figure 8.51).

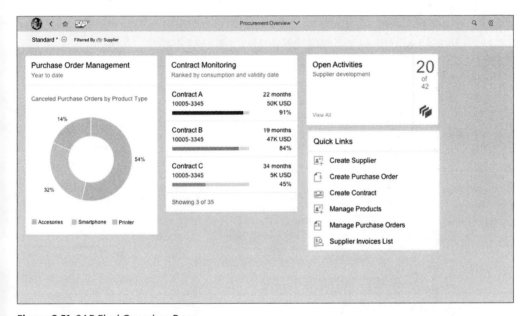

Figure 8.51 SAP Fiori Overview Page

Cards are containers for app content, and they represent an entry-level view of the most relevant app data for a given topic. The SAP Fiori overview page contains five types of cards, shown in Figure 8.52; each type of card allows users to visualize information in an interactive and efficient way:

1. **List**

   List cards display items in a vertical list.

2. **Link list**
   Link list cards display items as links or images that can navigate to a target or open a pop-up window with additional information.

3. **Table**
   Table cards display items in a table format.

4. **Stack**
   The stack card is a special type of card that displays a collection of single object cards. This type of card has two clickable areas; the left area navigates to the parent app, and the right area opens the object stream.

5. **Analytic**
   Analytic cards consist of two areas: a header area that displays the aggregated values of a KPI and a chart area that displays data in a graphical format.

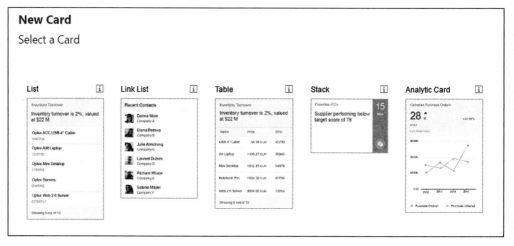

Figure 8.52 Card Types

8.4.2   List Report Floorplan

The second type of floorplan is the List Report application, a reusable floorplan template that allows users to work with large lists of items and act on each one (see Figure 8.53).

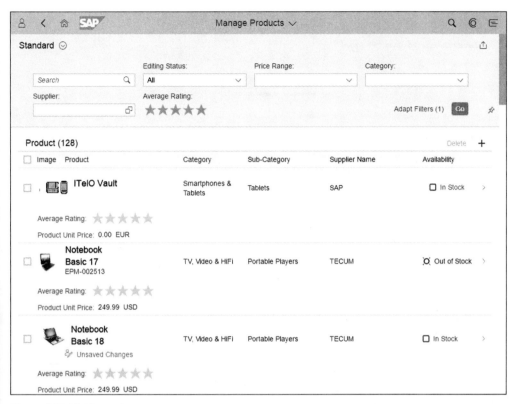

Figure 8.53 List Report

8.4.3 Object Page Floorplan

Object Page (as seen in Figure 8.54) is another type of floorplan template, which allows users to display, create, or edit an item. The Object Page floorplan can be implemented using the prebuilt SAP Fiori element.

Now that you understand the different floorplans available with the latest SAPUI5 release, we'll walk step-by-step through how to develop SAP Fiori apps using SAP Fiori elements.

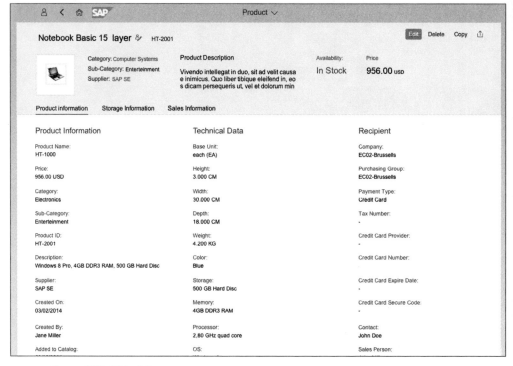

Figure 8.54 Object Page

8.4.4   Exercise

In this exercise, we'll cover the end-to-end scenario of developing a basic SAP Fiori overview page using SAP Web IDE and the deployment to your SAP Fiori launchpad. All the data in the overview page is based on the Supplier List OData service.

1. Login to SAP Web IDE.

2. Create a new project, and choose **New Project from Template**.

3. Select **SAP Fiori Elements** from the **Category** dropdown, select **Overview Page Application**, and click **Next** (see Figure 8.55).

4. Enter a **Project Name** and click **Next** (see Figure 8.56).

5. Select the **Service Catalog** and the **Server**.

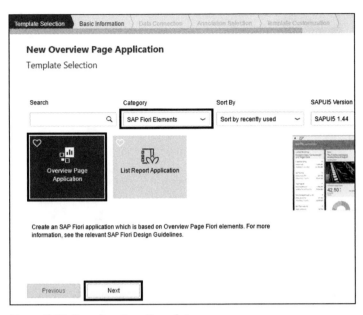

Figure 8.55 Overview Page Template

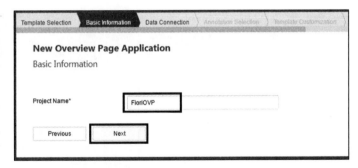

Figure 8.56 Project Name

6. Select the OData service on which you'd like to build the app, then click **Next**. In our example, we selected the **Supplier Invoice** OData service (see Figure 8.57).

7. In the **Annotation** window, for now, just click **Next** (see Figure 8.58). An annotation file is a semantic description of an OData service; in general, an annotation file should be populated, and you can create your own annotation file and upload it in this step in the future.

Figure 8.57 Data Connection

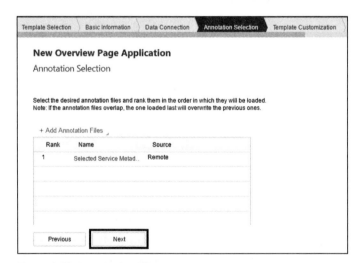

Figure 8.58 Annotation File

8. Enter **Technical** and **General** details, such as the **App Title** and **App Description**, then click **Finish** (see Figure 8.59).

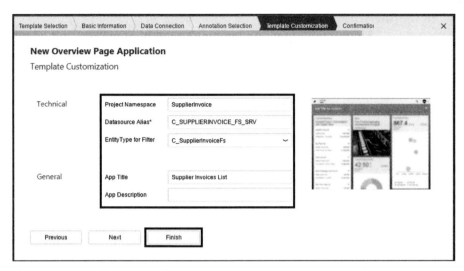

Figure 8.59 Template Customization

You've successfully created an SAP Fiori overview page project from a template. Next, let's create a card:

1. Right-click the project and select **New**, then click **Card** (see Figure 8.60).

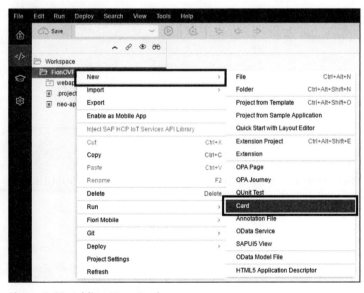

Figure 8.60 Adding New Card

2. Verify the datasource and click **Next** (see Figure 8.61).

Figure 8.61 Datasource

3. Select **List** from the list of cards and click **Next** (see Figure 8.62).

Figure 8.62 List Card

4. Select the **Entity Set** from the dropdown, and enter the **Title** and **Subtitle** (see Figure 8.63).

Figure 8.63 General Details

5. Scroll down to view **Annotations** and **Card Properties** (see Figure 8.64). Annotations are usually preselected. Select the card properties, then click **Next**.

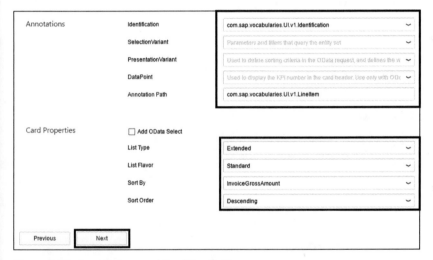

Figure 8.64 Annotations and Card Properties

6. Click **Finish**.

7. Right-click the project and select **Run**, then select **Run Configurations** (see Figure 8.65).

Figure 8.65 Run Overview Page

8. Select **Run Component.js**, then click **Save and Run** (see Figure 8.66).

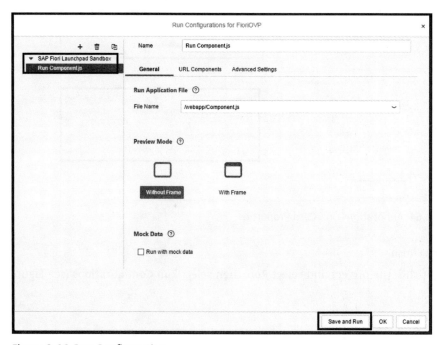

Figure 8.66 Run Configuration

9. You should now see the list card that you created in this exercise (see Figure 8.67).

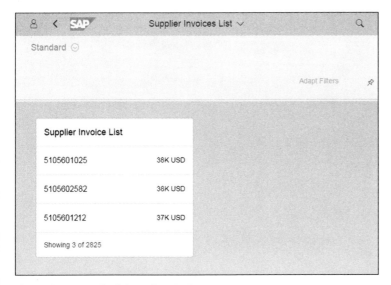

Figure 8.67 SAP Fiori Overview Page

To add more cards to the overview page, you can follow the same steps and add different types of cards. Once your overview page is ready to deploy, right-click the project and select **Deploy**, then select the desitination (e.g., SAPUI5 ABAP Repository or SAP Cloud Platform).

SAP Fiori Elements Help

For more information on SAP Fiori elements, go to *https://sapui5.netweaver.onde-mand.com* and click **Developing Apps with SAP Fiori Elements**.

8.5   Summary

In this chapter, we introduced you to SAP Web IDE and showed you how to set up SAP Web IDE with SAP Cloud Platform. At this point, you should understand the different phases of the development process and the options available in SAP Web IDE to develop an SAP Fiori app. We created our first SAP Fiori app using the master-detail standard template with an EDMX file as a source. In the next chapter, we'll explain how to create and extend transactional apps using SAP Web IDE.

Chapter 9

Creating and Extending Transactional Apps

This chapter demonstrates how to create and extend transactional apps. A complete example app is also presented to illustrate the extension process.

In Chapter 8, we discussed all the options available in SAP Web IDE to create or extend an SAP Fiori application, and in Chapter 7 we looked at the basic OData concepts and how to create an OData service. In this chapter, we'll begin tying all the pieces together as we walk through the end-to-end process of creating and extending transactional apps.

In the first part of this chapter, we'll explore the process of creating transactional apps (see Section 9.1). We'll start by outlining some basics of app creation using a template in SAP Web IDE, and then we'll cover the end-to-end process of creating a transactional app. In the second part of this chapter, we'll explore how to extend a transactional app. We'll start our discussion in Section 9.2 with an overview of the extension process and examine various extension layers in the architecture and the skills required to extend each of these layers. In Section 9.2.1, Section 9.2.2, and Section 9.2.3, we'll describe the end-to-end extension process for each layer of the architecture, with an example based on the My Quotations transactional app.

9.1 Creating Transactional Apps

In this section, we'll walk you through the step-by-step process of creating a transactional app with a template from SAP Web IDE. In the previous chapter, we examined the different templates available as part of SAP Web IDE. In this section, we'll focus on the UI layer of the transactional app. In a real-world scenario, you'll create an OData service and then create the UI layer. However, in Chapter 7, we covered the basics of

OData creation and the extension process, so you should be able to create an OData service by this point. In this section, we'll therefore use an existing OData service to create the app.

You can create simple to very complex apps using SAP Web IDE. The main purpose of this section is to show you how to create a transactional app and publish it to SAP Fiori launchpad. We'll use an SAP Fiori worklist application template and the SR018_ SO_TRACKING_SRV OData service to build the app.

9.1.1   Create a New Project Using a Template

In this step, we'll use a template in SAP Web IDE and integrate it with an existing OData service. Follow these steps:

1. Log in to SAP Web IDE.
2. Select **New Project from a Template**.
3. Select the **SAP Fiori Worklist Application** template, then click **Next** (see Figure 9.1).

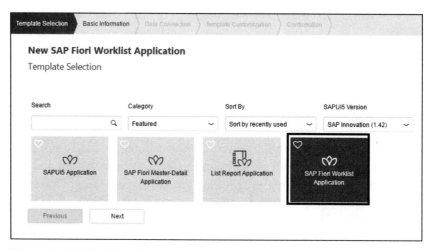

Figure 9.1 SAP Fiori Templates

4. Enter a **Project Name**, and click **Next** (see Figure 9.2).
5. Select the back-end server connection from the dropdown menu, then enter "SRA018_SO_TRACKING_SRV" in the **Search** field to search for the **SRA018_SO_TRACKING_SRV** OData service (see Figure 9.3).
6. Select the OData service and click **Next**.

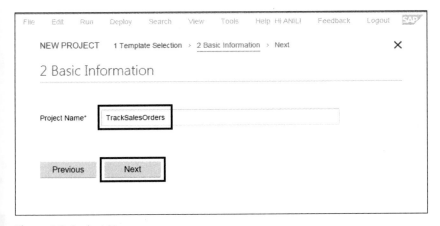

Figure 9.2 Project Name

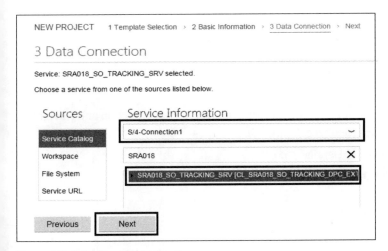

Figure 9.3 Selecting OData Service

7. Enter or select the following details in **Project Settings** and **Page 1 Section** (see Figure 9.4):
    - **Project Namespace**: "TrackSalesOrders"
    - **Title**: "Sales Order Tracker"
    - **OData Collection**: **SalesOrders**
    - **Item Title**: **SalesOrderNumber**
    - **Numeric Attribute**: **TotalAmount**

- **Units Attribute**: Currency
- **Status Attribute: ShippingStatusCode**
- **Attribute: OrderDate**

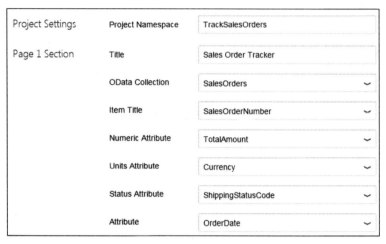

Project Settings	Project Namespace	TrackSalesOrders
Page 1 Section	Title	Sales Order Tracker
	OData Collection	SalesOrders
	Item Title	SalesOrderNumber
	Numeric Attribute	TotalAmount
	Units Attribute	Currency
	Status Attribute	ShippingStatusCode
	Attribute	OrderDate

Figure 9.4 Project Settings and Page 1 Section

8. Scroll down, enter or select the following details in **Page 2 Section** and **Navigation Section**, then click **Next** (see Figure 9.5):
   - **Title**: "Sales Order Details"
   - **Attribute 1: PO**

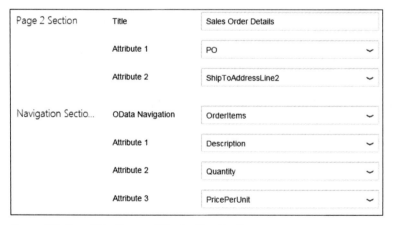

Page 2 Section	Title	Sales Order Details
	Attribute 1	PO
	Attribute 2	ShipToAddressLine2
Navigation Sectio...	OData Navigation	OrderItems
	Attribute 1	Description
	Attribute 2	Quantity
	Attribute 3	PricePerUnit

Figure 9.5 Page 2 Section and Navigation Section

- Attribute 2: ShipToAddressLine2
- OData Navigation: OrderItems
- Attribute 1: Description
- Attribute 2: Quantity
- Attribute 3: PricePerUnit

9. Click **Finish** to complete the project creation.

9.1.2 Test the App with Mock Data

In this step, you'll test the app you created in the previous step with mock data and check whether the fields are showing the data correctly. Follow these steps:

1. From the **TrackSalesOrder** project folder, right-click **index.html**, then select **Run ·
   Run with Mock Data** (see Figure 9.6).

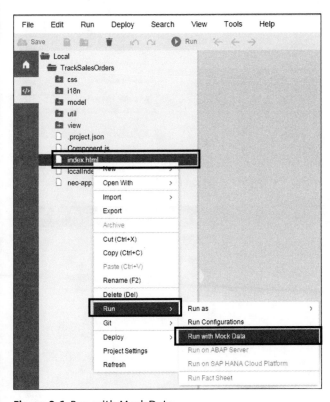

Figure 9.6 Run with Mock Data

The first screen shows the page 1 section (see Figure 9.7).

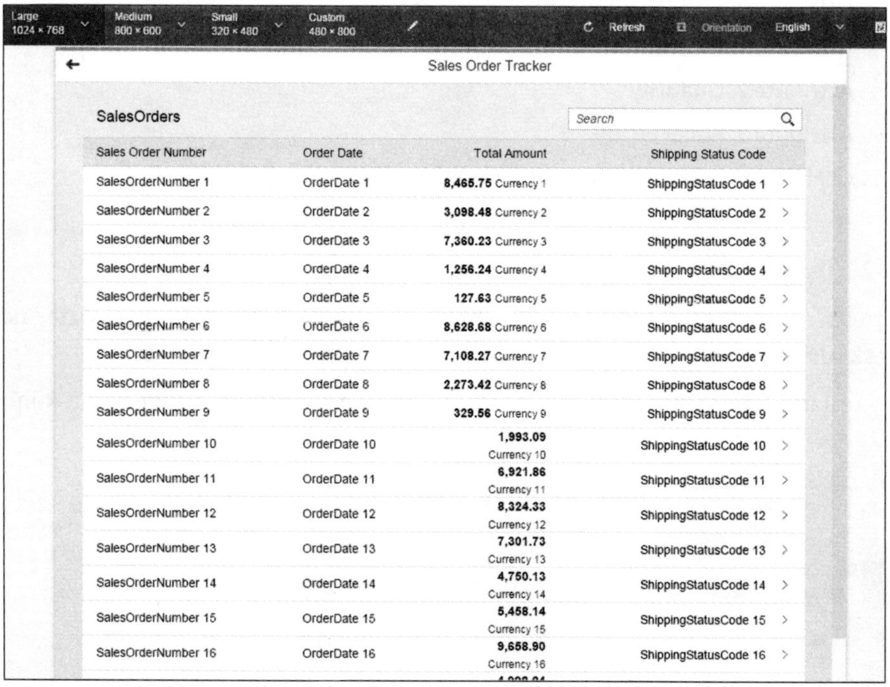

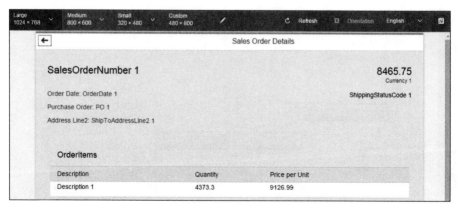

Figure 9.7 Page 1 Section

2. Clicking a sales order's row will take you to the second screen, which shows the fields from **Page 2 Section** and **Navigation Section** (see Figure 9.8).

Figure 9.8 Page 2 Section and Navigation Section Fields in App

9.1.3   Deploy the App to the ABAP Back-End Server

In the previous steps, you successfully created and tested the app. Next, we'll show you how to deploy the app to the back-end server. Follow these steps:

1. Right-click the project and select **Deploy · Deploy to SAPUI5 ABAP Repository** (see Figure 9.9).

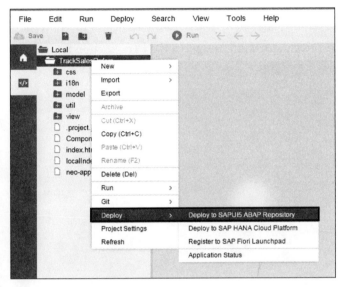

Figure 9.9 Deploying the App

2. Enter the **Name**, the **Description**, and a **Package**. Click **Next** (see Figure 9.10).

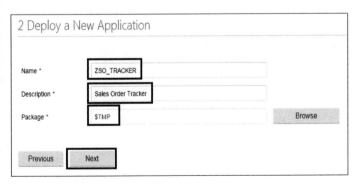

Figure 9.10 Application Details

3. Click **Finish** to complete the deployment.

You've now successfully created the app and deployed it to the back-end server. Next, you'll set up the app in SAP Fiori launchpad and create a catalog and tiles. You'll follow the same steps as in Chapter 4, Section 4.6, so we'll just include the high-level steps in the next section.

9.1.4   Publish the App to SAP Fiori Launchpad

In this step, you'll publish the new app to SAP Fiori launchpad. Follow these steps:

1. Log in to the back-end server, and check the service via Transaction SICF, which you deployed previously (see Figure 9.11).

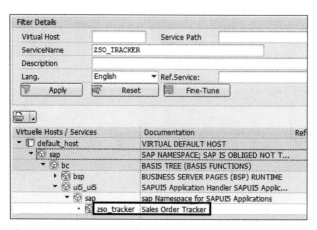

Figure 9.11 Maintain Service

2. Create a new launchpad via Transaction LPD_CUST (see Figure 9.12).

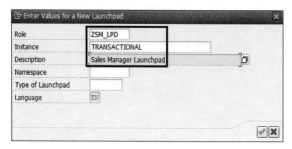

Figure 9.12 New Launchpad

3. Enter the application **URL** parameter of the service (see Figure 9.13).

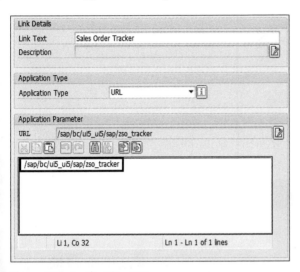

Figure 9.13 Application URL

4. Enter the **Application Alias** and the SAPUI5 component details (see Figure 9.14).

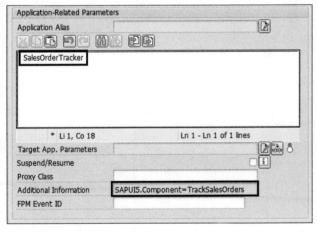

Figure 9.14 Application Alias

5. Log in to SAP Fiori launchpad designer and create a new catalog (see Figure 9.15).

Figure 9.15 New Launchpad Catalog

6. Add a new target mapping, and enter the following details (see Figure 9.16):
   - **Semantic Object**: "SalesOrders"
   - **Action**: "tracker"
   - **Launchpad Role**: "ZSM_LPD"
   - **Launchpad Instance**: "TRANSACTIONAL"
   - **Application Alias**: "SalesOrderTracker"

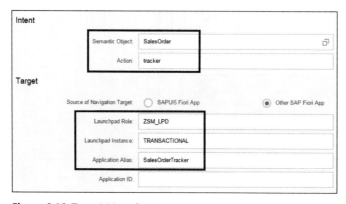

Figure 9.16 Target Mapping

7. Next, create a new tile with the following details (see Figure 9.17):
   - **Title**: Enter "Sales Order Tracker".

- **Icon**: Select an icon.
- **Semantic Object**: Enter "SalesOrders".
- **Action**: Enter "tracker".

General

Title:	Sales Order Tracker
Subtitle:	
Keywords:	
Icon:	sap-icon://Fiori2/F0006
Information:	

Navigation

Use semantic object navigation:	☑
Semantic Object:	SalesOrder
Action:	tracker

Figure 9.17 New Tile

8. Create a new role in the ABAP system, then assign the launchpad catalog and user to the role (see Figure 9.18).

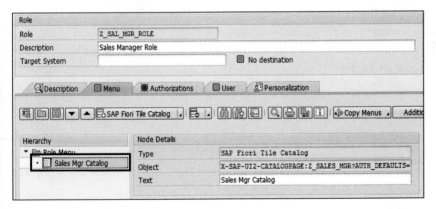

Role

Role	Z_SAL_MGR_ROLE
Description	Sales Manager Role
Target System	☐ No destination

| Description | Menu | Authorizations | User | Personalization |

SAP Fiori Tile Catalog   Copy Menus   Additic

Hierarchy	Node Details	
▼ Role Menu	Type	SAP Fiori Tile Catalog
· Sales Mgr Catalog	Object	X-SAP-UI2-CATALOGPAGE:Z_SALES_MGR?AUTH_DEFAULTS=
	Text	Sales Mgr Catalog

Figure 9.18 Maintain Role

9. Log in to SAP Fiori launchpad; you should now see the new **Sales Order Tracker** app in the catalog.

10. Add the app to your **My Home** group or any group, then launch the app (see Figure 9.19).

Figure 9.19 New Transactional App

You've successfully created and deployed a transactional app to the ABAP server and then published the app to SAP Fiori launchpad. Next, we'll explain how to extend a transactional app.

9.2   Extending Transactional Apps

Many customers want to customize their SAP Fiori apps beyond the standard applications delivered by SAP. The ability to extend transactional and other SAP Fiori apps is useful when, for example, you want to add a field, hide nonrelevant controls, replace a standard view with a custom view, or add a custom OData service. Depending on the application type and extension requirements, you can enhance one or multiple content layers.

Figure 9.20 shows the system landscape of a transactional app. The landscape is comprised of three main layers:

1. **SAP Business Suite layer**
   This layer contains the business logic and back-end data. You can extend the SAP Business Suite layer if the back-end logic and the content required for the app extension don't exist.

2. **SAP Gateway layer**
   This layer maintains the connections to the back-end system and allows users to create OData services. You can extend the SAP Gateway layer (OData) if the back-end logic and the content required for the app enhancement are present in the SAP Business Suite layer but not exposed to the SAP Gateway server.

3. **UI layer**

   This layer contains the product-specific UI add-ons, SAPUI5 control library, and SAP Fiori launchpad. You can extend the UI layer if the back-end logic and the content required for the app extension are present in the SAP Gateway layer but not exposed to the UI layer.

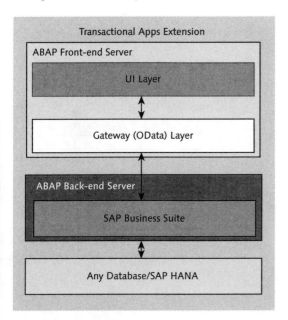

Figure 9.20 Architecture

Table 9.1 lists the knowledge/skill required to extend each of these layers.

Content Layer	SAPUI5	HTML5, JavaScript	SAP Fiori Specific UI Development	ABAP	SAP Gateway	SAP Business Suite
UI	Yes	Yes	Yes			
SAP Gateway				Yes	Yes	
SAP Business Suite				Yes		Yes

Table 9.1 Skill Matrix

Extending a transactional app end to end includes many different steps in each of the content layers; we've broken the app extension process down into nine steps (see Figure 9.21). Each of these steps can be performed by different teams based on existing skillsets.

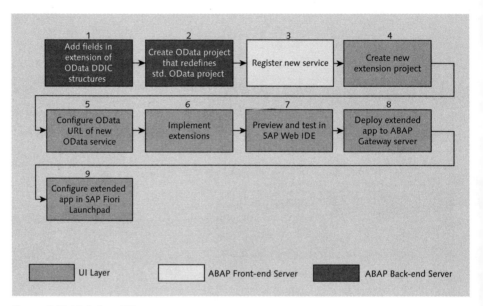

Figure 9.21 High-Level Steps

Extending transactional apps is modification-free with this approach, so any upgrade to standard SAP Fiori apps won't be impacted. We'll walk you through each of these steps in more detail in the next sections. However, let's first review the tools and transaction codes that you need to extend each layer:

- **ABAP back-end server**
  - Transaction SE80 (ABAP Object Navigator)
  - Transaction SE11 (ABAP Dictionary)
- **UI layer**
  - SAP Web IDE or Eclipse with ABAP Repository Team Provider
- **ABAP front-end server**
  - Transaction SEGW (Gateway Service Builder)

With that high-level introduction completed, let's dive straight into the steps for extending a transactional app by using an example based on the My Quotations transactional app. You'll extend the app by adding the **State** field to the standard app (see Figure 9.22); that is, you'll display the **State** field in **Ship to address**.

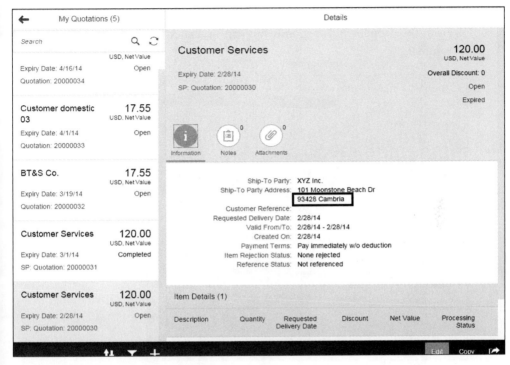

Figure 9.22 My Quotations Standard App

9.2.1   Extend the SAP Business Suite Layer

The first step in the extension process is to append the ABAP DDIC structure of the OData service with the new field in the back-end server (SAP Business Suite layer) so that you can use the new **Region** field in the UI layer.

> **Region/State**
>
> **Region** and **State** are the same. **Region** is the field from the DDIC structure, and **State** is the title that you're adding in the app.

To add a field to the app, you need to find the package and DDIC structure details. To do so, refer to the SAP Fiori app-specific online help at *http://help.sap.com/fiori* and navigate to the **App Extensibility** section of the My Quotations app information.

After you have the package details, follow these steps:

1. Log in to the ABAP back-end system.
2. Run Transaction SE80.
3. From the dropdown list, choose **Package**, and click the down arrow button (see Figure 9.23).

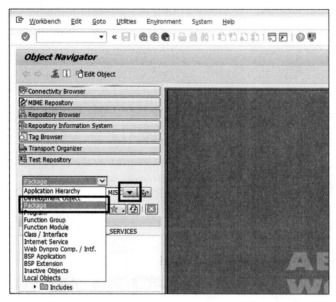

Figure 9.23 Object Navigator

4. Click the **Information System** button in the pop-up window.
5. Enter "*ODATA_MY_QUOTATION" in the **Package** field (see Figure 9.24).

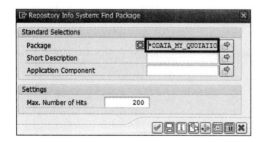

Figure 9.24 Search Package

6. Click **Continue** ✔, or press ⌈Enter⌋.

7. Select the **ERP_SD_ODATA_MY_QUOTATION** package and click **Continue** ☑ (see Figure 9.25).

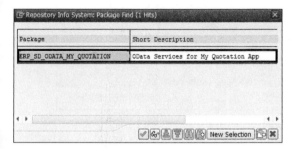

Figure 9.25 Select Package

8. On the left side, drill down to **Dictionary Objects · Structures** (see Figure 9.26).

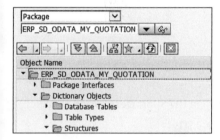

Figure 9.26 Navigate to Structures

9. From the list of structures shown in Figure 9.27, double-click **TDS_ODATA_QUO-TATION_PARTNER_IN** to view the structure details.

- TDS_ODATA_QUOTATION_OUTPUT
- TDS_ODATA_QUOTATION_OUTPUT_INC
- TDS_ODATA_QUOTATION_OUT_MSG
- TDS_ODATA_QUOTATION_OUT_MSG_IN
- TDS_ODATA_QUOTATION_PARTNER
- TDS_ODATA_QUOTATION_PARTNER_IN
- TDS_ODATA_QUOTATION_PRICE_COND
- TDS_ODATA_QUOTATION_PRICE_C_IN
- TDS_ODATA_QUOTATION_SEARCH
- TDS_ODATA_QUOTATION_SEARCH_INC
- TDS_ODATA_QUOTATION_SLINE
- TDS_ODATA_QUOTATION_SLINE_INCL
- TDS_ODATA_QUOTE_HEADER_SEARCH
- TDS_ODATA_QUOTE_HEAD_SEARCH_I

Figure 9.27 Selecting Partner Structure

10. Click **Append Structure** (see Figure 9.28).

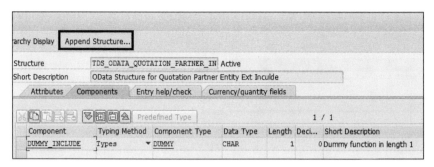

Figure 9.28 Selecting Append Structure

11. Enter "ZQUOTATION_PARTNER_EXTN" in the **Append Name** field (see Figure 9.29). Click **Continue** ✅, or press ⌨Enter⌨.

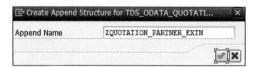

Figure 9.29 Append Name

12. Enter "Partner Extension for My Quotations" in the **Short Description** field.

13. Add the following details, as shown in Figure 9.30:
    - **Component**: "REGION"
    - **Typing Methods**: "Types"

14. Click the **Predefined Type** button to enable the **Data Type** and **Length** fields. Enter the remaining details, as follows (see Figure 9.30):
    - **Data Type**: "CHAR"
    - **Length**: "3"
    - **Short Description**: "Region"

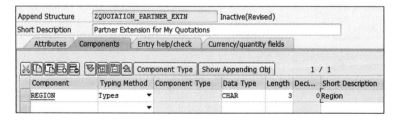

Figure 9.30 Adding New Fields

15. Check for errors by clicking 🔧.

16. Click **Save** 💾.

17. Click **Local Object/Package**.

18. Click **Save**.

19. Activate the structure by clicking **Activate** ✏️.

20. Now, check if the new field is added to the partner structure. Double-click **TDS_ODATA_QUOTATION_PARTNER**, and you should see the **Region** field added to the structure (see Figure 9.31).

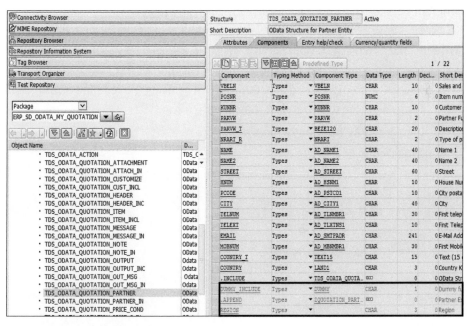

Figure 9.31 Appended Structure

You've successfully added a new field to the structure!

9.2.2   Extend the SAP Gateway Layer

In Chapter 7, we discussed OData concepts in general and walked through a simple OData service example. In addition, we looked at the different options for redefining an OData service created in SAP Gateway and external services such as BOPF, SAP BW queries, and GenIL. With SAP Gateway Service Builder, you can extend the OData service using the redefine technique, which lets you reuse the business objects and services from your existing SAP system landscape.

SAP Gateway Service Builder is an OData-compliant modeling environment that provides developers with a set of tools for creating and maintaining an OData service. This tool provides options for both experienced developers and less experienced developers. Experienced developers can define a new service, whereas less experienced developers can import existing definition files or use content generators to expose the data for simple consumption. In addition, this tool also empowers non-programmers to build applications using wizards and templates.

Redefine and Extend the OData Service

A standard SAP-delivered project will be the starting point for the extension project. Let's now look at how to extend an OData service by using the redefine technique in SAP Gateway Service Builder. Follow these steps:

1. Log in to the ABAP front-end server.

2. Run Transaction SEGW.

3. Create a new project by clicking the **Create Project** icon (see Figure 9.32).

Figure 9.32 Create New Project Icon

4. On the next page, enter the following project details (see Figure 9.33):
   - **Project:** "ZLORD_MY_QUOTATION"
   - **Description:** "OData Service Extension for My Quotation"

5. Click **Local Object**.

6. In the new project, right-click **Data Model Redefine** and select **OData Service (GW)** (see Figure 9.34).

7. Enter the following details (see Figure 9.35):
   - **Technical Service Name:** "LORD_MY_QUOTATION_SRV"
   - **Version:** "1"

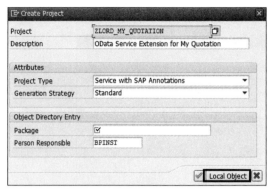

Figure 9.33 Selecting Package

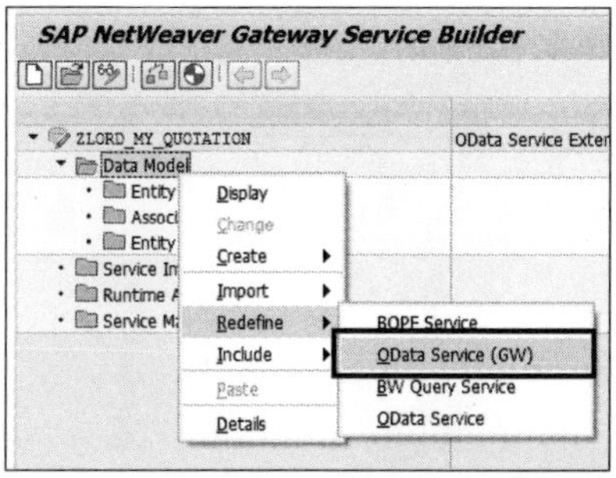

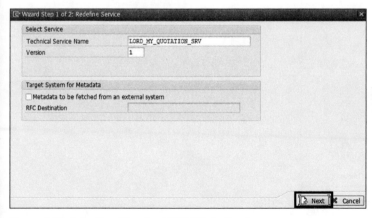

Figure 9.34 Redefining OData Service

Figure 9.35 Selecting Standard SAP OData Service

8. Click **Next**.

9.   Select all the fields by clicking 📄 (see Figure 9.36).

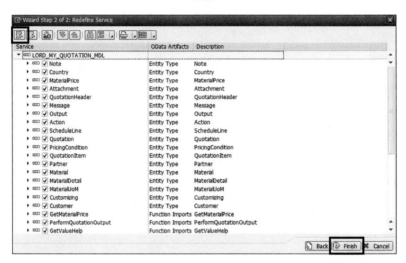

Figure 9.36 Selecting All OData Artifacts

10. Click **Finish**.

11. Expand **Data Model** · **Entity Types** · **Partner** (see Figure 9.37).

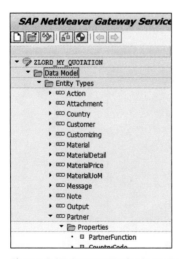

Figure 9.37 Partner Entity Type Properties

12. Double-click **Properties**.

13. Append a new row by clicking 📄.

14. Enter the following details in the new row (see Figure 9.38):
    - **Name:** "State". This is the property that is visible externally to the OData.
    - **EDM Core Type:** "Edm.String". This is the EMD data for each property.
    - **Max Length:** "25". This property is the length of the data type.
    - **Label:** "State". This field's content is used by OData.

    After you enter all the fields, your screen should look similar to the one shown in Figure 9.38.

Name	Key	Edm Core Type	Prec.	Scale	Max	Unit Property Name	Crea.	Upd.	Sort	Null	Fit.	Label	L	Comp. Type	ABAP Field Name	A
PartnerFunction	✓	Edm.String	0	0	2							Partner Functn	T		PARVW	
CountryCode		Edm.String	0	0	3					✓		Country	T		COUNTRY	
CountryDescription		Edm.String	0	0	15					✓			T		COUNTRY_T	
CellPhoneNumber		Edm.String	0	0	30					✓		Mobile Phone	T		MOBNUM	
Email		Edm.String	0	0	241					✓		E-Mail Address	T		EMAIL	
TelephoneNumbe_		Edm.String	0	0	10					✓		Extension	T		TELEXT	
TelephoneNumber		Edm.String	0	0	30					✓		Telephone	T		TELNUM	
City		Edm.String	0	0	40					✓		City	T		CITY	
PostalCode		Edm.String	0	0	10					✓		Postal Code	T		PCODE	
HouseNumber		Edm.String	0	0	10					✓		House Number	T		HNUM	
Street		Edm.String	0	0	60					✓		Street	T		STREET	
Name2		Edm.String	0	0	40					✓		Name 2	T		NAME2	
Name1		Edm.String	0	0	40					✓		Name	T		NAME	
PartnerNumber		Edm.String	0	0	10							Customer	T		KUNNR	
QuotationID	✓	Edm.String	0	0	10							Sales Document	T		VBELN	
PartnerFunctionD_		Edm.String	0	0	20					✓		Description	T		PARVW_T	
PartnerFunctionT_		Edm.String	0	0	2							Partner type	T		NRART_R	
State		Edm.String	0	0	3							State	T		REGION	

Figure 9.38 Adding New Field

15. Finally, on the same screen as the preceding options, select **Region** from the value help for **ABAP Field Name** (see Figure 9.39). With the ABAP Data Dictionary binding, you'll be able to know the EDM data type and the length of the entity type as well.

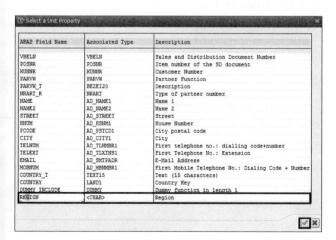

ABAP Field Name	Associated Type	Description
VBELN	VBELN	Sales and Distribution Document Number
POSNR	POSNR	Item number of the SD document
KUNNR	KUNNR	Customer Number
PARVW	PARVW	Partner Function
PARVW_T	BEZEI20	Description
NRART_R	NRART	Type of partner number
NAME	AD_NAME1	Name 1
NAME2	AD_NAME2	Name 2
STREET	AD_STREET	Street
HNUM	AD_HSNM1	House Number
PCODE	AD_PSTCD1	City postal code
CITY	AD_CITY1	City
TELNUM	AD_TLNMBR1	First telephone no.: dialling code+number
TELEXT	AD_TLXINS1	First Telephone No.: Extension
EMAIL	AD_SMTPADR	E-Mail Address
MOBNUM	AD_MBNMBR1	First Mobile Telephone No.: Dialing Code + Number
COUNTRY_T	TEXT15	Text (15 characters)
COUNTRY	LAND1	Country Key
DUMMY_INCLUDE	DUMMY	Dummy function in length 1
REGION	<CHAR>	Region

Figure 9.39 Selecting Region Field

16. Click the **Check Project Consistency** icon 🔄 at the top left to check for errors.

17. Click **Generate Runtime Objects** ⊕.

18. Verify the **Model Provider Class** (MPC), **Data Provider Class** (DPC), and **Service Registration** details, and click **Continue** ✅ (Figure 9.40).

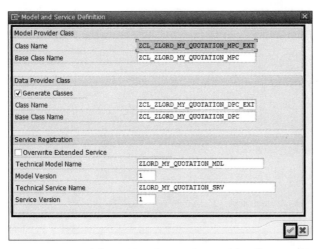

Figure 9.40 Model Provider Class, Data Provider Class, and New OData Service Registration

More Information

See Chapter 7, Section 7.2 for details about the MPC, DPC, and service definition.

19. Select **Local Object** on the next screen (see Figure 9.41).

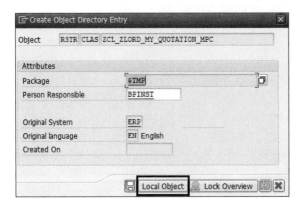

Figure 9.41 Local Object

20. SAP Gateway service builder will generate the following runtime artifacts (see Figure 9.42):

  – Data Provider Base Class

  – Data Provider Extension Class

  – Model Provider Base Class

  – Model Provider Extension Class

  – Registered Model

  – Registered Service

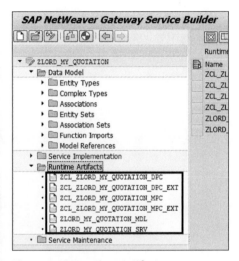

Figure 9.42 Runtime Artifacts

21. Whenever you redefine an OData service, SAP Gateway service builder generates the new OData service with the DPC and MPC. The DPC is used to code your CRUD methods and function import methods. You can define all back-end logic in redefined methods of the DPC extension class. The MPC is used to define the data model; using the code-based implementation methods, you can create entities, properties, and so on.

22. SAP Gateway Service Builder generates the base class and extension class after you generate a project. The base class inherits its code from the minimal SAP Gateway abstract class /IWBEP/CL_MGW_PUSH_ABS_DATA, and the extension class is created for both MPC and DPC by SAP Gateway Service Builder, which is inherited from the base class.

You've successfully extended the OData service! In the next section, we'll register the OData service.

Register the OData Service

The next step is to register the OData service. To expose the OData service you created in the previous step, you must create an entry in the service catalog in the SAP Gateway system (front-end server). A custom OData service is always developed on top of the SAP Gateway add-on installed in the back-end server. To register the service on the front-end server, follow these steps:

1. Select the **Service Maintenance** folder from your project.

2. Select your SAP Gateway hub system and click **Register** (Figure 9.43).

Figure 9.43 Registering Service

3. Select **Local Package**.

4. Click **Continue** ✔.

Test the OData Service

After the service is registered, the final step is to test the OData service. In the next steps, we'll test the service via a quotation ID available in the back-end system. You can select any quotation available in your back-end system to check if the OData service is responding correctly.

Follow these steps:

1. Run Transaction /IWFND/MAINT_SERVICE (on the SAP front-end server).

2. In the list, double-click the service you created in the previous section.

3. Click **Gateway Client** (see Figure 9.44).

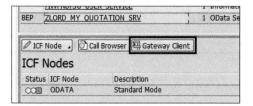

Figure 9.44 Running Gateway Client

4. In the line **Request URI**, replace "?$format=xml" with "$metadata".

5. You should now see the **State** property under the **Partner** entity type (see Figure 9.45).

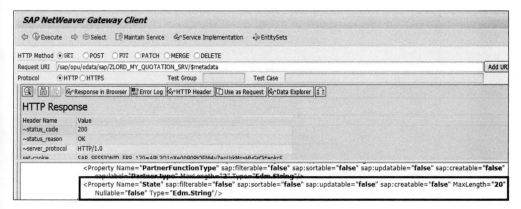

Figure 9.45 State Property

6. In the **Request URI** line, replace "?format=xml" with the following text: "QuotationHeaderSet('<your QuotationID>')?$expand=PartnerSet".

   – *For example*: QuotationHeaderSet('20000030')?$expand=PartnerSet

7. You should now see the **State** field populated with the data (see Figure 9.46).

> **Quotation ID**
>
> We'll be testing with quotation ID 20000030, but you can use any quotation ID available in the back-end you're using.

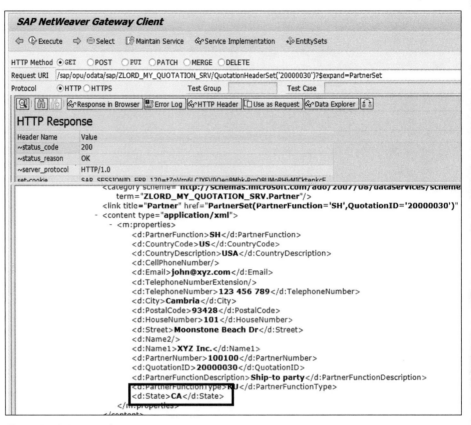

Figure 9.46 State Value

Now, let's verify the data with the back-end server. Follow these steps:

1. Log in to the SAP ERP back-end system.

2. Run Transaction VA23.

3. Enter any quotation ID available in your system and press [Enter].

4. From the menu bar, navigate to **Goto** · **Header** · **Partner.**

5. Double-click the partner function **Ship-to party**.

You should now see the same value in the **State** field in the back-end as well (refer to Figure 9.46 and Figure 9.47).

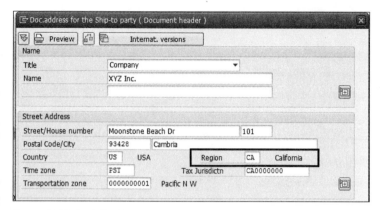

Figure 9.47 Back-End Data

9.2.3   Extend the UI Layer

The next step is to add the new field to the UI layer. SAP delivers the SAPUI5 project for every SAP Fiori transactional app. You can get the details of a specific app from the online help at *http://help.sap.com/fiori*. Figure 9.48 shows the SAPUI5 application details for the My Quotations transactional app.

SAPUI5 Application	
The ICF nodes for the following SAPUI5 application must be activated on the front-end server:	
Component	**Technical Name**
SAPUI5 Application	sd_myquotes

Figure 9.48 SAPUI5 Application

In Chapter 8, we covered all the basic options available in SAP Web IDE to extend an SAPUI5 app. Let's now explore those options in greater detail. In this section, you'll extend the My Quotations SAPUI5 app by adding the **State** field to the UI layer. SAP provides extension points for extending standard views of the application with custom content. You can get the extension points details from the app-specific help page (see Figure 9.49). In addition, the **Extension** wizard in SAP Web IDE lists all the extension points available for a specific view or fragment, as we'll discuss in our example.

Extension Points in Views		
View	**Extension Point**	**Use**
CreateQuotation.view.xml	extEditQuotationCustDetailsBottom	Allows you to add fields at the bottom of the customer details section in edit and create mode
	extEditQuotationCustDetailsTop	Allows you to add fields at the top of the customer details section in edit and create mode
	extEditQuotationDetailsBottom	Allows you to add fields at the bottom of the quotation details section in edit and create mode
	extEditQuotationDetailsTop	Allows you to add fields at the top of the quotation details section in edit and create mode
ItemDetails.view.xml	extDisplayQuotationItemDetailsBottom	Allows you to add fields at the bottom of item details in read-only mode
	extDisplayQuotationItemDetailsTop	Allows you to add fields at the top of item details in read-only mode
	extEditQuotationItemDetailsBottom	Allows you to add fields at the bottom of item details in edit and create mode
	extEditQuotationItemDetailsTop	Allows you to add fields at the top of item details in edit and create mode
ProductDetail.view.xml	extQuotationMaterialDetailBottom	Allows you to add fields at the bottom of the material details
	extQuotationMaterialDetailTop	Allows you to add fields at the top of the material details
S3.view.xml	extQuotationDetailsInfoBottom	Allows you to add fields at the bottom of the information tab in read-only mode
	extQuotationDetailsInfoTop	Allows you to add fields at the top of the information tab in read-only mode
	extQuotationDetailsTabs	Allows you to add an additional tab

Figure 9.49 Extension Points

In Chapter 2, we discussed the customizations that are supported in the standard SAPUI5 app. In this section, you'll implement the view extension by using extension points to insert custom content (i.e., you'll add the **State** field to the S3.view.xml view).

The following are the high-level steps that you need to follow to extend the UI layer for transactional apps:

1. Create a new extension project using the SAP-delivered standard application.
2. Replace the OData service with the custom OData service.
3. Identify extension points and views.
4. Publish the custom application to the ABAP Repository.
5. Configure the app on SAP Fiori launchpad.
6. Configure and test the application in SAP Fiori launchpad.

Create a New Extension Project

The first step in this process is to create a new extension project by importing the original SAPUI5 application for the My Quotations app. Refer to Figure 9.48 for the technical name of the SAPUI5 app. Follow these steps to create a new project:

1. Log in to SAP Web IDE.
2. Click **New Extension Project** from the welcome screen, or navigate to **File · New · Extension Project** from the menu bar (see Figure 9.50).

Figure 9.50 New Extension Project

3. Click **Remote**, then choose **SAPUI5 ABAP Repository** (see Figure 9.51).

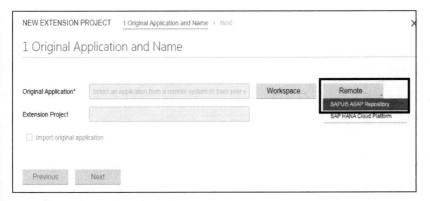

Figure 9.51 Selecting Remote System

4. Select your SAP Gateway system.
5. Search for "sd_myquotes" (see Figure 9.52).
6. Choose the **sd_myquotes** app, and click **OK**.
7. Enter the **Extension Project** name, and click **Next** (see Figure 9.53).

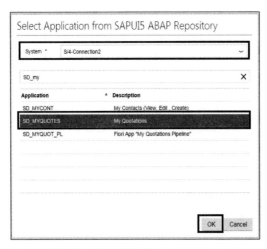

Figure 9.52 Selecting SAPUI5 Component

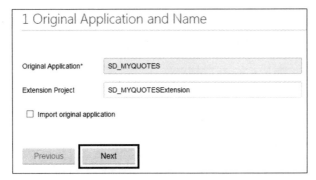

Figure 9.53 Extension Project

8. Uncheck the **Open extension project in extensibility pane** checkbox, and click **Finish** (see Figure 9.54).

Figure 9.54 Completing Extension Project

You've successfully created a new extension project using the original application, so you should now see the extension project created under your projects folder. Remember, modifications made to this project won't impact the actual application.

Replace the OData Service with the Custom OData Service

Next, you'll replace the OData service. The standard My Quotations app is developed using the standard LORD_MY_QUOTATION_SRV OData service. To add the new **Region** field to the app, you must replace the standard OData service with the custom OData service you created in Section 9.2.2. Follow these steps to replace the OData service:

1. Right-click the new project folder, then select **New · Extension** (see Figure 9.55).

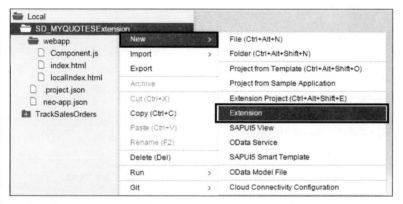

Figure 9.55 New Extension

2. Check your extension project name and click **Next** (see Figure 9.56).

Figure 9.56 Verifying Project

3. Choose **Replace Service** and click **Next** (see Figure 9.57).

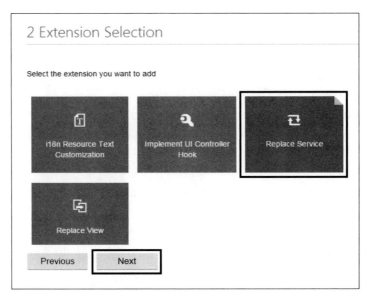

Figure 9.57 Choosing Replace Service

4. Choose **Service Catalog** from the listed sources.

5. Select the connection for your SAP system.

6. Search for "ZLORD_MY_QUOTATION_SRV" (see Figure 9.58). Click **Next**.

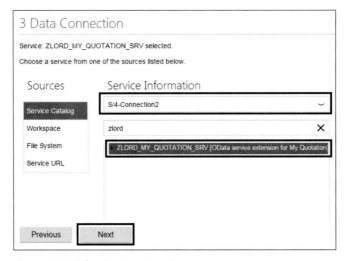

Figure 9.58 Selecting New Service

7. Drill down to check if the new field is displayed (see Figure 9.59). Click **Next**.

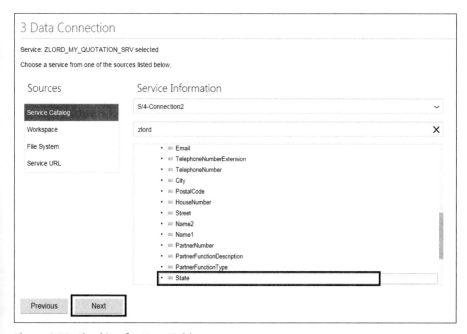

Figure 9.59 Checking for New Field

8. Click **Finish**.

Identify the Extension Points and Views

You've successfully created an extension project and replaced the OData service. Let's now add the new field to the UI layer. For that, you first need to identify the view and then the extension points of that view. Perform the following steps to add a field in the custom view:

1. Right-click your project, and select **New • Extension**.

2. Verify the extension project location and click **Next**.

3. Choose **Extend View/Fragment** and click **Next** (see Figure 9.60).

4. Select **S3.view.xml** from the **View/Fragment** dropdown list to display the extension points available for that view.

5. Select **Extension Point** and click **Next** (see Figure 9.61).

Figure 9.60 Extend View

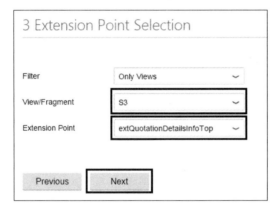

Figure 9.61 Extending S3 View

Extension Point Tag

The extension point tag in the XML view indicates the position at which you can insert your custom content.

---

6. Click **Finish**. You should now see the S3 extension point under sap.ui. viewExtensions in the component.js file (see Figure 9.62).

```
    customizing: {
"sap.ui.viewExtensions": {
    "cus.sd.myquotations.view.S3": {
        "extQuotationDetailsInfoTop": {
            className: "sap.ui.core.Fragment",
            fragmentName: "cus.sd.myquotations.SD_MYQUOTESExtension.view.S3_extQuotationDetailsInfoTopCustom",
            type: "XML"
        }
    }
}
```

Figure 9.62 Extension Point

Extension Configuration

The component.js file contains the extension configuration, which has the following properties:

- `sap.ui.viewExtensions`
  This is used to provide custom view content in standard SAP applications.

- `sap.ui.viewModifications`
  This is used for modifying certain properties of controls in standard SAP applications.

- `sap.ui.viewReplacements`
  This is used to replace a view with a custom view in standard SAP applications.

- `sap.ui.ControllerExtensions`
  This is used for replacing a controller with a custom controller in standard SAP applications.

7. You should now see a new extended view under the **Views** folder. Double-click the extended view to open it in the code editor (see Figure 9.63).

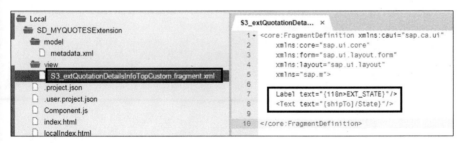

Figure 9.63 New Field

8. Add the following code:

```
<Label text="{i18n>EXT_STATE}" /><Text text="{shipTo>/State}" />
```

9. Click **Save**.

10. Right-click the project folder, then select **New · Folder**.

11. Create a folder with the name i18n.

12. Right-click the new **i18n** folder, then select **New · File**.

13. Create a file with the name i18n_custom.properties (see Figure 9.64).

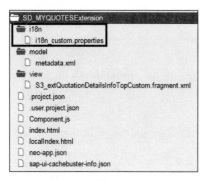

Figure 9.64 i18n Files

14. Double-click the **i18n_custom.properties** file, then enter "EXT_STATE=State".

15. Click **Save**.

Publish the Custom Application to the ABAP Repository

The next step is to publish your custom application to the ABAP Repository.

Right-click your project and select **Deploy · Deploy to SAPUI5 ABAP Repository** (see Figure 9.65).

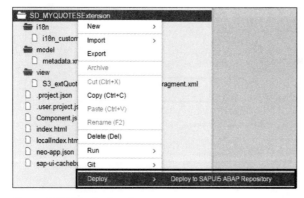

Figure 9.65 Deploying App

Configure and Test the App in SAP Fiori Launchpad

After the app is published to the ABAP Repository, you need to follow the same steps as in Chapter 4 to make this app available to users on SAP Fiori launchpad. After you publish and launch the app from SAP Fiori launchpad, you should see the new **State** field added to the app (see Figure 9.66).

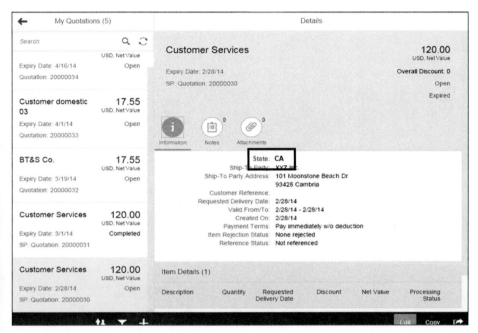

Figure 9.66 Extended App

9.3   Summary

In the first part of this chapter, we showed you how to create a transactional app using a template in SAP Web IDE. In the second part, we covered the extension process with an example based on the My Quotations app. This chapter provided detailed, step-by-step instructions for how to extend the different layers in the architecture to extend an SAP Fiori transactional app. This chapter should provide enough information to get you started with creating and extending transactional apps. In the next chapter, we'll explore in detail how to create and extend fact sheet apps.

Chapter 10
Creating and Extending Fact Sheet Apps

This chapter demonstrates how to create and extend a fact sheet app and provides a complete example app to illustrate the extension process.

In this chapter, we'll show you how to create and extend fact sheet apps. We'll start with a brief introduction into the various layers of the system landscape of fact sheet apps, and we'll highlight the steps to create and extend them. To recap, fact sheet apps display contextual information about central objects used in your business operations. You can drill down from one fact sheet to another fact sheet, and you can call fact sheets from SAP Fiori launchpad. Fact sheet apps run only on an SAP HANA database, and they require an ABAP stack.

Figure 10.1 shows the system landscape of fact sheet apps. The landscape is comprised of two layers: the UI layer that contains the product-specific UI add-ons, SAPUI5 control library, and SAP Fiori launchpad, and the SAP Business Suite layer that contains the search model.

Fact sheet apps are created or extended from annotation files in an XML format; these files are based on semantic and object structure information. A fact sheet app is represented by a combination of a search model, OData service, and Business Server Page (BSP) application. Fact sheet apps can be extended by enhancing one or multiple layers. As explained in Chapter 9, you can create new SAP Fiori apps from scratch or extend existing SAP Fiori apps.

Before we dig deep into the creation and extension process, we need to enable the SAP Web IDE fact sheet editor app, which is covered in Section 10.1. In Section 10.2, we'll teach you how to create a fact sheet app using an existing search model, and at the end of this section, we'll highlight the steps to deploy the app to the ABAP Repository. In Section 10.3, we'll move on to the extension process. Section 10.3.1 provides an example based on the Sales Order fact sheet app to show you how to extend a search model and create connectors using the search and analytics modeler and the connector administration cockpit tools. SAP Web IDE is still a young product, and it's being developed at full speed by SAP. The goal of this chapter is to introduce you to the templates you can use to create or extend SAP Fiori fact sheet apps. In Section 10.3.2, we'll show you how to enhance the app using the Existing Fact Sheet Application template and a Modification Free Fact Sheet Application template, and then we'll explain how to deploy the extended app in Section 10.3.3.

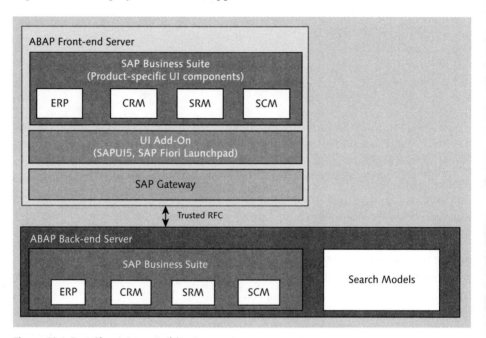

Figure 10.1 Fact Sheet Apps Architecture

Checklist

You'll use the following tools in this chapter:

- Search and analytics modeler
- Connector administration cockpit
- SAP Web IDE

10.1   Enabling the SAP Web IDE Fact Sheet Editor App

In Chapter 8, we introduced you to SAP Web IDE and walked you through the various options available with this tool. Next, we need to enable the SAP Web IDE fact sheet editor app to create or extend fact sheet apps. Follow these steps:

1. Log in to SAP Web IDE.
2. Navigate to **Tools · Preferences** from the menu bar (see Figure 10.2).

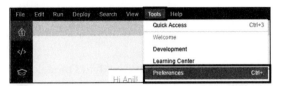

Figure 10.2 Adding Plugins from Preferences

3. Select **Plugins.**
4. In the pop-up page, enable the **Fact Sheet Editor** plugin, and click **Save** (see Figure 10.3).

Figure 10.3 Enabling Fact Sheet Editor Plugin

5. Refresh your browser to view the fact sheet app plugin.

You've successfully enabled the SAP Web IDE fact sheet editor app. Next, we'll dive into the fact sheet app creation process.

10.2   Creating Fact Sheet Apps

In this section, we'll highlight the steps required for creating a fact sheet app using an existing search model and OData service.

10.2.1   Create the Search Model

The processes for creating and extending a search model is very similar. In both cases, the system will take you through a similar sequence of screens to configure the search model. Therefore, refer to Section 10.3.1 on extending the search model for details.

To create a search model, simply select **Create** in the search and analytics modeler. To extend an existing search model, click **Edit** (see Figure 10.4). In Section 10.3.1, we'll show you how to extend an existing search model by adding a new field.

Figure 10.4 Create or Extend Search Model

In this fact sheet creation process, we'll assume that you already have a search model and have created a search connector, as we instructed in Chapter 5, Section 5.4. In the following sections, we'll look at the necessary steps to create a search model by creating and adding the necessary software components. These steps are also relevant for extension.

Create the Software Components

Before you create or extend a search model, you first need to create a customer-specific software component. Similarly, this is also necessary for the extension process to include all the SAP-standard software components and enhance them.

Proceed with the following steps:

1. Launch the search and analytics modeler tool by running Transaction ESH_MODELER from the ABAP system.

2. Select **Software Components**, then click **Maintain Software Components** (see Figure 10.5).

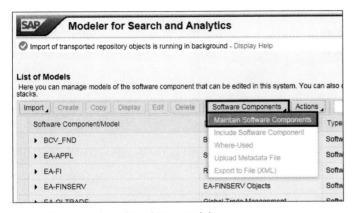

Figure 10.5 Search and Analytics Modeler

3. Create a software component by clicking **Create** (see Figure 10.6).

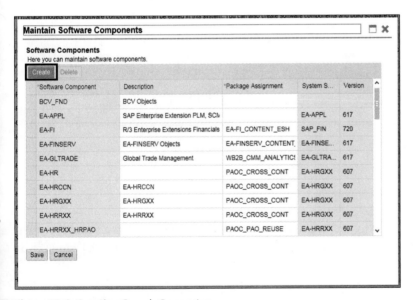

Figure 10.6 Creating Search Connector

4. Enter a name in the **New SW Comp** field.

5. In the **Package Assignment** field, assign a package by clicking 🗗, as shown in Figure 10.7 (you can create a new package in the Object Navigator via Transaction SE80).

6. Click **Create** to create the software component.

Figure 10.7 New Search Connector Component

7. You should now see the new software component in the list shown in Figure 10.8. Click **Save**.

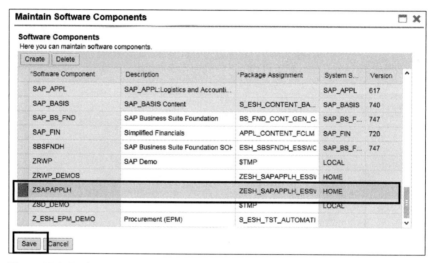

Figure 10.8 Saving Component

8. Next, you need to add the changes to a transport request. If a transport request exists, it will appear in the list, or you can create a new request by clicking **Create** (see Figure 10.9).

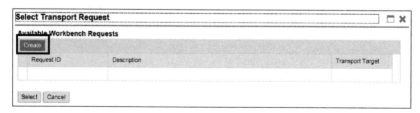

Figure 10.9 Creating Transport Request

9. Select the **Request ID**, then click **Select** (see Figure 10.10).

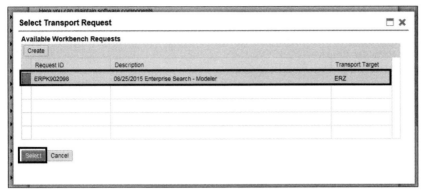

Figure 10.10 Assigning Transport Request

10. Save the software component by clicking **Save** (see Figure 10.11).

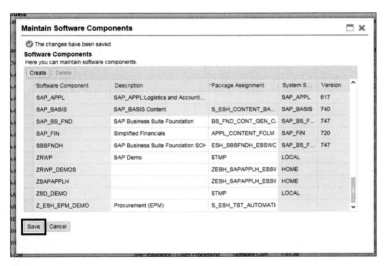

Figure 10.11 Saving Software Component

Add the Software Component to the Customer-Specific Software Components

Next, you'll add the software component to the customer-specific software components to enhance the model. Follow these steps:

1. From the search and analytics modeler tool, select the new customer-specific software component, click **Software Components**, then select **Include Software Component** (see Figure 10.12).

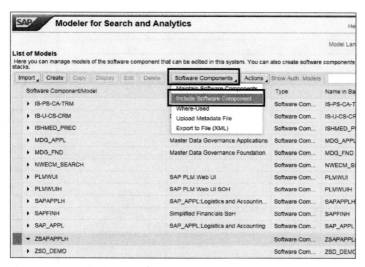

Figure 10.12 Including Standard SAP Component

2. Select the existing software component that you want to refer to—in our example, it's **SAPAPPLH**—and click **Select** (see Figure 10.13).

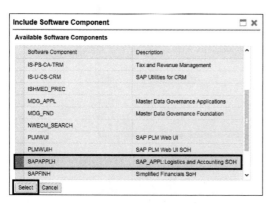

Figure 10.13 Selecting SAP Software Component

3. On the next screen, you can resolve conflicts (i.e., when there are any object types with identical names, they're displayed on this screen; the system automatically renames the technical objects and background functions).

4. In our example, there are no conflicts, so click **Close** (see Figure 10.14).

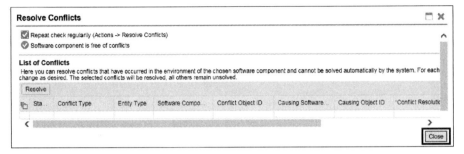

Figure 10.14 Resolve Conflicts

5. Select a transport **Request ID**, then click **Select** (see Figure 10.15).

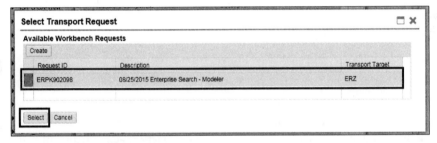

Figure 10.15 Assigning Transport

6. The software component **SAPAPPLH** will now appear below the customer-specific software component **ZSAPAPPLH**, as shown in Figure 10.16.

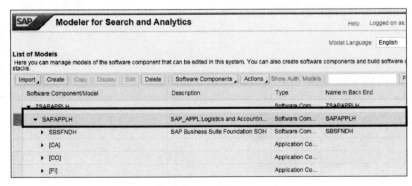

Figure 10.16 Customer-Specific Software Component

This completes the process of creating and adding the software components. As previously stated, the extension process is practically identical to creating search models. Therefore, refer to Section 10.3.1 for further information, or visit *https://help. sap.com/saphelp_nw73/helpdata/en/b6/e51604ca9a480bb8d58111a837b4ae/content.html*.

Creating an OData Service

In Chapter 7, we discussed the steps for creating an OData service. Simply follow the same process to do so again here.

10.2.2   Create the UI Layer

In this section, we'll show you how to create a new fact sheet app on the sales order search model. We'll use the CB_SALES_ORDER_SRV OData service (refer to Chapter 5, Section 5.2) to build the fact sheet app. Follow these steps:

1. Log in to SAP Web IDE, and click **New Project from a Template**.

2. You can either build an app using an existing fact sheet app or build the app from the scratch:
   - **Existing Fact Sheet Application**
     Use this template when you want to create a new fact sheet app using an existing fact sheet app as a template.
   - **New Fact Sheet Application**
     Use this template if you want to create a fact sheet app from scratch.

3. For this example, select **New Fact Sheet Application**, then click **Next** (see Figure 10.17).

Figure 10.17 New Fact Sheet Template

4. Enter the **Project Name** and click **Next** (see Figure 10.18).

Figure 10.18 Project Name

5. Select the connection name, and search for "CB_SALES_ORDER_SRV".

6. Select the **CB_SALES_ORDER_SRV** service and click **Next** (see Figure 10.19).

Figure 10.19 Data Connection

7. Enter the following details, as shown in Figure 10.20:
   - **Main OData Entity**: "SalesOrders"
   - **Fact Sheet Name**: "NB Sales"
   - **Name**: "VBELN_DESCR"
   - **Additional Name**: "SalesOrder"

   Click **Next**.

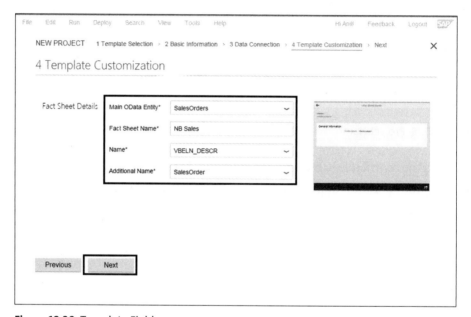

Figure 10.20 Template Fields

8. Click **Finish**.
9. Double-click the **CB_SALES_ORDER_SRV.anno** file to open it in the fact sheet app editor (see Figure 10.21).
10. Drag and drop fields from the **Available Fields** tab to the correct section in the design editor (see Figure 10.22):
    - Into **Key Facts Section**, drag and drop **NetAmount** and **OverallSDProcessStatus-Desc**.
    - Into **Facet Section**, drag and drop **SalesOrder**, **SoldToParty**, and **ShipTo-Party-Name**.

Figure 10.21 Annotation File

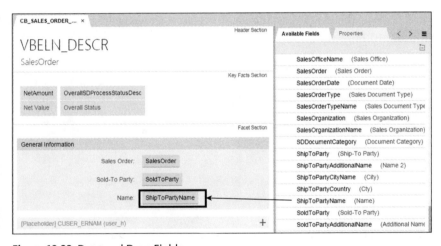

Figure 10.22 Drag and Drop Fields

11. Save the project by clicking the **Save** button.

12. Run the fact sheet app by right-clicking the ANNO file and selecting **Run • Run Fact Sheet** (see Figure 10.23).

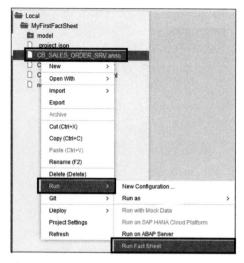

Figure 10.23 Preview Fact Sheet

You should now see the new Sales Order fact sheet app, showing data from the backend (see Figure 10.24).

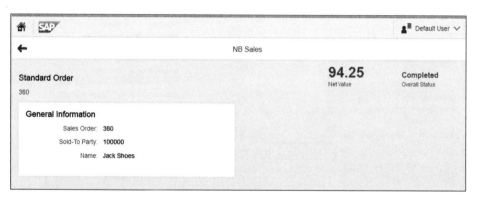

Figure 10.24 New Fact Sheet

We've successfully created a fact sheet app. Next, let's discuss how to deploy the app.

10.2.3   Deploy the Fact Sheet App

In this section, we'll deploy the project to the ABAP Repository by following these steps:

1. Right-click the project and select **Deploy · Deploy to SAPUI5 ABAP Repository** (see Figure 10.25).

Figure 10.25 Deploying to ABAP Repository

2. Enter the **Name** and **Description** and select a **Package**. Click **Next** (see Figure 10.26).

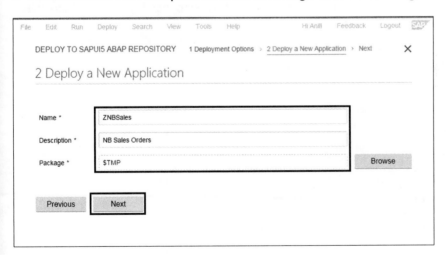

Figure 10.26 Application Details

3. Select the ABAP back-end system connection.

4. Select the **Deploy a New Application** radio button, then click **Next** (see Figure 10.27).

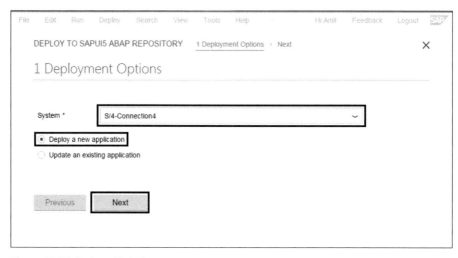

Figure 10.27 System Details

5. Click **Finish**.

You've successfully deployed a new fact sheet app to the ABAP Repository. Next, let's check whether the app and the service were created in the ABAP back-end server. Follow these steps:

1. Log in to the ABAP back-end server, and run Transaction SE80.

2. Search for the "ZNBSALES" BSP application, and check whether the objects are created (see Figure 10.28).

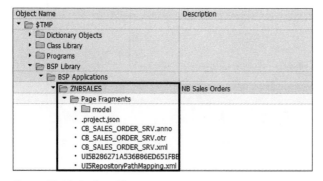

Figure 10.28 Project Files

3. Check whether the service was created by running Transaction SICF and searching for the "ZNBSALES" service (see Figure 10.29).

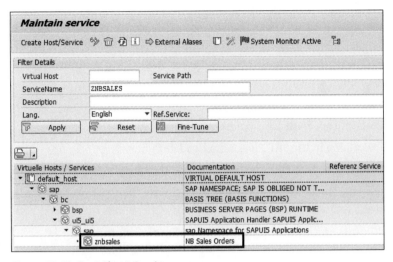

Figure 10.29 Fact Sheet Service

4. Provide access to the end user to the OData service that you used to build the fact sheet app. In Chapter 4, Section 4.4.2, we showed you how to assign a role to a user. You can follow the same process and assign the SAP_SD_SALESORDER_APP role to the end user (see Figure 10.30).

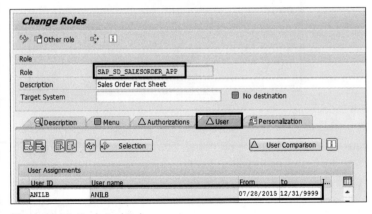

Figure 10.30 Back-End Role

Roles

You can create your own roles and assign an OData service and a user to your custom role.

5. The next step is to create a new launchpad and application using Transaction LPD_ CUST. Refer to Chapter 4, Section 4.6 to complete the following steps:

    – Create a new launchpad.

    – Create a new application under the new launchpad.

    – Create a new catalog in the SAP Fiori launchpad designer.

    – Add a new target mapping with the launchpad as the target.

6. To create a new launchpad and application, you can use the existing Sales Order fact sheet app as a reference (see Figure 10.31) and use the details from Steps 2 and 3 of this section.

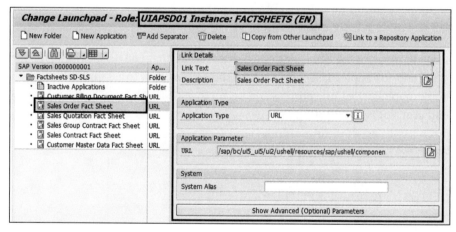

Figure 10.31 Fact Sheet Launchpad

7. Similarly, to create catalog and target mapping, you can use the existing Sales Order fact sheet's target mapping details as a reference while creating target mapping (see Figure 10.32).

Now that you understand the end-to-end process to create a fact sheet app, let's look at the fact sheet extension process.

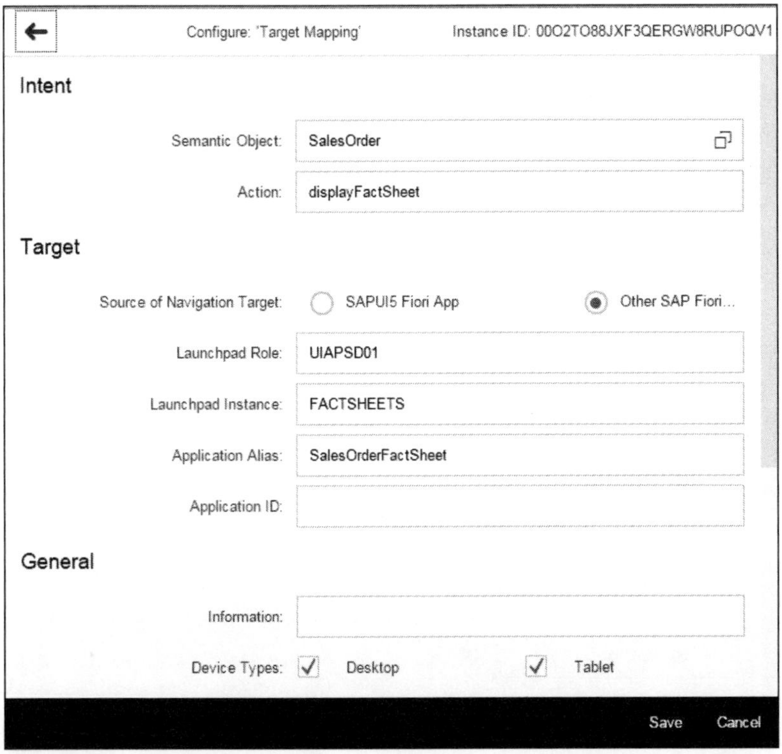

Figure 10.32 Target Mapping

10.3   Extending Fact Sheet Apps

You can extend a fact sheet when a standard fact sheet app delivered by SAP doesn't meet your requirements. The following are scenarios in which you can extend a specific layer of a system landscape for fact sheet apps:

- You can extend a search model when you want to add fields to the fact sheet app that aren't available in the search model.
- You can extend the UI layer if the back-end logic and the content required for the app extension are present in the SAP Gateway layer, but it's not exposed to the UI layer.

We'll use an example based on the Sales Order fact sheet app in this section. We'll walk you through extending both a search model and the UI layer by adding the new **Risk Category** field to the Sales Order app.

10.3.1   Extend the Search Model

The first step in the extension process is to extend the search model. From the SAP Fiori apps reference library, search for the Sales Order fact sheet app, and navigate to the **Configuration** section. Go to the **Search Connector** section to see a list of connectors for the Sales Order fact sheet app (see Figure 10.33). In Chapter 5, Section 5.4, we discussed how to create a connector on a search model and how to enable an app using these connectors. In this section, we'll show you how to extend a search model by adding a field.

Search Connector

The following search connectors need to be activated in the back-end system:

Search Component (Software Component)	Application Component	Search Model
EAAPPLH	SD-BIL	CUSTOMER_BILL_DOC_H
SAPAPPLH	LO-MD-BP-CM	CUSTOMER_H
	SD-SLS	CUST_QUOTATION_H
	LE-SHP	OUTBOUND_DELIVERY_H
	SD-SLS	SALES_ORDER_H
	BC-EIM-ESH	USER_H

Figure 10.33 Search Models

Search Models and Connectors

To get the complete list of search models and connectors for all SAP Fiori fact sheet apps, refer to SAP Note 1861013.

To extend a model, we use the search and analytics modeler, which is a component of SAP Enterprise Search. This tool allows developers to create or change models for search object connectors. You need to have extensive knowledge of the SAP Business Suite back-end technology to create or change any search model.

SAP Enterprise Search and the search and analytics modeler tool are big topics. In this chapter, we'll cover a very basic example, explaining how to enhance a search model by added a field to it. The sections that follow walk through the different steps for extending the search model.

Enhance the Model

In this section, we'll begin by enhancing our data model. As previously mentioned, most of the steps are similar when creating or enhancing a search object connector. In both scenarios, you'll follow the same sequence of screens:

1. Expand the **SD-SLS** component, then select **SALES_ORDER_H**.

2. Click **Edit** (see Figure 10.34).

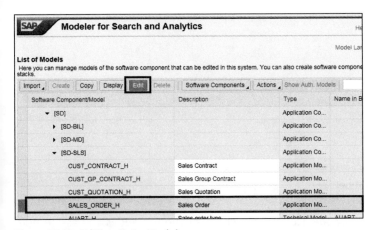

Figure 10.34 Editing Data Model

3. Click **Yes** to confirm the model enhancements, as shown in Figure 10.35.

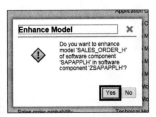

Figure 10.35 Enhance Model Confirmation Pop-up

4. Next, you'll be working through the roadmap steps. In the first step (**Model Properties**), the properties of the search object connector model are defined (i.e., the **Model Type** and the component properties). Click **Next** (see Figure 10.36).

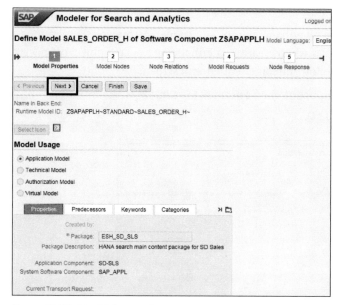

Figure 10.36 Model Properties

5. In the second step (**Model Nodes**), you create or modify nodes and assign node names and node attributes. From the **List of Nodes of 'SALES_ORDER_H'** section, select **SO_VBAK** (see Figure 10.37).

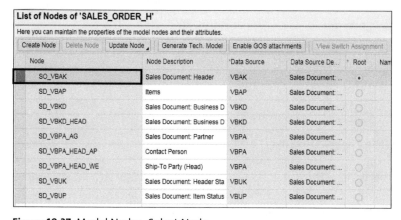

Figure 10.37 Model Nodes: Select Node

6. Scroll down to the **Details Attributes** section, and select the **CTLPC** (**Risk category**) attribute by checking the **Select for Node** checkbox. Click **Next** (see Figure 10.38).

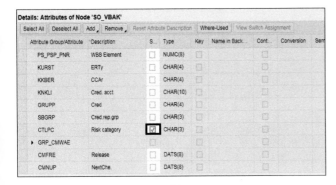

Figure 10.38 Selecting New Field

7. In the third step (**Node Relations**), all the nodes you selected in the previous steps and their relations are listed. Click **Next** (see Figure 10.39).

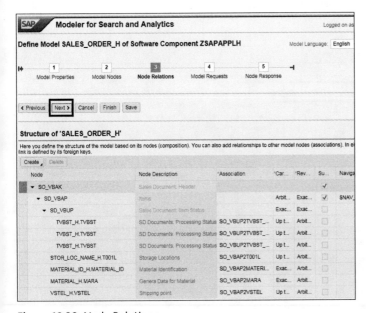

Figure 10.39 Node Relations

8. Now, you'll define the attributes and the search pattern or queries. After the attributes are selected, the system generates a default query with all the selected response attributes. In this step, you need to add "Risk category" as an attribute and define the query. Under the **Request Attributes** tab, click **Add**, then select **Attributes/Group from Node** (see Figure 10.40).

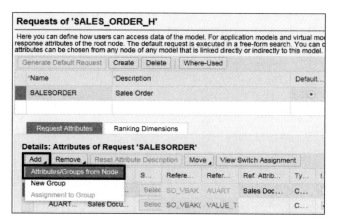

Figure 10.40 Adding Attributes

9. Select **CTLPC** from the **Details Attribute of Node**, then click **Select**. Click **Next** (see Figure 10.41).

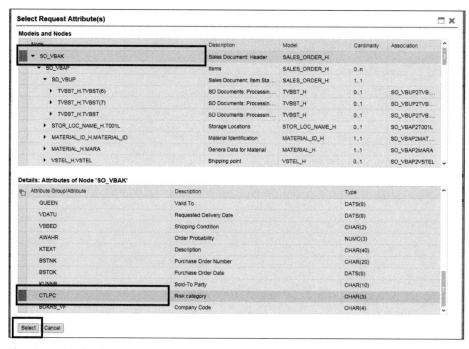

Figure 10.41 Selecting New Field

10. Finally, you'll define the optional settings for the search object model. In this step, you'll add **CTLPC** as a response attribute and define the properties. Under the **Request Attributes** tab, click **Add**, then select **Attributes/Groups from Node** (see Figure 10.42).

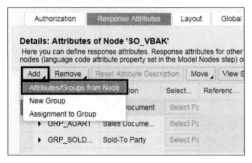

Figure 10.42 Adding Attribute

11. Select **CTLPC** from **Details Attributes of Node**, then click **Select** (see Figure 10.43).

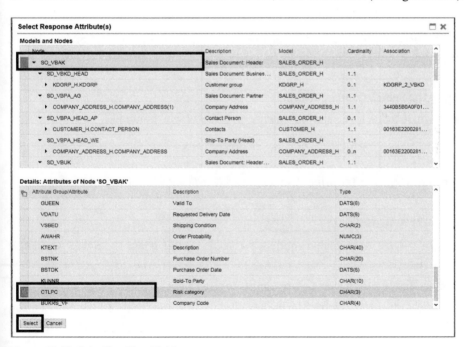

Figure 10.43 Selecting New Field

12. Select the **CTLPC** attribute, and define the response attributes. Check the **Details** and **Fact Sheet** checkboxes (see Figure 10.44).

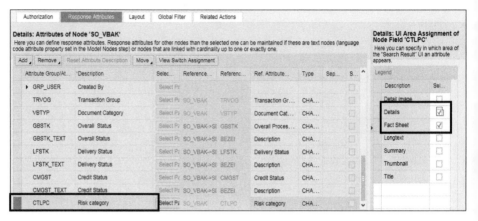

Figure 10.44 Selecting UI Area Assignment

13. Click **Save**, then click **Finish**.

You've successfully enhanced the search model by adding a new field and setting its properties.

Create the Search Connector

Next, you'll create the search connector on the new search model.

Important!

You need to follow the same steps as you followed to create a new fact sheet app.

Follow these steps:

1. From the list of available models, navigate to and select the **SALES_ORDER_H** search object.

2. Select **Actions**, then click **Create Connector** (see Figure 10.45).

3. The system creates a job in the background to create search object connectors. You can monitor the job in Transaction SE38, and the job name is ESH_<Client>_C_ <Unique Code>.

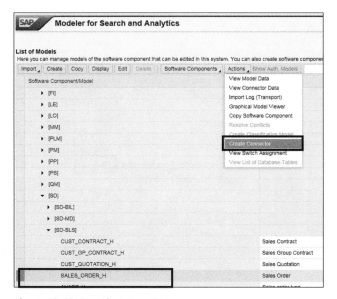

Figure 10.45 Creating New Connector

Schedule Indexing

Now that you've enhanced the model and created the search connector successfully, you must schedule indexing for the sales order search model, which is handled in the connector administration cockpit. The status of the newly created connector will be set to **Prepared**, so you need to schedule this connector to change its status to **Active**.

> **Important!**
>
> You need to follow the same steps as you followed to create a new fact sheet app.

Follow these steps:

1. Run Transaction ESH_COCKPIT.
2. Select **Sales Order.**
3. Click **Actions**, and select **Schedule Indexing** (see Figure 10.46).
4. To make the business objects fully searchable, you need to index **SAPScript long-texts** and select the **Start Immediately** checkboxes for both **ESH_SAPSCRIPT_TEXT** and **USER_AUTHORITY** (see Figure 10.47).
5. Click **OK.**

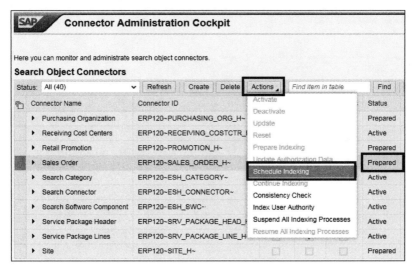

Figure 10.46 Schedule Indexing

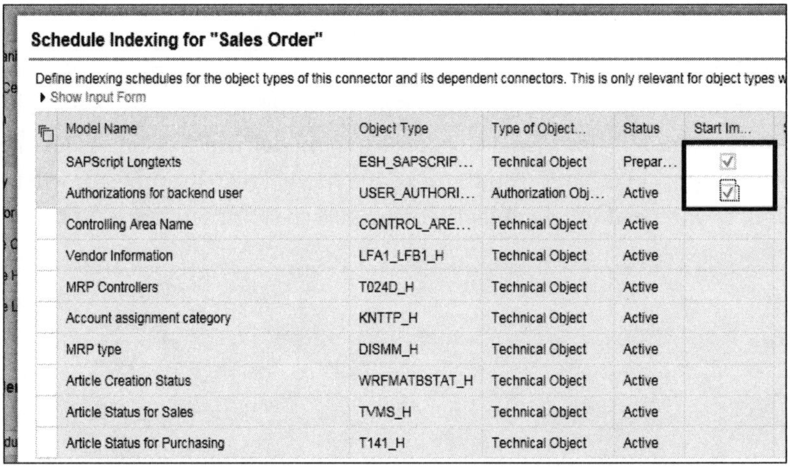

Figure 10.47 Starting Indexing

6. The system creates a job in the background to index search models. You can monitor the job in Transaction SE38. The job name is ESH_<Client>IX_<System ID + Client>_<Unique Code>.

7. After the index is started, the status of the connectors will change to **Indexing**; after the job is completed, the status will change to **Active** (see Figure 10.48).

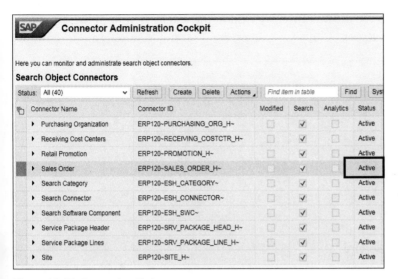

Figure 10.48 Connector Status

Test Embedded Search

After the status is changed to **Active**, you can test the embedded search via the Web Dynpro UI. You need to follow the same steps as you followed to create a new SAP Fiori fact sheet app:

1. Launch embedded search by running Transaction ESH_SEARCH from the ABAP system.

2. Enter "Sales Orders" in the **Search For** field, then click **Search** (see Figure 10.49).

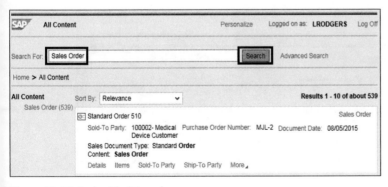

Figure 10.49 Embedded Search

3. Click **Details** to view the details of a sales order.

You should now see the **Risk category** field in the details view, with the data populated (see Figure 10.50).

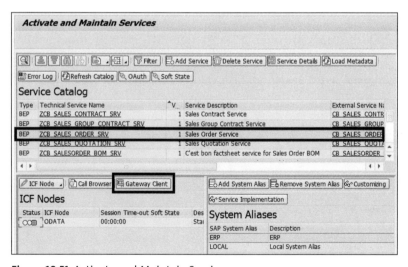

Figure 10.50 New Field

Test the OData Service

In this step, you need to check whether the OData service of the Sales Order fact sheet app is displaying the new field. You need to follow the same steps as you followed to create a new SAP Fiori fact sheet app:

1. Run Transaction /IWFND/MAINT_SERVICE.

2. Select **ZCB_SALES_ORDER_SRV**, then click **Gateway Client** (see Figure 10.51).

Figure 10.51 Activate and Maintain Services

3. In the **Request URI** field, enter "/sap/opu/odata/sap/CB_SALES_ORDER_SRV/ $metadata" (see Figure 10.52).

4. Click **Execute.**

5. Under **Sales Order Entity Type**, you should now see the new property, **CTLPC**.

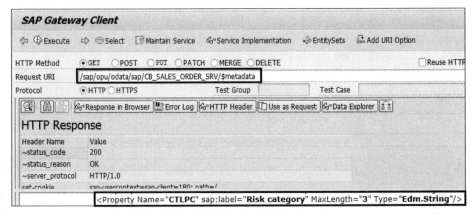

Figure 10.52 Testing OData Service

You've successfully completed the first part of the extension process by extending the sales order search model and adding the **Risk category** field. Next, we'll explore the UI layer of the Sales Order fact sheet app.

10.3.2   Extend the UI Layer

The next step in the process is to extend the UI layer. You can extend the UI layer when the back-end logic and content exist in the SAP Gateway layer, but aren't exposed to the UI layer. In our example, we have the risk category added to the search model and to the OData service; however, it's not added to the UI layer.

You have two options to extend a UI layer of a fact sheet app:

1. Extend a fact sheet app with SAP Web IDE.

2. Extend a fact sheet app manually.

The next two sections walk through these options.

Extend the UI Layer with SAP Web IDE

The SAP Web IDE fact sheet editor app allows developers to create fact sheets from scratch and extend existing fact sheets (refer to Section 10.1). The beauty of SAP Web IDE is that you can connect to the ABAP system and preview the fact sheet. In this section, you'll extend the fact sheet app with SAP Web IDE by following detailed steps.

10

Retrieve the BSP Application and Annotation File

Before we take a deep dive into this process, let's first get the details of the BSP application and the annotation file details of the Sales Order fact sheet app. Search for "Sales Orders" in the SAP Fiori apps reference library at *https://fioriappslibrary. hana.ondemand.com/sap/fix/externalViewer/index.html*, then navigate to the **Extensibility** section (see Figure 10.53).

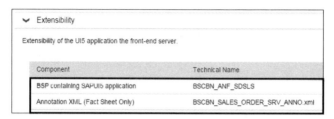

Figure 10.53 Sales Order Fact Sheet Technical Names

Select a Template

The next step is to extend the UI layer of the app using a standard SAP fact sheet app template. Follow these steps:

1. Log in to SAP Web IDE and click **New Project from Template** (see Figure 10.54).

Figure 10.54 Creating New Project from Template

2. You'll see three templates to create or enhance a fact sheet app (see Figure 10.55):
   - **Existing Fact Sheet Application**
     Use this template when you want to extend an existing fact sheet app. You can either deploy the app as a new application or overwrite the existing application.
   - **Modification Free Fact Sheet Application**
     Use this template when you want to extend an existing fact sheet app in the modification-free mode. After you change the XSL file and upload it to the back-end server, the fact sheet app will contain the changes from both the annotation file and XSL file you created using this template.

- **New Fact Sheet Application**
  Use this template if you want to create a fact sheet app from scratch.

Figure 10.55 Fact Sheet Application Templates

> **Templates**
>
> You can use either the **Existing Fact Sheet Application** or **New Fact Sheet Application** template to create a fact sheet app.

In our example, we'll use the existing Sales Order fact sheet app and enhance it with the new field.

When extending a fact sheet app, you can use either the **Existing Fact Sheet Application** option or the **Modification Free Fact Sheet Application** option. Let's begin by using the **Existing Fact Sheet Application** template:

1. Select **Existing Fact Sheet Application**, then click **Next** (see Figure 10.56).

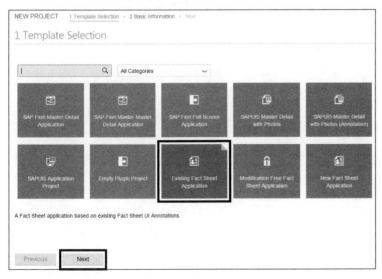

Figure 10.56 Existing Fact Sheet Application

2. Enter a **Project Name**, and click **Next** (see Figure 10.57).

Figure 10.57 Project Details

3. Select your ABAP system (refer to Chapter 8 to add a connection) from the drop-down list, then enter "Sales Orders Fact Sheet" in the **Search** field to search for the Sales Order fact sheet app.

> **Note**
>
> If you don't see the list of fact sheet apps, you may not have added the `WebIDEUsage` `bsp_execute_abap` property in the connection. Refer to Chapter 8 to review how to add properties in the connection.

4. Select **Sales Order Fact Sheet** and click **Next** (see Figure 10.58).

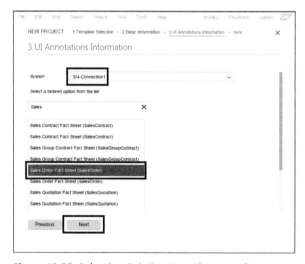

Figure 10.58 Selecting Existing Fact Sheet Application

5. Click **Finish** to confirm.

Now that we've looked at how to use existing fact sheet app templates, we'll move to the second template: **Modification Free Fact Sheet Application**.

You can use this template when you want to extend an existing fact sheet app without modifying it; that is, you don't want to change the XML code in the original file, but you still want to add new fields in the fact sheet app. Most of the steps are like those we've already discussed in this chapter; you'll just notice new files created, compared to app creation with the first template.

In this example, you'll use the same search model you enhanced by adding a new field (**Risk Category**) and will create a new modification-free fact sheet app. We'll just add screens that are specific to this template. If you get stuck while working on this extension, refer to the previous section; the process is similar between all the templates, although the initial screens look different. Follow these steps:

1. Log in to SAP Web IDE, and from the menu bar, select **File • New • Project from Template** (see Figure 10.59).

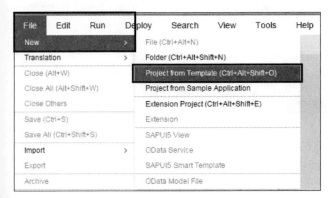

Figure 10.59 Creating New Project from Template

2. Select **Modification Free Fact Sheet Application**, then click **Next** (see Figure 10.60).
3. Enter a name in the **Project Name** field and click **Next**.
4. Select your ABAP system from the dropdown list, then search for the Sales Order fact sheet app by entering "Sales Orders Fact Sheet" in the **Search** field.
5. Select **Sales Order Fact Sheet** and click **Next**.
6. Click **Finish** to confirm.

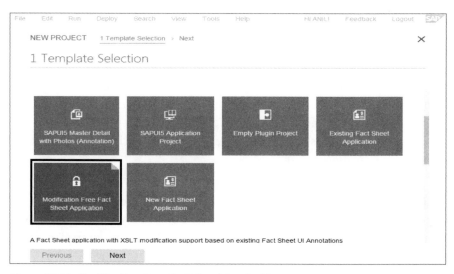

Figure 10.60 Modification-Free Fact Sheet Application

7. You should now see the annotation file under the new project folder (see Figure 10.61).

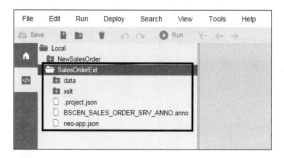

Figure 10.61 Editing Annotation File

8. Double-click the **BSCBN_SALES_ORDER_SRV_ANNO.anno** file to open it in the SAP Web IDE fact sheet editor app.

9. Drag and drop the **CTLPC** field to the **Facet Section/General Information** section.

10. Save the project by clicking the **Save** button. SAP Web IDE automatically generates the files required for the extension process (see Figure 10.62).

    Table 10.1 shows the list of files or folders generated when you use the **Modification Free Fact Sheet Application** template in SAP Web IDE.

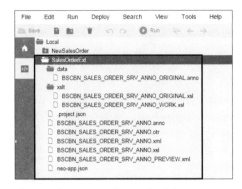

Figure 10.62 New Files and Folders

File/Folder	Description
data	This folder contains the original annotation file.
Original.xsl	This file contains the XSLT template that is generated exactly the like the original ANNO file. This file is used to track the changes that a user makes to the annotation file.
Work.xsl	This file contains all the changes made by a user in the design view. In our example, we added the **Risk Category** field, and that change will be captured in this file.
.project.json	This service file with .project.jso extension contains the service URL details and the main entity sets.
.anno	This is the original fact sheet annotation file.
.otr	This service file contains the Online Text Repository (OTR) aliases, with the labels and back-end availability status.
.xml	This service file contains the ABAP code for the OTR.
.xsl	This file with .xsl extension is used in the back-end system to apply changes to the matching fact sheet.
Preview.xml	The result of the XSL file and the original.anno file is saved in this preview.xml file.
neo-app.json	This service file contains settings to preview the fact sheet in SAP Fiori launchpad.

Table 10.1 Project Files

11. Test the extended fact sheet by right-clicking the ANNO file and navigating to **Run • Run Fact Sheet**.

12. Upload the XSL file to the back-end server to deploy the changes to the ABAP system.

The next time the user runs the Sales Order fact sheet app, it will contain both the changes from the annotation file and the XSL file changes you created using this template in SAP Web IDE.

Extension Project Properties

You've successfully created a project in SAP Web IDE using an existing template for the Sales Order fact sheet app. Before we show you how to enhance the UI layer, we'll show you some basic properties and components of an extension project.

You should see the annotation file under the new project folder (see Figure 10.63).

Figure 10.63 Fact Sheet Annotation File

The new project folder contains the following files:

- **project.json**
  This file contains the OData service URL and the entity set details of the fact sheet.

- **ANNO**
  This is the annotation file that you'll be working on to extend the fact sheet.

- **neo-app.json**
  This file contains settings to preview the fact sheet app.

Template Files/Folders

If you're using a different template—that is, **Modification Free Fact Sheet Application** or **New Fact Sheet Application** (refer to Figure 10.55)—you'll see a different set of files/folders under the main project folder.

Double-click the **BSCBN_SALES_ORDER_SRV_ANNO.anno** file to open it in the SAP Web IDE fact sheet editor app. On the next screen, you can switch between **Design** editor and **Source Code** editor (see Figure 10.64). Depending on your programing skills, you can decide the type of editor you want to use; for example, a nondeveloper can use the design editor to edit the annotation file.

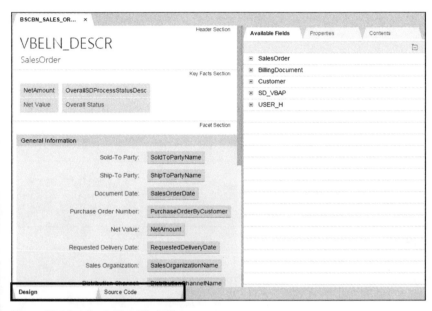

Figure 10.64 Annotation File Editors

The fact sheet app design editor contains three tabs on the right side of the screen:

- **Available Fields**
  This tab displays all the fields provided by the OData service, and you can drag and drop these fields into your fact sheet to enhance it (see Figure 10.65).

Figure 10.65 List of Available Fields

- **Properties**

  Upon clicking any of the fact sheet fields, facets, or key facts in the **Design** editor, you can view their properties on the right side. Figure 10.66 shows the properties of a fact sheet field.

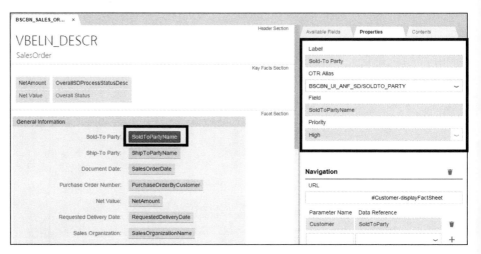

Figure 10.66 Fact Sheet Properties

The following fields are found under the **Properties** tab:

- **Label**

  This is the label of the field displayed in the fact sheet app.

- **Field**

  This is the back-end field provided by the OData service that you want to display.

- **Priority**

  This is the importance level of the fields, determining how they display on different devices or at different screen resolutions:

  - **High**: These fields are shown on the **General Information** section of the fact sheet overview page on all devices.

  - **Medium**: These fields are shown on the **General Information** section of the fact sheet only on larger devices.

  - **Low**: These fields are shown only on the **Details** page.

- **Navigation Target**

  This field defines the target object. When the user clicks on this field, it will navigate the user to the target location specified here.

In the **Key Fact Section**, select the **Net Value** key fact to display the following proper-ties (see Figure 10.67):

- **Label**
  This is the label of the field displayed in the fact sheet app.
- **Field**
  This is the back-end field provided by the OData service that you want to display.
- **Type**
  This is the key fact type.
- **Number of Fractional Digits**
  This is the number of decimals you want to display for this key fact.

Figure 10.67 Key Fact Properties

In **Facet Section**, select the **General Information** facets to display the following prop-erties (see Figure 10.68):

- **Title**
  This is the title of the facet.
- **Navigation Path**
  This is the navigation path of the facet.
- **Entity Type**
  This is the main entity type of the OData service.

Figure 10.68 General Information Properties

- **Contents**
  You can get the structure of the fact sheet from the **Contents** tab (see Figure 10.69).

Figure 10.69 Contents Tab

In addition, you can design a fact sheet app directly by using the **Source Code** editor tab (see Figure 10.70).

```
BSCBN_SALES_OR...   ×
 1  <edmx:Edmx xmlns:edmx="http://docs.oasis-open.org/odata/ns/edmx" Version="4.0">
 2      <edmx:Reference Uri="/sap/bc/ui5_ui5/ui2/ushell/resources/sap/ushell/components/factsheet/vocabularies/UI.>
 3          <edmx:Include Alias="UI" Namespace="com.sap.vocabularies.UI.v1"/>
 4      </edmx:Reference>
 5      <edmx:Reference Uri="/sap/bc/ui5_ui5/ui2/ushell/resources/sap/ushell/components/factsheet/vocabularies/Comm
 6          <edmx:Include Alias="vCard" Namespace="com.sap.vocabularies.Communication.v1"/>
 7      </edmx:Reference>
 8      <edmx:Reference Uri="http://docs.oasis-open.org/odata/odata/v4.0/cs01/vocabularies/Org.OData.Measures.V1.xm
 9          <edmx:Include Alias="CQP" Namespace="Org.OData.Measures.V1"/>
10      </edmx:Reference>
11      <edmx:Reference Uri="/sap/bc/ui5_ui5/ui2/ushell/resources/sap/ushell/components/factsheet/vocabularies/Comm
12          <edmx:Include Alias="Common" Namespace="com.sap.vocabularies.Common.v1"/>
13      </edmx:Reference>
14      <edmx:Reference Uri="/sap/opu/odata/sap/CB_SALES_ORDER_SRV/$metadata">
15          <edmx:Include Alias="CB_SALES_ORDER_SRV" Namespace="CB_SALES_ORDER_SRV"/>
16      </edmx:Reference>
17      <edmx:DataServices>
18          <Schema xmlns="http://docs.oasis-open.org/odata/ns/edm" Alias="CB_SALES_ORDER_SRVAnnotation" Namespace=
19              <Annotations Target="CB_SALES_ORDER_SRV.SalesOrder/NetAmount">
20                  <Annotation Path="TransactionCurrency" Term="CQP.ISOCurrency"/>
21              </Annotations>
22              <Annotations Target="CB_SALES_ORDER_SRV.SD_VBAP/NetAmount">
23                  <Annotation Path="TransactionCurrency" Term="CQP.ISOCurrency"/>
24              </Annotations>
25              <Annotations Target="CB_SALES_ORDER_SRV.SD_VBAP/NetPriceAmount">
26                  <Annotation Path="WAERK_NETPR" Term="CQP.ISOCurrency"/>
27              </Annotations>
28              <Annotations Target="CB_SALES_ORDER_SRV.SalesQuotation/SalesQuotationNetAmount">
29                  <Annotation Path="TransactionCurrency" Term="CQP.ISOCurrency"/>
30              </Annotations>
31              <Annotations Target="CB_SALES_ORDER_SRV.SalesContract/NetAmount">
32                  <Annotation Path="NetAmountCurrency" Term="CQP.ISOCurrency"/>
33              </Annotations>
34
Design              Source Code
```

Figure 10.70 Source Code Editor

Getting back to the extension process, you can extend three sections in the **Design** view (see Figure 10.71):

- **Header Section**
  This section contains the **Fact Sheet Name** and **Additional Name**.

- **Key Facts Section**
  This section contains the **Key Facts** about central objects used in your business operations.

- **Facet Section**

  This section shows the general information and other facets:

  - **General Information**

    These pages are the detail pages with the facet information; you can view them from the **Contents** tab.

Figure 10.71 Annotation Sections

Figure 10.72 shows the same sections in the actual Sales Order fact sheet app.

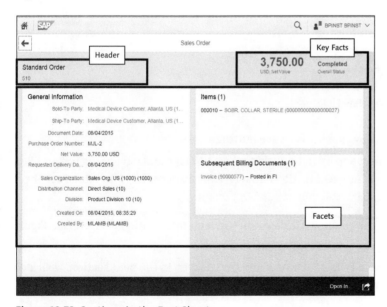

Figure 10.72 Sections in the Fact Sheet

Add the Risk Category

By now, you should be familiar with the SAP Web IDE fact sheet editor app options. Next, you'll add the **Risk Category** field to the **Facet Section** and then preview it. Follow these steps:

1. Drag and drop the **CTLPC** field to the **Facet Section/General Information** section (see Figure 10.73).

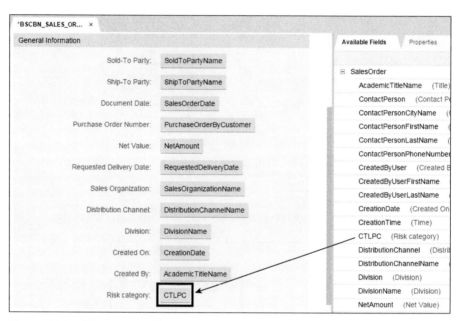

Figure 10.73 Adding New Field

2. Save the project by clicking the **Save** button.
3. Run the fact sheet app by right-clicking the ANNO file and navigating to **Run • Run Fact Sheet** (see Figure 10.74). Alternatively, you can use select **Run • Run Fact Sheet** from the menu bar.

You should now see the new fields in the **General Information** section (see Figure 10.75).

You've now enhanced the data model and the UI layer. In the next section, we'll look at the option for manually extending the UI layer.

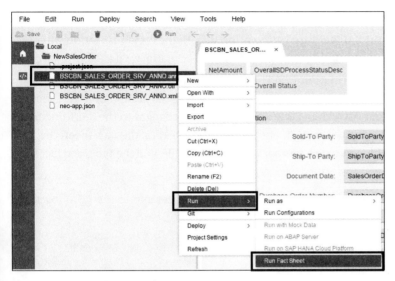

Figure 10.74 Running Fact Sheet App

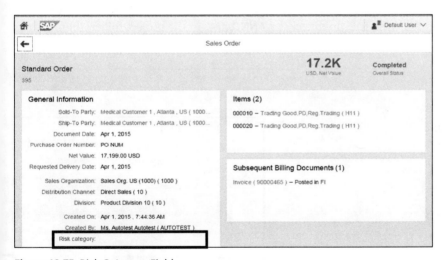

Figure 10.75 Risk Category Field

Extend the UI Layer Manually

In the previous section, we covered how to extend the UI layer using SAP Web IDE. Now, we'll discuss the manual extension process. You can extend the UI layer manually when you want to add more complex elements (e.g., Google Maps) to your fact sheet that can't be added via SAP Web IDE.

You have two options to extend the fact sheet manually:

1. Directly edit the SAP-delivered annotation files. In the previous section we copied the XML code generated in SAP Web IDE, in this scenario, we'll add our own code.

2. Create XSL Transformation (XSLT) documents to work in conjunction with the original SAP-delivered annotation files. The original annotation file remains unchanged, and you can include all the fact sheet changes to the XSLT document and then upload it to the back-end. When the user runs the fact sheet, the XSLT document generates a new temporary annotation file, and the rendered fact sheet is based on the transformed annotation file.

In the next section, we'll deploy the extended fact sheet app to the ABAP back-end server.

10.3.3   Deploy the Fact Sheet App

To deploy or make changes to the original annotation file in the ABAP system, follow these steps:

1. From SAP Web IDE, double-click **_ANNO.XML** in the project folder, then copy all the XML code (see Figure 10.76).

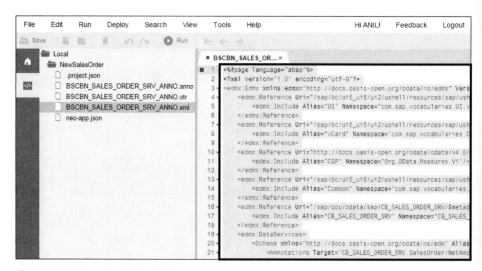

Figure 10.76 Copying XML Code

2. Run Transaction SE80 from your ABAP system.

3. Enter the BSP application name "BSCBN_ANF_SDSLS" and press [Enter].

4. Right-click the Sales Order fact sheet annotation file and select **Change** (see Figure 10.77).

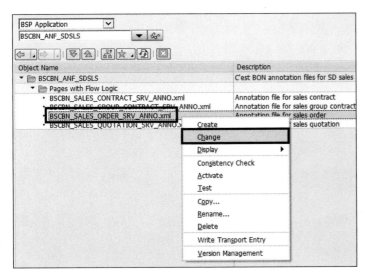

Figure 10.77 Editing Annotation File

5. Paste the code that you copied in Step 1, click **Save** 🖫, then click the **Activate** icon 🖉.

You've successfully extended the app by adding a new field and deploying the Sales Order fact sheet app.

10.4   Summary

In this chapter, we provided step-by-step instructions for how to create and enhance an SAP Fiori fact sheet app using SAP Web IDE. We discussed everything from how to enhance the search model to how to deploy the app to the ABAP systems. In addition, we showed you how to enhance an app using two different templates. We then gave you an overview on how to extend a fact sheet manually. In the next chapter, we'll explore the creation and extension process for analytical apps.

Chapter 11

Creating and Extending Analytical Apps

This chapter explains how to create and extend an analytical app and illustrates the process by walking through a complete example app.

In Chapter 1, we introduced you to the SAP Fiori system landscape with SAP HANA XS. You then learned how to implement a standard SAP Fiori analytical app with and without the SAP Smart Business modeler in Chapter 6. In this chapter, we'll focus on creating and extending an analytical app with an example based on SAP HANA Live views. All the SAP Fiori analytical apps are based on SAP HANA Live views, so we'll begin with an overview of SAP HANA Live before digging into the creation and extension process.

11.1 Introduction to SAP HANA Live

By now, you know that analytical apps only run on an SAP HANA database and that these apps are developed on query views from SAP HANA Live. Therefore, it's important to understand some basic concepts about SAP HANA Live before we look at creating or extending analytical apps. Because SAP HANA Live is a big topic, we'll keep the introduction brief. However, a basic understanding of SAP HANA Live is needed to get started with the app development. Figure 11.1 shows the logical architecture of the SAP Fiori landscape with SAP HANA Live (VDM).

What is SAP HANA Live? SAP HANA Live is a complete set of predefined virtual data models that expose the SAP Business Suite application data. SAP delivers SAP HANA Live packages for several SAP Business Suite application areas; for example, in Figure 11.1, you can see SAP HANA Live for SAP ERP, SAP CRM, and so on. Customers can download and install the specific packages they need.

In this section, we'll look at the important aspects of SAP HANA Live, including SAP HANA Live views, the SAP HANA Live Browser, and the process of exposing these views to SAP Fiori analytical apps.

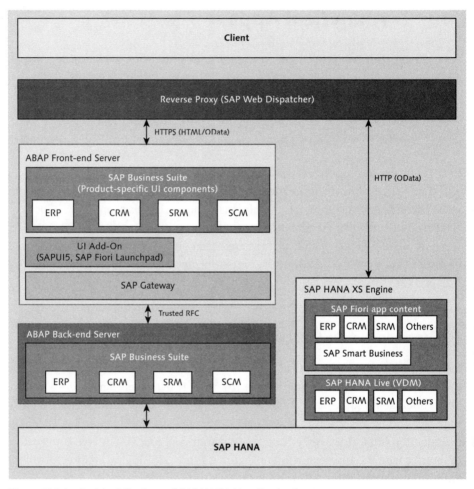

Figure 11.1 Logical Architecture of SAP HANA Live Content

11.1.1   SAP HANA Live Views

A VDM is a structured representation of an SAP HANA database view that follows consistent modeling rules. Data from SAP Business Suite is consumed into the analytical apps using these views. A VDM contains four types of SAP HANA Live views:

1. **Values help views**

   As the name implies, these views are used to populate value help, the dropdown lists in the applications that provide a full list of possible values for entities—for example, customers, materials, and so on.

2. **Private views**

   These views summarize certain SQL transformations on one or several database tables. A private view can be based on database tables, other private views, or reuse views. These are the SAP standard views that use SAP tables directly. No one can modify these views.

3. **Reuse views**

   These views expose business data from SAP Business Suite systems in a well-structured format. They are designed to be reused in other views, and they consist of one more private views.

4. **Query views**

   As previously mentioned, all analytical apps are developed on query views. These are the top level of views, designed to expose business data from the SAP Business Suite system and for direct consumption by the analytical apps.

Now that you know about the different views available in SAP HANA Live, let's look at how to browse and navigate those views.

11.1.2   SAP HANA Live Browser

SAP HANA Live Browser is a web application built using SAPUI5. With this tool, users can easily browse and navigate between the SAP HANA Live content views. You can access SAP HANA Live Browser at *http://<SAP HANA Server Host>:80<SAP HANA Instance>/sap/hba/explorer/*.

Figure 11.2 shows the landing page for SAP HANA Live Browser. On this screen, the content is organized by application components; users can navigate among **ALL VIEWS**, **MY FAVORITES**, **SEARCH**, and **INVALID VIEWS** tabs.

After selecting a view on the left-hand side of the screen, you can see the details of the selected view on the right side. The following icons are shown on the right side (from left to right):

- **Open Definition**

  Use this icon to view the metadata of the SAP HANA Live views.

- **Open Content**

  Use this icon to view the data of the SAP HANA Live views.

- **Open Cross Reference**

  Use this icon to view the tables and view cross references.

- **Add Tags**

  Use this icon to add personalized tags; select a view, then click the **Add Tags** button.

- **Generate SLT**

  Use this icon to generate the SAP Landscape Transformation file.

- **SAP Lumira**

  Use this icon to open the SAP HANA Live view in SAP Lumira and build storyboards using data from SAP HANA Live.

- **SAP BusinessObjects Analysis**

  Use this icon to open the SAP HANA Live view in SAP BusinessObjects Analysis to perform further detailed analysis on your data.

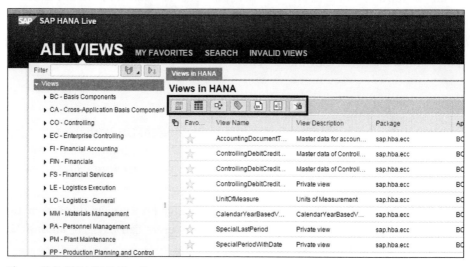

Figure 11.2 SAP HANA Live Browser

We've now covered the overview of both SAP HANA Live views and SAP HANA Live Browser. In the next section, we'll discuss how these views work in relation to SAP Fiori analytical apps.

11.1.3   Exposing SAP HANA Live Views to Analytical Apps

Views in SAP HANA Live can be exposed as an OData service. These services can integrate SAP HANA Live views with SAP Fiori analytical apps. By now, you're familiar with OData services and their concepts. An OData service for SAP HANA XS is defined in a text file with the suffix *.xsodata*. The data is transferred to analytical apps over HTTP using either the AtomPub (XML) or the JSON format.

A couple of advantages of using SAP HANA Live with analytical apps are as follows:

- Developers can build analytical apps directly on SAP HANA Live views without the need for additional software.
- All analytical apps run on the primary database, so there's no need for users to wait for the data-loading jobs to complete. The cycle time from recording to displaying in analytical apps is dramatically reduced.

In addition, when working with SAP HANA Live views in correlation with SAP Fiori analytical apps, it's important to keep the following points in mind:

- Private views should not be copied or modified.
- Use query views or reuse views for extensions by copying them. If you change the original views, then the changes will be lost the next time a new VDM is installed.
- The **Enforce SQL Execution** flag must be set to **True** for all graphical calculation views.
- Using attribute and analytical views must be avoided for better performance of the app.

Now that you have a basic understanding of SAP HANA Live and its views, let's walk through how to create or extend an analytical app using a view from SAP HANA Live. The creation and extension processes are very similar, so we'll first cover the creation processes in detail, and then we'll talk about the extension process from a high-level perspective.

Prerequisites

Several prerequisites must be met before you start creating or extending analytical apps:

- The correct version of SAP HANA must be installed on the SAP HANA server per the requirements for SAP HANA Live. Refer to the SAP Fiori apps reference library to find the exact versions.

- The standard SAP tables used by SAP HANA Live must exist and be populated with data by an appropriate data-replication mechanism.
- The SAP HANA client and SAP HANA Studio software must be installed on the client systems.
- A beginner's knowledge of SAP HANA data modeling is required.
- You must be familiar with or have access to the SAP HANA Live release notes.
- You need to have access to KPI modeler apps (see Chapter 6).

We highly recommend going through Chapter 6 if you haven't yet done so before you work on the examples in this chapter.

11.2 Creating Analytical Apps

In this section, we'll show you how to create an analytical app using an example based on a sales order calculation view. The first step in this process is to create the SAP HANA Live view.

11.2.1 Create the SAP HANA Live View

For the SAP HANA Live view, you can either create it from scratch or create it by copying an existing view.

In this example, you'll create a new view by copying an existing calculation view. Follow these steps:

1. Log in to your SAP HANA system from SAP HANA Studio.
2. Select the **Developers** perspective.
3. Create a new package by right-clicking either the **Content** folder or the existing package and selecting **New · Package** (see Figure 11.3).

Creating a Package

It isn't necessary to create a new package in the same location that you created an old package (see Figure 11.3). The new package can be located anywhere in the **Content** folder. However, it's important to keep in mind that the package you're creating should be included in SAP Web Dispatcher. For example, in our demo system, sap.hba is included in SAP Web Dispatcher (refer to Chapter 3, Section 3.1.2).

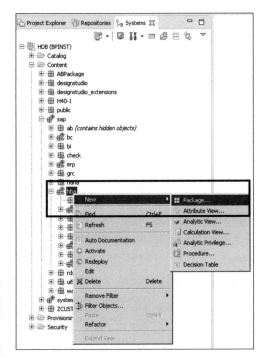

Figure 11.3 Create New Package

4. On the next screen, enter the package name, then click **OK** (see Figure 11.4).

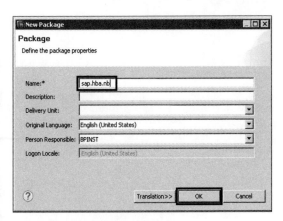

Figure 11.4 New Package Definition

5. Right-click the new package and select **New · Calculation View** (see Figure 11.5).

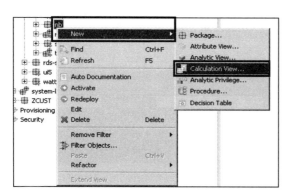

Figure 11.5 Create New Calculation View

6. Enter a name for the view in the **Name** field, then select the **Copy From** checkbox. Click **Browse** (see Figure 11.6).

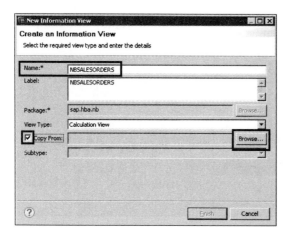

Figure 11.6 Copy Calculation View

7. Search for the word "salesorder", then select **SalesOrderQuery** from the results. Click **OK** (see Figure 11.7).

8. Click **Finish** (see Figure 11.8).

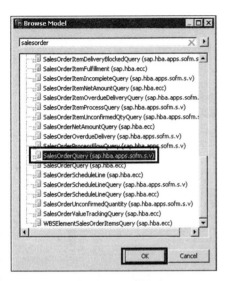

Figure 11.7 Selecting Standard View

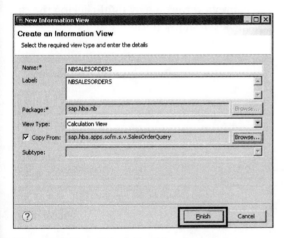

Figure 11.8 New Calculation View Parameters

9. Right-click the new calculation view, then click **Activate** (see Figure 11.9).

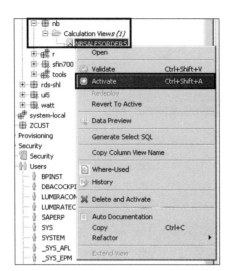

Figure 11.9 Activating New Calculation View

10. After the calculation view is activated, preview the data by right-clicking the calculation view and selecting **Data Preview** (see Figure 11.10).

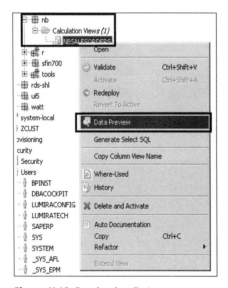

Figure 11.10 Previewing Data

11.   Enter the parameters (i.e., for the client), then click **OK** (see Figure 11.11).

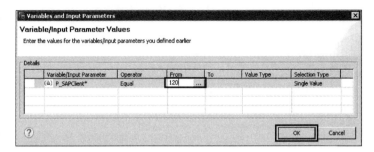

Figure 11.11 Enter Parameters

12.   You should now see the data under the **Raw Data** tab (see Figure 11.12).

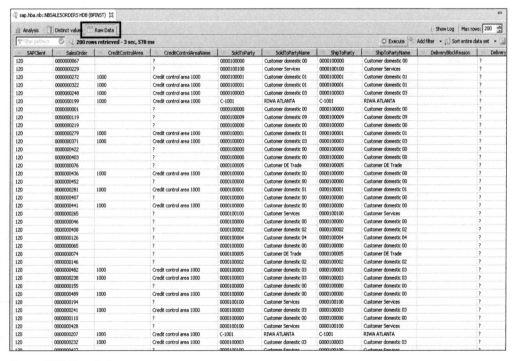

SAPClient	SalesOrder	CreditControlArea	CreditControlAreaName	SoldToParty	SoldToPartyName	ShipToParty	ShipToPartyName	DeliveryBlockReason	Delivery
120	0000000067		?	0000100000	Customer domestic 00	0000100000	Customer domestic 00		?
120	0000000229		?	0000100100	Customer Services	0000100100	Customer Services		?
120	0000000272	1000	Credit control area 1000	0000100001	Customer domestic 01	0000100001	Customer domestic 01		?
120	0000000322	1000	Credit control area 1000	0000100001	Customer domestic 01	0000100001	Customer domestic 01		?
120	0000000248	1000	Credit control area 1000	0000100003	Customer domestic 03	0000100003	Customer domestic 03		?
120	0000000199	1000	Credit control area 1000	C-1001	RIWA ATLANTA	C-1001	RIWA ATLANTA		?
120	0000000001		?	0000100000	Customer domestic 00	0000100000	Customer domestic 00		?
120	0000000119		?	0000100009	Customer domestic 09	0000100009	Customer domestic 09		?
120	0000000219		?	0000100000	Customer domestic 00	0000100000	Customer domestic 00		?
120	0000000279	1000	Credit control area 1000	0000100001	Customer domestic 01	0000100001	Customer domestic 01		?
120	0000000371	1000	Credit control area 1000	0000100003	Customer domestic 03	0000100003	Customer domestic 03		?
120	0000000422		?	0000100000	Customer domestic 00	0000100000	Customer domestic 00		?
120	0000000403		?	0000100000	Customer domestic 00	0000100000	Customer domestic 00		?
120	0000000076		?	0000100005	Customer DE Trade	0000100005	Customer DE Trade		?
120	0000000436	1000	Credit control area 1000	0000100000	Customer domestic 00	0000100000	Customer domestic 00		?
120	0000000452		?	0000100000	Customer domestic 00	0000100000	Customer domestic 00		?
120	0000000281	1000	Credit control area 1000	0000100001	Customer domestic 01	0000100001	Customer domestic 01		?
120	0000000407		?	0000100000	Customer domestic 00	0000100000	Customer domestic 00		?
120	0000000441	1000	Credit control area 1000	0000100000	Customer domestic 00	0000100000	Customer domestic 00		?
120	0000000265		?	0000100100	Customer Services	0000100100	Customer Services		?
120	0000000046		?	0000100000	Customer domestic 00	0000100000	Customer domestic 00		?
120	0000000408		?	0000100002	Customer domestic 02	0000100002	Customer domestic 02		?
120	0000000126		?	0000100004	Customer domestic 04	0000100004	Customer domestic 04		?
120	0000000065		?	0000100000	Customer domestic 00	0000100000	Customer domestic 00		?
120	0000000074		?	0000100005	Customer DE Trade	0000100005	Customer DE Trade		?
120	0000000146		?	0000100002	Customer domestic 02	0000100002	Customer domestic 02		?
120	0000000482	1000	Credit control area 1000	0000100003	Customer domestic 03	0000100003	Customer domestic 03		?
120	0000000238	1000	Credit control area 1000	0000100003	Customer domestic 03	0000100003	Customer domestic 03		?
120	0000000155		?	0000100000	Customer domestic 00	0000100000	Customer domestic 00		?
120	0000000489	1000	Credit control area 1000	0000100000	Customer domestic 00	0000100000	Customer domestic 00		?
120	0000000194		?	0000100100	Customer Services	0000100100	Customer Services		?
120	0000000241	1000	Credit control area 1000	0000100003	Customer domestic 03	0000100003	Customer domestic 03		?
120	0000000110		?	0000100000	Customer domestic 00	0000100000	Customer domestic 00		?
120	0000000428		?	0000100100	Customer Services	0000100100	Customer Services		?
120	0000000207	1000	Credit control area 1000	C-1001	RIWA ATLANTA	C-1001	RIWA ATLANTA		?
120	0000000232	1000	Credit control area 1000	0000100003	Customer domestic 03	0000100003	Customer domestic 03		?
120	0000000427		?	0000100100	Customer Services	0000100100	Customer Services		?

Figure 11.12 Raw Data

We've successfully copied an existing calculation view and created a new one. In the next section, we'll expose the calculation view by creating an OData service.

11.2.2   Create the OData Service

In the previous section, we created a calculation view, and now in this section, we'll show you how to create an OData service and expose the calculation view as an OData service. Follow these steps:

1. Log in to the SAP HANA system from SAP HANA Studio, then select the **Project Explorer** tab.

2. Before you can start the OData service development, you must create a project, which you'll use to group all your application-related artifacts. Next, you'll create an SAP HANA XS project. Right-click in the blank area and select **New · Project** (see Figure 11.13).

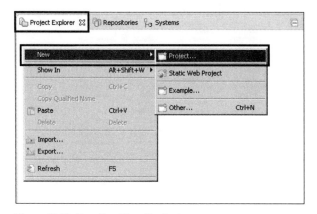

Figure 11.13 Creating New Project

3. From the wizard, select **SAP HANA · Application Development · XS Project**, then click **Next** (see Figure 11.14).

4. Enter a **Project name**, then click **Next** (see Figure 11.15).

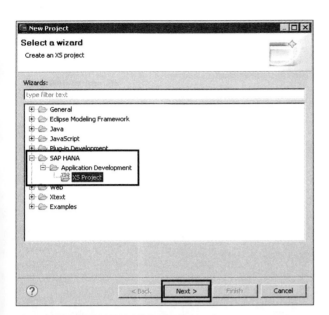

Figure 11.14 SAP HANA XS Project

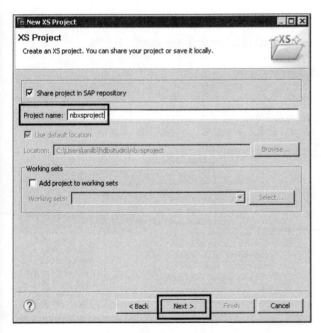

Figure 11.15 SAP HANA XS Project Name

5. Now, we'll add a workspace. You can skip this step and proceed to the next if you've already created a workspace. Otherwise, click **Add Workspace** (see Figure 11.16).

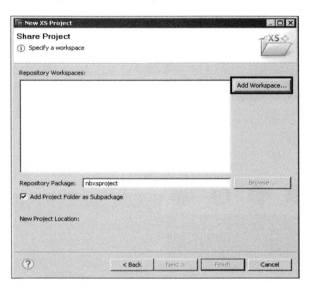

Figure 11.16 Adding Workspace

6. Select your SAP HANA system, then click **Finish** (see Figure 11.17).

Figure 11.17 Creating New Workspace

7. Select the workspace, then click **Browse** (see Figure 11.18).

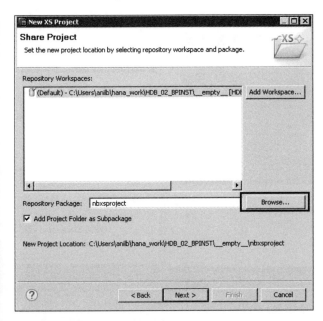

Figure 11.18 Share Project Dialog Box

8. Select the repository package you created in the first step and click **OK** (see Figure 11.19).

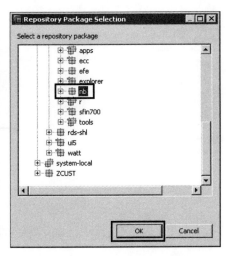

Figure 11.19 Selecting Repository Package

9. Uncheck the **Add Project Folder as Subpackage** checkbox and click **Next** (see Figure 11.20).

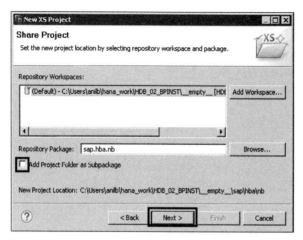

Figure 11.20 Unchecking Add Project Folder as Subpackage

10. Leave everything blank on this screen, and click **Finish** (see Figure 11.21).

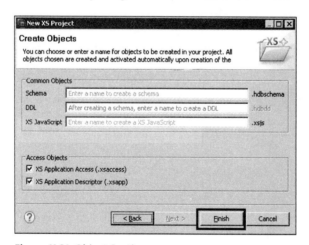

Figure 11.21 Object Section

A new project is created with the calculation view. Make sure the application access file (XSACCESS) and the application descriptor files (XSAPP) are automatically created. Next, we'll create the OData service file. Follow these steps:

1. Right-click the new project and select **New • XSODATA File** (see Figure 11.22).

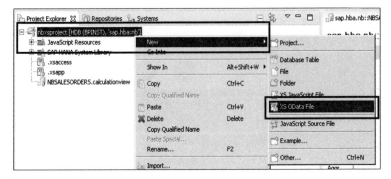

Figure 11.22 New SAP HANA XS OData File

2. Enter the OData service **File Name** and click **Finish** (see Figure 11.23).

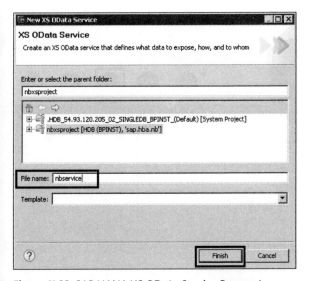

Figure 11.23 SAP HANA XS OData Service Parameters

3. Enter the code in for the new file you created (see Listing 11.1).

```
service
{
  "sap.hba.nb/NBSALESORDERS.calculationview" as "NBSalesOrderQuery"
  keys generate local "GenID"
  aggregates always
  parameters via entity "NBSalesOrderP"
  ;
          }

  annotations {
  enable OData4SAP;
  }
```

Listing 11.1 OData Service

In the listing, sap.hba.nb is the location of the calculation view, and NBSALESORDER is the view you created. Your screen should look like the one shown in Figure 11.24 after you enter the code.

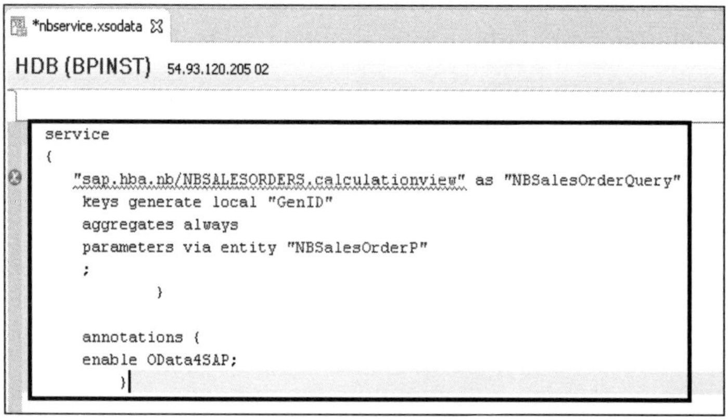

Figure 11.24 OData Service File

4. Click **Save**. Then, right-click the project and select **Team • Commit** (see Figure 11.25).

5. Activate the project by right-clicking the project and selecting **Team • Activate** (see Figure 11.26).

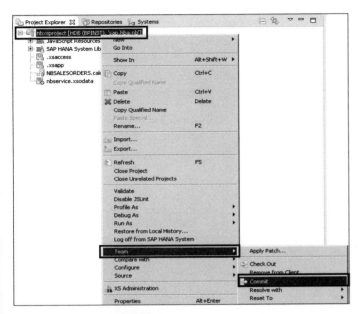

Figure 11.25 Committing Changes

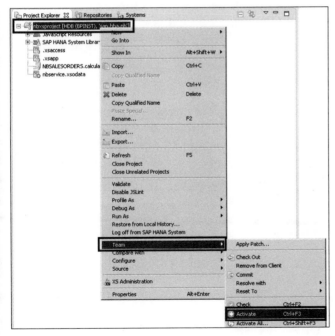

Figure 11.26 Activating Project

Next, let's test the newly created OData service. Follow these steps:

1. Right-click the XSODATA service file and select **Run As • XS Service** (see Figure 11.27).

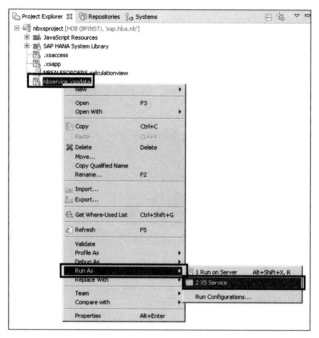

Figure 11.27 Running SAP HANA XS Service

2. After you log in, you should see something like what's shown in Figure 11.28.

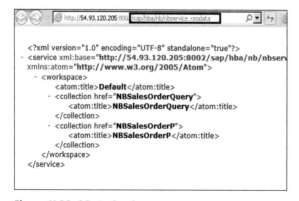

Figure 11.28 OData Service

3. Now, append the URL with "$metadata" and press ⌈Enter⌋.

4. You should see the metadata of the OData service you created (see Figure 11.29).

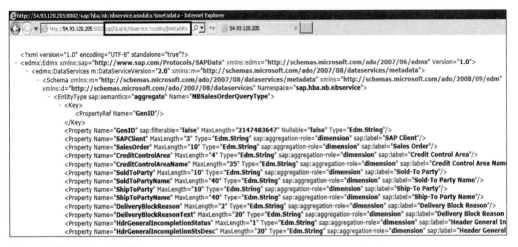

Figure 11.29 Metadata File

You've successfully created an OData service on the new calculation view. In the next section, we'll configure the KPI.

11.2.3   Configure the KPI

In this section, we'll show you how to create a KPI on the new calculation view and how to create a generic drilldown at a high level. In Chapter 6, Section 6.3, we covered the KPI creation process with step-by-step instructions. Refer to that chapter as needed to complete the following steps:

1. Log in to SAP Fiori launchpad.

2. Click the **Create KPI** app under the **KPI Modeler** group.

3. On the next screen, you need to fill in the mandatory **Title** field and add a **Description** for the KPI (see Figure 11.30).

4. Scroll down to the next section and select the values by clicking ⎙. Enter the information shown in Figure 11.31.

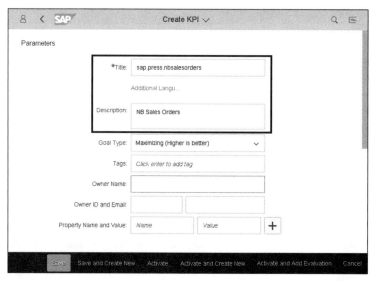

Figure 11.30 Create KPI

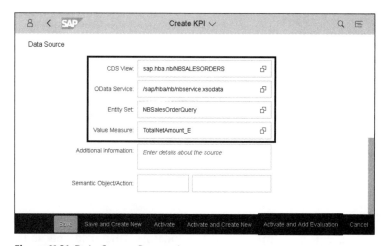

Figure 11.31 Data Source Parameters

Value Measure

If the **Value Measure** field list isn't populated, the package in which your OData service is saved won't be included in SAP Web Dispatcher. Therefore, be sure to include the package you created in Section 11.2.1 in SAP Web Dispatcher.

---

5. After the fields have been entered, click **Activate and Add Evaluation**. Enter a unique Evaluation name as shown in Figure 11.32 on the **Add Evaluation** screen.

Figure 11.32 Adding Evaluation

6. Scroll down to the **Input Parameters and Filters** section to input parameters that are expected in the calculation view.

7. Enter the SAP Client shown in Figure 11.33 in the **Input Parameters** section.

Figure 11.33 Input Parameters

8. Add the **Target, Thresholds, and Trend** values (see Figure 11.34):
   - **Target**: "50000000"
   - **Warning**: "50000000"
   - **Critical**: "5000000"

9. Click **Activate and Configure Tile**.

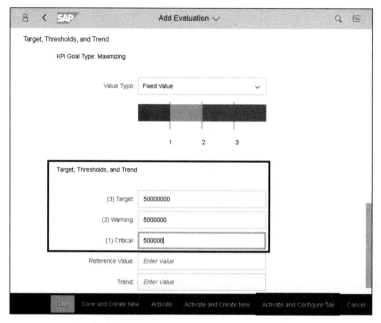

Figure 11.34 Threshold Values

10. Select your evaluation and click **Add Tile** (see Figure 11.35).

Figure 11.35 Adding Tile

11. Enter the **Tile Configuration** details, then click **Save and Configure Drill Down** (see Figure 11.36).

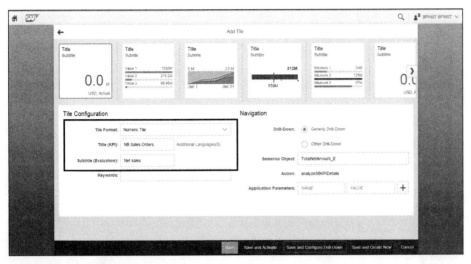

Figure 11.36 Saving Tile

12. Return to the home screen by clicking ⌂.

13. From SAP Fiori launchpad, click the **Configure KPI Drill-Down** link.

14. Select the evaluation and click **Configure** (see Figure 11.37).

Figure 11.37 Configuring Drilldown

15. Select the **Customer** from the dimensions list and click **OK**.

16. Enter **View ID** and **View Title**, then click **Save View** (see Figure 11.38).

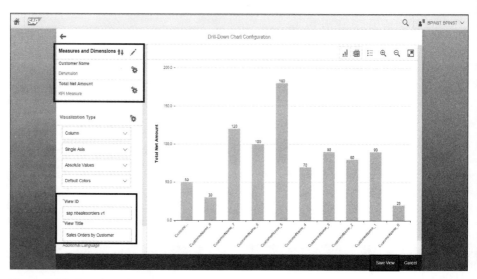

Figure 11.38 Creating View

17. Click **Save Configuration**.

You should now see the app in the catalog and be able to add the app from the catalog to your home group in SAP Fiori launchpad (see Figure 11.39).

Figure 11.39 Adding KPI Tile

You should now understand the end-to-end process of creating an analytical app. In the next section, we'll look at the extension process for an analytical app.

11.3   Extending Analytical Apps

You can extend an analytical app when the standard SAP Fiori analytical apps don't meet your requirements. In this section, we'll look at how to extend an app using an example based on the sales order query calculation view.

As previously mentioned, the SAP Fiori system landscape for analytical apps is comprised of two main layers: the SAP HANA layer and the UI layer. Depending on the individual analytical app extension requirements, you can extend one or multiple layers. Note the following when extending either of these layers:

- **SAP HANA layer**
  This layer is extended when the back-end content required for the analytical app extension is available in the SAP HANA models, but isn't exposed to the OData service.

- **UI layer**
  This layer is extended when the back-end content is exposed to the OData service later, but isn't exposed in the analytical app.

In the previous section, you learned that analytical apps are developed on predelivered SAP HANA objects such as views, and these views reside in SAP Business Suite on the SAP HANA server. These SAP HANA Live views can be extended by adding a field from a standard SAP table or a custom field.

For this example, you'll expose an additional back-end field from the SAP HANA database in the sales order query calculation view. To do so, you need to modify all the layers; we'll explain how in the following sections.

11.3.1   Extend the SAP HANA Live View

To extend SAP HANA Live views, you need to install the extensibility tool in SAP HANA Studio. The SAP HANA Live extensibility tool is an Eclipse plugin for SAP HANA Studio that can enhance standard SAP HANA views. With this tool, users can expose fields from a standard model, remove unnecessary fields from a view, or include custom tables and fields.

Follow these steps in SAP HANA Studio to install the SAP HANA Live extensibility tool:

1. Open SAP HANA Studio.
2. Go to **Help · Install New Software** from the menu bar (see Figure 11.40).

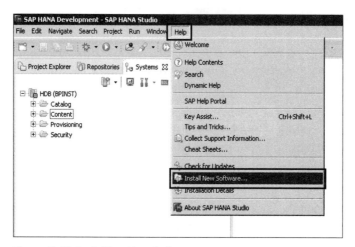

Figure 11.40 Installing New Software

3. Enter the following URL to access the tools, then click **Add**: *http://<HANAServer>:80<HANAInstance>/sap/hba/tools/extn*.

4. Select **SAP HANA Live Extensibility** and then click **Next** (see Figure 11.41).

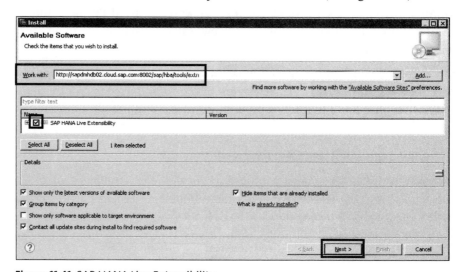

Figure 11.41 SAP HANA Live Extensibility

5. Click **Next**.

6. Select the radio button to accept the terms of the license agreement, then click **Finish** (see Figure 11.42).

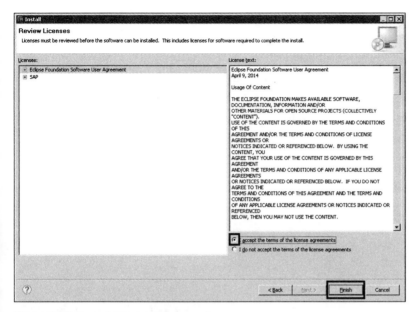

Figure 11.42 Accept License Agreement

7. Click **OK** in the security warning pop-up window (see Figure 11.43).

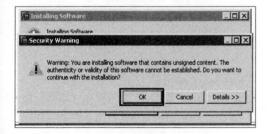

Figure 11.43 Security Warning Message

8. Click **Yes** to restart SAP HANA Studio for the changes to take effect (see Figure 11.44).

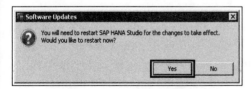

Figure 11.44 Restarting SAP HANA Studio

You've successfully installed the extensibility tool. After SAP HANA Studio is restarted, you need to grant access to users so that they can use the extensibility tool. Follow these steps:

1. Log in to the SAP HANA system from SAP HANA Studio.

2. Navigate to the **Security** folder. From the **Users** folder, double-click the user name of the user who needs access to the extensibility tool.

3. Add the following role in the **Granted Roles** tab: **sap.hba.tools.extn.roles::ExtensibilityDeveloper** (see Figure 11.45).

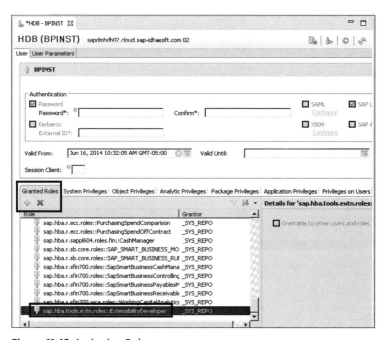

Figure 11.45 Assigning Roles

4. Add **REPO.READ, REPO.EDIT NATIVE OBJECTS**, and **REPO.ACTIVATE NATIVE OBJECTS** permissions to the package in which the new extended view will be created.

5. Click [◎].

With the preconfiguration of the extensibility tool out of the way, we'll now show you how to extend a standard sales order query view by adding new fields. As previously mentioned, SAP recommends that you don't reuse the standard query views; instead, use a copy in your own namespace and make the necessary modifications. A new view is automatically created in SAP HANA Studio when you extend a standard

SAP HANA Live view, and the original view isn't affected when you make any changes in the extended view.

Follow these steps to extend the view:

1. Log in to the SAP HANA system from SAP HANA Studio.

2. Under the **Content** folder, navigate to **sap · hba · ecc · Calculation Views** (see Figure 11.46).

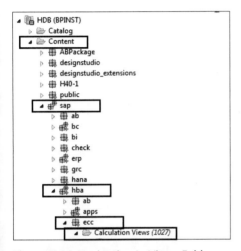

Figure 11.46 Navigating to Views Folder

3. Right-click **SalesOrderQuery**, then select **Extend View** (see Figure 11.47).

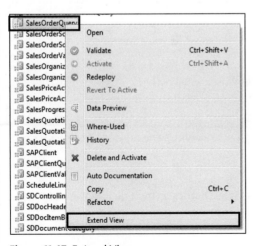

Figure 11.47 Extend View

> **Extend View**
>
> If you don't see the **Extend View** option, that means you've skipped the prerequisite to install the extensibility plug-in, noted at the beginning of this section. Go back and review those steps before proceeding.

4. Enter the new view name in the **Name of Copied View** field, then select the package in which you want to save this new view (see Figure 11.48).

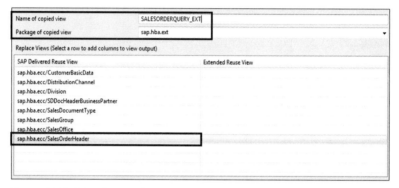

Figure 11.48 Selecting Replace View

5. The extensibility tool displays all the SAP-delivered reuse views. Upon clicking a view, the tool will display the unused fields.

> **Query View Extension**
>
> The following are important points to remember while you're working on query view extension:
>
> - You can't extend query views with unions.
> - You can't extend query views that have aggregation in the middle level, except for the top node below the semantics layer.
> - For some query views, the underlying reuse views can be replaced if there's a corresponding reuse view.

6. Select **SalesOrderHeader**, then choose **SalesDistrict** to include it in the output (see Figure 11.49).

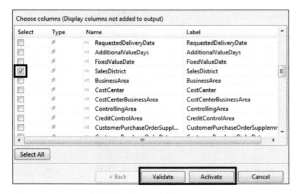

Figure 11.49 Selecting New Fields

7. Click **Validate**; after the validation completes successfully without any errors, click **Activate**.

8. After the activation is complete, the new extension view is created in the package you selected previously (Figure 11.50).

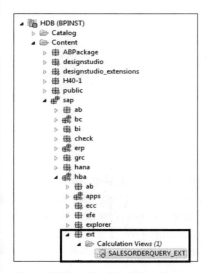

Figure 11.50 Activating New View

9. Activate the new calculation view and check whether the data is being populated.

We've successfully extended a calculation view by adding a new field and saving it to a new package. Next, you need to activate and create an OData service on the extended view.

11.3.2   Create the OData Service

You now need to create an SAP HANA XS project (see Figure 11.51) and then create an OData file on the extended calculation view. The OData process creation is just as described in Section 11.2.2. Repeat the same steps to create an OData service.

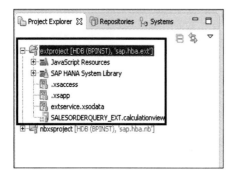

Figure 11.51 SAP HANA XS Project

11.3.3   Configure the KPI

The final step in the extension process is to configure and create a KPI tile. The steps to configure a KPI tile are the same as for both the creation and extension scenarios. Follow the same steps to create a new KPI tile based on the new OData service, as described in Section 11.2.3.

11.4   Summary

In this chapter, we walked through the processes involved in creating and extending an analytical app. We introduced SAP HANA Live and discussed its place in the SAP Fiori landscape. We then looked at the different views provided by SAP HANA Live and the benefits of exposing these views to analytical apps. From there, we described the necessary steps to either create or extend an analytical app.

In the next chapter, we'll look at modifying the workflow of SAP Fiori apps.

Chapter 12
Workflow and SAP Fiori

*The most common modifications to SAP Fiori apps involve workflow.
Accordingly, this chapter provides an overview of SAP Business Workflow, explains how and when to create a custom workflow, and shows
a step-by-step example based on the My Inbox app.*

A *workflow* is an orchestrated and repeatable pattern of a business activity. It can represent a sequence of operations, be declared as the work of a person or group, demonstrate staff structure, or be one or more simple or complex mechanisms.

This chapter starts with an introduction to workflow and the basic terminology used
in the workflow process in Section 12.1. We'll introduce you to the My Inbox app architecture in Section 12.2, and we'll discuss how the My Inbox application simplifies the
processing of workflow tasks for end users.

In Section 12.2.1, we'll discuss the prerequisites that need to be fulfilled before you
start implementing workflows and the My Inbox app. We'll walk you through how to
implement the **All Items** inbox tile in Section 12.2.2. We'll end the chapter in Section
12.2.3 with step-by-step instructions for how to define a workflow scenario and implement a scenario-specific inbox.

12.1 Workflow Basics

A workflow, as the name suggests, is a flow of work activities in a sequence that
results in an exchange of information. To better understand the workflow process,
we'll look at a simple example of a leave application: An employee submits a leave
application to the manager, and the manager checks the leave application. If everything looks good, he will approve the application; however, if something in the leave
application isn't correct, then the manager will reject it. If this process happened on
in traditional paper-based workflow, the process would take forever. SAP Business
Workflow streamlines the process in such scenarios.

SAP Business Workflow is a cross-application tool that automates business processes such as leave approval procedures and makes them quick and simple. SAP Business Workflow maps business processes in the SAP system and processes them under the workflow system. These workflows can be anything from a simple approval process to a more complex business process. Typically, SAP Business Workflow helps in situations in which work processes must be run repeatedly or in which several agents in a specific sequence are involved.

When a document is created, updated, or deleted, SAP Business Workflow creates events. These events represent an action in the system and are captured by SAP Business Workflow, which handles work items based on the defined workflow templates.

Let's look once again at the leave application example. When an employee submits a leave application, the manager receives a notification/request to approve or reject it. These requests are delivered to the manager's inbox as work items, and the person who executes a work item is called an agent. If the manager requests more information, then the employee receives a work item in his inbox.

Currently, enterprises across industries use multiple workflow engines as part of their landscapes to run their business processes. In addition, they use different types of inbox-like portals, or Universal Work Lists (UWLs), to track their day-to-day activities. The biggest challenge for end users is using multiple sources for work items because they need to be trained to interact with different task-management technologies. Inconsistent UX across different devices will impact their daily activities. From an IT perspective, setting up and configuring heterogeneous workflow engines and making all workflows accessible from mobile devices is the biggest challenge.

Customers want a unified inbox from which all business users can easily access and manage all work items, with a consistent UX across all devices. This will reduce complexity and increase productivity for end users. The My Inbox app in SAP Fiori is the solution that satisfies all these workflow needs.

In the next section, we'll look at creating standard and custom workflows using the My Inbox app in SAP Fiori.

12.2   Creating Standard and Custom Workflows with the My Inbox App

The My Inbox app is a full-blown workflow inbox for SAP Fiori. This transactional application can process workflow tasks based on decision options defined in the back-end server. The My Inbox app can process tasks from SAP Business Workflow, SAP Business Process Management (BPM), and third-party providers.

The following are some of the key features of the My Inbox app:

- Users can sort and filter the information displayed in the app.
- Users can select multiple requests and approve or reject them together.
- Users can add attachments and post comments.
- Users can share their tasks via SAP Jam or email.

Figure 12.1 shows the high-level system landscape of the My Inbox app. This app runs on SAP Gateway, similar to other SAP Fiori transactional apps, but a special service called the Task Gateway Service in the SAP Gateway server is the app's key component. This component harmonizes views from different task providers, such as SAP BPM, SAP Business Workflow, or third-party workflow engines. The task information is exposed from different task providers in a standard format called the *task consumption model*. This model can be extended with additional task providers via the task provider's API.

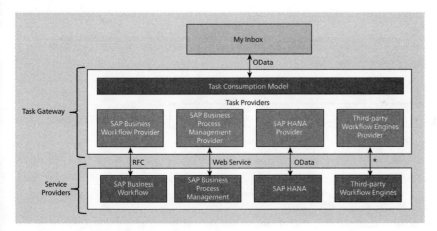

Figure 12.1 My Inbox Architecture

SAP provides out-of-the-box integration with SAP HANA Workflow, SAP Business Workflow and SAP BPM service providers. Third-party workflow engines are supported as well.

In the sections that follow, we'll look at the prerequisites for using the My Inbox app, how to create standard workflows with the **All Items** tile provided by SAP, and how to create custom workflows for a scenario-specific inbox.

12.2.1   Prerequisites

Before you start implementing the My Inbox app, several prerequisites need to be fulfilled:

- If your front-end server is on SAP NetWeaver 7.4, then you need the following components (see Figure 12.2):
  - *Component for app*: UIX01CA1 100 SP 05
  - *SAP Gateway component*: IW_PGW 100 SP 07
- If your front-end server is lower than SAP NetWeaver 7.4, then you need the following components in addition to UIX01CA1 and IW_PGW:
  - SAP Gateway 2.0 SPS 10
  - UI add-on 1.0 for SAP NetWeaver 7.03 SPS 10 or higher (UI5 1.26.0)
- On the back-end server, you need to be on SAP EHP 1 for SAP NetWeaver 7.3 SPS 15 (for SAP BPM support).
- If your back-end server is on an SAP NetWeaver version lower than 7.4, then you need to have the SAP IW BEP 200 SP 10 Gateway component installed on the back-end server.

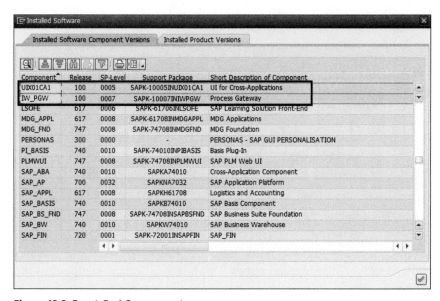

Figure 12.2 Front-End Components

Install or update all the required components before you proceed with the My Inbox app implementation.

My Inbox Release Information

Refer to SAP Note 2106212 for release information on the My Inbox app.

In addition to installing these components, you also need to define the system alias for the My Inbox app before proceeding. Follow these steps:

1. Run Transaction SPRO.

2. Navigate to **Manage SAP Systems Alias**, as shown in Figure 12.3.

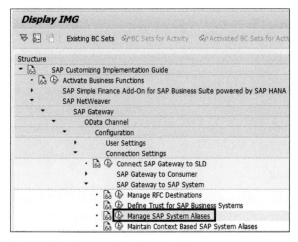

Figure 12.3 Manage SAP System Alias

3. Click on **New Entries** to create a new system alias, then enter or select the following details (see Figure 12.4):

- **SAP System Alias**: Enter "LOCAL_PGW".

- **Description**: Enter "LOCAL_PGW".

- **Local SAP GW**: Uncheck this box.

- **For Local App**: Check this box.

- **RFC Destination**: Leave this blank.

- **Software Version**: Enter "/IWPGW/BWF".

New Entries: Overview of Added Entries

SAP System Alias	Description	Local SAP ...	For Local App	RFC Destina...	Software Version
LOCAL_PGW	LOCAL_PGW	☐	✓		/IWPGW/BWF

Figure 12.4 /IWPGE/BWF Component

Central Hub Deployment

If your landscape deployment is a hub deployment, you need to fill the **RFC Destination** field as well.

The My Inbox app can process both standard and custom workflows based on the options defined in the back-end server. The SAP-delivered **All Items** tile for the My Inbox app enables users to easily process all tasks (standard workflow). In addition, you can configure a scenario-specific tile in SAP Fiori launchpad (custom workflow). In the remainder of this chapter, we'll teach you how to configure the **All Items** tile and scenario-specific My Inbox tiles.

12.2.2   All Items Tile for My Inbox

In this section, we'll look at steps for creating a standard workflow with the **All Items** tile. By now, you should be familiar with many of the screens and transactions we'll show.

Important!

Make sure that you have at least one workflow defined in the back-end server that can be used in the My Inbox app.

Follow these steps:

1. Activate the ICF service of the SAPUI5 application CA_FIORI_INBOX via Transaction SICF (see Figure 12.5). Navigate to **default_host · sap · bc · ui5_ui5 · sap**, right-click **ca_fiori_inbox**, and click **Activate**.

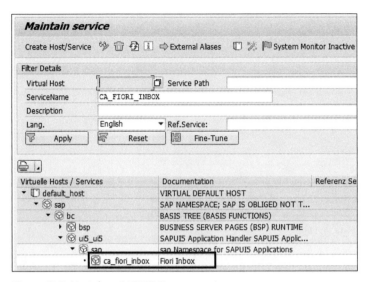

Figure 12.5 My Inbox SAPUI5 Component

2. Activate the OData service /IWPGW/TASKPROCESSING version 2 via Transaction /IWFND/MAINT_SERVICE (see Figure 12.6).

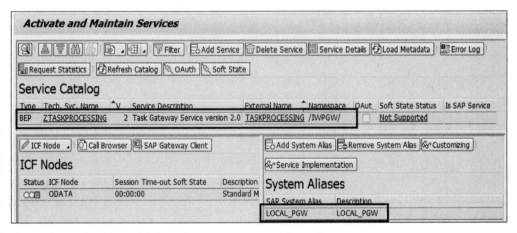

Figure 12.6 TASKPROCESSING Service

3. Assign the business role **SAP_FND_BCR_MANAGER_T** to the end user via Transaction PFCG (see Figure 12.7).

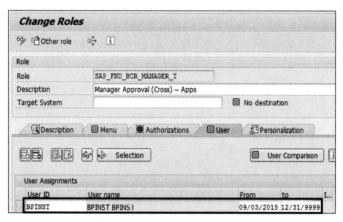

Figure 12.7 Assigning Role to User

4. Log in to the SAP Fiori launchpad designer and select the **SAP_FND_TC_T** catalog (see Figure 12.8).

Figure 12.8 Configuring Tile

5. Double-click the **My Inbox All Items** tile, then define the following parameter in the **Navigation** section: **allItems=true&listSize=150** (see Figure 12.9). The listSize property is set, by default, to **100** (i.e., the My Inbox app displays up to one hundred items in the list by default).

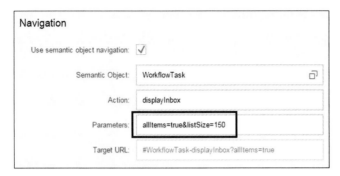

Figure 12.9 Adding Properties

6. In addition, you can define the following parameters:

  - **massAction**
    By default, this parameter is set to **True**. This property will let users process several tasks or mass actions of the same type at the same time.

  - **quickAction**
    By default, this parameter is set to **True**. This property will let users perform quick actions.

  - **sortBy**
    By default, this parameter is set to **CreatedOn**. This property will sort the list displayed in the app.

7. Log in to SAP Fiori launchpad, and add the **My Inbox** app from the tile catalog **Manager Approval (Cross)—Content**, as shown in Figure 12.10.

Figure 12.10 Adding My Inbox to SAP Fiori Launchpad

8. You should now see the **My Inbox** tile with the number of tasks that you have access to under the **My Home** group in SAP Fiori launchpad (see Figure 12.11).

Figure 12.11 All Items Tile

Most Common Issues

The following are some of the most common issues that you might come across while you're configuring the My Inbox app:

- **Issue 1**
  If you notice "Error" or "???" in the My Inbox tile or if an error log says "Task Facade not implemented for provider," you might not have configured the system alias correctly. Refer to Section 12.2.1 to verify your configuration.

- **Issue 2**
  Make sure you have at least one workflow created in the back-end. You'll notice errors in the tile when you don't have one.

- **Issue 3**
  If you see tasks in the back-end but your **My Inbox** tile shows **0** tasks, this may be because the task filter is activated in the back-end system. Run Transaction SPRO, navigate to **SAP NetWeaver • Gateway Service Enablement • Content • Workflow Settings • Enable Task Filter**, and click **Deactivate**.

---

9. You can now make important decisions from your My Inbox app. Clicking the tile opens the list of tasks you have access to. You can **Release**, **Forward**, or **Claim** a task. In addition, certain tasks will let you perform an **Accept** or **Reject** action, and so on, depending on the type of task (see Figure 12.12).

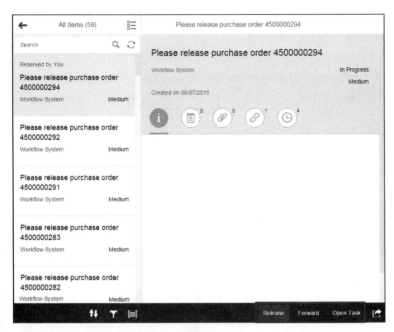

Figure 12.12 My Inbox App with All Items

10. To verify the tasks in the back-end system, log in to the back-end server, then run Transaction SBWP to view your inbox. You should see the same number of tasks (**59** in this example) in the back-end system as in the app (see Figure 12.13).

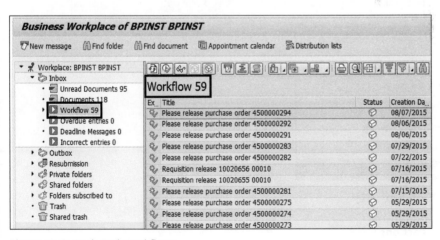

Figure 12.13 Back-End Workflows

Next, let's explore some of the key features of the My Inbox app. The following are some specialized tasks:

- **Search**

    You can search for a specific task from the list of tasks, and you can perform a free-text search (see Figure 12.14).

Figure 12.14 Search Functionality

- **Refresh**

    Click the **Refresh** icon to refresh the task list.

- **Multi-select**

    By clicking the icon, you can enable multiple selections, and then users can select and execute multiple tasks. Users first need to select the task type (see Figure 12.15).

Figure 12.15 Task Type

- **Mass actions**

    After you select the task type (see Figure 12.15), you can select multiple tasks and perform mass actions, as shown in Figure 12.16.

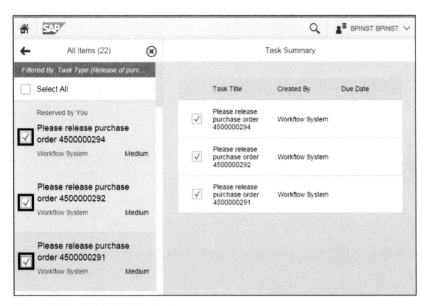

Figure 12.16 Multiselecting Tasks

- **Sorting**

  The sorting option at the bottom of the task list lets users sort tasks by **Created On (Newest on Top)**, **Created By (A on Top)**, **Priority (Highest on Top)**, or **Task Title (A on Top)** (see Figure 12.17).

Figure 12.17 Sort By Options

- **Filter By**

  To filter tasks by **Priority**, **Due Date**, **Task Type**, **Status**, or **Creation Date**, use the **Filter** icon ▼ (see Figure 12.18).

Figure 12.18 Filter By Options

- **Group By**
  The **Group By** icon groups tasks by **Priority**, **Task Type**, **Status**, or **Reservation** (see Figure 12.19).

Figure 12.19 Group By Options

- **Comments**
  After selecting a task, you can view the task details on the right and then view and post comments by clicking the **Comments** icon (see Figure 12.20).
- Users can view, upload, or delete attachments via the **Attachments** icon (see Figure 12.21).

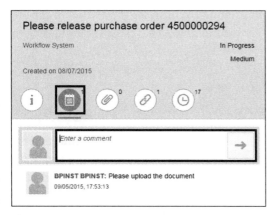

Figure 12.20 Viewing Comments

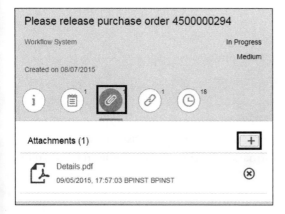

Figure 12.21 Attachments

- **Share** or **Send Email**

  Users can click share icon  to send emails or post tasks to a preconfigured SAP Jam site (see Figure 12.22).

Figure 12.22 Collaboration

Now that you have a clear understanding of how to configure the My Inbox app and its features, let's discuss some advanced features of workflow scenarios and custom, scenario-specific tiles.

12.2.3   Scenario-Specific Inbox

SAP delivers many standard approval scenarios. However, in real-world scenarios, the standard approval apps may not be sufficient for your business requirements. The My Inbox app allows you to define your own workflow scenario and create scenario-specific tiles in SAP Fiori Launchpad. Next, we'll provide an example with step-by-step instructions for how to add a custom workflow to the My Inbox app based on a purchase order approval process. The following tasks will be discussed:

1. Retrieve workflow template information.

2. Define workflow scenarios.

3. Configure the task decision.

4. Add the Business Add-In (BAdI) for task quotations.

5. Add the tile to SAP Fiori launchpad.

Retrieve Workflow Template Information

The first step in creating a custom workflow based on a purchase order approval process is to collect all the workflow information for the purchase order release. Follow these steps:

1. Log in to the back-end server, and run Transaction PFTC.

2. Select the **Workflow template** from the **Task type** dropdown, then enter "20000075" in the **Task** field (see Figure 12.23).

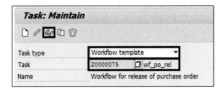

Figure 12.23 Workflow Template

3. Click 🔍 to view the workflow.

4. Click the **Workflow Builder** button to view the workflow of the purchase order release (see Figure 12.24).

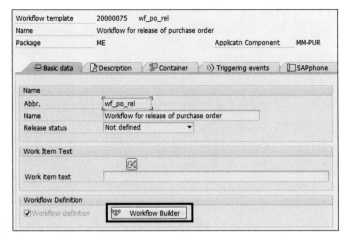

Figure 12.24 Workflow Builder

5. In the workflow, the approval or release of a purchase order occurs at Step 93. Double-click Step 93 to view the activity of this step (see Figure 12.25).

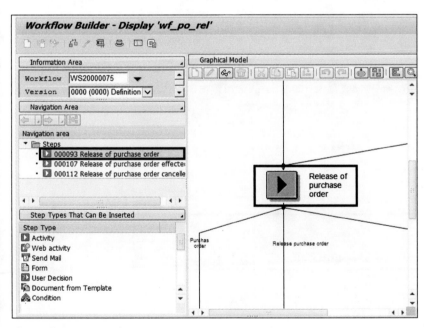

Figure 12.25 Approval Step

6. Go to the **Control** tab to view and take note of the task ID (see Figure 12.26).

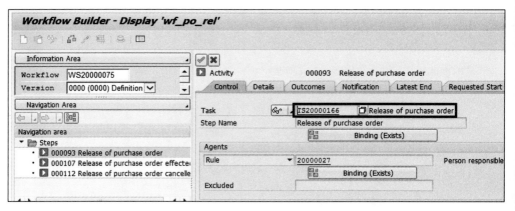

Figure 12.26 Task ID

7. Double-click the **Task** ID to view the **Object method** section. Make a note of the **Object Type** and **Method** (see Figure 12.27).

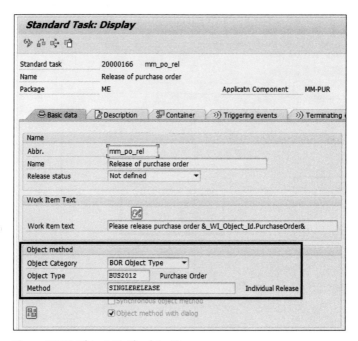

Figure 12.27 Object Method Section

8. Click the **Back** icon to return to the **Workflow Builder** screen.

9. Select the **Outcomes** tab (see Figure 12.28).

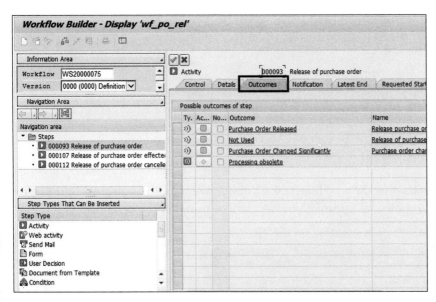

Figure 12.28 Outcomes

10. Double-click an outcome to view its events. First, select **RELEASED** in the **Event** field (see Figure 12.29), then make a note of the **Event** information, and then click **Continue** ✅.

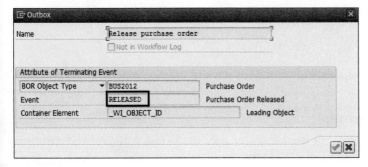

Figure 12.29 Event Type

11. Select **RESET** (**Not Used**) in the **Event** field in the **Outcomes** tab (see Figure 12.30), and click **Continue** ✅.

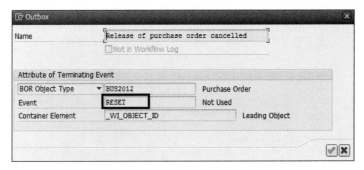

Figure 12.30 Event Type Outcome

You now have all the workflow, task ID, object methods, and outcomes information. Table 12.1 shows the information that you'll be using for the remainder of this exercise.

Fields	Details
Workflow Template ID	WS20000075
Approval Step ID	93
Step Type	Activity
Task ID	20000166
Business Object	BUS2012
Approval Method	SINGLERELEASE
Outcomes	RELEASED, RESET

Table 12.1 Workflow Information

Define Workflow Scenarios

In this step, you'll define the workflow scenarios in the task gateways and customizing in SAP Gateway. Follow these steps:

1. Run Transaction SPRO.

2. Click the **SAP Reference IMG** button.

3. Navigate to **SAP NetWeaver · SAP Gateway Service Enablement · Content · Task Gateway · Task Gateway Service · Scenario Definition**.

4. Click the **Scenario Definition** folder, then click the **New Entries** button.

5. Add the following scenario definition information (see Figure 12.31), then press Enter :

   - **Scenario Identifier**: "DEMO_PO_RELEASE"
   - **Scenario Display Name**: "PO Approval"
   - **Technical Service Name**: "/IWPGW/TASKPROCESSING"
   - **Version**: "2"

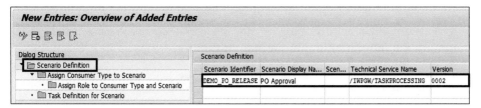

Figure 12.31 Scenario Definition

6. Select the scenario definition, then click **Assign Consumer Type to Scenario**.

7. Click **New Entries**, then add the consumer types, as shown in Figure 12.32.

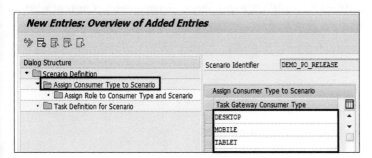

Figure 12.32 Consumer Type

8. Double-click **Task Definition for Scenario** (Figure 12.33), then click the **New Entries** button.

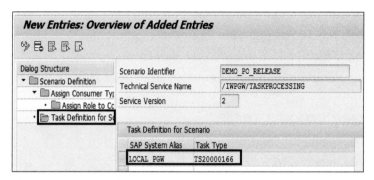

Figure 12.33 Task Definition for Scenario

9. Add the **System Alias** and the **Task Type**, then click **Save**.

You've successfully defined the workflow scenario!

Configure the Task Decision

In this step, you'll define the task decision, which involves maintaining the workflow tasks that need to be included in the task filter. Follow these steps:

1. Run Transaction SPRO.

2. Click the **SAP Reference IMG** button.

3. Navigate to **SAP NetWeaver · SAP Gateway Service Enablement · Content · Work Flow Settings · Maintain Task Names and Decision Options**.

4. Click the **Step Name** folder, and create a new entry with the following details (see Figure 12.34):

   – **Workflow ID**: "WS20000075"

   – **Step ID**: "93"

   – **Step Description**: "Approve Purchase Order"

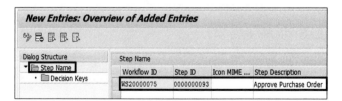

Figure 12.34 Workflow ID and Step ID

5. Select the step name, then create two new decision keys, as shown in Figure 12.35:

   – **Key**: "1"/"2"

   – **Decision Text**: "Approve"/"Reject"

   – **Nature**: "Positive"/"Negative"

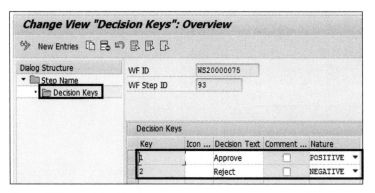

Figure 12.35 Decision Keys

Implement the BAdI for the Task Quotation

In this step, you'll implement the BAdI to update the user selections to the back-end. When the user selects **Approve** or **Reject** from the My Inbox app, this BAdI will update the user's decision in the back-end. Follow these steps:

1. Run Transaction SE18.

2. Enter "/IWWRK/BADI_WF_BEFORE_UPD_IB" in the **BAdI Name** field, then click **Display** (see Figure 12.36).

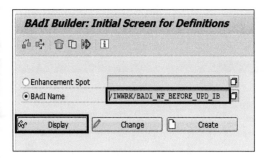

Figure 12.36 Standard BAdI

3. Right-click **Implementations** and select **Create BAdI Implementation** (see Figure 12.37).

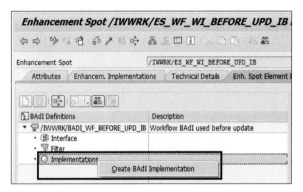

Figure 12.37 Create BAdI implementation Option

4. Create the new enhancement implementation by clicking [].
5. Enter the name and short text as shown in Figure 12.38, then click **Continue** .

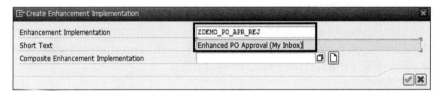

Figure 12.38 Enhancement Implementation

6. Select the local object.
7. Select the new enhancement implementation and click **Continue** (see Figure 12.39).

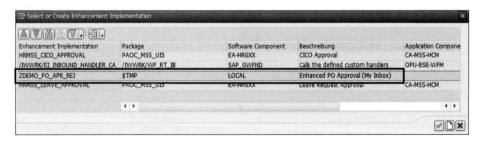

Figure 12.39 Selecting New Enhancement Implementation

8. Create the BAdI implementation by entering the details shown in Figure 12.40, then click **Continue** ☑.

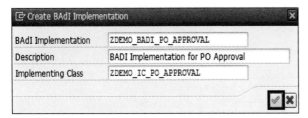

Figure 12.40 Creating BAdI Implementation

9. Double-click **Filter Val.**, then click ☐ Combination (see Figure 12.41).

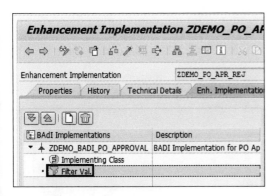

Figure 12.41 Filter Values

10. Select both **WORKFLOW_ID** and **STEP_ID**, then click **Continue** ☑ (see Figure 12.42).

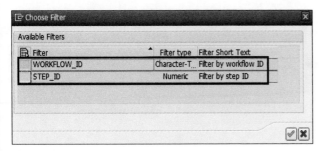

Figure 12.42 Selecting Filters

515

11. Double-click the filter values, and enter the **STEP_ID** and **WORKFLOW_ID** (see Figure 12.43):

   – **STEP_ID**: "93"

   – **WORKFLOW_ID**: "WS20000075"

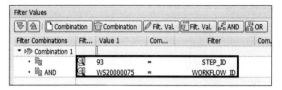

Figure 12.43 Workflow ID and Step ID

12. Click **Save**.

13. Click **Yes** to save the enhancement implementation.

14. Double-click the **Implementing Class** folder, then click the value in the **Implementing Class** field (see Figure 12.44).

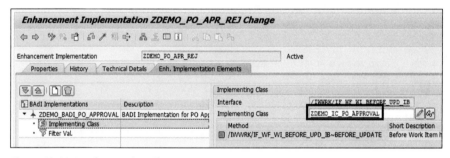

Figure 12.44 Implementing Class

15. Double-click the **Method** field value, as shown in Figure 12.45.

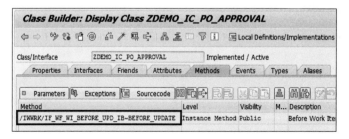

Figure 12.45 Method Field

16. Enter the code shown in between the **Method** and **End Method.**

```
"1. Variables
DATA abs_object TYPE swr_obj_2.
DATA abv_retcode TYPE sy-subrc.
DATA abt_container TYPE TABLE OF swr_cont.
DATA abs_container_line TYPE swr_cont.
DATA abt_msg_lines type sapi_msg_lines.
DATA abt_msg_struc type sapi_msg_struc.
DATA FORMNUMBER TYPE SWXFORMABS-FORMNUMBER.
DATA abs_formabs TYPE swxformabs.

"2. Get Workitem Details
CALL FUNCTION 'SAP_WAPI_GET_OBJECTS'
  EXPORTING
    WORKITEM_ID           = is_wi_details-wi_id
*   LANGUAGE              = SY-LANGU
*   USER                  = SY-UNAME
*   BUFFERED_ACCESS       = 'X'
IMPORTING
*   LEADING_OBJECT        =
    RETURN_CODE           = abv_retcode
    LEADING_OBJECT_2      = abs_object
TABLES
*   OBJECTS               =
    MESSAGE_LINES         = abt_msg_lines
    MESSAGE_STRUCT        = abt_msg_struc
*   OBJECTS_2             =
        .
"3. Get Document Number
MOVE abs_object-instid TO formnumber.

*4. Get Decision Based on the Workitem ID
CALL FUNCTION 'SAP_WAPI_READ_CONTAINER'
  EXPORTING
    WORKITEM_ID           = is_wi_details-wi_id
*   LANGUAGE              = SY-LANGU
*   USER                  = SY-UNAME
*   BUFFERED_ACCESS       = 'X'
IMPORTING
```

12

```
   RETURN_CODE                      = abv_retcode
*    IFS_XML_CONTAINER               =
*    IFS_XML_CONTAINER_SCHEMA        =
TABLES
   SIMPLE_CONTAINER                 = abt_container
   MESSAGE_LINES           = abt_msg_lines
   MESSAGE_STRUCT          = abt_msg_struc
*    SUBCONTAINER_BOR_OBJECTS        =
*    SUBCONTAINER_ALL_OBJECTS        =.

"5. Get Application Data
select single * from swxformabs into abs_formabs where formnumber =
 formnumber.

"6. Set Decision Value
CASE iv_decision_key.
  WHEN 0001. "Approved
    abs_container_line-value = 'A'.
    abs_formabs-procstate = 'A'.
  WHEN 0002. "Rejected
    abs_container_line-value = 'R'.
    abs_formabs-procstate = 'R'.
ENDCASE.

"7. Set Result Value Based on Decision
abs_container_line-element = '_WI_RESULT'.
"Update Container rows
MODIFY abt_container INDEX 3 FROM abs_container_line TRANSPORTING value.

"8. Update Container
CALL FUNCTION 'SAP_WAPI_WRITE_CONTAINER'
  EXPORTING
    WORKITEM_ID                      = is_wi_details-wi_id
*    LANGUAGE                        = SY-LANGU
*    ACTUAL_AGENT                    = SY-UNAME
    DO_COMMIT                       = 'X'
*    IFS_XML_CONTAINER               =
*    OVERWRITE_TABLES_SIMPLE_CONT    = ' '
*    CHECK_INBOX_RESTRICTION         = ' '
```

```
IMPORTING
   RETURN_CODE                         = abv_retcode
TABLES
   SIMPLE_CONTAINER                    = abt_container
   MESSAGE_LINES              = abt_msg_lines
   MESSAGE_STRUCT             = abt_msg_struc
   .

"9. Update App Data
abs_formabs-approvdate = sy-datum.
abs_formabs-approvby = sy-uname.
update swxformabs from abs_formabs.

*10. Complete the Task
CALL FUNCTION 'SAP_WAPI_WORKITEM_COMPLETE'
   EXPORTING
   WORKITEM_ID                     = is_wi_details-wi_id
*   ACTUAL_AGENT                    = SY-UNAME
*   LANGUAGE                        = SY-LANGU
*   SET_OBSOLET                     = ' '
   DO_COMMIT                       = 'X'
*   DO_CALLBACK_IN_BACKGROUND       = 'X'
*   IFS_XML_CONTAINER               =
*   CHECK_INBOX_RESTRICTION         = ' '
IMPORTING
   RETURN_CODE                     = abv_retcode
*   NEW_STATUS                      =
TABLES
*   SIMPLE_CONTAINER                = abt_container
   MESSAGE_LINES              = abt_msg_lines
   MESSAGE_STRUCT             = abt_msg_struc
   .

*11. Set Confirm
CALL FUNCTION 'SAP_WAPI_WORKITEM_CONFIRM'
   EXPORTING
   WORKITEM_ID                     = is_wi_details-wi_id
*   ACTUAL_AGENT                    = SY-UNAME
*   LANGUAGE                        = SY-LANGU
```

12

```
    DO_COMMIT                        = 'X'
*   CHECK_INBOX_RESTRICTION          = ' '
IMPORTING
    RETURN_CODE                      = abv_retcode
*   NEW_STATUS                       =
TABLES
    MESSAGE_LINES            = abt_msg_lines
    MESSAGE_STRUCT           = abt_msg_struc
```

Listing 12.1 BAdI to Capture User's Decision

17. Click **Save**, and then click **Activate**.

Add the Tile to SAP Fiori Launchpad

In this step, you'll add a new dynamic tile and the custom workflow to the My Inbox app. Follow these steps:

1. Log in to the SAP Fiori launchpad designer.

2. Select **SAP_FND_TC_T**, and add a new dynamic tile.

3. Use the following details in the **General** section, as shown in Figure 12.46:

    – **Title**: Enter "My Inbox".

    – **Subtitle**: Enter "PO Approval".

    – **Keywords**: Enter "Workflow, Inbox, PO Approval".

    – **Icon**: Select an icon.

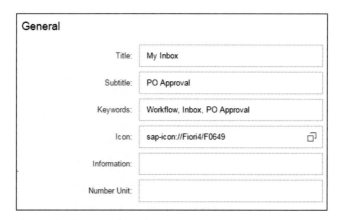

Figure 12.46 General Section

4. Enter the **Service URL** details in the **Dynamic Data** section:

"/sap/opu/odata/IWPGW/TASKPROCESSING;mo;v=2/ScenarioCollection?$filter=
key eq *<your scenario ID>*".

In this example, the *scenario ID* is DEMO_PO_RELEASE (see Figure 12.47).

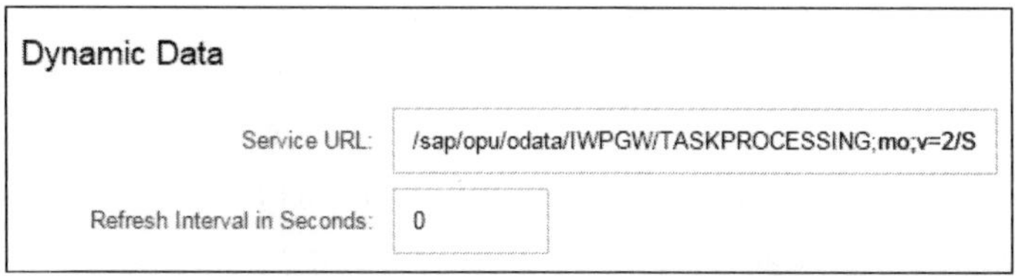

Dynamic Data

Service URL: /sap/opu/odata/IWPGW/TASKPROCESSING;mo;v=2/S

Refresh Interval in Seconds: 0

Figure 12.47 Dynamic Data

5. Enter the following details in the **Navigation** section (see Figure 12.48):
   - **Semantic Object**: "WorkflowTask"
   - **Action**: "displayInbox"
   - **Parameters**: "scenarioId=*<your scenario ID>*"

Navigation

Use semantic object navigation: ✓

Semantic Object: WorkflowTask

Action: displayInbox

Parameters: scenarioId=DEMO_PO_RELEASE

Target URL: #WorkflowTask-displayInbox?scenarioId=DEMO_PO_RI

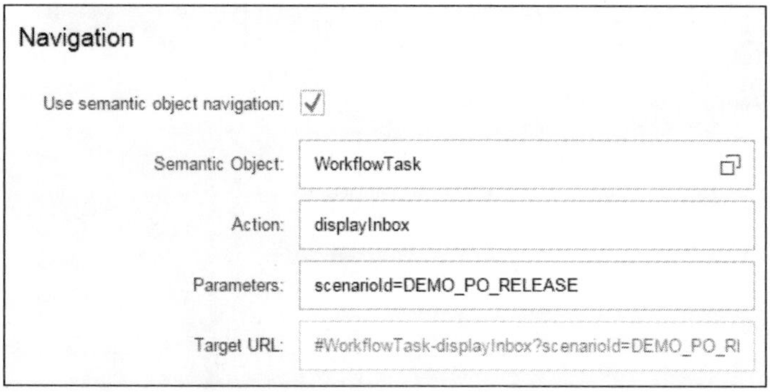

Figure 12.48 Navigation Section

6. Click **Save**.
7. Log in to SAP Fiori launchpad, and add the new **My Inbox** tile from the SAP_FND_TC_T catalog (see Figure 12.49).
8. Click the **My Inbox PO Approval** tile and open it (see Figure 12.50).

521

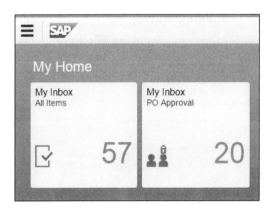

Figure 12.49 All Items Tile and Scenario-Specific Tile

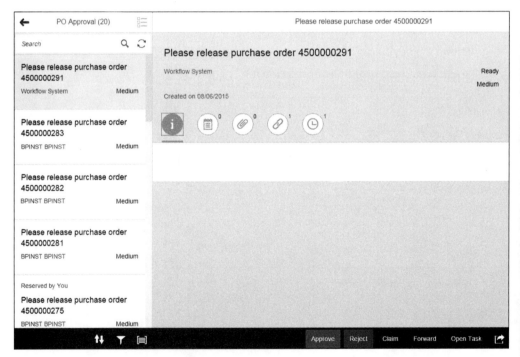

Figure 12.50 Scenario-Specific App

Users can now approve and reject purchase orders from the My Inbox app.

12.3   Summary

Workflows are important for carrying out daily business activities. In this chapter, we discussed the basics of the workflow process and how to integrate SAP Business Workflows with the My Inbox app in SAP Fiori. Specifically, we configured the **All Items** tile, which shows all the workflow tasks that you have access to in the back-end system. We concluded the chapter by creating a custom workflow for a scenario-specific tile.

In the next chapter, we'll look at integrating SAP Fiori apps with other SAP products.

12

Chapter 13
Integration with Other SAP Products

This chapter provides an overview of how SAP Fiori launchpad can be integrated with SAP BusinessObjects Lumira, SAP Jam, and SAP BusinessObjects BI reports and dashboards.

The SAP Fiori landscape can be integrated with SAP products such as SAP Jam, SAP BusinessObjects Lumira, and SAP BusinessObjects BI In this chapter, we'll cover the integration steps for these pieces of software.

We'll start with an introduction on how to leverage SAP Jam in conjunction with SAP Fiori in Section 13.1, including how this tool can help business users collaborate with each other by using tiles in SAP Fiori launchpad or from an SAP Fiori application. We'll begin by looking at prerequisites for integration in Section 13.1.1. In Section 13.1.2, we'll show you how to configure a social media catalog, and we'll leverage SAP Jam tiles in SAP Fiori launchpad to collaborate with teams in Section 13.1.3. We'll end the SAP Jam and SAP Fiori integration section with an overview of different collaboration components in Section 13.1.4.

Next, in Section 13.2, we'll introduce you to SAP's self-service visualization tool—SAP BusinessObjects Lumira. We'll start with the roles and authorizations required for a user to access SAP BusinessObjects Lumira in SAP Fiori (Section 13.2.1), and then we'll introduce the different tiles available in SAP Fiori from the SAP BusinessObjects Lumira perspective (Section 13.2.2). We'll end the section by showing you how to create an SAP Fiori tile from an SAP BusinessObjects Lumira story (Section 13.2.3).

The chapter concludes with a discussion on integrating SAP Fiori launchpad with the reports and dashboards from SAP BusinessObjects BI platform in Section 13.3. We'll start with the high-level configuration to integrate SAP BusinessObjects BI Platform and the SAP front-end server in Section 13.3.1. We'll end the chapter with an exercise that walks through how to build an SAP Fiori app using the open document URL of an SAP BusinessObjects Design Studio application, and then publish the app to SAP Fiori launchpad with custom roles and custom catalogs.

13

13.1   SAP Jam

SAP Jam is a powerful enterprise social network solution with which users can collaborate with teams to brainstorm issues related to specific business objects or share knowledge within the organization. SAP Jam solves problems and improves decision making. In addition, SAP Jam can now be integrated with SAP Fiori via either of the following methods:

- Social media tiles in SAP Fiori launchpad
- Collaboration components

To better demonstrate how the integration between these two products can help businesses, let's look at an example. Say that you're a sales manager viewing sales orders in the Track Sales Order app in SAP Fiori. During your review, you realize something's wrong with a particular sales order. The next thing you do is share this information with your team members, who can help solve this problem as quickly as possible. SAP Fiori and SAP Jam integration makes it easy to share the issue with team members via SAP Jam, which can lead to not only solving your issues with your subject matter experts quickly but also improving your decision making. After the problem is solved, you'll receive a notification in SAP Fiori launchpad. The beauty of SAP Jam is that all this social collaboration happens securely across your entire organization, directly from SAP Fiori launchpad.

Several prerequisites must be fulfilled to integrate SAP Jam and SAP Fiori. We'll highlight the prerequisites in the next section. You'll then configure the social media catalog to provide user access to SAP Jam tiles. Finally, we'll highlight collaboration components that are integrated within SAP Fiori applications.

13.1.1   Prerequisites

The Social Media Integration (SMI) function integrates SAP Jam social collaboration platform tiles and SAP Fiori. The collaboration features of SMI aren't only useful for integration between SAP Jam and SAP Fiori; they can also be integrated with other web technologies, such as Web Dynpro, ABAP, and SAPUI5.

You need to configure ABAP SMI to allow SAP Fiori apps and SAP Fiori launchpad to use the SMI functions developed for SAP Fiori. SMI offers functions that run within the SAP Fiori app and functions that run as an SAP Fiori tile. For more information, go to *http://help.sap.com/nw-uiaddon* and choose **SAP Jam Integration**.

In addition, you need to fulfill the following prerequisites:

- Purchase an SAP Jam license.
- Ensure that every SAP Fiori user has an SAP Jam account.
- Import SAP Jam server certificate sapjam.cer into the SAP Fiori front-end server via Transaction STRUST.
- Configure SAML 2.0 authentication and the OAuth client.

13.1.2   Configuration

In this section, we'll walk you through various configuration steps required to integrate SAP JAM and SAP Fiori. We'll start with SAP ABAP SMI configuration in the front-end server.

1. Log in to the front-end server, and run Transaction CLB2_PLATF.
2. Click **New Entries**, and add the following new entries (see Figure 13.1):
   - **Serv. Provider Type**:"Jam"
   - **Server**: "Jam productive"
   - **Service Provider**: "cubetree.com"
   - **Server URL**: "https://integration3.sapjam.com"

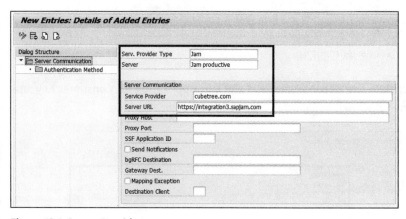

Figure 13.1 Server Provider

3. Double-click **Authentication Method**, then click **New Entries**.
4. Add the following entries (see Figure 13.2), and click **Save**:
   - "APPLI": "OAUTH_10_SHA1"

- "APPUSR": "OAUTH_10_SHA1_3"
- "NONE": "NONE"
- "USER": "SAML_20"

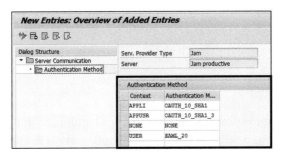

Figure 13.2 Authentication Methods

5. Run Transaction CLB2_APPLI_ PLATF.

6. Click **New Entries**, and add the **Application ID, Service Provider Type**, and **Server** shown in Figure 13.3.

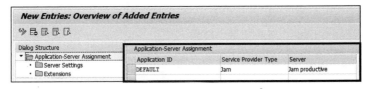

Figure 13.3 Server Assignment

7. Double-click **Server Settings**, and add the **Ext. Application ID, Consumer Key**, and **HTTP Timeout** shown in Figure 13.4. Click **Save**.

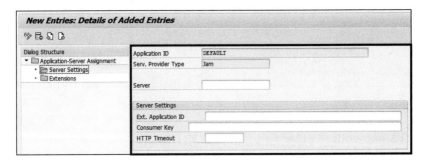

Figure 13.4 Server Settings

8. Run Transaction SICF, and activate the `rest_tunnel` service (see Figure 13.5).

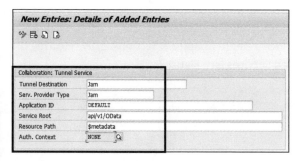

Figure 13.5 REST Tunnel Service

9. Run Transaction CLB2_TUNNEL, click **New Entries**, then add the **Tunnel Destination**, **Serv. Provider Type**, **Application ID**, **Service Root**, **Resource Path**, and **Auth. Context** as shown in Figure 13.6. Click **Save**.

13

New Entries: Details of Added Entries

Collaboration: Tunnel Service

Tunnel Destination	Jam
Serv. Provider Type	Jam
Application ID	DEFAULT
Service Root	api/v1/OData
Resource Path	$metadata
Auth. Context	NONE

Figure 13.6 Tunnel Services

Let's examine the tunnel destinations in Table 13.1.

Tunnel Destination	Service Provider Type	Application ID	Service Root	Resource Path	Authentication Context
Jam	Jam	DEFAULT	api/v1/OData	$metadata	NONE
Jam	Jam	DEFAULT	api/v1/OData		USER

Table 13.1 Tunnel Destinations

Tunnel Destination	Service Provider Type	Application ID	Service Root	Resource Path	Authentication Context
Jam	Jam	DEFAULT	api/v1/feed/post		USER
Jam	Jam	DEFAULT	/v1/single_use_tokens	$metadata	USER

Table 13.1 Tunnel Destinations (Cont.)

After the SAP Jam and SAP ABAP SMIs are configured, you can configure SAP Jam tiles in SAP Fiori. The *social media catalog* is used to group SAP Jam–related tiles for SAP Fiori launchpad. Like other catalogs, the social media catalog should be associated with a PFCG role as well. We'll now show you how to create a catalog and how to add this catalog to a new role. Most of these steps are like those you've seen in previous chapters.

Follow these steps:

1. Add the **SM_CATALOG_SRV** service (refer to Chapter 4, Section 4.2) by selecting the service and clicking **Add Selected Services** (see Figure 13.7).

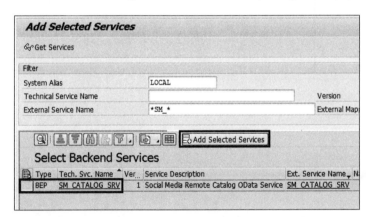

Figure 13.7 Adding Services

2. The next step is to activate the OData services (refer to Chapter 4, Section 4.2). Select the **SM_INTEGRATION_V2_SRV** and **SM_CATALOG_SRV** OData services via Transaction /IWFND/MAINT_SERVICE, and run them by clicking **Call Browser** (see Figure 13.8).

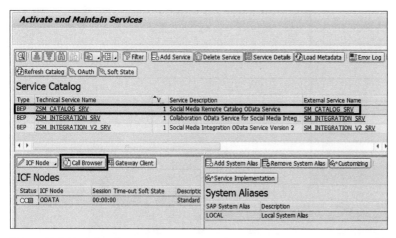

Figure 13.8 Test Service

3. Next, you need to create a remote catalog in the SAP Fiori launchpad designer. First, log in to the SAP Fiori launchpad designer (see Chapter 4, Section 4.6).

4. Select the **Catalogs** tab, then click **+** at the bottom of the screen to add a new catalog.

5. Select **Remote**.

6. Enter the following details, then click **Save** (see Figure 13.9):
   - **Title**: "Social Media Catalog"
   - **ID**: "Jam"
   - **Remote ID**: "SMCatalog"
   - **System alias**: "LOCAL"
   - **Base URL**: "/sap/opu/odata/sap/SM_CATALOG_SRV/"

7. Next, you need to create and assign the role to a user (refer to Chapter 4, Section 4.6). Run Transaction PFCG, enter "ZSM_CATALOG_ROLE" in the **Role** field, and then click **Single Role** (see Figure 13.10).

13

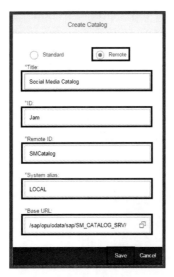

Figure 13.9 Create Catalog Screen

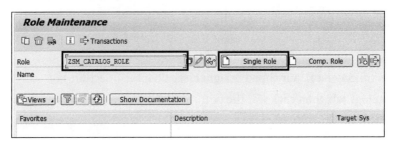

Figure 13.10 Creating Role

8. Enter a **Description**, then click **Save**.

9. On the menu bar, from the **Transactions** dropdown list, select **SAP Fiori Tile Catalog**.

10. Select **Remote Catalog** from the **Catalog Provider** dropdown box (see Figure 13.11).

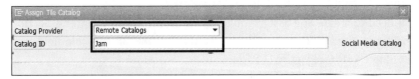

Figure 13.11 Assign Tile Catalog Screen

11. Select the catalog you created earlier and press [Enter].

12. To enable access to the catalog, you must assign a user to this role. Go to the **User** tab, enter a username, and press [Enter] (see Figure 13.12).

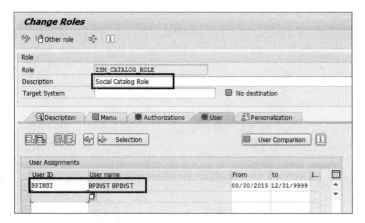

Figure 13.12 Assigning User to Role

13. Click **Save**.

You should now see the **Social Media Catalog** in SAP Fiori launchpad (see Figure 13.13).

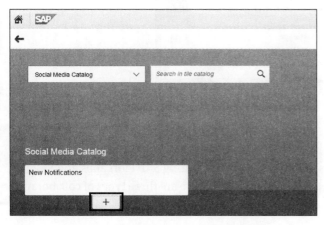

Figure 13.13 Adding Tile from Social Media Catalog

You've successfully created the social media catalog and assigned a user to the catalog role. Next, we'll explore the SAP Jam tiles available in SAP Fiori.

13.1.3   SAP Jam Tiles

There are two types of SAP Jam–based SAP Fiori tiles that can initiate collaboration directly in your SAP Fiori launchpad:

1. **Group tiles**

   You can add tiles in SAP Fiori launchpad for any SAP Jam group you belong to. The group tile displays the group name, group icon, time since last activity, and the content, updated every five minutes. For example, Figure 13.14 shows the **Project Manager Group**, with an activity recorded one minute ago.

2. **Notification tiles**

   You can add a notification tile in SAP Fiori launchpad to view notifications received in an SAP Jam account. The notification tile displays the notification sender's name and photo, notification type, notification message, and group name if the notification is from a group. This tile can display up to 10 notifications and show new notification content in 10-second intervals. For example, Figure 13.14 shows the last notification, which was created by user **Anil B**, responding to user **Larry R**'s question.

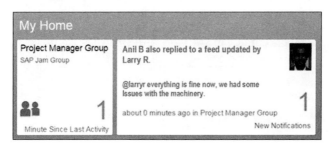

Figure 13.14 SAP Jam Tiles

13.1.4   Collaboration Components

Collaboration components are available for integrating SAP Fiori apps and SAP Jam (these components are part of the application). There are three types of collaboration components:

1. **Social timeline**

   Using this component, you can directly display some of the main features of SAP Jam, such as a user's photo, notifications from other users, and so on, in the SAP Fiori app.

2. Discuss

Using this component, you can display and contribute to SAP Jam through a feed (see Figure 13.15).

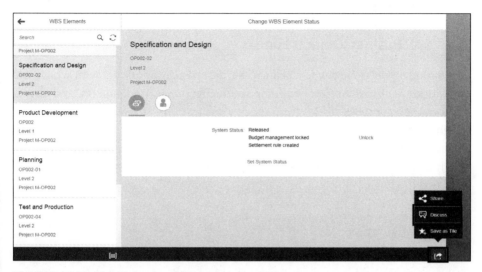

Figure 13.15 Discuss Dialog Component

3. Share

This component lets you share attachments, business objects, and comments about business objects with SAP Jam groups (see Figure 13.16). This feature is available in apps of all types: transactional, analytical, and fact sheet.

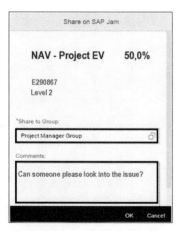

Figure 13.16 Share Component

You should now have a better understanding of which type of component to use for your SAP Fiori project with an SAP Jam integration. Next, we'll discuss SAP Fiori's integration with SAP BusinessObjects Lumira.

13.2   SAP BusinessObjects Lumira

SAP BusinessObjects Lumira is a self-service data visualization tool with which you can quickly and easily create stunning interactive maps, infographics, and charts. You can then compose stories from those visualizations, analyze trends, and share insights with a team via the SAP BusinessObjects Lumira server. In this section, we'll discuss the integration between SAP Fiori and SAP BusinessObjects Lumira and show you how to access and share SAP BusinessObjects Lumira stories from SAP Fiori launchpad.

13.2.1   Configuration

In this section, we'll walk through the configuration steps for the integration, and we'll look at the roles that must be assigned to an administrator and end users to view and run SAP BusinessObjects Lumira stories in SAP Fiori launchpad. In Chapter 2, Section 2.6.4, we showed you how to assign roles to a user in SAP HANA Studio. Follow the same steps to assign the following roles:

1. Assign administrator roles to SAP Fiori administrators; for this example, assign the following role to the **LUMIRATECH** user (see Figure 13.17):

   – **sap.bi.common::BI_TECH_USER**

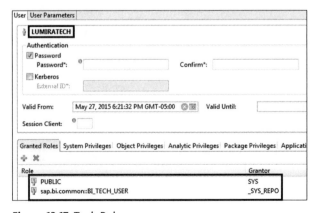

Figure 13.17 Tech Role

2. Assign administrator roles to SAP Fiori administrators; for this example, assign the following roles to the **FIORIADMIN** user (see Figure 13.18):
   - **sap.bi.admin::BI_ADMIN**
   - **sap.bi.admin::BI_CONFIGURATOR**

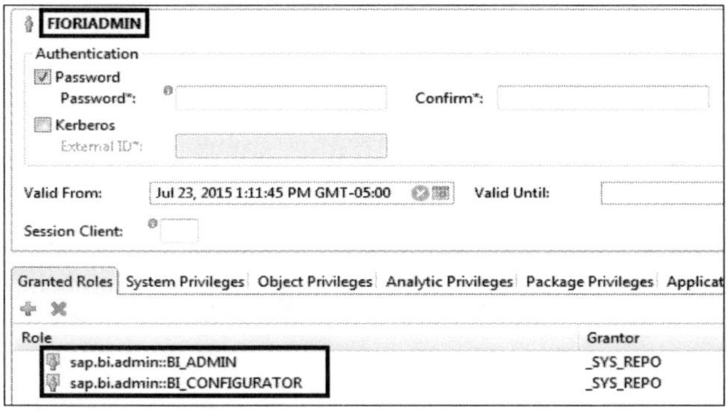

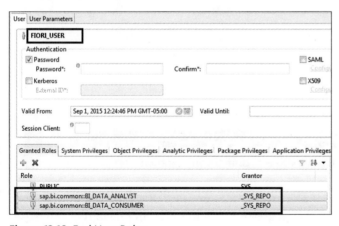

Figure 13.18 Admin Roles

3. Similarly, assign end user roles to SAP Fiori end users (see Figure 13.19):
   - **sap.bi.common::BI_DATA_ANALYST**
   - **sap.bi.common::BI_DATA_CONSUMER**

Figure 13.19 End User Roles

4. Next, you need to configure the SAP BusinessObjects Lumira Server in SAP Fiori launchpad. Log in to the SAP Fiori admin launchpad via *http(s)://<SAPHANAServer>:<Port>/sap/bi/launchpad/fiori*.

5. Add the **Configuration SAP Lumira Server** tile from the tile catalog, then launch the app (see Figure 13.20).

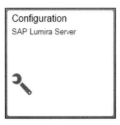
Configuration
SAP Lumira Server

Figure 13.20 Configuration Tile

6. Enter the **Technical user** and the **Password** (which you created in Step 1), and click **Run Configuration** (see Figure 13.21).

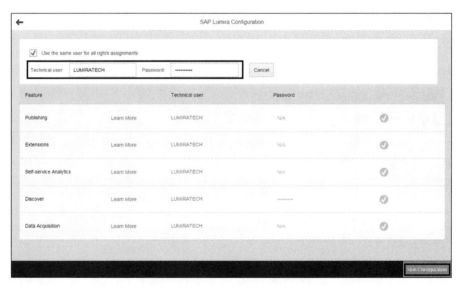

Figure 13.21 Running SAP BusinessObjects Lumira Configuration

7. Assign the SAP_LUMIRA_TCR role to FIORI_USER and FIORIADMIN in the ABAP front-end server. We showed you how to assign a role to a user in previous chapters (see Chapter 4, Section 4.42). Follow the same steps to add users to this role via Transaction PFCG (see Figure 13.22).

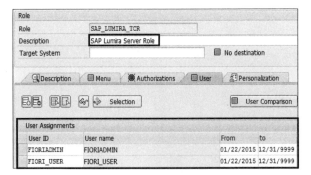

Figure 13.22 SAP BusinessObjects Lumira Roles on ABAP Server

You've now successfully completed the configuration required to integrate the SAP BusinessObjects Lumira Server and SAP Fiori.

Next, we need to integrate SAP BusinessObjects Lumira with SAP Fiori. SAP Fiori provides the capability to integrate with SAP BusinessObjects Lumira in three different ways: the **All Stories** tile, the **SAP Lumira** static tile, and via a KPI drilldown. In the next section, we'll start by discussing the SAP BusinessObjects Lumira tiles. We'll then look at how to create a KPI tile with a drilldown to an SAP BusinessObjects Lumira story using the KPI modeler.

13.2.2 SAP BusinessObjects Lumira Tiles

In this section, we'll focus our attention on the two tiles provided with SAP Business-Objects Lumira to integrate with SAP Fiori launchpad. Follow these steps to add these tiles from the SAP BusinessObjects Lumira catalog in SAP Fiori launchpad:

1. Log in to SAP Fiori launchpad, and click ▤ to open the menu.

2. Click **Tile Catalog**, then select **SAP Lumira** from the dropdown list.

3. Click the **+** sign below each tile to add the tile to the **SAP Lumira** group. You should see all the SAP BusinessObjects Lumira tiles in your SAP Fiori launchpad (see Figure 13.23).

> **Stories**
>
> All the stories displayed in SAP Fiori come from SAP BusinessObjects Lumira Server, which runs on SAP HANA.

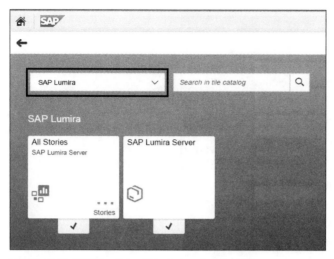

Figure 13.23 SAP BusinessObjects Lumira Catalog

You've successfully added the SAP BusinessObjects Lumira tiles. Next, let's explore each one:

- **All Stories**
  Figure 13.24 shows the **All Stories** launch tile, which displays the number of stories that a user has access to. Clicking this tile opens a list with all the available stories, which you can sort, filter, and search.

Figure 13.24 All Stories Tile

- **SAP Lumira static tile**
  Figure 13.25 shows the static tile, which launches SAP BusinessObjects Lumira in a new window. From SAP BusinessObjects Lumira, you can create and share stories.

Figure 13.25 SAP BusinessObjects Lumira Static Tile

You should now have a clear understanding of how SAP BusinessObjects Lumira and SAP Fiori products are integrated. Next, we'll show you how to access an SAP BusinessObjects Lumira story from SAP Fiori launchpad and how to create a tile from that story. Proceed with the following steps:

1. In SAP Fiori launchpad, select the **All Stories** tile.

2. Select a story from the list of stories available (left side), in this example we selected **Profitability Analysis – US**, and click **Open** (see Figure 13.26).

Figure 13.26 Selecting SAP BusinessObjects Lumira Story

3. Filter for a particular product, and in this example we selected **FIN100-P1,MTO-VC,F**, click [icon], and choose **Save as Tile** (see Figure 13.27).

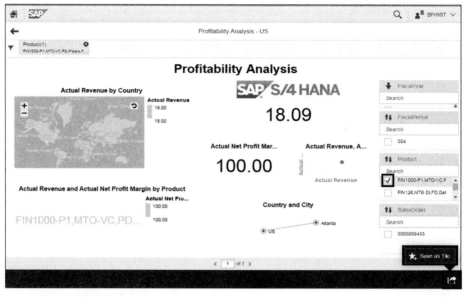

Figure 13.27 Filtering Story

4. Enter the **Title** and **Subtitle**, then click **OK** (see Figure 13.28).

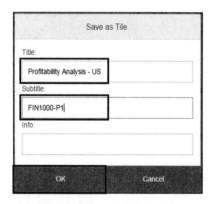

Figure 13.28 Save as Tile Screen

5. Return to the home screen by clicking 🏠.

6. You should now see a new SAP BusinessObjects Lumira story tile. Click the tile to open the SAP BusinessObjects Lumira story in SAP Fiori launchpad (see Figure 13.29).

Figure 13.29 New SAP BusinessObjects Lumira Story Tile

You've seen throughout this section the powerful combination of SAP Business-Objects Lumira and SAP Fiori and how both tools are integrated seamlessly. In the next section, we'll look at configuring a KPI tile with a drilldown to SAP Business-Objects Lumira.

13.2.3   Configure a KPI Tile with a Drilldown to SAP BusinessObjects Lumira

In addition to launching an SAP BusinessObjects Lumira story from a tile, you can also configure a KPI tile with a drilldown to an SAP BusinessObjects Lumira story. In Chapter 6, we explained how to implement an analytical app using the Days Sales Outstanding app as an example. You can follow the same steps to implement the KPI tile to drilldown to an SAP BusinessObjects Lumira story. In Chapter 6, Section 6.3.4, we created a generic drilldown. Now, instead creating a generic drilldown, you need to select an SAP BusinessObjects Lumira story as a drilldown in the **Navigation** section (see Figure 13.30). Proceed with the following steps:

1. Login to SAP Fiori Launchpad and select the Configure KPI Tile from the KPI Modeler group.

2. Under the **Navigation** section, select the **Other Drill Down** radio button.

3. Select **SAP Lumira** from the **Select Drill-Down** dropdown options

4. Select the SAP BusinessObjects Lumira **Story ID** from the list, then click **Save and Activate**.

> **Important!**
> You will be able to view only those SAP BusinessObjects Lumira story IDs (in the value help) that are available for the SAP HANA view your KPI is based on.

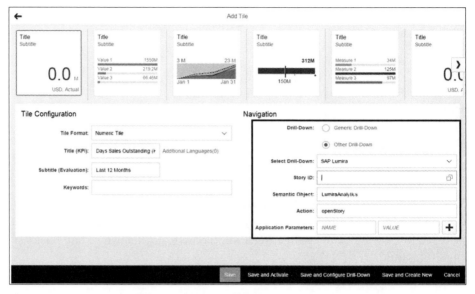

Figure 13.30 SAP BusinessObjects Lumira Drilldown

This concludes the SAP Fiori and SAP BusinessObjects Lumira integration process. Next, we'll see how SAP Fiori integrates with SAP BusinessObjects BI platform.

13.3   Integrating SAP BusinessObjects BI and SAP Fiori Launchpad

The SAP BusinessObjects BI suite is a complete business intelligence solution. It offers a set of tools for content developers, business analysts, executives, and data scientists. The following are some of tools in SAP BusinessObjects BI:

- *SAP BusinessObjects Design Studio*: Create dashboards, analysis applications, and planning applications intuitively based on SAP BW, SAP HANA, and universes.
- *SAP BusinessObjects Lumira*: Explore data.
- *Crystal Reports*: Create highly formatted reports.
- *Web Intelligence reports*: Useful for ad hoc report development.

These powerful tools allow you to put decision-ready information within a business user's reach. In this section, we'll explain the steps to seamlessly integrate these SAP Business Objects BI tools with SAP Fiori launchpad. Before we move on to the technical configuration, let's look at the high-level architecture in Figure 13.31.

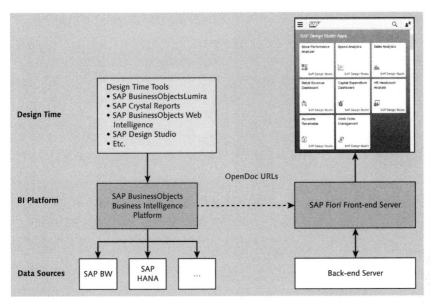

Figure 13.31 SAP BusinessObjects BI and SAP Fiori Launchpad Integration

On the left side in Figure 13.31 are design-time tools such as SAP BusinessObjects Design Studio, SAP BusinessObjects Lumira, WebI, and Crystal Reports on the BI platform, which can connect to pretty much any data source, like SAP S/4HANA, SAP BW, and so on. You can integrate these with the SAP Fiori front-end server through OpenDoc URLs.

In the following sections, we'll highlight the steps to integrate SAP Business Objects BI and SAP Fiori launchpad and to publish a dashboard to the SAP Fiori launchpad.

13.3.1   Configuration

In this section, we'll highlight the most important steps that you need to follow to integrate SAP BusinessObjects BI platform and SAP Fiori. We highly recommend working with your SAP BusinessObjects BI administrator to perform most of these steps.

Configure SAP Web Dispatcher

When a user clicks on a tile in SAP Fiori launchpad, SAP Web Dispatcher forwards the calls from the SAP Fiori front-end server to SAP BusinessObjects BI. To enable this call forwarding from SAP Web Dispatcher to SAP BusinessObjects BI, we need to add the following parameter in the SAP Web Dispatcher profile file and restart SAP Web Dispatcher:

wdisp/system_<number> = SID=BOE, EXTSRV=<BI Platform https hostname> : < BI Platform port>, SRCSRV=:<reuse same port with Fiori Launchpad>, SRCURL=/BOE/.*

Configure SSL

If your SAP BusinessObjects BI platform's web application server certificate is signed by the same certificate authority as SAP Web Dispatcher, you can then skip this step. Otherwise, proceed as follows:

1. Export a key certificate for the key store file from the SAP Business Objects BI server by running the following command at a command prompt:

   ```
   keytool –export -alias <certificate_alias> -keystore <keystore_file> -file <cer-
   tificate_file> -storepass <password>.
   ```

2. Import the certificate into SAP Web Dispatcher:
   - Log on to the SAP Web Dispatcher OS.
   - Launch a command prompt, and navigate to the sapgense file location: <Install_dir>\usr\sap\<SID>\SYS\exe\nuc\NTAMD64.
   - Run the following command: `sapgenpse.exe maintain_pk -p <Client_PSE> -a <Tomcat_certificate>`.
   - Restart Tomcat.

Configure SAP BusinessObjects BI Authentication

In this step, we'll add your SAP system, then import roles from SAP to SAP BusinessObjects BI:

1. Create an SAP user account that authorizes access to connect the SAP BusinessObjects BI platform and your SAP system.
2. Add your SAP entitle system in SAP BusinessObjects BI from Central Management Console (CMC).
3. Import the user and roles from the SAP system to SAP BusinessObjects BI.

Setup SSO between SAP Systems

In this step, we generate a key store file and a corresponding certificate, then add the generated certificate to your SAP ABAP front-end, SAP ABAP back-end, and the SAP BusinessObjects BI platform:

1. Login to the SAP BusinessObjects BI server and then generate a key store file by running the following command in command prompt: java -jar PKCS12Tool.jar.

2. Export the public key certificate by running the key tool program from a command prompt: keytool -exportcert -keystore <keystore> -storetype pkcs12 -file <filename>-alias <alias>.

3. Import the certificate file to the SAP ABAP front-end system and SAP ABAP back-end system via Transaction STRUSTSSO2.

4. Import the certificate into SAP BusinessObjects BI from the **Authentication Management** area in CMC.

Enable SSO for OpenDocument

Set the default authentication to SAP in the OpenDocument.properties file in *SAP BusinessObjects\SAP BusinessObjects Enterprise XI 4.0\warfiles\webapps\BOE\WEB-INF\config\default.*

Create RFC Destination

Create an RFC destination to connect SAP Fiori launchpad and SAP Web Dispatcher:

1. Login to the SAP Fiori front-end server, and run Transaction SM59.

2. Create a new connection.

3. Enter the **RFC Destination** name, and select **H** for the **Connection Type** (see Figure 13.32).

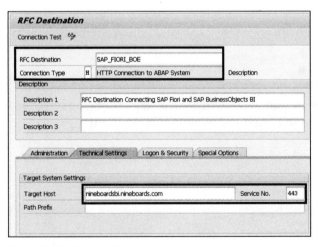

Figure 13.32 RFC Destination

4. Enter the fully qualified SAP Web Dispatcher name in **Target Host** and the SAP Fiori launchpad port in the **Service No.** field (see Figure 13.32).

You've successfully configured SAP Fiori and SAP BusinessObjects BI. In the next section, we'll show you how to deploy a dashboard to SAP Fiori launchpad.

13.3.2   Create an SAP Fiori App

This section walks you through the steps to integrate an SAP BusinessObjects Design Studio application called *Liquidity Forecast* with SAP Fiori launchpad; you can follow the same steps to integrate any report or dashboard from SAP BusinessObjects BI platform into SAP Fiori launchpad. Most of the steps are like those we've covered in previous chapters, so we'll just highlight the main steps.

First, you need to generate the OpenDoc URL from the SAP BusinessObjects BI Launchpad. Log in to the SAP BusinessObjects BI launchpad, and right-click the report or SAP BusinessObjects Design Studio app you want to make available in SAP Fiori launchpad. Click **Document Link** (see Figure 13.33), and copy the URL.

Figure 13.33 Open Document Url

Next, you need to create the semantic object. In the SAP ABAP front-end server, run Transaction /UI2/SEMOBJ and add a new semantic object, as shown in Figure 13.34.

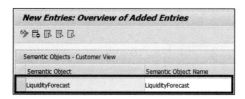

Figure 13.34 Adding Semantic Object

Now, create a new catalog:

1. Log in to SAP Fiori launchpad designer from your browser via the following URL: *http://<server>:<port>/sap/bc/ui5_ui5/sap/arsrvc_upb_admn/main.html?sap-client=<client>?scope=CUST.*

2. Create a new catalog, and click **Save** (see Figure 13.35)

Figure 13.35 Create Catalog

3. Click **+** to add a tile to the new catalog (see Figure 13.36).

Figure 13.36 Add New Tile

4. Add the static tile by clicking **+** (see Figure 13.37).

Figure 13.37 Static Tile

549

Next, you'll create a new tile and perform target mapping, as seen in Figure 13.38:

1. Enter the following information in the **General** section:
   - **Title**: "Liquidity Forecast"
   - **Information**: "Design Studio"
2. In the **Navigation** section, select **LiquidityForecast** from the **Semantic Object** list by clicking 🗗.
3. In the **Action** field, enter "display".

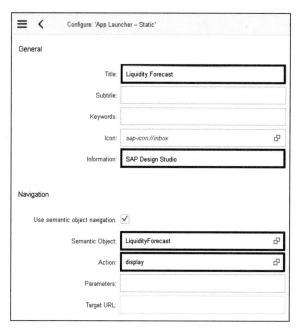

Figure 13.38 App Launcher

4. Click **Save**.
5. Add a target mapping by clicking the **Target Mapping** icon, then click **Create Target Mapping**, as shown in Figure 13.39.
6. In the **Intent** section, select **LiquidityForecast** from the **Semantic Object** list by clicking 🗗.
7. In the **Action** field, enter "display".

Figure 13.39 Creating Target Mapping

8. In the **Target** section, select **URL** from the **Application Type** dropdown list, then enter the following (see Figure 13.40):

- **Title**: Enter "Liquidity Forecast".
- **URL**: Paste in the URL you generated previously. Ignore the host and port; just paste it from /BOE/Open...
- **System Alias**: Enter "SAP_FIORI_BOE". This is the same RFC destination that you created in the configuration section.

Figure 13.40 Target Mapping

Next, let's create a custom group and add the tile which we created in the previous step:

1. Create a new group (see Figure 13.41) by adding a **Title** and **ID,** (in our example "SAP BusinessObjects BI" and "ZSAP_BI_GROUP") and then click **Save.**

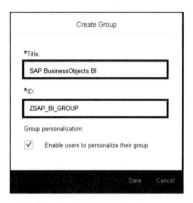

Figure 13.41 Creating Group

2. Select the catalog you created previously. In this exercise, we created a catalog with the name SAP BusinessObjects BI.
3. Click **+** to add the app (i.e., **Liquidity Forecast**) to the new group.

Figure 13.42 Adding App to Group

Next, you'll create a new role for the catalog and group:

1. Log in to the ABAP back-end server, then create a new role via Transaction PFCG.
2. Add the new catalog (see Figure 13.43), which you created previously.

3. Add the new group (see Figure 13.43), which you created in previously.

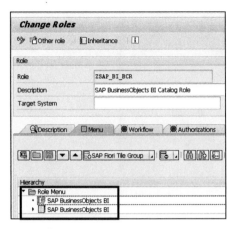

Figure 13.43 Creating New Role

4. Add the username (for whoever needs access to this app) in the **User** tab (see Figure 13.44).

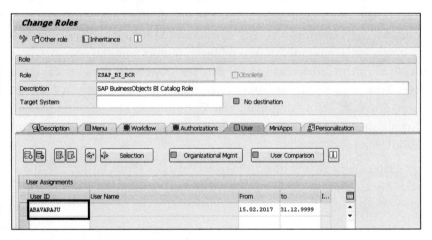

Figure 13.44 Assigning Users to Role

5. Click **Save**.

To test the app, log in to SAP Fiori launchpad; you should see the **Liquidity Forecast** app under the **SAP BusinessObjects BI** group (see Figure 13.45).

Figure 13.45 SAP BusinessObjects BI Group in SAP Fiori Launchpad

13.4   Summary

In this chapter, we introduced SAP Jam, SAP BusinessObjects Lumira, and SAP BusinessObjects Design Studio, and we showed how each of these tools can be integrated with SAP Fiori. We also discussed how you can collaborate with team members directly from SAP Fiori launchpad via SAP Jam standard tiles. We explored different options to configure standard SAP BusinessObjects Lumira tiles and discussed how to create a KPI tile with a drilldown to an SAP BusinessObjects Lumira story using the KPI modeler. Finally, we highlighted steps to configure the SAP BusinessObjects BI platform and SAP Fiori Front-end server, and then we ended this chapter with an exercise to publish an SAP BusinessObjects Design Studio application as an SAP Fiori app in the SAP Fiori Launchpad.

In the next chapter we'll discuss how SAP Screen Personas allows business to transform classic SAP screens into SAP Fiori-inspired designs.

Chapter 14

Introduction to SAP Screen Personas

In this chapter, we'll discuss how SAP's UX strategy relates to the SAP Screen Personas solution. We'll also explain how SAP Screen Personas allows you to transform classic SAP screens into SAP Fiori-inspired designs.

Although incorporating the SAP Fiori UX is the ultimate goal for SAP S/4HANA, SAP is still on the journey to get there; therefore, SAP introduced a powerful tool in 2012 called *SAP Screen Personas* to transform the classic SAP screens into SAP Fiori-inspired designs. Several customers are now using SAP Screen Personas to improve adoption of SAP by personalizing screens for different groups. SAP Screen Personas allows you to personalize and transform the classic SAP screens to meet your business needs, without changing them fundamentally and while leaving the system as untouched as possible.

In Section 14.1, we describe SAP Screen Personas and its components to give you a grounding in the product. You'll used what you learned in Section 14.2 to help you create your first SAP Screen Personas project. Then, in Section 14.3, we'll cover some more advanced techniques and elements of SAP Screen Personas flavors. Section 14.4 will cover key administrative tasks associated with flavors. Finally, Section 14.5 walks you through how to deploy your SAP Screen Personas flavors to SAP Fiori Launchpad.

When should you implement SAP Screen Personas? The flowchart in Figure 14.1 provides guidelines. Basically, when there is no standard SAP Fiori app that meets your requirements, and when there is a standard SAP GUI or WebDynpro ABAP option that does meet your requirement, you can use SAP Screen Personas.

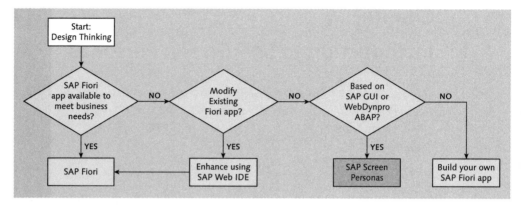

Figure 14.1 SAP Screen Personas Decision Flowchart

SAP Screen Personas is a visual product that lets users create flavors; a *flavor* is a specific, personalized screen of a specific, classic SAP transaction screen, and every transaction can have more than one flavor, depending on the business needs. SAP Screen Personas developers can create flavors by dragging and dropping components in the WYSIWYG HTML5 editor and can deploy them easily.

With SAP Screen Personas, you have an easy way to personalize screens by role, so your business users will see only what they need. A developer can edit screens directly in the browser, and end users can access the simplified screens from the browser or SAP GUI.

In addition, SAP Screen Personas lets companies refresh SAP screens without any disruption; that is, the existing functionality and authentication models are retained, and the changes are applied as a delta to the existing screens.

14.1   SAP Screen Personas 3.0 Architecture and Navigation

SAP Screen Personas is an add-on for SAP ERP, SAP Business Suite powered by SAP HANA, and SAP S/4HANA. The installation requires no additional servers and, the best part, it's nondisruptive to the IT landscape.

The latest version of SAP Screen Personas is 3.0 SP 04. Figure 14.2 shows the high-level architecture for SAP Screen Personas components.

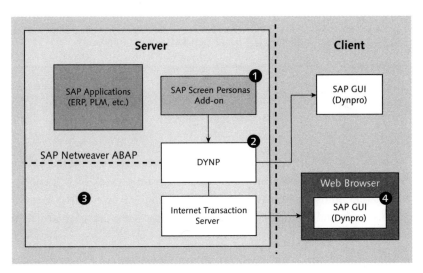

Figure 14.2 SAP Screen Personas Architecture

1. The SAP Screen Personas add-ons layer stores the flavors that are created/updated by users.

2. The SAP NetWeaver basis component layer is a foundation layer for all SAP ERP applications. It contains the ABAP components that are part of every SAP NetWeaver ABAP installation. The minimum supported SAP NetWeaver versions are 700 SP 25, 701 SP 10, 702 SP 09, 731 SP 07, and 740 SP 03 or higher for installing SAP Screen Personas.

3. Screen Personas can be installed on the Kernel versions 7.22 or 7.42 or higher. This layer contains the key component of SAP Screen Personas—that is, the internet transaction server (ITS), which provides the standard SAP screen definitions for each transaction code accessible via browsers.

4. SAP Screen Personas Client is a JavaScript application that runs in a browser.

> **Note**
>
> Your system must have the SAPUI 750 SP 0 component installed to use the SAP Screen Personas for Web Dynpro ABAP applications.

Now, let's navigate the SAP Screen Personas 3.0 screens in runtime and editing mode. Follow these steps:

14

1. Log in to SAP Easy Access.

2. Click the SAP Screen Personas Icon ![P] to launch SAP Screen Personas.

3. You'll see the **My Flavors** bar. Typically, you provide access to couple of flavors for each user or role based on what they want to do; in some cases, IT will choose default flavors for end users. However, if you're running SAP Screen Personas for the first time, you should see an **Original Screen** button to view the original screen (see Figure 14.3).

Figure 14.3 My Flavors Main Menu

4. Now, let's explore the options in the SAP Screen Personas flavor editor. To enter the editor, select a flavor and click **Edit** (see Figure 14.4).

Figure 14.4 Edit Flavor

5. Edit mode contains editing tabs, an **Information** area, controls, and so on, allowing you to personalize the look and feel of the current SAP standard transaction screen. Let's discuss the options available:

- **Home**
  From this tab (Figure 14.5), you can format the text of a selected control, add background images, or assign icon to a button.

Figure 14.5 Home Tab

- **Insert**
  From this tab (Figure 14.6), users can insert buttons, images, and labels, and add screen events.

Figure 14.6 Insert Tab

- **Tables**
  If your SAP screen has a table, you can customize it with the options available from this tab (Figure 14.7), such as hiding columns, changing column text, moving columns, or applying conditional formatting.

Figure 14.7 Tables Tab

- **Design**
  From this tab (Figure 14.8), developers can create or edit a template and can add it to a flavor as well. You can add shapes and can apply styles to multiple objects.

Figure 14.8 Design Tab

   – **Release**

     From this tab (Figure 14.9), developers can manage different versions of the flavors. Here, you can maintain a history of changes, and once the flavor is ready, you can lock it to signify that it's ready for transport.

Figure 14.9 Release Tab

Now that you understand the basics of the SAP Screen Personas flavor editor, in the following sections we'll set up an SAP Screen Personas project, build a theme, and assign the theme to flavors.

14.2   Creating Your First SAP Screen Personas Project

In this section, we'll create an SAP Screen Personas project and discuss some of the basic options while creating themes and flavors.

14.2.1   Create a Theme

The SAP Screen Personas theme editor allows you to change visual properties that apply to multiple screens; for example, you can set background colors for all buttons, change all the label colors, and so on. To get started, follow these steps:

1. Log in to SAP GUI.
2. Start SAP Screen Personas by clicking .
3. Click the **Themes** button, then click **Create New Theme** (see Figure 14.10).

Figure 14.10 Themes

4. Enter the theme **Name** and **Description**, and click **Done** (see Figure 14.11).

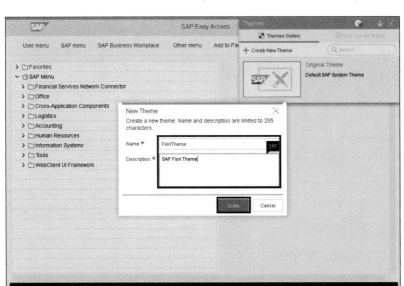

Figure 14.11 New Theme Details

5. Select **General Theme**, then select **Label** from the dropdown box (see Figure 14.12). You can select different components from the dropdown list to customize.

6. Each component from the dropdown will have customization options. For this example, let's change the label font color (see Figure 14.12).

Figure 14.12 General Theme Properties

7. In the **General Theme** tab select **Label**, and then click **A** to the right of the **Font Color** box and select a color from the available options.

8. Click the **Control Specific Styles** tab and click the components that you want to hide to select them (see Figure 14.13).

9. Select **Hidden** from the **Visible** dropdown box (see Figure 14.13).

10. Once you've set all the theme customizations you need, click **Save** (see Figure 14.13).

Figure 14.13 Hiding Components

14.2.2   Assign the Theme to a Role and Transaction

In this section, we'll create a role and assign the theme we created in the previous section to that role and a transaction.

1. Log in to the SAP front-end server, and run Transaction /PERSONAS/ADMIN.

2. Click the **Display/Search** icon 🔍 under the **User and Role Administration** section (see Figure 14.14).

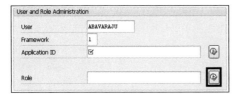

Figure 14.14 User and Role Administration

3. Click **Add Role**, then enter the **Role** technical name; click **Save** (see Figure 14.15).

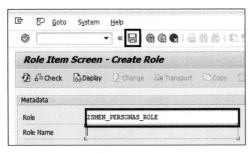

Figure 14.15 Creating Role

4. Now, return to the **SAP Screen Personas Administration** screen by clicking the back button.

5. Select the theme we created in the previous section, then click **Display/Search** ⊕ (see Figure 14.16).

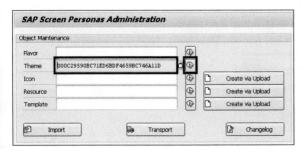

Figure 14.16 Theme Maintenance

Next, we'll enter the role name we created previously and then enter the transaction to which we want this theme to be assigned. In our example, we're assigning the theme to Transaction SMEN. Follow these steps:

1. Click **Change**, then enter the **Role** name and **Transaction** code in the **Assignment** section (see Figure 14.17).

2. Click **Assign Theme** (see Figure 14.17).

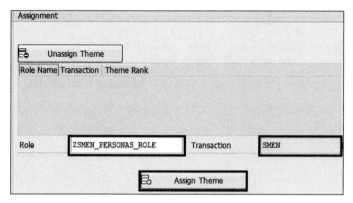

Figure 14.17 Assigning Theme

14.2.3   Create a Flavor

In this section, we'll create a new flavor for the SAP Easy Access screen by customizing the UI.

1. Start SAP Screen Personas from the SAP Web GUI. Click **+** to add a new flavor.

2. Enter the flavor **Name** and **Description**, then click **Create** (see Figure 14.18).

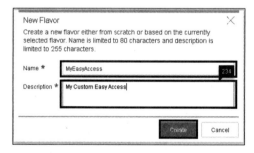

Figure 14.18 New Flavor

3. Next, let's add a logo in the top-left corner. Select the **Insert** tab, then click **Image** (see Figure 14.19).

Figure 14.19 Inserting Image

4. Select the image you want to add and click **Insert Image**. Click **Upload Image** to upload an image if you don't see what you need in the image gallery (see Figure 14.20).

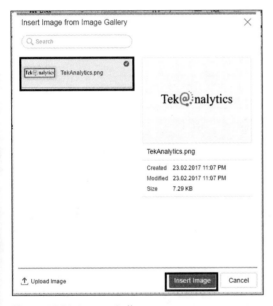

Figure 14.20 Image Gallery

5. Next, let's insert a button that invokes a transaction code. Click **Transaction Button** from the **Insert** tab.

6. Enter a **Label** (in this example, "User Maintenance") and transaction **Code**, ("SU01") then click **Done** (see Figure 14.21).

7. Follow the previous two steps to add two more transaction buttons, one for Create Sales Order (tcode VA01) and another for Release a Sales Order (tcode VL01N).

Figure 14.21 New Transaction Button

8. Select all the transaction buttons, and then resize, and align the buttons using the align options under the Home tab (see Figure 14.22).

Figure 14.22 Transaction Buttons

9. Next, let's add a button to log off. Click **Menu Items Button** under the **Insert** tab, and select the **System/Log Off** item from the **Menu Items** dropdown box. Click **Done** (see Figure 14.23).

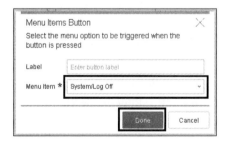

Figure 14.23 Log Off Button

10. Now, let's add an icon to the System/Log Off button we added in the previous step, select the new **System/Log Off** button, then click the **Assign Icon** button.

11. Select an icon from the gallery and click **Done** (see Figure 14.24).

Figure 14.24 Inserting from Icon Gallery

12. Format the three transaction buttons, formatting options are available from the **Home** tab (see Figure 14.25).

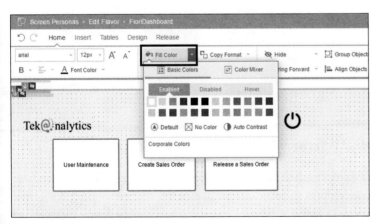

Figure 14.25 Formatting Options

13. Select all the transaction buttons and add a background color by clicking the Fill Color option under the **Home** tab.

14. Increasing the font size by selecting the font size from the formatting section under **Home** tab.

15. Drag and drop the Transaction box from the SAP Menu, to the personas screen (see Figure 14.26).

16. In Section 14.3, we'll cover some advanced features in SAP Screen Personas, so we need to add more components to the flavor here first.

17. Create a tile with a Text Field box, and rename text field to **Sales Order Lookup**

18. Add 3 Text input boxes. Add a script buttons, and rename the button as "GO". For now, these text button, text boxes, and the script button are just dummy components, but we'll use these in the next sections.

19. Once you add all the components, your screen should look something like the one in Figure 14.26.

20. Save the flavor by clicking **Save**, and click **Exit**.

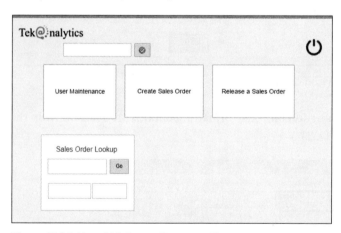

Figure 14.26 New SAP Screen Personas Flavor

14.3   Advanced SAP Screen Personas Flavor Concepts

In this section, we'll explore advanced options such as scripting. *Scripting* is a powerful tool that allows developers to automate or manipulate a screen action. We'll cover some basic scripting tasks using JavaScript and show you how to create more engaging SAP screens.

In the following exercise, we'll cover navigation of scripting windows, moving around the SAP Screen Personas script editor, and using JavaScript events to enrich screens. Follow these steps:

1. Launch SAP Screen Personas.

2. Select your custom flavor, then click **Scripting** (see Figure 14.27).

Figure 14.27 Scripting

3. Click ⛭ to create a new script, enter a script name (for example: **SalesOrder_ Lookup**) and press ⌁Enter⌁ (see Figure 14.28).

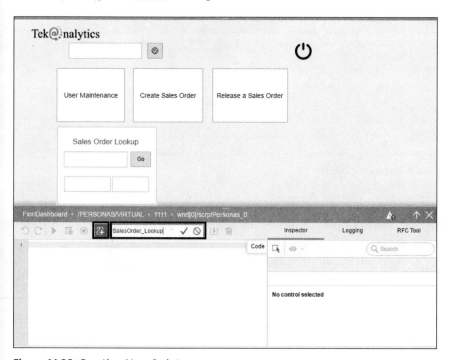

Figure 14.28 Creating New Script

4. Click **Start Recording** in the script window, this captures the screen actions that you perform in the following steps.

5. We'll first capture the screens of the VA03 (Display Sales Order) transaction. In the command field enter the transaction code **VA03** and click the green checkbox (see Figure 14.29).

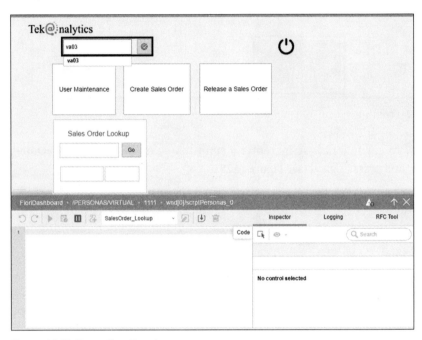

Figure 14.29 Recording Events

6. You should now see the event captured in the script window (see Figure 14.30). The following is an example of a recorded script:

```
session.findById("wnd[0]/tbar[0]/okcd").text = "VA03";
session.findById("wnd[0]").sendVKey(0);
```

7. While the script window is open, enter a sales **Order** number, then press ⌷Enter⌷ (see Figure 14.30). The following is an example of a recorded script:

```
session.findById("wnd[0]/usr/ctxtVBAK-VBELN").text = "14800";
session.findById("wnd[0]/usr/ctxtVBAK-VBELN").setFocus();
session.findById("wnd[0]").sendVKey(0);
```

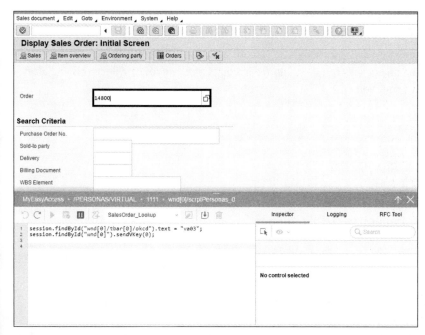

Figure 14.30 Captured Transaction Code Event

8. Click the **Object Selector** 🔍 from the **Inspector** tab, then click the **NetValue** field (see Figure 14.32).

9. Grab the text field by clicking ✎ next to the text field (see Figure 14.31)

Figure 14.31 Text Field

10. Define the SONetVal variable as follows:

    Var SONetVal = session.findById("wnd[0]/usr/subSUBSCRFFN_HEADER:SAP-MV45A:4021/txtVBAK-NETWR").text; (see Figure 14.32).

> **Important!**
> Remember to add a semicolon (;) at the end of every text element you capture using the object selector. If you notice in your script window ; will be missing after the .text function.

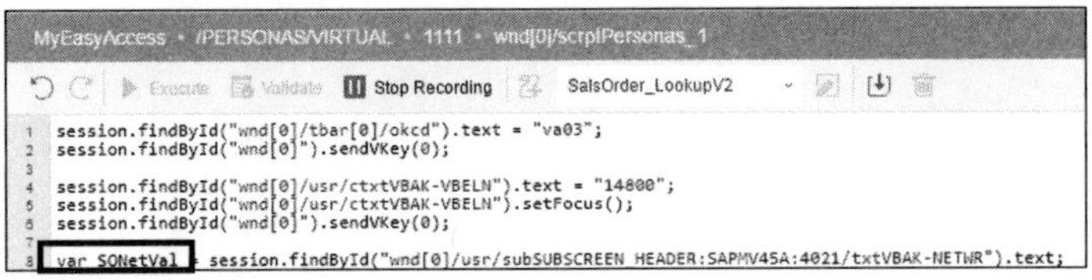

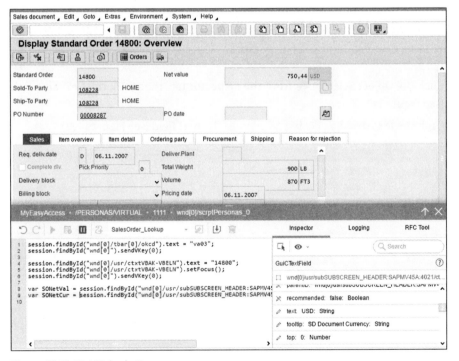

Figure 14.32 Object Selector

11. Again, with the object selector, select the currency field **USD** (see Figure 14.33), then click ✐ to capture the text. Define the SONetCur variable.

Figure 14.33 Net Value's Currency

12. The following is an example of a recorded script; remember to add ; at the end of the script:

```
Var SONetCur = session.findById("wnd[0]/usr/subSUBSCREEN_HEADER:SAP-
MV45A:4021/txtVBAK-NETWR").text;
```

13. Navigate back to the initial screen, and click **Stop Recording**.

14. We defined text input fields in the previous section; now, click ⌕ **Object Selector**, then select the input field in **Sales Order Lookup** box (see Figure 14.34).

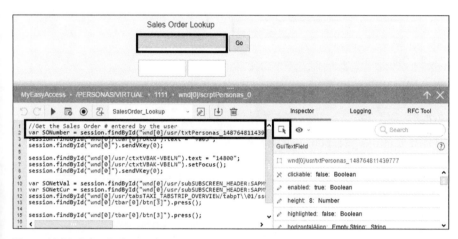

Figure 14.34 Sales Order Lookup

15. Click ✎ to capture the user's sales order number input.

16. Now, assign the selection to the SONumber variable.

17. Your script should look something like the following:

```
//Get the Sales Order # entered by the uservar
SONumber = session.findById("wnd[0]/usr/txtPersonas_148764811439777").text;
```

18. Now, pass the user-entered sales order number by using the variable we created in the previous step (see Figure 14.35):

```
//Pass the user entered SO Numbersession.findById("wnd[0]/usr/ctxtVBAK-
VBELN").text = SONumber;
```

19. Similarly, capture the other two text boxes (see Figure 14.35 and Figure 14.36), and pass the variables we created, SONet and SONetCur in Steps 9 and 11:

```
//Fill the Netvalue and Currency
fieldssession.findById("wnd[0]/usr/txtPersonas_148764813406176").text =
```

```
SONetCur;session.findById("wnd[0]/usr/txtPersonas_148764812672532").text =
SONetVal;
```

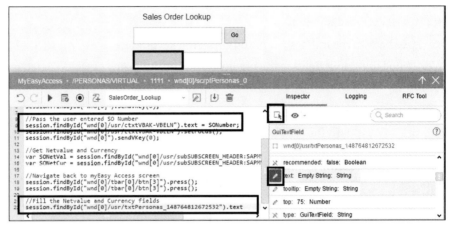

Figure 14.35 Capturing Text Box to Pass Net Values

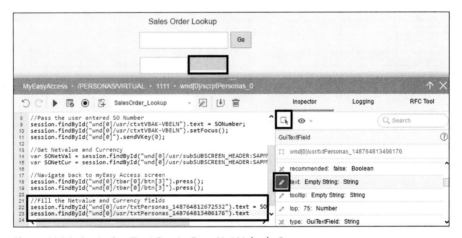

Figure 14.36 Capturing Text Box to Pass Net Value's Currency

20. Check your final script:

```
//Get the Sales Order # entered by the uservar
SONumber = session.findById("wnd[0]/usr/txtPersonas_148764811439777").text;
//Go to Transaction
VAO3session.findById("wnd[0]/tbar[0]/okcd").text = "va03";
session.findById("wnd[0]").sendVKey(0);
```

```
//Pass the user entered SO
Numbersession.findById("wnd[0]/usr/ctxtVBAK-VBELN").text = SONumber;
session.findById("wnd[0]").sendVKey(0);
//Get Netvalue and Currencyvar
SONetVal = session.findById("wnd[0]/usr/subSUBSCREEN_HEADER:SAPMV45A:4021/
ctxtVBAK-WAERK").text;
var SONetCur = session.findById("wnd[0]/usr/subSUBSCREEN_HEADER:SAP-
MV45A:4021/txtVBAK-NETWR").text;
//Navigate back to myEasy Access
screensession.findById("wnd[0]/tbar[0]/btn[3]").press();
session.findById("wnd[0]/tbar[0]/btn[3]").press();
//Fill the Netvalue and Currency
fieldssession.findById("wnd[0]/usr/txtPersonas_148764813406176").text =
SONetCur;
session.findById("wnd[0]/usr/txtPersonas_148764812672532").text = SONetVal;
```

21. Click ⬇ to save the script.

22. Validate the script by clicking 🗏, and make sure there are no errors.

23. Now, let's test the script. Enter a sales order number, and click **Execute**.

24. You should now see the net value and the currency displayed in the text boxes
(see Figure 14.37).

Figure 14.37 Execute Script

Now, we'll enable the **Go** button to run the script we created in the previous steps.

1. To start, select the **Go** button, and navigate to **Events** • **Script Events** • **onClick** (see Figure 14.38).

2. Select the **SalesOrder_Lookup** script we created in the previous steps (see Figure 14.38).

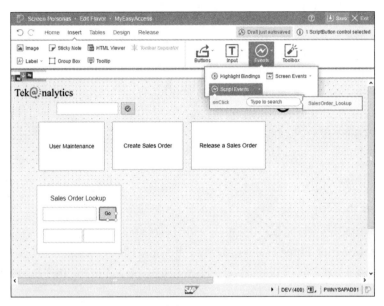

Figure 14.38 Script Events, onClick

3. **Save**, then **Exit**. You should now be able to check the net values and currency of a particular sales order (see Figure 14.39).

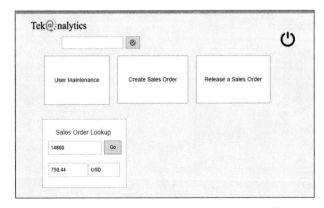

Figure 14.39 Custom Easy Access Screen Personas Flavor

We've successfully created our first screen persona flavor and then add explored some advanced scripting options as well. Next, we'll explore the SAP Screen personas administrative tasks.

14.4   SAP Screen Personas Administrative Tasks

In this section, we'll highlight core administrative tasks for SAP Screen Personas, such as maintaining flavors, themes, templates, and the overall SAP Screen Personas environment. Launch the SAP Screen Personas Administration by running the transaction /PERSONAS/ADMIN from the SAP GUI (see Figure 14.40).

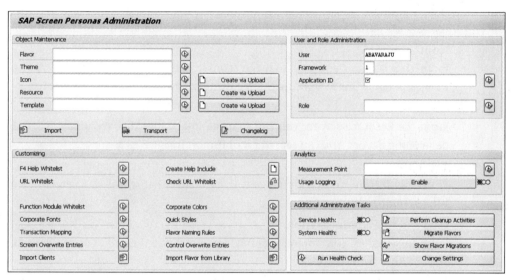

Figure 14.40 SAP Screen Personas Administration

Admin Role

An SAP Screen Personas administrator should have the /PERSONAS/ADMIN_ROLE role assigned to his or her user ID.

You can perform the following functions as an SAP Screen Personas administrator:

> **Note**
>
> You can launch the below functions from the Object Maintenance area of the SAP Screen Personas Administration (see Figure 14.40).

1. **Flavor**
   From the **Flavor** screen, you can manage the flavors available in the system; you can copy, delete, export, and share them, for example.
2. **Theme**
   From the **Theme** screen, you can manage the themes: find new themes, importing themes, assign/unassign themes to a role or transaction, and delete themes.
3. **Icon**
   From this section, you can manage icons: change their descriptions, change images, assign icons to a group, change owners, and show where icons are used.
4. **Resource**
   From the **Resource** screen, you can manage image files that are uploaded while developing flavors. You can search for or import image files as well.
5. **Template**
   From this section, you can manage the templates; that is, you can search for or import multiple templates.
6. **User and role administration**
   From this section, you can manage business users and their roles assigned to different SAP Screen Personas.

You can perform some additional tasks from the SAP Screen Personas administration, such as transporting SAP Screen Personas objects between environments, adding corporate fonts and colors, and running a health check tool that checks if the various SAP Screen Personas' relevant configurations have been implemented correctly.

> **Useful SAP Screen Personas Transaction Codes**
>
> The following transaction codes are useful for developers or administrators who are working on SAP Screen Personas.

- Transaction /PERSONAS/ADMIN(SAP Screen Personas Administration)
- Transaction /PERSONAS/USERS(User Maintenance)
- Transaction /PERSONAS/ROLES (Roles Maintenance)
- Transaction /PERSONAS/FLAVORS (Flavor Maintenance)
- Transaction /PERSONAS/THEMES (Theme Maintenance)
- Transaction /PERSONAS/ICONS (Icon Maintenance)
- Transaction /PERSONAS/RESOURCES (Resource Maintenance)
- Transaction /PERSONAS/TEMPLATES (Template Maintenance)

In this section, we've highlighted some of the administrative tasks that you can perform as a Personas administrator. In the next section, we'll show you how to deploy a Flavor in SAP Fiori Launchpad.

14.5   Deploying SAP Screen Personas Flavors in SAP Fiori Launchpad

In the previous sections, we showed you how to create an SAP Screen Personas flavor for a transaction code; in this section, we'll show you how to deploy an SAP Screen Personas flavor in the SAP Fiori launchpad as a tile. In Chapter 4, Section 4.6.1, we explained how to deploy an SAP Fiori app, follow the same steps here to deploy the SAP Screen Personas flavor in SAP Fiori launchpad:

1. Login to SAP Web GUI, and launch SAP Screen Personas.
2. Select the flavor you want to publish, then click the **Link** icon 🔗 to generate a URL (see Figure 14.41).

Figure 14.41 Generating Flavor URL

3. Copy the link, and click **Close** (see Figure 14.42).

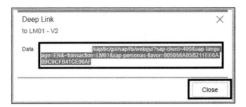

Figure 14.42 Copying Link

4. Now, follow the steps from Chapter 4 to create a new launchpad.

5. Most of the steps are the same as those in Chapter 4, Section 4.6.1, but in Step 8, paste the flavor URL you copied in Step 2 in this section into the **Application Parameters** section (see Figure 14.43).

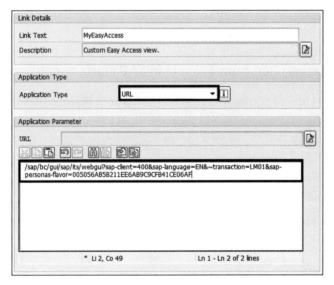

Figure 14.43 Application Parameter Section

6. Once you complete all the steps, you should be able to launch the SAP Screen Personas flavor from the SAP Fiori launchpad.

14.6   Summary

In this final chapter, we discussed how SAP Screen Personas allows you to transform classic SAP screens into SAP Fiori-inspired designs. We took a closer look at the SAP

Screen Personas 3.0 options and created a project covering some of the basic and advanced options. As you can see, SAP Screen Personas allows you to apply similar design factors that you would find in an SAP Fiori app to other SAP screens, extending the SAP UX strategy across SAP products.

This concludes our discussion on of the implementation and development of SAP Fiori applications. The next two appendices explore the SAP Fiori Client and custom themes in SAP Fiori Launchpad.

14

Appendices

A SAP Fiori Client 585

B Customizing SAP Fiori Launchpad 593

C The Author 603

Appendix A
SAP Fiori Client

Although one of the main selling points of SAP Fiori is that it's browser-based and can automatically adjust its layout depending on your device (desktop or mobile), there's also a native SAP Fiori app (version 1.4) for iOS, Android, and Windows 10 available. This appendix briefly introduces the native app, SAP Fiori Client, and discusses the pros and cons of using it as opposed to running SAP Fiori in a mobile browser.

A.1 Overview

SAP Fiori Client is a mobile app that can be downloaded from the app stores for iOS, Android, and Windows. This mobile app provides additional native functionalities, such as a barcode scanner, camera, geolocation, cache mechanism, and so on. Currently, the app works on devices running Android 4.3 through 5.x, iOS 7.1 through 9.x, and Windows 8.1 or 10. SAP Fiori Client was developed on the Apache Cordova architecture, with the APIs added through the Cordova plugins. Some of the common device features, such as the barcode scanner, the camera, and geolocation, work on all three OS types.

SAP Fiori Client implements an asset cache management strategy that allows the native app to maintain its own cache of SAP Fiori application assets. When the user runs the app for the first time, the application assets are cached in the device. The next time the user reopens the app, it uses the local cached assets while loading—unlike the mobile browser cache, which is purged every couple of hours.

> **Cache Management**
> Cache management isn't supported on Windows devices.

A.2   Download and Log In to SAP Fiori Client

Now that you have an overview of SAP Fiori Client, we'll look at using the app itself. In this section, we'll walk you through the application download and login on an iOS device, and the process is very similar on the other devices. Follow these steps:

1. Download the SAP Fiori Client app from the app store. Figure A.1 shows the SAP Fiori app icon.

Figure A.1 SAP Fiori App

2. Open the app by clicking its icon.
3. You can either click **Log In** to connect to your SAP Fiori landscape, or you can select **Demo Mode** to try out the SAP Fiori app. For this example, click **Log In** (see Figure A.2).

Figure A.2 Welcome Screen

4. Enter the SAP Fiori URL or email parameters provided by your administrator, and click **OK** (see Figure A.3).

5. Next, you'll see a passcode screen on which you can set the app password to protect your application from unauthorized access. You can reset the password if you've forgotten it; however, you'll have to reconfigure the application with your SAP Fiori launchpad details. With the integration of the SAP Mobile Platform into SAP Fiori, you can create a much more secure environment and manage the mobile environment for SAP Fiori very efficiently (see Figure A.4).

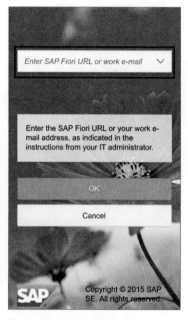

Figure A.3 Server Details

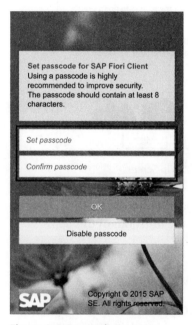

Figure A.4 Passcode Screen

6. After you're logged in, you'll see tips on some of the functionalities available (see Figure A.5). Click **Continue**.

7. On the next screen, you need to enter your login credentials and click **Log On** (see Figure A.6).

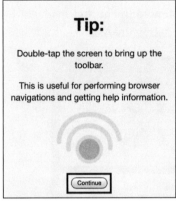

Figure A.5 Tip Screen

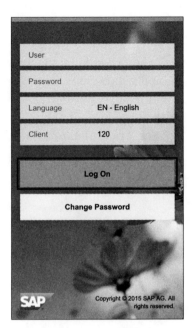

Figure A.6 Login Credentials

You should now see the SAP Fiori apps that you have access to. Next, we'll explore some of the functions of this app.

A.3   Functions

SAP Fiori Client houses the apps you have access to on your SAP Fiori landscape. Figure A.7 shows the SAP Fiori Client home screen.

By clicking ▤ at the top left, you can open the SAP Fiori catalog groups (see Figure A.8). You can navigate between these groups; for example, we selected the **Field Sales Representative** group to view the apps under that group.

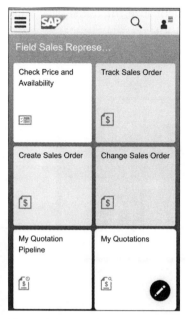

Figure A.7 Home Screen

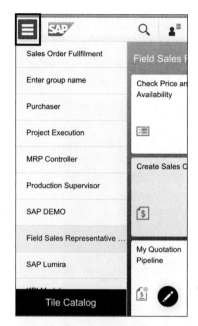

Figure A.8 Groups Catalog

You can search apps or objects that you have access to by clicking $\mathbb{Q}$ (see Figure A.9). For example, if you want to see the Sales Order fact sheet app for a particular order, just type the sales order number and click **Search** to view the fact sheet app.

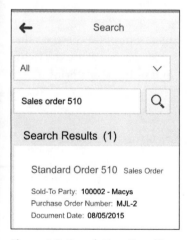

Figure A.9 Search Functionality

Clicking 👤☰ opens a menu from which you can personalize the home page, hide groups, set user preferences, and log out (see Figure A.10).

You can create new groups, edit the title and subtitle of an app, or remove apps by clicking 🖊️, as shown in Figure A.11.

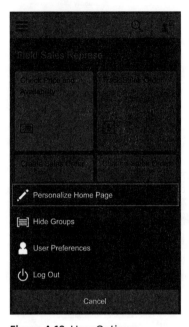

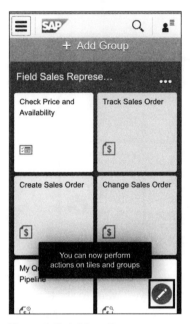

Figure A.10 User Options

Figure A.11 Adding Groups

On double-tapping the screen (iOS), SAP Fiori Client opens an options screen that allows you to navigate to a previous screen; refresh the current page; use the **Home** button to navigate to the main page; adjust help, logs, and settings; and print.

> **Screen**
>
> The Windows 10 options screen can be opened by swiping up from the bottom.

The **Settings** button under the options screen in SAP Fiori Client allows you to change the URL. You can also set the **Log Level** to **Error**, **Warn**, **Info**, or **Debug**, as well as clear the cache and all app settings (see Figure A.12).

You can also view attachments within SAP Fiori Client instead of opening them in a separate app. This option currently works in iOS only (see Figure A.13). On Windows and Android devices, attachments are opened using an external application.

Figure A.12 Options

Figure A.13 Attachments

Useful Links

There are some helpful links to references about supported apps and security you should be aware of:

- **Supported apps**
  A list of all the features that are supported by different OS versions can be viewed at *http://help.sap.com/fiori-client*; once there, navigate to **SAP Fiori Client Feature Matrix**.

- **Security**
  For security configuration information, go to *http://help.sap.com/fiori-client* and choose **SAP Fiori Client User Guide • Security Configuration**.

Appendix B
Customizing SAP Fiori Launchpad

SAP Fiori launchpad is a shell page from which all SAP Fiori apps can be accessed. It can be customized using a tool called the *UI Theme Designer*. The UI Theme Designer isn't just for SAP Fiori, but also functions as a tool for cross-theming scenarios, supporting many platforms and technologies. For example, when you create a theme for SAP Fiori launchpad, you can apply the same theme to SAP Fiori applications, Web Dynpro ABAP, Floorplan Manager (FPM), and SAP Business Client.

B.1 UI Theme Designer Overview

UI Theme Designer is a browser-based tool with a WYSIWYG designer (what you see is what you get); therefore, any change that you make can be viewed immediately in the browser. Using the UI Theme Designer, you can create your own themes to reflect your corporate identity, corporate colors, and company logo.

Figure B.1 shows the SAP Fiori launchpad architecture with the UI Theme Designer. The top layer shows the UI Theme Designer built on SAPUI5. The UI theme repository on the ABAP front-end server contains SAP standard themes and custom themes. Each time you create a custom theme, UI Theme Designer generates LESS files, CSS files, and images, which are saved into the repository. These files are received via HTTP calls. The application is loaded with the CSS files from a chosen custom theme.

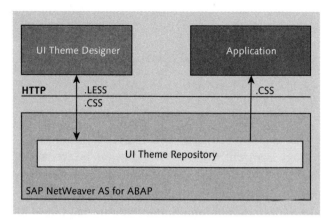

Figure B.1 UI Theme Designer Architecture

The following are the transaction codes you'll be using while working with UI Theme Designer:

- **Transaction UI5/THEME_DESIGNER**
  This transaction is used to create, edit, copy, delete, or rebuild/upgrade a theme.
- **Transaction UI5/THEME_TOOL**
  This transaction is used to delete, export, import, transport, and analyze theme content.
- **Transaction UI Theme Repository**
  This tool is used to export or import single files, or to analyze theme content.

Now that you have an overview of UI Theme Designer, let's look at how to create themes for SAP Fiori launchpad.

B.2   Creating a Custom Theme

In this section, we'll show you how to create a new theme for SAP Fiori launchpad and how to apply it to the default template. To do so, follow these steps:

1. Log in to your ABAP front-end server.
2. Run Transaction UI5/THEME_DESIGNER to open UI Theme Designer.
3. Select a theme, and click **Open** (see Figure B.2).

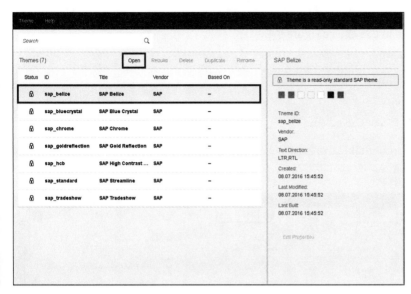

Figure B.2 UI Theme Designer

Base Theme

You can create a custom theme only on a base theme. For example, in the previous step, to create a new custom theme we started with the SAP Belize theme.

4. Enter the link to the application. In our example, we want to change the theme of SAP Fiori launchpad, so enter the SAP Fiori launchpad URL (see Figure B.3). You can also provide a name for the application, but doing so is optional.

Figure B.3 Application Link

UI Theme Designer provides various options for theming, depending on the developers skill level in CSS ❶ (see Figure B.4).

- Quick theming
- Expert theming*
- Color palette*
- Manual LESS or CSS editing

*These experimental features, which aren't for productive use, may be changed by SAP at any time.

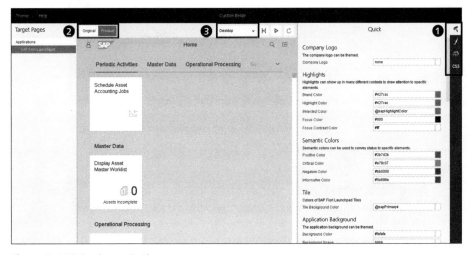

Figure B.4 UI Designer Options

You can toggle between **Original** and **Preview** modes to compare your changed version with the original version ❷.

You can select between different layouts—**Desktop**, **Mobile**, or **Tablet**—to simulate your changes on different device types ❸.

Next, let's look at some of the options in Quick theming that can help you change the look and feel of SAP Fiori launchpad.

B.2.1   Quick Theming

With the Quick theming option, you can change background colors, fonts, and images. Here, we'll add a custom logo using the Quick theming tool (see Figure B.5) and replace the standard SAP images. Similarly, you can change the text colors, fonts, and so on (see Figure B.6).

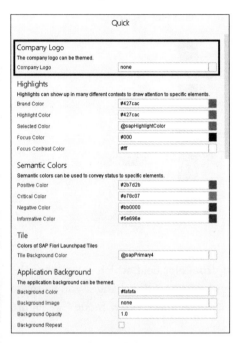

Figure B.5 Quick Theming Tool

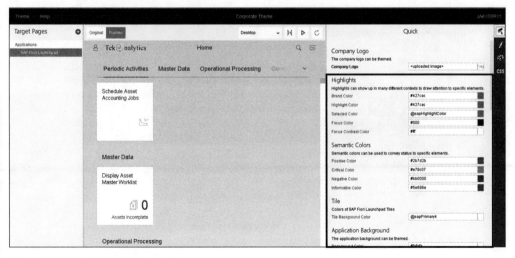

Figure B.6 Graphical Options

B.2.2   Expert Theming

Next, let's look at the Expert theming tool. To use this tool, select the **Expert** option, then enter "icon" in the search box to filter the objects (see Figure B.7).

Figure B.7 Expert Theming

You can change the color for the **sapContent_IconColor** field, which will change the color of the icons in a tile. Your output should reflect all the changes you've made until now, and you can toggle between the **Original** and **Preview** mode (see Figure B.8).

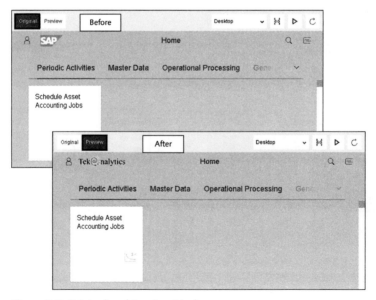

Figure B.8 Original and Preview Modes

B.2.3 Save and Build

The next task is to save and publish the changes to the ABAP front-end server. Follow these steps:

1. Click on **Theme • Save & Build** (see Figure B.9).

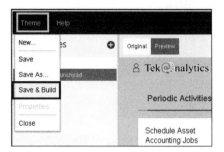

Figure B.9 Save and Build

2. Enter the **Theme ID** and the **Title**, then click **OK** (see Figure B.10).

Figure B.10 Theme Details

3. After the custom theme is saved and built, you should see a message something like the one in Figure B.11. Click **OK**.

Figure B.11 Saved Theme

B.2.4   Test the Custom Theme

You've successfully created a custom theme and uploaded it to the ABAP front-end server. Next, you'll have to test the custom theme by following these steps:

1. Log in to the ABAP front-end sever, and run Transaction UI5/THEME_TOOL.

2. Scroll down or search for your custom theme.

3. Double-click **Info** (see Figure B.12).

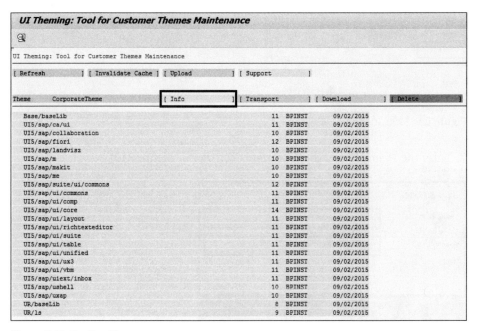

Figure B.12 Testing Theme

4. Copy the URL and paste it at the end of the SAP Fiori launchpad URL, prefaced by an ampersand (&).Your url should look something similar to what we have below, and once you run this url in the browser, you should see the new custom theme applied to your SAP Fiori Launchpad:

    https://<host>.<domain>:<port>/sap/bc/ui5_ui5/ui2/ushell/shells/abap/Fiorilaun-chpad.html?sap-theme=CorporateTheme&http://nbcloud.nineboards.com:50000/sap/public/bc/themes/~client-120/~cache-2VCj7NrjFnVxuDZ8vm6HqrJVPsI

5. The next step is to overwrite the standard theme with the custom theme, which you created in the previous steps. Run Transaction /UI2/NWBC_CFG_SAP.

6. Set the **SAP_FLP** parameter value to the name of the custom theme you created previously (see Figure B.13).

You should now see SAP Fiori launchpad with the new theme in place.

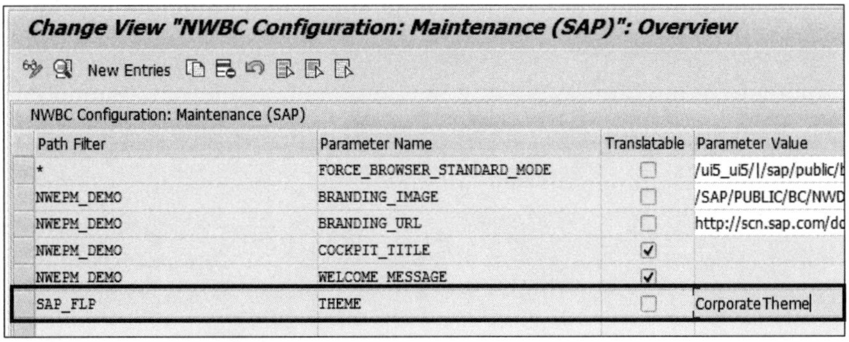

Path Filter	Parameter Name	Translatable	Parameter Value
*	FORCE_BROWSER_STANDARD_MODE	☐	/ui5_ui5/l/sap/public/b
NWEPM_DEMO	BRANDING_IMAGE	☐	/SAP/PUBLIC/BC/NWD
NWEPM_DEMO	BRANDING_URL	☐	http://scn.sap.com/do
NWEPM_DEMO	COCKPIT_TITLE	☑	
NWEPM_DEMO	WELCOME_MESSAGE	☑	
SAP_FLP	THEME	☐	Corporate Theme

Change View "NWBC Configuration: Maintenance (SAP)": Overview

New Entries

NWBC Configuration: Maintenance (SAP)

Figure B.13 Overwite Standard Theme

Important!

Whenever you apply a patch, make sure you check whether your custom theme is working without any issues. If you come across any issues, you may have to rebuild your theme with UI Theme Designer.

Appendix C
The Author

Anil Bavaraju has been working with SAP enterprise software since 2004, specializing in SAP Fiori, SAPUI5, SAP HANA, and SAP BusinessObjects BI products. His current focus is on SAP S/4HANA and SAP Fiori at his consulting company. Over the past three years, he has had the opportunity to help several clients implement SAP Fiori on SAP S/4HANA, and on SAP Business Suite as well. He has experience in managing development teams, as well as architecting, developing, and deploying highly scalable and available systems, acquired while working on global enterprise implementations for large, multinational companies. He is an SAP Certified Solution Consultant for SAP Business Intelligence, and an SAP Certified Application Associate for SAP HANA. You can follow Anil on Twitter at *@anilbavaraju* or connect via LinkedIn at *https://www.linkedin.com/in/anilbavaraju.*

Index

A

ABAP
    class 118
    environment 78
    servers 31, 155
ABAP back-end
    component 94
    copy business role 193
    server 45, 80, 123, 158, 175, 375, 382
ABAP Data Dictionary 292, 391
ABAP front-end
    components 494
    server 36, 44, 78, 89, 117, 120, 152, 153,
        158, 175, 382
ABAP Repository 398, 406, 422
Action 264
Activate services 178
Add node 187
Add-on 94
Administrator role 127
Adopting reference 127
Aggregation 488
AJAX 57
All Stories 540
All Views tab 459
Analytical app 55, 173, 231, 232, 457
    architecture 56
    creating 462
    extending 483
    nonsmart 232, 270
    prerequisites 233, 461
    SAP HANA layer 483
    SAP HANA Live 461
    SAP Smart Business modeler 232, 235
    UI layer 483
Analytical view 461
Android 30, 47
ANNO 446
Annotation file 440, 447
    edit 455
Anonymity 43

Apache reverse proxy 153
API 57, 69, 340
App
    information 353
    parameters 262
    registration 355
Apple 46
Application 27, 125
    access file 472
    alias 198, 377
    descriptor file 472
    details 423
    link 595
    parameter 198
    type 197
Approve Purchase Orders app 337
Apps reference library 28, 88, 218, 270
Architecture 30
AS ABAP 58
AS Java 58
Association 280, 284
Atom Publishing protocol
    (AtomPub) 68, 276
Attachments 505, 591
Attribute
    add 432
    view 461
Authentication
    process 169
Authorization
    change 190
    default 114, 187
    process 169
    roles 114
    start 186
Available fields 447

B

Backend
    database 80
    server 31

BAdI 513
   implementation 514
   standard 513
   user decisions 520
BAPI 73
Barcode scanner 585
Base class 393
Blue Crystal 595
Bootstrapped 66
BOPF 310
BOR 297, 298
Browser 30, 44
BSP application 409, 440, 455
Business 29
   engine 312
   function 130
Business Object Processing Framework
   (BOPF) 309
Business role
   assign 191
   copy 185, 193
   custom 195
   edit 187

C

Cache 585
Calculation view 462
   activate 466
   copy 464
   create 464
   sales order 462
Call browser 109
Catalog 185, 206, 263, 355, 378, 482, 531
   create 201
   group 588
   ID 267
   new 201
   role 272
CB_SALES_ORDER_SRV 419
Central hub deployment 85, 496
Central User Administration (CUA) 170
Certificate request 162
Change Sales Order app 185, 195
Check Price and Availability app 185
Class load 58

Client 30, 44, 78, 155
Coherent 30
Collaboration 505
   components 526, 534
Collections 70
Color palette 596
Comments 504
Communication channels 44, 152, 154
   security 152
Comparison tile 243, 244
Component
   download 99
   version 92, 98
Conceptual Schema Definition
   Language (CSDL) 277
Configuration 108
   scope 199
   tile 538
Configure Drill-Down app 246
Conflicts 417
Connector 221, 434
   automatic 225
   manual 223
Connector Administration Cockpit 223,
   410, 435
Consume 72
Consumer
   layer 73
   type 511
Contents 450
Controller 60
Create Sales Order app 176, 185, 194
Create, read, update, delete (CRUD) 70
CRUD 72, 179, 280
CSS 57
   files 593
Custom
   business catalog 195
   role 206, 261
   scope 199
   view 260
Custom theme 594
   overwrite 601
   save and build 599
   test 599
Customer Invoices app 185

D

Data
  binding 60
  model 71, 289, 318
  replication 82
  visualization tool 536
Data Model from File 290
Data Provider Base Class (_DPC) 393
Data Provider Class (DPC) 393
Data Provider Extension Class
  (_DPC_EXT) 287, 393
Data source 478
  attribute 301
  map 301
data-sap-ui-libs 67
data-sap-ui-resourceroots 67
data-sap-ui-theme 67
Days Sales Outstanding app 231, 232, 235,
  266, 543
DDIC structure 292
  import 294
Decimal precision 239
Decision
  keys 513
  text 513
Default language 128
Delightful 30
Delta indexing 225
Deployment 85, 122, 351
Design innovation 29
Destination 331
Development 333
Deviation tile 243
Dictionary objects 385
Dimensions 247
Discuss 535
Drilldown 239, 246
Dual tile 244
Dynamic
  data 521
  tile 204

E

Eclipse IDE 327
EDMX file 339, 341
Email 505
Embedded deployment 85
  advantages 87
  disadvantages 87
Embedded search 128, 223, 437
  UI services 129
Embedded service
  authorization 129
Enable 28
Entity 280
  requests 281
  sets 70, 277, 279, 285
  types 279, 284, 297
Entity Data Model (EDM) 277
EntityContainer 279
Evaluation 238, 479
Event type 509
Existing Fact Sheet Application ... 410, 418, 440
Expert Theming 596, 598
Explore systems 95
Extension 338
  class 393
  points 398, 403
  project 399
  views 403, 487, 488
External service name 109

F

Facets 420, 444, 451
Fact sheet app 54, 133, 172, 409
  ABAP back-end role 220
  ABAP back-end server tasks 213
  annotation file 446
  architecture 55, 409
  authorization 172
  creating 412, 434, 435
  deploy 422, 454
  editor plugin 411
  extending 427
  implementation 213
  run 228, 453

Fact sheet app (Cont.)

   Sales Order app 427

   SAPUI5 component 218

   search 33

   template 336

   UI layer 439, 453

Filter 253, 503, 515

flavor 556

flavor editor 560

Flower 28

Full indexing 225

G

Gateway client 277

General section 520

Generic Interaction Layer 312

Generic role 116

GenIL 312

GetList 298

Git 327

Granted roles 256

Graphical user interface (GUI) 28

Group 265, 590

   add 39

   by 504

   drag and drop 40

   tile 534

GUI 111, 165

H

Hash 111, 112

   key 182

Hierarchy 113, 178

HTML requests 44

HTML5 57

HTTP 155, 160

   connection 154

   response 307

Human values 29

Hypermedia as the engine of application state

   (HATEOAS) 70

I

ICF nodes 109, 112

Identity Provider (IDP) 165

Images 597

Implementation 78, 122, 125

Implementing class 516

INA search request 44

Indexing 225, 436

   clear 227

   keep 227

   real-time 227

Input parameters 241, 479

Installation 89

Instance profile 158

Integration 30, 525

Intent 202, 264

Internet Communication Framework

   (ICF) 161

Internet Communication Manager

   (ICM) 176

Internet-facing scenario 152

iOS 30

J

JavaScript 57, 60

jQuery library 57

JSON 60

Juno 328

K

Kepler 328

Kerberos/SPNego 163, 164

Key facts 420, 449

KPI 231, 232, 235

   configure 477, 490

   create 478

   framework 135, 234

   header 252

   modeler 92, 135, 462, 477

   modeling framework 56

   parameters 237

   tile 242, 482, 490

KPIs 51

L

Landscape 154
Landscape Planner 95
Launchpad 261, 426
   new 196
   role 196
LESS files 593
Lines of business (LOB) 27, 232
Lines of business (LOBs) 50
listSize 498
Load balancing 43
Local object 109, 392
Logon language 128

M

Mac 30
Maintain services 181
Maintenance Optimizer 95
Manage Products app 337
massAction 499, 502
Master-detail app 339
Microsoft Active Directory 164
Mini chart 253
Mobile app 585
Mock data 349, 373
Model 59, 224
   composition 289
   edit 429
   enhance 429
   node 430
   properties 430
Model Provider Base Class (_MPC) 287, 393
Model Provider Extension Class
   (_MPC_EXT) 287, 393
Model-view-controller (MVC) 59
Modification Free Fact Sheet
   Application 440, 444
Multiselect 502
MVC
   concept 59, 60
My Inbox app 96, 97, 491, 492
   All Items 496, 501
   architecture 493
   common issues 500

My Inbox app (Cont.)
   prerequisites 494
   release information 495
My Marketing Budget app 52
My Quotations app 170, 382, 397

N

Namespace 197
Navigation
   properties 284
   section 521
   target 448
neo-app.json 446
Network layer 152
New 28
   field 433, 452, 489
   project 388, 468
   view 489
New Extension Project
   method 334
   option 338
New Fact Sheet Application 418, 441
New Project from Sample Application 336
   method 334
New Project from Template 64, 335, 339,
   370, 440
   method 334
News tile 204
Notification tile 534
Numeric tile 242

O

Object
   method 508
   navigator 384
OData 68, 160, 175, 179, 276, 483
   activate service 179, 304
   add service 305
   advantages 69
   artifact 390
   consume service 70
   custom service 401
   generate service 315
   import service 290

OData (Cont.)
model 60
model service 288
redefine service 309, 389
register service 303, 394
requests 44, 80
SAP HANA Live view 461
service 45, 82, 186, 213, 219, 275, 311, 313, 321, 369, 438, 468, 473
service basics 276
test service 306, 394, 476
Online Text Repository (OTR) 445
Open Data Protocol (OData) 68
OpenAJAX 57
Operational performance indicators (OPIs) 233
Orion 327

P

Package 384, 389, 462
definition 463
select 471
Partner structure 385
Password 164
Personal Security Environment (PSE) 157
PFCG role for business catalog 185
Ping Federate 165
Predefined task list 137
Prerequisites 77
Preview 348, 596
Private view 459, 461
Product System Editor 95
Products 72
Product-specific UI 83
Profile 126
Profit Analysis app 231, 270, 273
Project
activate 475
create 297
properties 446
using a template 370
project.json 446
Properties 448
add 499
Propose mapping 301

Protocol 153
Prototyping 73

Q

Quality of Protection (QOP) 160
Query view 459, 461
extension 488
Quick Theming 596
quickAction 499

R

Raw data 467
Redefinition 288
Refresh 502
Registered Model (_MDL) 287, 393
Registered Service (_SRV) 287, 393
Release Campaigns app 52
Renew 28
Representational State Transfer (REST) 69
Resource identification 70
Responsive 29
REST 68, 72, 275
Reuse view 459, 461, 488
Reverse proxy 31, 42, 152, 155
server 80
RFC
connection 45, 123, 154, 159
generation 288
RFC/BOR interface 295
Risk category 438, 452
Role-based 29
Roles 426
administrators 537
assign 486
change 207
copy 186
end user 537
maintenance 126
technical 536
template 126
Runtime
artifacts 286, 318
objects 302, 392

S

Sales Order app 222, 228, 589
Sales Order Fulfillment app 273
Sales Order Tracker app 379
SalesDistrict 488
SalesOrderQuery 487
SAML 163
   authentication 166
Sample application 337
SAP Advanced Planning and
   Optimization (SAP APO) 107
SAP Analytics Foundation 107
SAP Basis 139
SAP BEx query 314
SAP Business Process Management
   (BPM) 493
SAP Business Suite 55, 56, 77, 79, 170, 483
   integration 123
   layer 73, 380
   powered by SAP HANA 232
SAP Business Warehouse
   query 312
SAP Business Workflow 491–493
SAP BusinessObjects Design Studio 233, 545
SAP BusinessObjects Lumira 536, 540
   configuration 536
   configuration tile 538
   KPI tile drilldown 543
   stories 536
   tiles 539
SAP BusinessObjects Lumira Cloud 536
SAP BusinessObjects Lumira Server 536
SAP Cloud Platform 36, 58, 326, 329, 351
SAP Cloud Platform cloud
   connector 327, 331
SAP Cryptographic Library 157
SAP Customer Relationship Management
   (SAP CRM) 106
SAP Enterprise Portal 36
SAP Enterprise Search 428
SAP Enterprise Warehouse Management
   (SAP EWM) 107
SAP ERP 106, 396
SAP Event Management (SAP EM) 106
SAP Financial Closing Cockpit (SAP FCC) 106

SAP Fiori 77
   app 586
   apps reference library 88
   architecture 30, 457
   basics 27
   communication channels 44
   configuration 77
   history 27
   installation 77
   integration 30
   landscape 154
   name meaning 28
   related technologies 57
   SAP ERP apps 93
   security 151
   supported browsers and OS 45, 47
   template 370
   timeline 50
   user roles 51
   UX design principles 29
   workflow 491
SAP Fiori Client 585
   download and login 586
   functions 588
   security 591
   tips 588
SAP Fiori launchpad 30, 32, 108, 111, 139,
   151, 170, 176, 235, 246, 272, 407, 477, 481, 526
   add tiles 520
   architecture 593
   change theme 41
   custom theme 33, 594
   customization 593
   deployment 36
   designer 426, 498
   embedded search 128
   features 37
   homepage 32, 37
   implementation 37
   keyboard shortcuts 42
   login screen 117, 120
   My Inbox app 499
   publish app 376
   responsiveness 35
   search 33
   user options 590

SAP Foundation (SAP FND) 107
SAP Gateway 36, 68, 79, 85, 122, 139, 170,
    171, 175, 177, 234, 275, 319, 327, 494
    architecture 73
    capabilities 72
    component version 90
    integration 123
    layer 73, 380
    SAP Business Suite 73
SAP Gateway client 395
SAP Gateway Service Builder 275, 283, 388
SAP Governance, Risk and Compliance
    (SAP GRC) 106
SAP HANA 55, 78, 80, 165, 167, 173, 254
    application development platform 74
    Application Lifecycle Manager
      (HALM) 234
    data modeling 462
    database 31
    role 271
    server 106, 234
    view 237
SAP HANA Client 462
SAP HANA cockpit 326, 339
SAP HANA Live 74, 78, 84, 106, 457
    advantages 461
    extend view 483
    extensibility tool 483
    package 457
    views 108, 458, 462
SAP HANA Live Browser 107, 459
SAP HANA Studio 134, 255, 462
    extensibility tool 483
SAP HANA XS 31, 43, 45, 74, 77, 105, 153,
    161, 175, 457, 461
    analytical apps 74
    architecture 81, 84
    build apps 74
    engine 58
    project 469
SAP Jam 340, 493, 526
    collaboration components 534
    tiles 534
SAP logon ticket 163, 167
SAP Maintenance Planner 95–97
SAP Marketplace 98

SAP Mobile 587
SAP NetWeaver 494
    component 90
    version 91
SAP Product Lifecycle Management
    (SAP PLM) 107
SAP S/4HANA Finance 107, 232
SAP Screen Personas 28, 555, 557
SAP Screen Personas Administration 577
SAP Smart Business 234
    app 232
    component 84
    framework 136
    SAP S/4HANA Finance 232
SAP Smart Business Modeler 134, 136, 231,
    257, 457
SAP Software Download Center 99
SAP Transportation Management
    (SAP TM) 107
SAP UX strategy 28
SAP Web Dispatcher 31, 42, 54, 80, 105, 152,
    153, 155, 161, 234, 478
    capabilities 43
    uses 43
SAP Web IDE 61, 325, 326, 369, 399, 439, 443
    advantages 327
    create 334, 335
    deployment 351
    development 333, 340
    environment 325
    import an application 338
    local version 61
    preview 348
    SAP Cloud Platform 328
SAP_ESH_LOCAL_ADMIN 222
SAP_ESH_SEARCH 222
sap.ui.ControllerExtensions 405
sap.ui.viewExtensions 405
sap.ui.viewModifications 405
sap.ui.viewReplacements 405
SAPUI5 .... 28, 57, 161, 271, 327, 335, 593
    ABAP Repository 338
    application 177
    architecture 58
    build app 67
    component 218

SAPUI5 (Cont.)
control library 175
create app 64
data binding 60
features 57
layer 381
preview 68
script 66
sapUshellTileColor 598
Scaling factor 239
Scenario definition 511
Scenario-specific inbox 506
Schedule indexing 435
Scope 151
Scripting 568
Search 33, 40, 502, 589
Search and analytics modeler 410, 412, 413,
    416, 428
Search connector 173, 221, 413, 428
indexing 225
Search for Software 99
Search help 295, 296
Search model 221, 409
create 412
extend 428
software components 412
Secure
network layer 158
protocol 160
Secure Network Communications 154
Secure Sockets Layer (SSL) 154
Security 43, 124, 151
session protection 161
Security Assertion Markup Language 165
Self-service scenarios 50
Semantic 264
layer 488
object 238, 378, 550
Service
catalog 306
development 288
document 277, 278
generation 288
implementation 286, 289
maintenance 287, 289, 304
metadata document 277

Share 505
dialog 535
Shop app 337
Simple 30
Simulator 349, 350
Single sign-on 158
SNC 159
connection 160
snc/enable 159
snc/gssapi_lib 159
snc/identity/as 159
snc/r3int_rfc_secure 159
Social media
catalog 525, 530, 533
tile 526
Social Media Integration (SMI) 526
Social timeline 534
Software components 412, 415
customer-specific 415
Software-as-a-service (SaaS) 36
sortBy 499
Sorting 503
Source code editor 450
SSL encryption 43
SSO 163, 169
authentication 167
Standard view 465
Static tile 204
Story 542
Subscription 329
Support package 98
download 101
upload 101
Support Package Manager 98
System
alias 125, 126, 495
status 91
tracks 95

T

Table
TADIR 188
USOBHASH 111
Target 203, 479
mapping 202, 264, 378, 426, 427

Task 139
   consumption model 493
   decision 512
   definition 512
   list 168
   processing 497
   quotation 513
Technical service name 180
Technology 29
Template 336, 420, 440, 441
   create project 370
theme editor 560
Theming 57
Threshold 480
Tiles 525
   activate and configure 479
   All Items 522
   All Stories 539
   catalog 38, 39, 267, 532, 539
   configuration 354
   format 245
   KPI Drilldown 539
   new 379
   parameters 245
   remove 38
   static 539
Track Sales Order app 185
Transaction
   /IWFND/MAINT_SERVICE 108, 179, 276,
     304, 319, 394, 497
   ESH_COCKPIT 221, 435
   ESH_MODELER 412
   ESH_SEARCH 227, 437
   LPD_CUST 196, 376
   PFCG (Role Maintenance) 114, 126, 135,
     172, 185, 191, 193, 206, 257, 267, 531,
     538, 552
   RZ10 158
   SAINT (SAP Add-On Installation Tool) 98
   SBWP 501
   SEO1 199
   SE11 (ABAP Dictionary) 382
   SE16 .... 111, 182
   SE18 513
   SE80 (ABAP Object Navigator) 382, 384,
     413, 424, 454

Transaction (Cont.)
   SEGW (Gateway Service Builder) 283,
     297, 382
   SICF (Maintain Services) 112, 117, 120,
     128, 376, 496
   SM59 .... 123, 159
   SMT1 124
   SPAM 101
   SPRO 122, 512
   STCO1 (ABAP Task Manager) 137, 225
   STCO2 138
   SUO1 .... 116, 130, 193
   UI5/THEME_DESIGNER 594
   UI5/THEME_TOOL 594, 599
   VA23 396
Transactional app 53, 105, 172, 369
   ABAP back-end roles 192
   ABAP front-end roles 184
   architecture 381
   components 54
   create 369
   deploy 375
   details 375
   extend 380–382
   OData services 179
   prerequisites 175
   publish 376
   run 194
   SAPUI5 component 176
   template 336
   test 373
Transport Layer Security (TLS) 154
Transport request 199, 414
Trend tile 243

U

UI
   add-on 79
   control library 57
   development toolkit 57
UI Theme Designer 33, 593, 595
   options 596
   transaction code 594
UI Theme Repository 594
Uniform Resource Identifier (URI) 69

Union 488
Universal Work List (UWL) 492
URI 276, 277, 308
URL rewriting 161
User 269
   authentication 163
   authorization 169, 170
   experience 27
   maintenance 116, 134
   management 169
   mapping 167
   role 193
USOBHASH 182
UX 27
   benefits 29
   design principles 29
   design services 29
   strategy 28

V

Value measure 478
Values help view 459
Variant 240
Views 60
   create 482
   extend 404
   replace 488
Virtual data model (VDM) 31, 74, 106, 231,
   457, 458, 461
   reuse content 57
Visualization 249

W

Web
   acceleration 43
   browser 153
Web application
   firewalls 43
   security 43
Web Dynpro 73, 133
What you see is what you get
   (WYSIWYG) 340, 593
Windows 30, 45
Workflow 491
   basics 491
   builder 507, 508
   custom 492
   ID 512
   scenarios 510
   standard 496
   template 492, 506
Workspace 470

X

X.509 certificate 168
XML 60
   code 454
   view 404
XSL Transformation (XSLT) 454

Interested in reading more?

Please visit our website for all new
book and e-book releases from SAP PRESS.

www.sap-press.com